Celluloid
MAVERICKS

Celluloid

MAVERICKS

The History of American Independent Film

By Greg Merritt

THUNDER'S MOUTH PRESS

Published by
Thunder's Mouth Press
841 Broadway, Fourth Floor
New York, NY 10003

First edition

Library of Congress Cataloging-in-Publication Data
Merritt, Greg, 1965-
    Celluloid mavericks: the history of American independent film /
by Greg Merritt,—1st ed.
        p. cm.
    Includes bibliographical references.
    ISBN 1-56025-232-4
    1. Motion pictures—Production and direction. 2. Low budget motion
pictures—United States—History. 3. Independent filmmakers—
United States—Biography. I. Title.
PN1995.9.P7 M418 2000
791.43'75'0973 21—dc21

                                                                                99-043696

Manufactured in the United States of America

Book Design by Pauline Neuwirth, Neuwirth & Associates, Inc.

Distributed by Publishers Group West
1700 Fourth Street
Berkeley, CA 94710
(800) 788-3123

In memory of
Donald Merritt
1931–1980

Contents

Acknowledgments

Many people and institutions helped transform an ambitious idea into a completed book. Principal research was conducted at the Margaret Herrick Library of the Academy of Motion Picture Arts and Sciences. I also wish to acknowledge the libraries of the American Film Institute, Loyola Marymount University, and the University of California, Los Angeles, and the Los Angeles Public Library system (especially the Culver City branch). For assistance with photographs, thank you to the staffs of Collectors Book Store, Cinema Collectors, Eddie Brandt's Saturday Matinee, the Margaret Herrick Library, and The Sundance Institute.

David Craig was an early and tireless supporter of this work. He has my sincere thanks. Editor Rob Vickerman as well as Neil Ortenberg and Daniel O'Connor of Thunder's Mouth Press helped sculpt a lengthy manuscript into a more user-friendly book. I also wish to acknowledge agent Victoria Sanders, Tim Braine of Popular Arts Entertainment, and attorney Mark Litwak.

Indie maven John Pierson provided advice and encouragement. Ken Nunney has discussed films with me for a decade. (He thought *Leaving Las Vegas* was vapid.) LaVonya Sturges brightened my life. (She thought *Ganja & Hess* was too bloody.) In my other writing job, Peter McGough of Weider Publications provided editorial guidance and support. And thanks to Rose Merritt for always believing.

Introduction

It's everywhere. It's playing at the local multiplex and filling the shelves of the neighborhood video store. It has its own magazines, its own award show, its own celebrities, its own television channels. Independent film became big business in the nineties. Not coincidentally, somewhere along the way, the term nearly lost all meaning.

The truth is there are a lot of so-called *independent films* out there that just aren't. As *sex, lies, & videotape*, Quentin Tarantino, and the Sundance Film Festival became household names, the word "independent" was usurped by entertainment factories big and small and applied to all manner of in-house productions. It had happened before. In fact, throughout cinema's long history there has rarely been a time when the word has been clearly defined.

In trying to establish terms, we can at least agree that a film like *Titanic* is not an independent. At a cost of more than $200 million, it was developed, financed, and released by Hollywood corporations (there were actually *two* studios involved). It tells a conventional romance with computer animation, grand sets, costumes, and schmaltz.

On the other end of the spectrum, *David Holzman's Diary* was financed with the director's own $2,500 and created and distributed entirely outside the studios. It's a mock-documentary storytelling experiment, featuring mostly a man talking to his camera. It would be difficult for anyone to argue that *David Holzman's Diary* is not an independent.

Between these two extremes there are hundreds, perhaps thousands, of films whose designations are less precise. Though everyone agrees that independent movies are produced outside the major studios, it's not the only variable they use. Issues of content, creative control, and financing are all criteria that different people use to define the term. Between *Titanic* and *David Holzman's Diary*, what is independent? Where does it begin and where does it end?

This book defines an **independent film** as any motion picture financed and produced completely autonomous of *all* studios, regardless of size. (A studio is a company that both produces and distributes movies.) Such films do not have a prior distribution arrangement (other than from a company owned by the filmmakers). *Reservoir Dogs*, financed and produced autonomously but later purchased and distributed by Miramax when it was completed, is an independent film.

What is defined in this book as a **semi-indie** film is not produced directly by a major studio (such as Paramount or Fox), but it does have a guarantee of distribution before it's produced, and it may be made by a smaller studio (such as Miramax or Gramercy). Again, content is not a consideration. *Pulp Fiction* (financed, produced, and distributed by Miramax) is a semi-indie film.

These definitions cut through the Hollywood marketing and codify what an independent film is and what it is not. They distinguish a motion picture made for $50,000 cobbled together with cash advances from credit cards (independent) from one made for $5 million at a smaller studio (semi-indie) from the typical $50 million major studio production (studio).

The problem with all other independent film definitions is that they are too slippery. They adopt the "I know it when I see it" standard, a widely held belief that independence is determined not by financing but by "spirit," by professing an alternative vision. Those well-intentioned souls voting for the indie Oscars, appropriately entitled the Spirit Awards, adopt this ambiguous yardstick. They annually bestow their top prizes on movies made by smaller studios. But "spirit" is an intellectual quagmire, based on arbitrary decisions about what constitutes art and, in previous decades, what constituted exploitation. It leads to a movie like *Fargo*, produced and distributed by a smaller studio, receiving indie credibility. If *Fargo* is called independent because of content, then why isn't *Forrest Gump*? The latter, made by a major studio, is at least as quirky and "spirited" as the former. One might argue, then, that the disqualifier here is the size of the studio.

But this logic is flawed, too, because today the biggest of the so-called indie studios are owned by the biggest media conglomerates. Why should films produced and distributed by such entities be given the same independent tag as those financed with tip money and credit cards? To do so is a disservice to genuinely self-sufficient rebels. The independent label should not be contingent upon on a mushy term like "spirit," nor on the size of the studio producing the movie.

Labels are about marketing. In the thirties, "independent" was an insult, synonymous with grind-house dreck. At the beginning of a century, the word has become trendy and sexy. The entertainment industry sells its difficult-to-categorize, low-budget films as the next indie event. Studios funnel them into their art-house divisions. This, in turn, has spawned a collective laziness in which all releases from one company are given the same label. The hope of this book is that its definition will strip away the marketing hype and map out the gray area between *Titanic* and *David Holzman's Diary*.

"Independent" as defined here makes this book both narrower and broader than many would anticipate. It is narrower because it does not delve extensively into what are defined here as semi-indies. On the other hand, it's broader because it is not limited to merely "spirited" art-house fare. Such genres as ethnic, horror, and pornography are given their fair due. Their importance must not be underestimated. For much of American cinema's long history, exploitation and specialized markets represented the best avenues for turning a profit outside the studios.

This book's definitions do not eliminate all problems. There's still a blurry line where independence ends and Hollywood begins. This is especially true when a film is purchased by a studio before completion. Additionally, there are transitional periods when it is difficult to tell a production company (which produces movies) from a small studio (which produces and distributes).

Geographic borders also confound the definition process. Essentially, films that were financed primarily by foreign sources but shot on US soil or vice versa may be included in these pages. Movies that were shot with foreign financing in a foreign country are not.

Renegades like Orson Welles and Alex Cox have regretfully been left out because they've created their unconventional works primarily for studios, foreign companies, or in the semi-indie realm. Still, any history that makes room in the same chapter for *Eraserhead, Gates of*

Heaven, The Adventures of the Wilderness Family, I Spit on Your Grave, My Dinner With Andre, and *Debbie Does Dallas* is certainly inclusive.

This book is all-embracing because so is independent cinema. All are welcome: vanguard artists, eccentrics, polemicists, and pornographers. The one quality such filmmakers share, past and present, is a willingness to do what the studios don't or won't. Sometimes the motive is economic. Sometimes it is a ploy to get noticed.

On still other occasions it is born from an authentic desire to tell an overlooked story, regardless of the costs or risks.

The off-Hollywood arena is American cinema's laboratory, proving ground, and launching pad. It's also its sideshow, filled with burlesque queens and bloodthirsty geeks. Over and over again nonstudio motion pictures have blazed a successful path that Hollywood has then followed, sometimes paving it over with a superhighway. Other times, the major studios decide—perhaps wisely—not to venture down that trail at all. In all but big-budget scenarios, independent movies lead the way.

This book will chart the entire history of American independent film. The story begins more than a century ago with the first flickering images, followed by much remarkable experimentation in the silent era. Between the Depression and the end of World War II, the Hollywood studio system was at its peak, but, still, brave mavericks persevered on the outside. Through the fifties, there were increasingly more opportunities, especially in exploitation. The sixties brought crucial art-house experimentation that led to the cinematic revolution of the Vietnam era. In the late seventies and the eighties, the modern independent scene took shape, creating the new indie system of recent years.

Throughout celluloid history, the most enthralling production tales have come from the nonstudio sector. From Winsor McCay to Neil LaBute, directors with a vision have begged and borrowed to capture original stories without the luxury of substantial budgets or the confidence of knowing whether their ultimate creation would ever see the dark of a commercial theater. That's the story of this book—the overriding passion of people working entirely separately of all studios to craft a special motion picture.

Why do they do it? Despite the odds, money is certainly a prime motivation. The lure of Hollywood drives many a renegade—the hope that by forging a successful feature on the outside they will then be invited through the studio gates. There have always been a few independent filmmakers who break through to huge paydays.

But there's something else that fuels independent filmmakers. It's the freedom of telling one's own story one's own way, of fulfilling a vision free of all the meetings and all the compromises. And it's the thrill of moviemaking itself, of preserving life with mirrors and light, whether trekking thousands of miles to document native people, pushing the boundaries of acceptable content, or laying bare one's own fears and desires. This book recounts the history of artists and entrepreneurs, of experimenters and impresarios, of celluloid mavericks who captured on film their wildest fantasies, their darkest nightmares, and their greatest dreams.

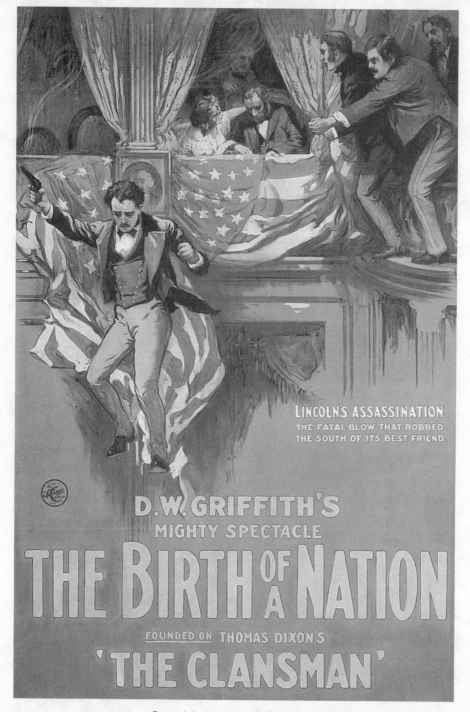

Rare original poster from *The Birth of a Nation*.

1896-1916

BIRTH

The moving picture, although a growth of only a
few years, is boundless in its scope and endless in
its possibilities.

—D. W. GRIFFITH

The last light dimmed. From out of the black abyss below came the
first note of the forty-piece orchestra. It wrenched something deep in
his soul. He would later describe this "throb through the darkness" as
the "low cry of the anguished South being put to torture."[1] The curtain went up.

It was the week of Valentine's Day, 1915. The Liberty Theater
screen looked down upon the stage where Thomas Dixon's play had
been performed nine years earlier. Though popular in the writer's
beloved South, *The Clansman* was lambasted by New York critics in
1906 and had bombed on Broadway. Fearing the worst, Dixon sat
alone in the balcony on that February morning so he could escape
unnoticed if the silent, celluloid version of his popular and controversial novel and play failed to stir emotions.

Not counting the orchestra and the chorus of singers, there were
less than a hundred people in the Liberty for the private screening.

Among them was one of the greatest film directors in the world, a few weeks past his fortieth birthday. The director, D. W. Griffith, had been at the premiere screening in Los Angeles the week before, where the audience had showered him with ovation after ovation. Griffith was confident of his creation.

Dixon sat mesmerized as his Confederacy was ravaged by Civil War, as the defeated Southerners returned home, as President Lincoln was assassinated, and as the Ku Klux Klan grew to avenge the vilest caricatures of African-Americans and their allies. In the coming months, when the KKK was framed in silhouette against the setting sun, stampeding to the rescue accompanied by the heroic sounds of "In the Hall of the Mountain King," viewers would stand and cheer, but on this February morning the theater was large, the audience was small, and the orchestra drowned out any applause. The square-jawed writer was moved almost to tears, but he could scarcely see or hear another soul.

He was overjoyed with the screen adaptation of his novel; he'd been swept away by its epic splendor. But he wondered if his judgment was impaired, like that of parents blind to the faults of their child. So when the lights came up and the curtain went down, he descended the stairs carefully, cautiously, frightened by the prospect of men and women quietly pulling on hats and gloves, sighing as they stepped out into the daylight.

When he reached the lobby, he was greeted by what he would later describe as "the loudest uproar I ever heard from seventy-five people."[2] He grinned. He shook a hand. A hand slapped his back. And he gazed across the regal room to the director, D. W. Griffith, the man who had risked his financial future and creative reputation to bring such an explosive tale to the screen. Dixon told Griffith that *The Clansman* was too tame a title for so powerful a story: "It should be called 'The Birth of a Nation.' "[3]

Dixon had been a North Carolina legislator, a minister, a lecturer, and, finally, a rabidly racist scribe. His friend of thirty years that he met while in graduate school had been a professor, Princeton administrator, governor of New Jersey, and, in 1912, was elected President of the United States. On February 18, 1915, the writer went to Washington, D.C. and persuaded Woodrow Wilson to watch *The Birth of a Nation*. This poisonous fable of the KKK rescuing America is believed to be the first film to play at the White House. Afterwards,

Wilson reportedly told Dixon, "It is like writing history with lightning. And my only regret is that it is all so terribly true."[4]

At a time when many venues changed films daily, *The Birth of a Nation* played at New York's Liberty Theater for eleven months. When the price of most tickets was fifteen cents, it commanded two dollars. The film stirred up controversy wherever it went, and it went almost everywhere, distributed on a state's-rights basis, traveling as a special attraction, an event not to be missed. The best estimates are that it made $60 million in its initial marathon run, a staggering sum (nearly $1 billion in today's dollars). It was the world's first movie blockbuster. Three hours long, in sweeping scope, with a synched musical score and single tinted colors, it launched the feature film, revolutionized motion picture production, and wrote much of the language of movies.

It was also inescapably racist, a depiction of the basest hatred, a propaganda piece that resurrected the Ku Klux Klan and launched them to their greatest power. It would be picketed, protested, censored, editorialized against, and banned. It was a work of art, a bold gamble that paid off, and a twisted exploitation flick. And like the majority of the most daring and controversial landmarks of cinema, it was made outside the studios, financed by two freelancing brothers, hundreds of individuals, and, occasionally, when film stock ran low, the contents of Griffith's hat after it was passed around a room.

It was, for better and for worse, America's first major independent film.

In the Beginning

The earliest publicly screened motion pictures in America were shown at Koster and Bial's Music Hall in New York on April 23, 1896. On that day popular cinema was born with a series of one-minute flicks screened between vaudeville acts. They were mostly burlesque and theatrical vignettes, each shot in a single unedited take with a stationary, hand-cranked camera. One flick, featuring a shot of waves breaking on a beach, caused the audience to recoil with fears of getting drenched.

That day's extravaganza had been produced by Thomas Edison, "The Wizard of Menlo Park," inventor of the carbon microphone, the phonograph, the incandescent lamp, and the profit-at-any-cost, slash-and-burn motion picture studio. Edison was never an independent. He took credit for creation of the moving-picture camera and peepshow-viewing apparatus when he patented them in 1891, but they were actually invented by his employee, W. K. L. Dickson. When the Lumière brothers of France publicly screened moving pictures in the final days of 1895, Edison, ever the business visionary, scrambled for his own projector. He arranged to manufacture and promote (as the "Edison Vitascope," no less) a projector developed by Thomas Armat.

That is how "The Wizard" came to screen the umbrella dance and crashing waves on Broadway in April of 1896. By the hottest days of summer there were half a dozen theaters in New York showing moving pictures, and a Vitascope Parlor had opened in Los Angeles. Three companies emerged that would produce most of the earliest films: Edison, Biograph, and Vitagraph. They were the first studios, with talent under contract and a monopoly on equipment. Because the studios each peddled their own projection systems, they had to keep churning out something to project. Prints were purchased by theaters for the same low price (around $5) regardless of quality.

Lawyers were the greatest beneficiaries of these early films, as the three New York studios battled each other with patent claim lawsuits. Meanwhile, a number of independent producers dodged the Big Three's attorneys, utilizing bootlegged equipment or imports from Europe which were prone to patent suits. Inventors, portrait photographers, vaudeville and circus people, all manner of men made movies. Most were also their own projectionists. Screening their creations in tents or any available public building, they traveled where the Big Three wouldn't tread. They went to all forty-five states, and the territories too, from cotton plantations in Mississippi to the gold camps of Juneau, Alaska. These adventures brought the wonder of movies to rural America. While a renegade would usually disappear the moment one of the Big Three threatened litigation, others soon emerged to take his place, out for a fast buck in an exciting new industry.

The earliest films were often just scenic shots, brief vignettes from existing theatrical presentations, or depictions of everyday life. These flicks quickly lost their novelty and were relegated to the role of vaudeville "chaser," a segment that signaled to the audience that the real show was over and it was time to go. Cinema as art and commerce was in danger of dying before it had truly begun.

One unique, if marginal, form of independent film premiered at the St. Louis Exhibition of 1904 when George C. Hale, former Kansas City fire chief, presented *Hale's Tours and Scenes of the World*. A mock "conductor" stamped patrons' tickets as they entered a viewing area that resembled a railway coach. As the car rumbled and swayed, images were projected on the front wall using scenic footage that had been shot from an actual moving train. *Hales Tours* appeared in scattered cities as a short-lived precursor to storefront theaters with five-cent admissions.

It was the phenomenal success of Edison's *The Great Train Robbery* (1903), directed by Edwin Porter, that aimed motion pictures towards their future: longer length, a story structure, motivated editing, and violent crime.

Nickelodeons sprouted up across the country between 1905 and 1910. These venues either consisted of rows of hand-cranked machines that showed movies to one viewer at a time or they projected flicks overhead in red rooms containing less than 200 chairs (to avoid expensive licensing regulations). All catered primarily to the urban working class and the millions of recent immigrants who could respond to the universal sign language of chases and pratfalls even if they couldn't read the intertitles.

The business structure also took shape. In the earliest years of the twentieth century, motion pictures were sold outright to exhibitors. With multi-flick programs that often changed daily, exhibitors were forced to buy a lot of celluloid. Exchanges were set up to act as middle-men, purchasing films and renting them to one theater after another, allowing everyone from the studio to the exhibitor to make a profit. Independent companies were often left out of this arrangement or received an exchange's lowest rate.

Business Matters

The major studios had been suing each other for a decade. They finally declared a truce and, in September of 1908, Edison, Biograph, and Vitagraph pooled their patents and formed the Motion Picture Patents Company, joined by several major signatories who paid royalties and fees to the Kodak company. This Trust with a capital "T" (a title the companies smugly accepted despite a popular tide against big business) was created to maximize the profits of the Big Three and squash their smallest competitors. Only the ten signatories of the

Trust could utilize an American camera or projector, purchase Kodak film stock, or sell to the most desirable exchanges.

What was intended as a roadblock instead opened up new trails. Between 1907 and 1910 the number of nickelodeons in America multiplied from 3,000 to 10,000.[5] As the Trust tried in vain to attract middle-class viewers, exchanges needed movies—any movies. Companies (many owned by European immigrants) leaped into the fray to supply the poorest theaters with products. Fox, Keystone, Thanhouser, Rex, and the Independent Motion Picture Company (IMP) were among the key challengers to the Big Three. It was still possible for independents to find a national exchange to distribute their films, but some genuine mavericks found other ways.

The cinematic roadshow was one such route. Through this method, which had roots in the earliest days of film, a motion picture toured with its own company: an advance man to stir up interest, a lecturer/projectionist, and a manager who secured opera houses and town halls. In 1912, actress Helen Gardner became the first star to form her own production company. She produced and performed the title role in *Cleopatra*, which her husband, Charles Gaskill, wrote and directed. They circulated it as a roadshow attraction with much fanfare. "Event pictures" and exploitation flicks relied on the roadshow for decades to come.

An important distribution method was developed by an unlikely man named Pliny P. Craft. Craft had been a publicist for Buffalo Bill's Wild West Show, a popular touring event that had earlier featured Sitting Bull and Annie Oakley. Inspired by the successful moving picture of the 1910 Johnson-Jeffries boxing match, Craft convinced Buffalo Bill to let him film the western show. When national exchanges rejected the unique event picture, Craft found showmen throughout the country willing to book it. *Buffalo Bill's Wild West and Pawnee Bill's Far East Show* was a hit in 1911. Its release strategy of leasing to small exchanges in regional territories (usually individual states) became known as "state's-rights," and it was popular in the teens before the studios developed their own exchanges. Through the 1970s, state's-rights remained a common method of circulating independent features.

Craft went on to import and distribute two Italian epics using roadshows. His perfected exhibition strategy included souvenir programs, novelty merchandising, and two-dollar tickets. After he exhausted the roadshow potential, he sold off the state's-rights. Others followed Craft's lead.

Meanwhile, the Big Three stubbornly clung to the rules from their earliest days, when selling projectors took precedence over the quality of film that clattered through them. As a policy, in order to squelch the salaries of nameless talent, the Big Three did not present credits on-screen. This allowed them to market their pictures solely on the strength of their company's lofty reputation. In 1910, defiant Carl Laemmle, head of IMP, hired Florence Lawrence away from Biograph. She was famous until then only as "The Biograph Girl," but Laemmle splashed her name everywhere. Soon audiences weren't so concerned with companies. They wanted their favorite actors. And the star system was born.

The Trust also held onto the dated nickelodeon formula that moving pictures should be one reel (approximately fifteen minutes) or less and shown as part of a program. It was those battling the Trust who released three-reelers. Then, in 1912, independent producers created the feature film: a photoplay long enough to stand alone. H. A. Spanuth presented his five-reel *Oliver Twist*, starring Broadway's Nat Goodwin. To much greater fanfare, Adolph Zukor's new Famous Players Company (later Paramount) released an import from France,

The Silent Experience

You sit in a dark theater and watch. On-screen dialogue is kept to a minimum. When an actor speaks or when exposition is necessary, it appears in an intertitle with ornate letters and borders. Most silent films are black-and-white, but the print you view is tinted in single hues. Sunlit scenes are gold, night scenes are blue, the dramatic confrontation is red.

In a ninety-nine seat Nickelodeon, the program ranges from ten minutes to a half-hour and runs continuously, repeating dozens of times each day. An organist tries to fit generic tunes to on-screen action. The full show may include a singer or vaudeville act to kill time while reels are changed. Lantern slides (slide photographs with titles) are projected between reels. These have a whimsical tone and instruct you to remove your hat, refrain from smoking, and return again.

continued

The Silent Experience
continued

In a post-Nickelodeon movie palace with more than a thousand seats, a musical score matches the on-screen action. The score was shipped with the feature, and it's played on an ornate pipe organ or an "orchestra machine." The organist may also have a Kinematophone for adding sounds like kisses, gunshots, and baby cries, but it's more likely he or his assistant approximates on-screen noises with tools (example: knocking coconuts together for hoofbeats). In the end, after the curtain falls, he plays the feature's refrain as you return your hat to your head and make your way up the crowded aisle.

■   ■   ■   ■   ■   ■   ■   ■

the four-reel *Queen Elizabeth*, starring European stage legend Sarah Bernhardt. Its monumental success rocked the industry.

By 1913, six-reelers were not uncommon, and the twelve-reel *The Birth of a Nation* was right around the corner. Features attracted the middle class and women to legitimate theaters. Ticket prices soared to fifteen cents or more. Movie palaces with velvet curtains, ornate pipe organs, and pseudoclassical names were constructed to show longer photoplays, while musky storefront nickelodeons with flat floors and rows of folding chairs closed in droves. Profits ballooned as the country went movie mad. Between 1908 and 1914, motion picture attendance in America virtually doubled.[6]

In 1912 the so-called "independent" companies matched the output of the Trust. As the patent war raged on, Edison slapped the larger outsiders with lawsuit after lawsuit. The Big Three hired detectives to monitor renegades. They sent thugs to break equipment and sometimes to break bones. "Independents" countered with armed security and occasionally went to great lengths to avoid lawsuits. Because the technology to make the sprocket holes was among the many thing patented by the Trust, the Eclair Company actually had an employee work full-time in a dark room hand-punching holes into the borders of negative film![7]

The need to escape the physical and legal assault of the Trust led some as far from New York as they could get—to a place with year-round sunshine, terrain that could fit most any story, cheap labor, and a nearby Mexican border to flee to in case someone paid a visit with a summons or a shotgun. Before the filmmakers arrived in a dusty town called Hollywood, the dirt roads through its orange and lemon groves were more likely to be traveled by a horse than a horseless buggy.

The motion picture business was passing the Big Three by. In a role reversal, the lawsuit-happy Trust members were named as defendants, charged with violating the Sherman Antitrust Act. The Trust lost the lengthy case in 1915 and the appeal in 1918. By then, however, most of its companies, including Edison and Biograph, were already out of business.

Things changed fast. The renegade "independents" soon deposed the Big Three as the new Goliathlike studios (precursors to the modern Universal, Fox, and Paramount); Los Angeles had replaced New York as the motion picture production center; once nameless performers like Mary Pickford and Charlie Chaplin were achieving world fame; and the feature film, playing in legitimate theaters in respectable neighborhoods, was pulling in a mass audience of all ages and classes, achieving ever greater popularity.

Winsor McCay

As a young man, Winsor McCay (1871–1934) painted posters for traveling circuses. In 1898 he worked as a staff cartoonist for a newspaper in Cincinnati, and in 1903 was hired by a New York tabloid, achieving fame with his detailed, hallucinatory comic strips "Little Nemo in Slumberland" and "Dreams of a Rarebit Fiend." He entered the vaudeville circuit in 1906, fast-drawing cartoons on stage. Edwin Porter directed a live-action version of *Dreams of a Rarebit Fiend* that year, and cofounder of Vitagraph and ex-cartoonist J. Stuart Blackton made the first truly animated film, *Humorous Phases of a Funny Face.*

Shortly thereafter, encouraged by his friend Blackton, McCay began the tedious task of bringing his cartoon creations to life. The short animated photoplay *Little Nemo* was produced with 4,000 separate drawings created in toto (no repeating backgrounds) on rice paper. Each was hand-colored, though shot in black-and-white. Filmed at the Vitagraph studios in 1909 and distributed by that studio, this dream-logic combination of live action and cartoons was shown as part of McCay's vaudeville act in 1911. Assisted only by his teenage neighbor, John Fitzsimmons, McCay followed with *The Story of a Mosquito* (1912), another mixture of live action and moving drawings. McCay sold it to IMP with the stipulation that it couldn't be shown in America while he utilized it in his vaudeville act.

His most famous movie, *Gertie the Dinosaur* (1914), is a short made up of 16,000 outline drawings inspired by his invitation from the American Historical Society to bring to life skeletons of prehistoric animals through pictures. During McCay's traveling show, he stood onstage in front of the screen (often a sheet) and appeared to work in tandem with the friendly brontosaurus. Dressed as an animal trainer wielding a whip, he barked out commands to which Gertie responded. The highlight was when he tossed a real apple to the dinosaur and she appeared to catch and eat it on-screen.

The fact that McCay toured with his first films while still under contract to produce newspaper cartoons severely limited their circulation in America (though not in Europe, where they enjoyed greater fame). When news tycoon William Randolph Hearst ordered his employee to stay in New York City, McCay gave up the circuit, and his movies went into wider release.

McCay's next photoplay was distributed by Universal, and it too was a groundbreaker. *The Sinking of the Lusitania* (1918) is a somber, documentary-style recreation of the tragic 1915 event that became a rallying cry for the United States entering World War I. It took nearly two years to painstakingly create. Comprised of 25,000 drawings and presenting a variety of angles, *The Sinking of the Lusitania* features McCay's most distinctive animation: detailed views of the ship going under and bodies bobbing helplessly in the waves.

All told, McCay made ten animated shorts. He capped off his film career with the inventive series *Dreams of a Rarebit Fiend* (1921), which brings fantasies to life in three shorts. In *Bug Vaudeville* there are boxing beetles and ballet-dancing butterflies. In *The Flying House* a husband and wife fly into outer space in their home. And *The Pet* features a dog that turns into a giant monster, devouring everything in its path.

McCay inspired other pioneering animators such as John Randolph Bray, Earl Hurd, Max Fleischer, and Paul Terry, who invented crucial timesaving techniques. By the mid-teens, animation studios has sprung up. The absence of sound and color impairs early cartoons, and character movements are often jerky by modern standards (McCay's are smoother than those of his contemporaries), but the results are monuments to persistence that defined much of the unique logic of the animated genre. Winsor McCay was a tireless and skilled craftsman and a true motion picture pioneer.

Literary Adaptations

With the Trust fading and the feature film rising, a number of enterprising independents leaped into production. Hobart Bosworth (1867–1943), an actor who starred in the first film shot entirely in Los Angeles (the Selig company's *The Power of Sultan*, 1909), had run away to the sea at the age of twelve and later labored on a ranch in the 1880s. Such a résumé made him the perfect candidate to bring the rugged works of Jack London to the screen. Bosworth formed his own production company in 1913. There was much fanfare regarding his acquiring the rights to London's popular novels.

The first of the adaptations, released in late 1913, was *The Sea Wolf*, an ambitious seven-reel adventure shot in Southern California, much of it at sea. Bosworth directed and stars as Wolf Larson, the ship captain who goes blind, is deserted by his crew, and runs ashore on Endeavor Island, where some of his crew has fled. The capture of a shark is a highlight. London appears in an introductory passage; his words appear in intertitles. Well reviewed, *The Sea Wolf* was a state's-rights success. It was followed in 1914 by the Bosworth/London features *The Valley of the Moon*, *Martin Eden*, and *John Barleycorn*. The last is a plea for temperance from the alcoholic and drug-addicted novelist that stars future independent director Elmer Clifton. After 1915, Bosworth returned to acting and performed supporting roles into the sound era. Jack London died in 1916, reportedly from morphine or alcohol; he was forty.

Prolific author and political activist Upton Sinclair was an early cinema enthusiast. His 1906 muckraking novel *The Jungle* shocked the nation and led to the passage of pure-food and meat inspection laws. In 1914 Sinclair helped adapt his book to celluloid; he also appears as himself. The five-reel feature exposed the horrendous working conditions in the Chicago stockyards. Despite the publicity the film gained when it was banned in Chicago, it failed to match the impact of the book. After its initial release, Sinclair secured the rights and screened *The Jungle* at Socialist Party meetings until the last print was lost.

Another famous writer explored moving pictures. Eager to bring his work to the screen, L. Frank Baum, author of the "Oz" books, opened the Oz Film Manufacturing Company in Los Angeles in June 1914. For inspiration, a composer played the piano as the first two features, *The Patchwork Girl of Oz* and *The Magic Cloak of Oz* (both 1914), were shot. The company disbanded in November of 1914 after those two films were shot, though Baum later returned to film production. Another short-lived independent company, Chadwick, produced an interesting silent version of *The Wizard of Oz* in 1925, with the Tin Woodsman played by Oliver Hardy (the year before teaming with Stan Laurel), but it would take MGM, sound, and Technicolor to truly bring Oz to life.

Ethnic

One key to independent film success has always been to do what the studios don't. And the studios have always provided ample opportunities. Racism was rarely as central to a plot as it was in *The Birth of a Nation*, but it prevailed during the silent era through degrading stereotypes. Using caricatures, popular cinema labeled minorities as inherently inferior to the Anglo majority. They were stripped of their love lives, faith, families, work ethic—all things that made them dimensional and human.

Beginning then and through today, it has been independent cinema's responsibility and privilege to fill the void. By picking up cameras to tell their own stories, American minorities of all skin tones, ethnicities, beliefs, and persuasions have been able to circumvent the pigeonholes of Hollywood. Unfortunately, for decades few people knew of such movies because of weak distribution. This often led to the quick failure of a noble dream.

William Foster, a black man living in Chicago, had worked as a show business press agent. In 1910 he produced *The Pullman Porter*, the first film with an African-American cast. His Foster Photoplay Company subsequently made shorts like *The Grafter and the Maid* (1913), and he produced a series at Pathé Studios starring the comedy team of Buck and Bubbles. These films were crudely made and hindered by the scarcity of exhibition venues. Their impact was minimal, but William Foster was a true pioneer at a time when most black roles were performed by whites in blackface and when virtually all African-American plots were demeaning. Foster forged a path towards self-empowerment. In just a few years, race pictures would grow into an important independent industry, though it would be more than half a century before the first African-American directed a studio feature.[9]

In 1914, the Japanese-American Film Company moved its operations from Japan to America. Its first feature, *The Oath of the Sword* (1915), is a love story about a Japanese man who returns from college to find his Japanese girlfriend has married an American philanderer. It was not a success.

Sidney Goldin immigrated to the United States from the Ukraine as a child. In 1911, he began crafting films with Jewish themes, both autonomously and for Carl Laemmle's Independent Motion Picture Company. Titles include *The Sorrows of Israel* (1911), about a Jew who flees Russia for America, *How the Jews Take Care of their Poor* (1913), which highlights philanthropic work in Jewish hospitals and agencies, and *The Terrors of Russia* (1914), an indictment of Russian anti-Semitism. In 1921, Goldin moved to Austria, where he became the father of Yiddish cinema.

Women

The earliest female director, Alice Guy Blaché (1873–1968), was an independent. A secretary to the Lumière brothers, the French film pioneers, she sometimes directed movies, which was seen at the time as just another office chore. She helmed *La Fée aux Choux* in France in either 1896 (making her the first director of a "story-film") or 1900. Guy married Englishman Herbert Blaché in 1907, and they immigrated to America soon thereafter and formed their own New York production company, Solax.

Between 1910 and 1914, Guy Blaché personally directed approximately half of Solax's more than 300 films (mostly one- and two-reelers). Some are noteworthy. *Canned Harmony* (1912) showcases triple-screen effects. At one point a suitor is in one screen while his girlfriend is in a screen on the opposite side with a symbolic empty road between them. *Dick Whittington and His Coat* (1913) had a large cast, twenty-six sets, and a substantial budget. Guy Blaché and Solax earned a reputation for quality productions. While some filmmakers turned to lustful tales, the Mother of Movies took pride in her "clean pictures."

In 1914, having produced only two four-reelers and unable to adapt to the feature film, Solax ceased production. During the teens, Guy Blaché opened and closed two production companies and worked sporadically for the studios, but her husband's career jealousy ended their marriage and a series of bad reviews halted her career. She returned to France in 1922. Alice Guy Blaché's cinematic pioneering was virtually forgotten until the French government bestowed on her the Legion of Honor in 1953.

As Guy Blaché blazed a trail for future female directors, women were finding their voice in other areas. Women's suffrage was rooted in the abolition and temperance movements of the first half of the nineteenth century. By 1912 it was a national force, with nine mostly Western states (including California) granting women the right to vote. There were more than 500,000 signatures on a petition for federal legislation. As the debate raged, the studios split along the patent war battle line, with the new "independents" in favor of women voting (Eclair's *Suffrage and the Man*, 1912, and Selig's *Your Girl and Mine*, 1914) and the Trust dinosaurs against (Edison's devilishly titled *When the Men Left Town*, 1914).

The suffrage leaders themselves stepped in front of the cameras for two independent productions. Hull House cofounder and winner of the 1931 Nobel Peace Prize, Jane Addams, stars with activist Dr. Anna Shaw in *Independent Votes for Women* (1912), directed by Hal Reid. The parable presents the two suffragists converting a US Senator to their cause by first persuading his fiancée to join them. It concludes with footage of an actual Manhattan suffragist parade.

In 1913, the Uneek Film Company produced *Eighty Million Women Want*, written by future producer B. P. Schulberg and helmed by Will Lewis. It stars suffragist leaders Emmeline Pankhurst and Harriot Stanton Blatch in the story of a female sleuth who exposes a corrupt political machine. Feminists had high hopes for *Eighty Million Women Want* and *Independent Votes for Women*, but the films mostly preached to the converted and failed to sway significant numbers of people. It was not until 1920 that women were finally granted the right to vote.

Sexploitation

The final months of 1913 were rocked by two features with the same controversial theme: forced prostitution. The first, *Traffic in Souls*, was one of the earliest releases from Universal Pictures (formed by merging several "independents," most notably IMP). The other was *The Inside of the White Slave Traffic*, written and produced by Samuel H. London, a former Director of the Secret Service (then the federal agency combating vice). Directed by Frank Beal, *The Inside of the White Slave Traffic* was shot in New York, New Orleans, and

Denver and features authentic footage of red-light districts, giving it a seamy, documentary feel.

In its first weeks, *The Inside of the White Slave Traffic* out-grossed *Traffic in Souls*, but its success was quickly halted by objections to its controversial content. It wasn't as though London hadn't seen trouble coming. In an effort to shelter his film from censorship, Mr. Samuel H. London himself appears in the film's opening, speaking to the camera as America's former chief vice buster. The following footage, he explains, is based on his official investigations, a pretense that enabled him to stamp the sordid content "For Educational Use." And in a tactic used by future exploitation producers, he named his production outfit The Moral Feature Film Company and distributed the film through The Sociological Research Film Corporation. But his cover was soon blown. *The Inside of the White Slave Traffic* was beset by legal problems and London, once America's top vice cop, was convicted in New York of holding an exhibition tending to corrupt morals.[10] Theaters were frightened away from any further bookings. Meanwhile, *Traffic in Souls* benefitted greatly from such controversy. Made for a mere $5,700, it grossed more than $500,000, and its unexpected windfall helped build Universal City.

White slave pictures are hardly shocking by today's standards. The exploitation racket was always about the *promise* of the forbidden. Delivering, however, could mean censorship or jail. Such flicks were sold by their sensational titles and lurid posters and through hype generated by outraged editorials often penned by authors who hadn't even seen the supposedly sinful celluloid. Once projected, many "SHOCKING TRUTH!" movies such as the innocuous *Damaged Goods* (1914) or *The Sex Lure* (1917) proved to be nothing more than tepid melodrama.

Still, a few films did deliver the goods, sometimes under the guise of "art." *Hypocrites* (1915), scripted and directed by Lois Weber (covered in the next chapter) and produced by Hobart Bosworth, tells an allegorical tale of corruption and features a "nude" woman (in a body stocking) as the all-knowing "Naked Truth." D. W. Griffith's mainstream epic, *Intolerance* (1916), presents unclothed bathing beauties in the Babylon sequence. Most brazen of all was the deceptively titled *Purity* (1916), directed by Rea Berger. Now a lost classic, *Purity* stars the curvaceous Audrey Munson as an artist's model who appears nude—sans body stocking—in fantasy scenes while artists imagine her in famous works of art. Because the production recreated classic paintings, censors were not eager to ban the Italian Renaissance, and *Purity* slipped into theaters. Box offices were crowded with men who'd never heard of Botticelli but knew a naked dame when they saw one.

As a result of editorials about perceived impurities in *Purity*, censorship boards cracked down on nudity in any guise. It would be a long time before legitimate films again featured the naked essentials. The illegitimate was another matter. Shortly after man invented the motion picture, he invented the pornographic movie. Hard-core stag loops in the silent era were produced for the then respectable price of $100 to $200 each. Surviving examples show frolickers, often in bad disguises, participating in the indoor sports men and women always have. Such "smokers" were typically shown at stag parties or at password screenings in "closed" movie houses. Numerous theaters and distributors were raided by police, but the market for forbidden fruit would only grow.

True Crime

The feature film in its early years was an exciting new medium possessing great power to influence the general public. Then as now, it was fascinated by fame and the infamous. A few in the latter category, novices to entertainment but not to tabloid front pages, decided to exploit the movies for all they were worth.

Herman Rosenthal owned several New York gambling houses. When they failed after repeated raids, he threatened to spill the beans on the police protection racket. In 1912, Rosenthal was murdered, and four of his competitors—Bald Jack Rose, Harry Vallon, Bridgie Webber, and Sam Schepps—admitted to hiring the gunmen. Notoriously crooked Police Lieutenant Charles Becker was pinned with the blame. The four gamblers cooperated with the District Attorney and went free; Becker and the killers went to the electric chair. The New York newspapers gave the enthralling case more coverage than any previous crime story.

In 1913, three of the unconvicted accomplices to murder (all but Webber) capitalized on their fame by starring in *The Wages of Sin*, a three-reel independent. Made by David Horsley, the picture has nothing explicitly to do with the Rosenthal case, but it does feature thievery, blackmail, and murder. The stars' notorious names appeared everywhere in connection with this poorly realized film, causing a great wave of indignant editorializing and selling thousands of tickets.

William "Plain Bill" Sulzer was the reformist governor of New York who learned the hard way you can't fight city hall. New York City's Tammany machine fought back, and "The People's Governor," too proud to properly defend himself, was impeached in 1913 on charges of financial corruption. His friend, former US senator James Barcus, wrote a book and play about Sulzer. In 1915 it was brought to the screen as *The Governor's Ball*, directed by Charles Davenport and starring Sulzer as himself. The film focuses on the ex-governor's experiences in Albany, his fight with Tammany boss Charles Murphy, and his impeachment. There is much emphasis on Tammany corruption: blackmail, forgery, vote stealing, bribery, and rape. *The Governor's Ball* is topped off with a wishful conclusion: the decadent machine's defeat. Sulzer's career was also the inspiration for Preston Sturges's directing debut, *The Great McGinty* (1940). The Tammany machine reached its apex in the late twenties and was brought down by its own graft soon thereafter.

D. W. Griffith

D. W. (David Wark) Griffith (1875–1948), raised in the defeated South, was the son of a revered Confederate colonel who died from the lingering effects of a Civil War wound. After a stint as a journalist, Griffith took up stage acting and barely sustained himself for a decade, traveling in stock companies and performing odd jobs. In 1906, he and his actress wife moved to New York City and worked in a play written by Thomas Dixon.

In 1907, Griffith broke into film acting and writing. He directed his first flick for Biograph the following year. Between 1908 and 1913, the prolific D. W. Griffith directed virtually every significant production at the Biograph studios, more than 450 in total (not one of them displayed his name on-screen). Week after week, he brought one-reel stories to life, and his style evolved. Before Griffith, most movies resembled filmed stage plays, but the man from Kentucky freed the camera, brought subtlety to acting, and helped define the language of editing. Billy Bitzer, the pioneer of cinematography, usually assisted. An aide to W. K. L. Dickson and a moving-picture cameraman since 1896, Bitzer teamed up with Griffith in 1908 and remained behind the lens for the next two decades.

In September of 1913, feature films were all the rage, and Biograph found itself on the losing side of a protracted war. Yearning to make a full-length photoplay, Griffith left the studio. Unable to turn to other Trust companies, he approached the Aitken brothers, Harry and Roy. Harry had been a theater owner who'd organized against the Big Three, forming the Majestic Motion Picture Company in 1911 and promptly signing actress Mary Pickford (after a few shorts she returned to Biograph). The following year he'd created the Mutual Film Corporation, an exchange that distributed the output of non-Trust companies. By 1913, busy with these concerns and producing the films of directors Mack Sennett and Thomas Ince, Harry Aitken was overextended (Roy maintained a lesser role), but found he couldn't pass up an opportunity to sign the great D. W. Griffith.

Nineteen thirteen was also the year Griffith read Thomas Dixon's novel *The Clansman*. He eagerly proposed it to the Aitkens, but the brothers had a lot of capital invested in various features and had not yet realized the kind of return necessary to fund an expensive flick like *The Clansman*. Dixon wanted an unprecedented $25,000 and 25 percent of the producer's gross; the production itself was budgeted at more than $40,000. Harry presented it to the Mutual board, but its members balked. Undeterred, Griffith charged ahead. He researched the Civil War and Reconstruction; he rented land for battle scenes; he secured costumes and horses. In the summer of 1914, without a dime raised for production, Griffith began casting and rehearsing actors.

Dixon admired Griffith's audacity and respected his Southern roots. He lowered his asking price to $2,000 up front with the same 25 percent of the producer's gross (a percentage that would eventually make him a millionaire). Finally, the Aitkens put up their own $25,000 and set up a corporation, Epoch, selling stock to raise additional funds for the sole purpose of producing and releasing what would become *The Birth of a Nation*. Majestic paid most of the production salaries, including Griffith's, but no Majestic stockholder ever benefited from *The Birth of a Nation*'s eventual windfall.[11] With $40,000, Griffith was ready to shoot, though he must have known that what he envisioned would cost much more.

Though Griffith and Frank E. Woods, Jr. are credited with adapting the story, the three-hour epic was shot without a detailed script. It was rare even in the silent era not to have a script that contained scenes and actions and shot descriptions. Griffith worked from notes;

the actors worked from his instructions. Billy Bitzer and Karl Brown were the cinematographers. Future directors Erich von Stroheim, Raoul Walsh (who also plays John Wilkes Booth), and Jack Conway were among the assistants. The principal actors were Henry B. Walthall, Lillian Gish, Elmer Clifton, Miriam Cooper, and Ralph Lewis. Shooting began, fittingly, on Independence Day, 1914. Shortly thereafter, Griffith was over budget.

During the early years of Hollywood, motion picture executives like the Aitken brothers remained in New York where the money was. Without visiting the set, they shelled out a final $19,000. When the money ran out again, Griffith, in the midst of shooting what he was certain would be a masterpiece, began selling stock in Epoch to anyone and everyone, diluting its original value. Theater owner W. H. Clune invested $15,000. Billy Bitzer put in his own life savings, $7,000 (he made it back four times over). Restauranteurs, the film's costumer, and some people who have never been identified bought stock. During production, Griffith would appear at the newsroom of the *Los Angeles Herald* and, with permission from the drama critic, pass his hat around in order to collect cash to meet the payroll.[12] Not counting prints, advertising, and distribution expenses, *The Birth of a Nation* cost over $100,000.

The completed film premiered at Clune's Auditorium in Los Angeles on February 8, 1915 and was screened at the Liberty in New York City the following week. On February 18 it played at the White House. And the rest is history with lightning.

The Birth of a Nation still wields great power. The battle scenes are impressively shot and edited, and the assassination of Lincoln is one of the most thrilling sequences of silent film, building suspense through artful cutting between the President's theater box, the blissful audience, and the approaching assassin. But the unabashed racism of *Birth* overwhelms the second half of the film. Dixon and Griffith perpetuate the cruelest stereotypes and most ignorant hatreds to position the Ku Klux Klan as America's heroes and to unite whites of the North and South against the black race.

Most white critics of the era praised *The Birth of a Nation* as history's greatest motion picture. *Variety* reviewed it four times between 1915 and 1930, always fawning. In 1922 it stated: "It looks very much as if this were the standard film of all time. No matter how often seen, there's always that little 'kick' or thrill involved that no other special

A portion of the colossal Babylon set in *Intolerance*.

feature or general release has held."[13] Through the years the racist elements were defiantly defended as "based on fact."

But many found the film's explicit racism not so easy to dismiss. The NAACP protested the film. Editorial writers and preachers, black and white, condemned it. *The Birth of a Nation*, frequently censored, was banned from five states and nineteen cities and has been legally challenged more than any other film in history—even as recently as 1978.[14]

Griffith appears to have been genuinely shocked by the negative response. He felt that he was merely presenting a Southern perspective on history and had tempered the most racist elements of Dixon's novel. Stung, he composed a treatise against censorship. The film's explosive controversy brought millions of Americans to see the world's first not-to-be-missed event picture. In the South, where it enjoyed its greatest success, it was advertised with the line "It will make you hate." In the following year two independents (*Free and Equal* and *Broken Chains*) tried to duplicate some of *Birth*'s box office receipts by mimicking its bigotry. Both failed.

Of the estimated $60 million *The Birth of a Nation* earned on its initial run, it returned to Epoch around $5 million, slightly less than a standard state's-rights percentage. *Birth* was rereleased several times, though never without protest. In 1930 it was edited to less than two hours and distributed with a soundtrack of music and effects. This version shamelessly concludes after the KKK rescue with an inserted sequence: a color shot of a billowing American flag shown while the national anthem plays, complete with the lyrics on-screen and encouragement to sing along.

In July 1915, Harry Aitken broke from Mutual to form the Triangle Film Corporation, which had separate production companies for Griffith, Ince, and Sennett. Griffith, at the height of the phenomenal success and swirling controversy of *The Birth of a Nation*, fixated on another epic he felt would both dwarf his previous work and answer its "intolerant" critics. *Intolerance* would tell four stories of woe: a modern account of poverty and injustice, Christ's crucifixion, the sixteenth century massacre of the Huguenots, and the fall of Babylon. Planning it, Griffith obsessed over historical minutiae. Actor/assistant/future director Joseph Henabery served as researcher, compiling an eight-pound scrapbook of design details that Griffith lugged everywhere.

Because *Intolerance* was beyond the scope of Triangle, Griffith and Harry Aitken set up the Wark Producing Corporation (as in David *Wark* Griffith) to create and distribute this single film. More than 80 percent of Wark was controlled by Aitken and Griffith via their *Birth of a Nation* profits and a wink-of-the-eye loan from Majestic. The remainder was raised through $1,000 certificates that sold themselves in the midst of *Birth*'s phenomenal success.

Despite exaggerations that *Intolerance* cost more than $2 million, it was actually made and released for $525,000 (still a gargantuan amount in 1916, forty times the cost of the average feature).[15] It remains today one of the most lavish productions in the history of cinema. The first spectacular "crane shot" (made with a platform elevator) of the Babylon court—an intricately designed set that was 300 feet tall and nearly a mile deep, filled with thousands of costumed extras—is perhaps the single greatest jaw-dropping sight on celluloid. Cinematography was again by Billy Bitzer and Karl Brown. Assistants included future respected directors Tod Browning, W. S. Van Dyke (both of whom also perform), and Erich von Stroheim.

Among the long list of actors are Lillian Gish, Donald Crisp, Mae Marsh, Douglas Fairbanks, Elmer Clifton, Howard Gaye (as Jesus), and Constance and Natalie Talmadge.

Griffith wanted to release *Intolerance*, originally edited to an overwhelming length of forty-eight reels, in two four-hour parts to be shown on consecutive nights. When no exhibitors agreed to the program, he trimmed it to three hours (some surviving versions are as short as two hours). The completed film is visually dazzling on a big screen, brimming with emotional power and beauty, but its theme feels trite, its intertitles are often insipid, and its structure is awkward, linking the four stories with the forced convention of Lillian Gish rocking in a chair.

Reviews at the time reflected its mixed qualities. Alexander Woollcott wrote in *The New York Times*: "Unprecedented and indescribable splendor of pageantry is combined with grotesque incoherence of design and utter fatuity of thought . . ."[16] *Intolerance* was distributed as a roadshow attraction. It played the best theaters, always accompanied by a full orchestra. For the first few months its box office kept pace with *The Birth of a Nation*'s early numbers, but the elaborate roadshow expenses ate up any profits. And then attendance trailed off.

Intolerance was a financial flop, an elephantine, big-budget saga that set out to alter the course of cinema but instead stumbled over its creator's ego. Griffith's temptation to follow a huge success with something even greater was an impulse felt by many future filmmakers, from Orson Welles to Michael Cimino, who would similarly fall into a pit of their own making.

When the most expensive film ever made bombs, it makes a loud explosion. Triangle filed for bankruptcy in 1917, and the Aitken brothers retreated to Wisconsin, where they sustained a living rereleasing *The Birth of a Nation*. Contrary to accounts, Griffith was not financially ruined, but he did take a major hit and was chastened enough to sign with a studio. The urge for independence would lead him on a different path in the not-too-distant future.

Meanwhile, the largest movie set ever constructed—a tribute to exuberance, to excess, and to dreams fulfilled and then crushed—was not torn down until 1917. For more than a year the walls of Babylon dominated the Hollywood skyline.

Notes

[1] Cook, Raymond Allen, *Fire from the Flint: The Amazing Careers of Thomas Dixon* (Winston-Salem, NC: John F. Blair, 1968), 168.

[2] Cook, 168.

[3] Quoted variously. By the time of the screening, "The Birth of a Nation" was already a subtitle in some advertising for "The Clansman."

[4] Quoted variously. Through a secretary, Wilson later denied making this remark.

[5] MacGowan, Kenneth, *Behind the Screen: The History and Techniques of the Motion Picture* (New York: Delacorte, 1965), 129.

[6] Merritt, Russel, "Nickelodeon Theaters 1905–1914: Building an Audience for the Movies," *The American Film Industry*, ed. Tino Balio (Madison: Univ. of Wisconsin, 1976), 75. Ticket sales went from twenty-six million per week in 1908 to at least forty-nine million in 1914.

[7] Brownlow, Kevin, *Hollywood: The Pioneers* (New York: Alfred A. Knopf, 1979), 56.

[8] *Rochester Post*, 2 April 1912.

[9] Gordon Parks became the first African-American to direct a feature for the studios when he adapted his own autobiographical novel, *The Learning Tree*, for Warner Bros. in 1969.

[10] *Variety*, 16 Jan. 1914.

[11] Schickel, Richard, *D. W. Griffith: An American Life* (New York: Simon and Schuster, 1984), 222–223.

[12] St. Johns, Adela, *The Honeycomb* (Garden City, NY: Doubleday, 1969), 56.

[13] *Variety*, 8 Dec. 1922.

[14] De Grazia, Edward and Roger K. Newman, *Banned Films: Movies, Censors and the First Amendment* (New York: R. R. Bowker, 1982), 5–6.

[15] Schickel, 326. The cost of production was $386,000 with an additional $139,000 for promotion, distribution, and guaranteed interest. Griffith's personal investment was $127,000.

[16] *New York Times*, 10 Sept. 1916.

EXPLORATION

The idea completely engulfed me. . . . By the time my train had reached the Middle West I had dressed my dream mouse in a pair of red velvet pants with two huge pearl buttons, had composed the first scenario and was all set.

—WALT DISNEY

February came, cold but glowing clear and calm. Then we began our films.

—ROBERT FLAHERTY[1]

The second half of the silent era was a period of tremendous creative growth. The new Hollywood studios continued to expand, though they hadn't yet perfected their system for stifling independence. There was ample room for mavericks, especially in emerging genres: race films, political propaganda, exploitation flicks, documentaries, the avant-garde. Furthermore, with the Trust defeated, film equipment was now readily available to all. It was a time when a whaling society could forge an adventure classic, a research scientist could conduct a storytelling experiment, and a mining explorer could turn the life of an Eskimo into one of the most influential works in the history of cinema.

Ethnic

There continued to be independent films made by and/or for a specific ethnicity. As in earlier years, limited exhibition channels and a shortage of capital often sentenced such companies to a quick death. A few were able to survive long enough, to compile a significant body of work. Most faded into obscurity.

In the twenties, Yiddish was still the first language for most American Jews, many of whom also rejected secular Hollywood cinema. Imported Russian, Polish, and Austrian flicks with traditional Yiddish themes and intertitles began to play New York venues. Maurice Schwartz, director of the Yiddish Art Theater, had acted in *Yisker* (1924), a film made in Poland by the expatriate Sidney Goldin. In 1926, Schwartz set out to star in and create the first American Yiddish feature. The result, *Tsebrokhene Herster* (Broken Hearts), a romantic melodrama about a Russian immigrant in New York, is amateurish and overly theatrical. It is also the only American-made silent film with Hebrew intertitles.

James B. Leong came to America from China in 1913 and served as assistant and interpreter on D. W. Griffith's *Broken Blossoms* (1919). He formed his own company and produced one movie, *Lotus Blossom* (1921), from a Chinese legend about a girl who gives her life so that a sacred bell will have a sweet tone. Leong went on to act in numerous B movies.

Sessue Hayakawa (1889–1973), a descendant of samurai, was the first non-Caucasian Hollywood star. Born and raised in Japan, he attended the University of Chicago, graduating in 1913 with a degree in political science. On the return trip to Nippon, Hayakawa changed plans and remained in Los Angeles. He joined a theater troupe and was signed to a film contract by producer/director Thomas Ince. In 1914 Hayakawa acted in Ince's *The Wrath of the Gods* and *The Typhoon*, both directed by Reginald Barker, both very successful.

The next year Hayakawa was the villain in Cecil B. DeMille's *The Cheat*, a racist worldwide sensation. He received praise for his powerful yet restrained acting (dubbed "Zen Method" by modern observers). Starring roles followed, casting him as Chinese, Hawaiian, Mexican, Indian, Arab, and, occasionally, Japanese. Hayakawa became a popular celebrity. With his wife, actress Tsuru Aoki, he built a castlelike home in Bel-Air and entertained his fellow Hollywood elite. In 1918, craving independence from frequently demeaning roles, Hayakawa formed a production company with writer/director William Worthington. They named it Hayworth (combining their last names).

Hayworth made more than twenty films. All were produced by and starred Hayakawa; most costarred his wife and were directed by Worthington. Their first film, *His Birthright* (1918), an espionage drama set around the then raging world war, features a US rear admiral who has an illegitimate son with a Japanese woman. The admiral's name is Milton, and, inadvertently insulted, rear admiral John B. Milton had the movie seized by naval officers. Charges didn't stand up, but publicity tainted the film and its immigrant star.

Hayworth mostly avoided making films with overtly Japanese themes, believing they'd have limited appeal. The most significant exception is *The Dragon Painter* (1919), in which a mad genius artist (Hayakawa) obsesses over a princess (Aoki). For the production, the city of Hakone, Japan, including its famous Shinto gates, was recreated in Yosemite Valley, California. Even at his own company, Hayakawa could not escape stereotyping and in 1919 played the role of the sinister "Chinaman" in *The Tong Man*, a film protested by the Chinese government and banned in Chinese-American communities.

The critics were sometimes kind to Hayworth's productions, but by the dawn of the Jazz Age the public had moved on to comedy and romance superstars. Hayakawa had only one comedic role, and as for romance, even when he played a "half-Japanese" he never won the white woman. He signed with Robertson-Cole in 1921 and continued to produce and act. In 1923, fed up with narrow minds in and out of the entertainment industry, the Hayakawas left America. He starred in European features, made a brief stab at a Hollywood comeback in character roles in the late forties, and was nominated for an Oscar for his acting in *The Bridge on the River Kwai* (1957). When his wife died in 1961, Hayakawa settled in Japan and lived as a Zen Buddhist priest. Sessue Hayakawa was a proud and intelligent man and a gifted performer who labored in and out of the Hollywood system. Disciplined and independent, he remains American cinema's only samurai.

African-American

The poison of *The Birth of a Nation* galvanized several black men to create a big-screen antidote. Emmet J. Scott had been the secretary to Booker T. Washington for more than twenty years. With Washington's death in 1915 and with Griffith's epic storming the nation, Scott proposed a filmed counterattack to *Birth*'s racism which would cite accomplishments of African-Americans. He raised money from wealthy blacks for a short entitled *Lincoln's Dream*, which could play after *The Birth of a Nation*. The script soon grew to feature length.

Shooting in Chicago and Tampa was plagued by bad weather, an inexperienced cast and crew, and inadequate equipment. When the money ran out, Scott turned to white investors who diluted the film's focus to a more universal tolerance. None of this stopped the completed picture, retitled *The Birth of a Race*, from running an excruciatingly long three hours. When it was finally released in 1918, it proved to be neither an effective answer to Dixon and Griffith's racist "history" nor an adequate tribute to African-American accomplishments. It opened strong but soon vanished.

D. W. Griffith's landmark also sparked the formation of the Frederick Douglass Film Company in New Jersey. Its first production, *The Colored American Winning His Suit* (1916), follows a hard-working black man. Its second, *The Scapegoat* (1917), was based on a story by the acclaimed black poet Paul Lawrence Dunbar. Both were directed by Traverse Sprague. The producers also made a documentary about African-American soldiers fighting in World War I. Unable to secure further bookings, the Frederick Douglass Film Company soon folded.

The same year as *The Birth of a Nation*, the Lincoln Motion Picture Company was formed by the imposing black actor Noble B. Johnson and his brother George, a postman. Backed by $75,000 from African-American investors, the company's stated mission—"to picture the Negro as he is in his every day, a human being with human inclination, and one of talent and intellect"—hints at how sorry the prevalent image of blacks was in the silent era.[2] Lincoln's first release, *The Realization of a Negro's Ambition* (1916), follows a Tuskegee graduate who strikes it rich in the oil fields of California. Its second, *The Trooper of Troop K* (1916), tells the true account of a black US regiment that fought in the Mexican-American War. Noble Johnson starred in both.

Johnson also starred in *The Law of Nature* (1916) while under contract to the burgeoning giant Universal Pictures, which perceived tiny Lincoln as a challenger and forced him to cease acting in the company. He went on to have a long career within the studio system, but after 1916 his roles were mostly small and demeaning: a savage Indian, a thieving Latin, a grunting jungle tribesman. His next-to-last role was as the Native American "Red Shirt" in the classic *She Wore a Yellow Ribbon* (1949).

The Lincoln Motion Picture Company persevered without Noble Johnson in front of the camera. It produced films starring Clarence Brooks (until then Lincoln's secretary) and one that featured Booker T. Washington, Jr. George Johnson, still a postman but also a visionary, spawned an independent film exchange for race pictures, hiring black newspapermen throughout America to book Lincoln's movies into "colored" theaters.

As the feature film surged in popularity and cinema palaces sprouted up, legal segregation in the South and de facto segregation in the North divided the movie-going audience along racial lines. A number of black venues opened to meet the demand, primarily in big-city ghettoes. Most were storefront dumps; some were vaudeville palaces. In 1921 there were more than 300 theaters catering almost exclusively to African-Americans. That number would grow, but with capital scarce and auditing of exhibitors nearly impossible, the profit margin for race picture producers remained slim. The Lincoln Motion Picture Company ceased operations in 1923. A flu epidemic that year closed many theaters—both black and white—and killed off several production companies.

Chicago's white-owned Ebony Film Corporation made one-reel slapstick comedies starring black vaudeville personalities. Most of them, like *Black Sherlock Holmes* (1918), spoofed popular Hollywood vehicles. Though they featured interracial casts, Ebony's flicks were criticized by black newspapers as insensitive and exploitive. The company folded in 1922.

At the dawn of the Harlem Renaissance in the early twenties, the Reol Motion Picture Corporation, which was headed by white Robert Levy and featured Harlem's Lafayette Players, tried to establish Edna Morton as the first black movie star, advertising her as "the colored Mary Pickford." The name didn't catch on.

Regional companies did a better job of capturing the diversity of the black experience, but like the others, they found it tough to turn a profit. The Norman Film Manufacturing Company produced race westerns. Their best known, *The Crimson Skull* (1921), was shot in the all-black town of Bosley, Oklahoma. It starred "thirty colored cowboys," including legendary rodeo star Bill Pickett. San Antonio had two companies that made black westerns, and there was a similar enterprise in Kansas City. A business in New York made black-themed newsreels. More than forty race picture companies came and went. Most of their films are long since lost.

By 1928 there were approximately 700 theaters catering almost exclusively to African-Americans. Some of these were owned by whites whose venues had gradually become predominantly African-American, and some of these owners made films for their new audience. One such man was David Starkman, who formed the Colored Players Company in 1926. Their first release, *A Prince of His Race* (1926), is a drama about the black bourgeoisie. The Colored Players made what is regarded as the best African-American silent picture, *Scar of Shame* (1928). It's a melodramatic tale of stratification within black society. When a light-skinned black pianist (Harry Henderson) marries a darker-skinned nightclub singer (Lucia Lynn Moses), the union is doomed by color. Starkman was the writer, Frank Perugini the director. The one African-American behind the camera was producer Sherman Dudley. Production values are slim, but in composition and theme *Scar of Shame* compares favorably with typical Hollywood productions of the era.

The race picture industry was virtually wiped out by the Depression and the advent of sound, which made production and projection prohibitively expensive. Only one company survived into the thirties. It was the same company that withstood the flu epidemic of 1923 and the growth of radio entertainment throughout the twenties and that would persevere in one form or another to create an unprecedented forty-six black-cast features in four decades, its entire output produced, directed, written, and distributed by a single black man.

The grandson of slaves, Oscar Micheaux (1884–1951) was raised in Illinois, one of thirteen children. In 1909, while searching for adventure, he homesteaded a farm in lily-white South Dakota. In a few years he had acquired more than 500 acres. Spring, summer, and fall were filled with planting and harvesting, but the cold winters provided idle time. Micheaux began to write. Beginning in 1913, he self-published semi-autobiographical novels and sold them door-to-door. When Micheaux lost his farm in 1915 due to the financial malfeasance of his brother-in-law, he moved to Iowa. He continued to write books and toured wide sections of the country hawking them.

In 1918 George Johnson read Micheaux's *The Homesteader*, and he summoned him to the Lincoln Motion Picture Company to negotiate a screen adaptation. Micheaux was interested in breaking into moving pictures, but the Johnson brothers balked at letting him direct. So

Oscar Micheaux
Presents
The
Gunsaulus
Mystery
WITH
EVELYN PREER —
— DICK ABRAMS
L. DE BULGER —
LAWRENCE CHENAUī
and a notable supporting
colored cast

Writer/director/producer Oscar Micheaux pictured on a lobby card for
The Gunsaulus Mystery (1921). This film is now lost.

Micheaux kept the rights to his novel, formed the Micheaux Film and
Book Company, and raised capital from farmers and businessmen. He
hired a chauffeur to drive his cast and crew—piled into one car—from
Chicago to a farm in Winner, South Dakota. The picture they made
was no timid two-reeler. Instead, Oscar Micheaux, a total novice to
filmmaking, produced *The Homesteader* (1919) in eight reels. It tells
Micheaux's personal tale of a lone black man farming in the West. *The
Homesteader* was a success.

Micheaux followed his debut with his most controversial picture,
Within Our Gates (1920). This was the first film to depict lynching from
a black perspective. Challenging *The Birth of a Nation*, the film depicts
a white Southerner about to rape a black woman. He stops only when
he realizes she's his illegitimate daughter. *Within Our Gates* was like a
keg of dynamite in 1920. The year before was "Red Summer," so
named for the bloody antiblack riots in several cities. Fearing the
worst, many theaters refused *Within Our Gates*, and Micheaux excised
the most inflammatory material from some screenings. Despite a slow

first hour, for sheer bravery, *Within Our Gates* remains the essential Oscar Micheaux movie. In 1992 it was named to the National Film Registry of the Library of Congress.

Even after forty films, Micheaux would not be an adept artist, but from the very beginning he was the consummate salesman. He toured from city to city with a film print and advertising material. A tall and handsome man who dressed extravagantly, he was a charmer. Micheaux convinced theater owners to show one of his movies while getting them to invest in his next, all the while peddling his novels. One film led to another. Shooting in Chicago, New Jersey, and New York, he averaged nearly three race pictures a year through 1927.

In 1924, Micheaux made *Body and Soul*. A case against crooked preachers (a recurring Micheaux theme), it features the debut of football star/singer/law school graduate Paul Robeson. In future decades, through his film roles, vibrant stage career, and martyrdom as a leftist, Robeson would be the first African-American actor exalted as a legend.

Micheaux films featured few such captivating performers. With budgets of less than $15,000, most scenes could only be filmed in one take. Yet Micheaux's films rose above the sloppy editing, sparse production design, and dull cinematography. Unlike most race picture producers in the silent era, he did not take the easy path of merely grinding out ebony versions of Hollywood moneymakers. Instead, he addressed controversial black themes for black urban audiences, including intermarriage, prostitution, the numbers rackets, racially motivated injustice, and the Ku Klux Klan. Micheaux stated in 1925: "It is only by presenting those portions of the race portrayed in my pictures in light and background of their true state that we can raise our people to greater heights."[3]

When the movies learned to talk and the Depression stung the hardest, Micheaux's contemporaries closed up shop. The race picture industry was virtually wiped out. The silent legacy is mixed. Saddled with the slimmest of budgets, mute African-American movies are mostly crude productions with stilted acting and artless plots. Many of them perpetuated stereotypes and often focused on passing for white as a worthy aspiration. But on many dimly lit screens in ghetto theaters during the silent era, blacks could see positive representations of themselves as soldiers, cowboys, judges, intellectuals, beauties, and heroes. Better than any other genre in the history of cinema, the silent race pictures of men like William Foster, Emmet J. Scott, the Johnson brothers, and Oscar Micheaux represent an ethic of self-empowerment, of people circumventing an ignorant and ignoble Hollywood to take control of their own stories and their own destinies.

True Crime

True crime continued to be a small but delightfully unpredictable independent category. Al Jennings headed the infamous band of cattle rustlers and train robbers known as "The Long Riders." Out of prison and going (sort of) respectable, he played himself in *Beating Back* (1914), based on his own moral conversion. In 1918, Jennings formed a movie company to tell real tales of Western banditry featuring himself and his brother Frank, another ex-Long Rider going (sort of) respectable; he was a practicing attorney. Former Griffith assistant and future MGM "one-take" director W. S. Van Dyke directed the productions. The first, starring Corinne Grant and Al Jennings, was *The Lady in the Dugout* (1918). Others followed, of marginal quality and success. Al Jennings acted in assorted pictures until the end of the silent era.

Clara Harmon admitted to killing her husband, oil tycoon Jacob Harmon, but she was acquitted of the Oklahoma murder in 1920. Though she was able to persuade a jury of her innocence, the general public was not so easily swayed, so she decided to star in and produce a motion picture that would tell her story. Aided by promoter W. C. Weathers, an extravagant budget of $200,000 was raised primarily from Jacob Harmon's spiteful competitors in the oil business. But Hollywood, having been rocked by the sordid manslaughter case of actor "Fatty" Arbuckle, wanted nothing to do with Harmon. Technicians were ordered not to work on the film. Andre Barlatier accepted the hefty fee of $500 a week as cameraman, but it cost him his membership in the prestigious American Society of Cinematographers.[4] Hollywood outsider John W. Gordon signed on as screenwriter and director for the hyperinflated salary of $75,000. During production a romance developed between Gordon and Clara Harmon. They were married in August 1921 (and divorced four years later).

The completed film, *Fate* (1921), is Clara's version of events. Director John Ince (brother of the more famous filmmaker, Thomas) plays Jacob Harmon. She's a teen; he's middle-aged. He strikes it rich in oil, drinks, grows brutal. She shoots him in self-defense, flees to Mexico, returns to face trial, and is acquitted, to the joy of courtroom observers. *Fate* premiered in the Oklahoma town where the events took place, and it had the desired effect, swaying opinion there towards Clara. A number of local women even contributed from their own purses to help with distribution.

But the film immediately ran into trouble elsewhere, mostly from outraged men. James Quirk in *Photoplay* wrote: "Despite the clearly voiced opinion of the country that Clara Harmon . . . should not try to capitalize her disgusting notoriety on the screen, she proceeded to make a picture . . . No decent distributor would handle it [and] any exhibitor that showed it in his theater should be run out of town."[5] Newspapers wouldn't advertise it and venues wouldn't screen it. *Fate*, a flawed but intriguing true crime tale, drifted into obscurity, as did its leading lady.

A Man in a Million (1922) was a twist on the true crime independent. The fashionable young Madalynne Obenchain divorced her husband Ralph to pursue Los Angeles aristocrat J. Belton Kennedy, with whom she was having an affair. Kennedy then spurned her. One night Obenchain called Kennedy to a cabin where a gunman—allegedly Arthur Burch—shot and killed him. Both Obenchain and Burch stood trial for murder. Obenchain received much press attention for her implausible defense: she lost her memory the moment she heard the gun fire.

Amid much evidence of her infidelity and implication in a premeditated killing, Ralph Obenchain testified to his ex-wife's good character and offered to marry her again. Taking loyalty to an extreme, he financed the three-reel *A Man in a Million*. Directed by Charles Seeling, Ralph plays himself in this sugarcoated story of his romance with Madalynne. He made personal appearances wherever the film was shown and insisted that all profits go towards his ex-wife's defense.

After two trials and a year in jail, Madalynne Obenchain and Arthur Burch were released. She studied acting with the unfulfilled hope of breaking into film. She and her man in a million never remarried.

Directing Debuts

Independent films have always been a way for outsiders to squeeze their way inside. If the studios won't hire you, the belief goes, find a company small enough to give you a shot. If nobody will hire you, do it yourself. Many of America's greatest cinematic artists have launched their career's this way.

King Vidor (1894–1982), born and raised in Galveston, Texas, worked in a nickelodeon as a teenager and shot Houston events for newsreel companies. In 1914, at the age of twenty, Vidor set up the Hotex Motion Picture Company to make one- and two-reelers. Unable to secure proper distribution, the business quickly failed. The next year Vidor and his new wife, Florence Arto, moved to Hollywood. She worked as an actress; he was an actor and screenwriter. His first script sold to Vitagraph for $30.

Around this time, Willis Brown, a juvenile court judge in Salt Lake City, established a system of orphanages known as Boy Cities. In 1914, eager to dramatize the experiences of these young men, Judge Brown wrote, directed, and starred as himself in *A Boy and the Law*, a true parable of an immigrant youth benefiting from a Boy City. The film was a moderate success (the *Chicago Herald* made arrangements for kids under sixteen to see it for free), but Judge Brown wasn't much of a filmmaker. So he hired the young and eager King Vidor.

In 1918 Vidor called the shots on ten two-reelers for the Boy City Film Corporation. Each moving picture opens with the parents of some unruly youth presenting a problem to the judge. As Vidor explains, "Judge Brown would always prescribe some unorthodox but deeply human remedy. The main film story would concern itself with the manner in which these intensely human problems worked themselves out."[6]

It was just the start Vidor needed. In 1919, with $9,000 from some of the same physicians who'd backed Judge Brown, King Vidor launched Brentwood Films. He wrote and directed *The Turn in the Road*, a melodrama that featured elements of Vidor's Christian Science faith. *The Turn in the Road* opened at a bankrupt theater in downtown Los Angeles. Word of mouth spread through Christian Science circles, and eleven weeks later there were still lines around the block. The picture was picked up for distribution by Robertson-Cole and went on to gross a very healthy $350,000.

Vidor was ordained the new boy wonder. He followed later in 1919 with a simple love story, *Better Times*, featuring ZaSu Pitts, and two social dramas starring his wife that preached compassion for the destitute, *The Other Half* and *Poor Relations*. In 1920, for $15,000, he bought a square block in Hollywood and built his own studio with permanent small-town sets. It was dubbed "Vidor Village." Vidor also published "A Creed and a Pledge" in *Variety*, stating that he would utilize the motion picture medium only to uplift humanity, always for good, never for evil, an ideal sometimes at odds with the bottom line.

Two additional "problem pictures" followed: *The Family Honor* (1920) preaches against gambling and drinking; *The Jack-Knife Man* (1920) is a touching tale of a vagrant who makes good. Neither was successful. Vidor loved his creative freedom, but independence brought one debt after another. *The Sky Pilot* (1921), a melodrama about a young minister on a ranch, was shot on location in the Northwest. Plagued by bad weather, it went dangerously over budget. Vidor Village soon faced a court-ordered seizure of its property. *Love Never Dies* (1921), a domestic melodrama, could only be finished when Thomas Ince took over financing.

Financially beleaguered but still craving the autonomy to tell his own stories, Vidor signed a four-picture deal with Associated Exhibitors that made his wife (then a leading player at Paramount) executive producer. The first three films were *The Real Adventure, Dusk to Dawn,* and *Conquering the Woman.* All are dramas directed by Vidor and released in 1922; all star his wife. By the time the fourth movie went into production, the Vidor marriage was breaking up. The following year King Vidor produced *Alice Adams* (1923), a domestic tale starring his soon-to-be-ex-spouse, but it was directed by Rowland V. Lee.

Vidor succumbed to the studios in 1922, and under contract at MGM he created his silent antiwar masterpiece, *The Big Parade* (1925). A populist who would eventually make films on both sides of the political spectrum, King Vidor was one of the earliest mavericks to compile a significant body of work devoted to social themes. He wasn't done with independence, either. In the early years of the sound era, when no studio would finance it, King Vidor set out on his own to forge one of the most radical social works in the history of American cinema.

Gregory La Cava started as an animator in 1917. His live-action directorial debut is *His Nibs* (1921), which features Colleen Moore in an inventive comedy about a Southern theater owner who explains (in intertitles) a titleless movie. *His Nibs* was an independent production, as were La Cava's next two features: the domestic melodrama

Restless Wives and the rural comedy *The New School Teacher* (both 1924). La Cava went on to helm such studio classics as *My Man Godfrey* (1936) and *Stage Door* (1937).

Other moviemakers, established in the studios, did independent work between better-paying gigs. Tod Browning was a director at Universal before crafting a pair of suggestive exploitation pictures, *The Dangerous Flirt* and *Silk Stocking Sal* (both 1924), both starring the popular Evelyn Brent, both poorly reviewed. He returned to studio back lots and later made such gothic classics as *Dracula* (1930) and *Freaks* (1932).

Maurice Tourneur, a trained painter, acted and directed in France before he came to Hollywood to work for the studios. Between 1918 and 1921 Tourneur directed seven independent productions. The first was *Sporting Life* (1918), a suspense melodrama. *Variety* overly praised the romantic *The White Heather* (1919) as "an absolute masterpiece of motion picture direction and photography. . . ."[7] The best of Tourneur's autonomous productions is *While Paris Sleeps* (1923, shot in 1920). A gothic tale set in France, it stars the legendary Lon Chaney (between studio gigs) as a murderous waxworks attendant. The other indies are *Woman* (1918), *The Broken Butterfly* (1919), a first-rate version of *The Last of the Mohicans* (1920), and *The Foolish Matrons* (1921); the final two were codirected with Clarence Brown. Ever the renegade, Tourneur felt creatively stifled when he returned to studio stages. After an artistic squabble with MGM, he repatriated to France in 1927 and made films there throughout the forties. Son Jacques Tourneur surpassed his father, directing several Hollywood classics.

Socialism

During the first three decades of the twentieth century, socialism was a significant political movement in America. In the presidential election of 1920, Eugene Debs—while in prison for protesting World War I—received nearly one million votes (more than 6 percent) as the Socialist Party candidate. In this climate, when it was still possible to make one- and two-reelers cheaply, nearly a dozen radical groups adopted the popular medium of motion pictures to promote their cause. The most prolific group was the Labor Film Service, whose most widely seen motion picture was *The Contrast* (1921). Financed by coal miners, it's a love story that compares the lives of the rich with those of the poor. Backed by the Federation Film Corporation, *The*

New Discipline (1921) presents a World War I hero who leads workers in taking control of the mills. Such films were shown primarily at union meetings, often shrouded in secrecy.

On the other end of the political spectrum, in 1920, anticommunist Herbert Hoover, then in charge of the American effort to alleviate famine in Europe, backed the nonfiction feature *Starvation*. Produced and financed by Navy lieutenant commander George Baker and shot, directed, and edited by newsreel cameraman George Zimmer, the movie is a rebuke of socialism. It features footage of Bolsheviks being hanged and shot (which had the opposite of the intended effect, making audiences sympathetic), and it documents the famine that followed communism. The dawn of the twenties was a bad time for a movie called *Starvation*; World War I had sent American food prices soaring. Baker lost $11,000 on the venture and advised other capitalists against investing in cinema. Herbert Hoover was elected president in 1928. Famine followed.

In October of 1925, textile workers in Passaic, New Jersey staged a walkout in response to a wage cut. It was the first American strike openly initiated and led by the Communist party, and it soon spread to other mills, bringing the total number of strikers to 16,000. Alfred Wagenknecht, head of the strikers' relief committee, proposed a film to raise money. He explains, "We then bought a movie camera and a projector, got together a staff from the strikers and photographed the real happenings. It was dangerous but it was genuine adventure, not the warmed-over thrills carefully dolled up by Hollywood methods.[8]

The Passaic Textile Strike, which features staged and actual footage, including real gassing and clubbing of picketers by the police, was shown in Passaic in October 1926. The film played at labor events throughout the country in an effort to raise relief funds. The strike finally ended in February 1927, and though the wage cut was rescinded, thousands of strikers were not rehired. All had lost more than a year's wages, and the area was devastated. *The Passaic Textile Strike* was considered lost until a print was discovered in the eighties. It remains today an early document of ordinary citizens utilizing popular cinema for their cause.

Though socialist films were little seen, they highlight a role independent cinema has always filled: to tell the sort of politically charged (almost always leftist) tales the studios assiduously avoid. From Upton Sinclair and King Vidor to Lizzie Borden and Michael Moore, not having to answer to corporate bosses is intellectually liberating. As will be seen in the next section and throughout this book, independent filmmakers often make movies to argue for a political cause.

Women

In the era of the flapper, of short skirts and bobbed hair, social mobility was big news. "The fairer sex" was entering previously all-male domains like colleges, offices, and taverns (then speakeasies). As women won the right to vote, learn, work, and play, female filmmakers forged their own opportunities to an extent not seen before or since.

Margaret Sanger was born in 1883, one of eleven children. She became a nurse, married an architect, and had three children. As a nurse, she specialized in obstetrics and saw firsthand the need among the poor for reliable advice about contraception. Under the Comstock Law of 1873, it was illegal to distribute information on birth control (as well as merely to mention in print the names of sexually transmitted diseases). But after learning of a poor pregnant woman who committed suicide rather than bring another child into a life of poverty, Sanger could no longer remain silent.

Beginning in 1914, Sanger would be arrested numerous times for publishing and mailing contraceptive advice. In 1916 she opened America's first birth control clinic. She was jailed, but won her appeal, clearing the way for doctors to disseminate such information in New York City. With the dream of reaching a mass audience, Sanger wrote a screenplay with Frederick Blossum on the subject of contraception. Financed by an associate of Blossum and boldly titled *Birth Control* (1917), the film stars Sanger in her personal story of political enlightenment. It ends with her imprisonment and the intertitle "No matter what happens, the work shall go on."

Variety noted *Birth Control*'s contrasts of the uninformed poor with the wealthy: "The average observer is electrified with the intense convictions of the propagandist, taken hither and thither throughout New York's teeming child streets, to the almost childless precincts of the informed wealthy."[9] Predictably, the New York Film Commission denied *Birth Control* a license, calling it "immoral, indecent, and directly contrary to public welfare."[10] For years *Birth Control* was seen by those attending Sanger's lectures. Not until 1965 did the US Supreme Court overturn state laws making the dispersal of birth control information a crime. In 1921, Margaret Sanger founded the American Birth Control League, which would later become Planned Parenthood. She advocated contraceptive rights throughout the world until her death in 1966.

Another favorable film biography of Sanger was released in 1917. Entitled *The Hand that Rocks the Cradle*, its producer, director, and star was female filmmaking pioneer Lois Weber. The film caused much less controversy than Weber's pro-contraception (and antiabortion) picture of the previous year, *Where Are My Children?* Neither film was an independent, though Weber would soon begin working outside the studio walls.

Lois Weber (1882–1939) devoted most of her filmmaking career to social issue dramas. Born in Allegheny, Pennsylvania, she ran away to New York City as a teenager and endured the kind of poverty she would later so vividly portray in her films. At one point she sang in the streets for food. Weber labored as a social worker in the slums and as a missionary to prisoners. She married Phillips Smalley in 1905; both acted in early photoplays. Weber began directing in 1912. Because her one-reelers were knocked out in a week or less, she compiled a filmography that nearly rivaled D. W. Griffith's, directing, writ-

Censorship

The independent arena has had a long and stormy relationship with censors. While *Birth Control* was banned from New York, *The Spirit of '76* (1917) opened in Los Angeles. This independent epic patriotically depicts the events of the American revolution, including the brutality of British soldiers, and yet the film was seized and producer Robert Goldstein (a backer of *The Birth of a Nation*) was charged with violating the Espionage Act. Incredibly, courts held that *The Spirit of '76* was calculated to encourage disloyalty towards Britain, a US ally during World War I. Goldstein was sentenced to ten years in prison and fined $5000.

The ironic case of *The Spirit of '76* is an extreme example, but hundreds of independent filmmakers have faced suppression. Beginning in 1909, most states and major cities established censorship boards. Boards were either part of the police department or they were elected tribunals of concerned (or overly concerned) citizens. Many were phased out after the Production Code was enforced in the early thirties. Others persisted for decades, meeting privately to screen movies

continued

Censorship

continued

and pass judgment. Censors objected most-ly to sexual content, but motion pictures were also suppressed because of profanity, sacrilege, the depiction of police corruption, and, in either the North or the South, the presentation of racial disharmony or racial harmony. Among the independent films that were officially banned from communi-ties are: *The Birth of a Nation, The Forgotten Village, Lost Boundaries, The Connection, The Garden of Eden, Titicut Follies*, and *Deep Throat*.

ing, producing, or starring in more than 400 moving pictures.

Lois Weber was the first woman to direct a feature (*The Merchant of Venice*, 1914) and, following the publicity surrounding *Hypocrites*, became one of the top-salaried filmmakers in Hollywood, signing at Universal for $5,000 per week. It was money well spent; *Where Are My Children?* grossed $3 million. Weber explained, "I like to direct because I believe a woman, more or less intuitively, brings out many of the emotions that are rarely expressed on the screen."[11] Like Vidor, Weber was a Christian Scientist, and she said of filmmak-ing, "Now I can preach to my heart's content."[12] And preach she did. Weber made movies against capital punishment, alcohol, divorce, and promiscuity and for the rights of women and the elimination of poverty.

In 1919, at the height of her popularity, Weber signed a contract with Paramount for $50,000 per picture and half of the profits, a deal that allowed her to pursue independent productions. Her first indie was *To Please One Woman* (1920), a preachy melodrama that shows how one woman's selfishness affects those around her. It died at the box office. For the lead role Weber cast Clara Viola Cronk, whose experience consisted of one appearance as an extra. Weber dreamed up Cronk's new name—Claire Windsor—and a (minor) star was born.

Weber's next independent, the society melodrama *What's Worth While?* (1921), barely made a splash. It was followed by her most famous feature: *The Blot* (1921). Using a special lighting technique (invented by her cameraman, Del Clawson) that enabled her to shoot in real homes, *The Blot* documents a gloomy small-town reality rarely seen in studio productions. *The Blot* plot is another melodrama: a librarian (Claire Windsor) falls in love with a clergyman, but her father, an underpaid college professor, steers her towards a wealthy

Lois Weber.
Courtesy of the Academy of Motion Picture Arts and Sciences.

student because he fears for her financial future. Addressing the genteel poverty of teachers and clergy, it was advertised as "a great American drama of today." It flopped.

Weber's final independent was *What Do Men Want?* (1921), a melodramatic sermon. A man deserts his wife (Claire Windsor) and children for Bertha the Unfortunate. When he later deserts her, too, she kills herself, and the contrite husband returns to his family. In 1921 Lois Weber said, "I'll never be convinced that the general public does not want serious entertainment rather than frivolous."[13] Big mistake. Jazz Age audiences were not interested in being preached to. Though Weber directed a few additional pictures, by the mid-twenties she'd lost her company, divorced Smalley (in spite of her moral convictions), and suffered a nervous breakdown. Once one of the highest-paid directors in Hollywood, two decades later she died lonely, broke, and virtually forgotten. Weber's funeral expenses were paid by screenwriting great Frances Marion.

After women were granted the right to vote, the suffragist film *Mothers of Men* (1917) was remade as *Every Woman's Problem* (1921). Both were independents directed by and featuring Willis Robards. They tell of a woman who is elected to a judgeship and must sentence her husband to death. The husband is saved at the last minute when the real killer confesses. The lasting value of these pictures is that they star Dorothy Davenport and her husband, Wallace Reid.

The son of director Hal Reid, Wallace began acting in films in 1910. Featured in both *The Birth of a Nation* and *Intolerance*, Wallace Reid was a popular thirty-two-year-old leading man when he died of morphine addiction in 1923. Dorothy Davenport, who had called a press conference when she admitted her husband to a sanitorium, was quick to capitalize on his scandalous death. She adopted the name Mrs. Wallace Reid (1895–1977) and went on to act in the lost classic *Human Wreckage* (1923), an exposé of the dangers of drugs, famous for the deranged buildings featured in the hallucination scene. After a cross-country tour lecturing on drug addiction and promoting *Human Wreckage*, Mrs. Reid, professional widow, embarked on a career as independent producer and occasional director and actress.

In contrast to Lois Weber, Mrs. Reid feigned morality, but her films were barely couched exploitation. *Broken Laws* (1924) criticizes neglectful parents but mostly details the debauchery of their children. Her most famous production is *The Red Kimono* (1925), which marks the directorial debut of stage veteran Walter Lang. According to accounts, Reid sat next to Lang on the set and approved each shot. After opening with a brief allegory of Hell, Mrs. Reid introduces the tale of Gabrielle (Priscella Bonner), a prostitute in New Orleans whose boyfriend has gone to Los Angeles to marry someone else. Gabrielle follows him, sees him buying a diamond ring, and kills him. At the trial she recounts her history, that of an innocent girl lured into white slavery. The jury acquits. Unable to find work,

Gabrielle returns to the red lights of New Orleans only to be rescued by the love of a chauffeur. Mrs. Reid appears again to wrap it all up with a Bible quotation.

With cheap production values and an overly melodramatic plot, *The Red Kimono* hasn't aged well, except as an interesting document of what once passed for shocking. Upon its release, *Variety* said: "It seems the day when 'the line' can be shown in pictures is long since passed."[14] One line Reid should not have passed was basing her script on an actual case and not changing names. The real Gabrielle sued and won $50,000, nearly bankrupting Mrs. Reid.

The next year Walter Lang again called the shots on a Reid production, *The Earth Woman* (1926), starring Mary Alden. The title card dedicates it "to pioneer women who helped build this country," but it's a standard melodrama featuring murder, attempted rape, and lynching.

When Walter Lang made *The Satin Woman* (1927) for Sam Sax Productions, he returned a favor to Reid, casting her in the starring role. It was not well reviewed. Mrs. Reid directed her first feature, *Linda*, in 1929. As Dorothy Reid, she continued to sporadically write, produce, and direct marginal movies for independent companies and Poverty Row studios. Her acting career essentially ended when sound arrived, but she directed as late as 1955 (*Footsteps in the Fog*) and produced a feature in 1966 (*Terror in the City*). Walter Lang made a few additional indies before signing with the studios. He went on to helm more than fifty pictures, including such musical extravaganzas as *State Fair* (1945) and *The King and I* (1956).

Natasha Rambova and Alla Nazimova remain two of the most fascinating enigmas in silent cinema. Beginning in 1916, the Russian-born Nazimova performed in numerous features, some of which were produced and financed by herself and directed by her common-law husband, Charles Bryant. The most compelling is *Salome* (1923), based on Oscar Wilde's play of the same name. Reinterpreting the Biblical tale, Nazimova plays the title character who, enraged at Jokaanan's refusal of a kiss, will dance for Herod if he will bring her Jokaanan's head on a silver platter. Herod grants her request but, outraged at the sight of Salome kissing Jokaanan's head, has her killed.

Salome's set designer, costumer, writer (using the pseudonym Peter M. Winters), and, some film historians say, true director was Natasha Rambova, wife of the legendary screen heartthrob Rudolph Valentino and supposed lover of Nazimova. Based on the hedonistic drawings of Aubrey Beardsley, the set design is sumptuously artificial.

Along with the perverse plot and impressive sets and costumes, what is fascinating about *Salome* is that the entire cast was rumored (some say touted by Nazimova) to be gay. A 1914 independent, *A Florida Enchantment*, by Sidney Drew, dealt with sex changes, but *Salome* is today regarded as America's first gay feature. Reviewers made no mention of this upon release (after censors excised several sequences), but *Salome*'s notoriety grew, doing much damage to the careers of Nazimova, Rambova, and even Valentino.

Nazimova was financially ruined when *Salome* flopped. Acting offers disappeared, though she did make a brief stab at a comeback in the early forties (she died in 1945). Blamed for crafting Rudolph Valentino's increasingly effeminate image, Rambova slipped into relative obscurity. Valentino was arrested for bigamy and hounded by press insinuations about his sexuality (the *Chicago Tribune* editorialized against him under the headline "Pink Powder Puff"). He suffered a perforated ulcer in 1926 and died of complications at the age of thirty-one.

Masterpieces?

In 1922, *Motion Picture News* stated: "What will be written in screen history as a masterpiece of its kind is offered in Elmer Clifton's *Down to the Sea in Ships*."[15] This unique production, while not quite a masterpiece, does stand today as a true adventure classic. The historical seafaring romance was initiated by its producer/director Elmer Clifton, an actor in such films as *John Barleycorn* and *The Birth of a Nation* and director of more than fifty features between 1917 and 1950. John L. E. Pell penned the script.

Down to the Sea in Ships (1922) was financed by the Whalemen's Association of New Bedford in order to preserve a historical document of their work and lifestyle. The townspeople of New Bedford, Massachusetts embraced the idea. An advisory council of ship captains assisted, and the *Charles W. Morgan*, the oldest ship afloat, was enlisted. James A. Tilton, a seaman with forty years of experience, was cast as the schooner's captain. All houses on-screen are actual homes, some of them Quaker domiciles dating as far back as 1714.

The tale follows Thomas Dexter (Raymond McKee), who loves Patience Morgan (Marguerite Courtot) but cannot marry her until he becomes a Quaker and has killed a whale. The first obligation is easy enough to meet; the second requires much effort. Because the whaling expedition was genuine, production lasted a full year. The cast and crew sailed on an extended voyage south of Haiti. Actor Raymond McKee actually harpoons the whale killed on-screen. Adding to the film's sense of authenticity, an on-set romance developed between McKee and Courtot, and they were married before filming wrapped. The completed yarn features Clara Bow (who went on to become the "It" girl, a Roaring Twenties icon) and a shipload of intertitles from *Moby Dick*. Despite a predictable plot, *Down to the Sea in Ships* is a rousing quest and a unique celluloid document. It was remade by Fox in 1949.

Another independent historical "masterpiece" has not fared so well. *The Dramatic Life of Abraham Lincoln* (1924, aka *Abraham Lincoln*), produced and distributed by the Rockett-Lincoln Film Company and helmed by the prolific Phil Rosen, is a detailed story of Lincoln's life from birth to death. George A. Billings is convincing as the sixteenth president, and the use of Honest Abe's quotes for intertitles is effective, but the screenplay tries to cover too much and thus ends up covering very little. Though at the time it was widely hailed as the best American film of 1924, today, it seems boring and unfocused.

Documentary

Robert Flaherty (1884–1951) was born the son of a miner and divided his early years between Iron Mountain, Michigan and the Canadian wilderness. He began working as a prospector in 1907 and in 1910 the railroad baron Sir William MacKenzie sent him into the subarctic around the Hudson Bay in search of iron ore. That's when he first met an Eskimo. In 1911 he set out on another frozen odyssey that lasted nineteen months. Assisted by four Eskimos, his was the first expedition to cross the barren Ungava region.

In 1913 MacKenzie arranged for him to go North on an even longer excursion. The explorer remembers, "Just as I was leaving, Sir William said to me casually, 'Why don't you get one of those newfangled things called a motion picture camera?' So I bought one with no other thought really than of taking notes on our exploration. We were going into interesting country, we'd see interesting people."[16]

Flaherty took a three-week course in cinematography from the Eastman Company. He bought a camera, some film, and a portable developing and printing machine. He sailed a thousand miles to Baffin Island and set up camp with the Eskimos to wait out the ten months of winter. Then, in 1914, he traveled via sled to Amadjuak Lake and filmed his surroundings. On the way back, Flaherty's sled broke through the ice and all the film was lost.

The man from Iron Mountain was willing to try again. He journeyed to the Belcher Islands in the summer of 1915. Waterproofing his film boxes with sealskin, Flaherty captured the Northern Canadian scenery. In 1916 he cut it into a film. But again fate was against him, and while working in his Toronto editing room one day, he dropped a lit cigarette onto the highly combustible negative and the whole film went up in flames. Flaherty consoled himself by saying the film had been merely a series of nature shots.

Flaherty soon had a new idea: "Why not take . . . a typical Eskimo and his family and make a biography of their lives through the year? What biography of any man could be more interesting? Here is a man

The star of *Nanook of the North*.
Courtesy of the Academy of Motion Picture Arts and Sciences.

who has less resources than any other man in the world. He lives in a desolation that no other race could possibly survive. His life is a constant fight against starvation. Nothing grows; he must depend utterly on what he can kill; and all of this against the most terrifying of tyrants—the bitter climate of the North."[17] Flaherty tried for years to secure financing. He finally convinced a French furrier to foot the bill (which would eventually total $50,000) in exchange for the credit "Revillon Frères presents" in the opening titles.

Flaherty took two new cameras to Northern Canada along with equipment to develop, print, and project the celluloid. In order to process the film, Eskimos kept a hole chiseled through six feet of ice and hauled water to their American friend in barrels pulled by sled. In order to dry the film, the explorer built an annex onto the hut with a stove, a room where he would spend a year of his life. When Flaherty first projected rushes, one viewer, Nanook, the film's star, harpooned the screen in an attempt to kill the image of a walrus. Every native in the room grabbed the rope to make sure the celluloid mammal didn't get away.

As Flaherty intended, the completed film, *Nanook of the North* (1922), is an engaging document of an utterly unique life. In an age of timid travelogues, it presented a vivid protagonist triumphing over a hostile environment, building shelter with ice and hunting for his family's next meal. We feel the isolation of the Eskimo clan (and Flaherty) in the depth of shots and the length of single-camera sequences. Moving moments include Nanook diving deep into snow to pull a fox from a trap, crafting an ice window for an igloo, and smiling with pride after his family eats a walrus he harpooned.

Nanook of the North opened in the summer of 1922. Greeted by positive if sometimes patronizing reviews, it went into wide release in North America and Europe. In 1947, United Artists rereleased it with music and hokey narration in place of the intertitles (this version has been widely seen ever since). *Nanook*'s images, structure, and theme reverberated for decades, defining the documentary feature and influencing cinema throughout the world. Less than two years after shooting wrapped and while the movie was still in theaters, Nanook, the Eskimo beloved throughout the world, died of starvation while on a hunting trip.

Riding high on worldwide acclaim, Flaherty was hired by Paramount to make a nonfiction feature in the sunny South similar to the one he'd shot in the frozen North. *Moana of the South Seas* (1926) beautifully captures the Samoan culture, but it lacks the power of *Nanook*. When British philosopher (and future documentarian) John Grierson saw *Moana*, he coined the term "documentary" to describe its "creative treatment of actuality."

Flaherty went on to film two nonfiction shorts, *The Pottery Maker* (1925) and *Twenty-Four Dollar Island* (1927), a cityscape of Manhattan. He started shooting but then quit MGM's fictional *White Shadows in the South Seas* (1928) and then bailed out of a Pueblo Indian story he was making for Fox. In both cases it was because the studio forced too many "Hollywood elements" into the script. The struggle between fiction and nonfiction and between money and creative control would forever shadow Robert Flaherty.

World War I veterans Ernest Schoedsack and Merian Cooper claimed they'd heard of *Nanook of the North* but hadn't seen it when they set out to document a rare adventure. The pair had shot footage in North Africa but lost it in a ship fire. Now they enlisted thrill-seeking investor Marguerite Harrison, who contributed half of their $10,000 budget. She joined them as they covered the annual migration of 50,000 Bakhtiari tribesmen herding half a million animals over treacherous terrain to summer grazing grounds in southwest Persia (now Iran).

To cross a half-mile-wide river, the Bakhtiari inflated goatskins and tied them together as rafts. Over six days, two men and countless animals died in river whirlpools. The tribesmen carried animals up a sheer rock wall and tramped down snow for others with bare and bleeding feet. Schoedsack, Cooper, and Harrison were the first foreigners to make the trek, and they captured it all in *Grass: A Nation's Battle for Life* (1926). Artfully edited, with many fascinating moments, the movie was acquired and released by Paramount. *Grass* has been overshadowed by *Nanook* in film history books, and though it lacks the emotional power of Flaherty's debut, it deserves to be remembered as a true nonfiction adventure classic.

Cooper and Schoedsack followed with *Chang* (Siamese for "elephant") in 1927. Shot in Siam (now Thailand), it tells of native life in the jungle and features many groundbreaking wildlife scenes, including one of a herd of elephants. Upon release, *Variety* called it "the best wild animal picture ever."[18] *Chang* was a popular success that influenced fictional jungle films of the thirties.

Cooper and Schoedsack easily made the transition to screenplays, studios, and sound. In 1933, they codirected and coproduced the ultimate wildlife adventure, *King Kong*. Over the next three decades, alone or in tandem, their names appeared on some of Hollywood's greatest films. Cooper became a studio executive, returned to the Army to serve as a general in World War II, and coproduced some of John Ford's classics.

Nonfiction features before Flaherty's debut were primarily guidebook-style travelogues. For a decade after, they were mostly adventurous travelogues. But with *Nanook* and *Grass*, the groundwork had been laid for the documentary genre. These compelling films would continue to reverberate, inspiring explorers daring enough to conquer new cinematic territory.

Indie Companies

A few successful actors of the silent era established themselves through the studios and then, in search of greater creative and financial freedom, formed their own production companies. This still happens today, though rarely are such companies truly independent. Usually they are set up under the wing of a studio that provides distribution, financing, and creative input.

One of the three great screen comedians of the Prohibition era, Buster Keaton, appeared to have total freedom, though in fact, he had none. Joe Schenck had been producing "Fatty" Arbuckle comedies when he signed Keaton in 1919. When Arbuckle was arrested for manslaughter, Schenck changed the name of the company to Buster Keaton Productions. This put Keaton in a curious position. He had his own impressive Buster Keaton Studio in Hollywood, and he wrote, starred in, and codirected some of the greatest comedies ever, including *Sherlock, Jr.* (1924), *The Navigator* (1924), and *The General* (1926), but he was a salaried contract player (for $2,000 per week) at what was nominally his own production company. The business of Buster Keaton Productions was fully controlled by Joe Schenck. In 1928 Schenck effectively sold Keaton to MGM.

The second member of pantomime comedy's triumvirate, Harold Lloyd, had a much more rewarding arrangement. After the success of his classic *Safety Last* (1923), he broke with the Hal Roach Studios, leased his own stages, and formed the Harold Lloyd Corporation. Lloyd had the financial strength to demand creative control from

Pathé, the distributor of his first three productions: *Girl Shy* (1924), *Hot Water* (1924), and *The Freshman* (1925). At the height of his popularity, Lloyd signed a distribution deal with Paramount, which offered him an unprecedented 77½ percent of the domestic gross and 90 percent of the foreign, as well as complete creative control. (Lloyd took only acting credits, though he essentially directed and produced his films.) In 1926 Lloyd was the most successful movie star in the world, earning more than $2 million. In total he made seven comedies released through Paramount, including the excellent *The Kid Brother* (1927), but he began to falter when sound arrived. Harold Lloyd gave up his autonomy to sign with Paramount in 1936, but he worked only sparingly thereafter, his fortune and reputation firmly secured.

The third member of the trinity took a different route. Charlie Chaplin had done well by the studios. By 1916 he was the world's most popular actor and making more than $10,000 per week. In 1918 he signed a million-dollar contract with First National. He then teamed up with three other giants of the era, actress Mary Pickford, actor Douglas Fairbanks, and—still the world's most successful filmmaker—D. W. Griffith. They made an announcement that shook the entertainment world. They were truly freeing themselves from the constraints of the Hollywood studios by creating their own "studio" with no contract players, no back lots, no acres of costumes and props. United Artists was born on February 5, 1919. Over the next seven decades it was one of the most important forces in cinema. Most of its productions were nominally independent.

The concept of United Artists was that the inmates would run the asylum. Each of the four principals would produce and finance three films per year. The problem was that Griffith, Pickford, and Chaplin were still under other studio contracts, and no one was motivated to meet the yearly quota. The first UA release was Fairbanks's *His Majesty, the American* in 1919, but the first film starring Chaplin, his classic *The Gold Rush*, didn't appear until 1925. Many great pictures were created by UA's founders during the silent era: Griffith's *Way Down East* and *Orphans of the Storm*, Fairbanks's *The Mark of Zorro* and *The Thief of Baghdad*, and Chaplin's *A Woman of Paris* and *The Circus*. Quality was not a problem. Quantity was. In order to survive, United Artists had to attract other capable producers.

The man assigned that duty was none other than Joe Schenck, who was elected chairman of the United Artists board in 1924. He attached to UA his own Buster Keaton Productions and the production company of his wife, actress Norma Talmadge. He also brought in the companies of acting legends Rudolph Valentino (who died in 1926) and Gloria Swanson, the prolific Samuel Goldwyn (who'd been ousted from his own Goldwyn Pictures when it merged to form MGM), tycoon Howard Hughes, and mogul-in-waiting Darryl Zanuck. United Artists was, in effect, a film exchange for various producers. As such, it avoided the bloated overhead expenses of the Hollywood studios, which were by then rapidly expanding into virtual cities unto themselves.

During its long history, United Artists would occasionally acquire and distribute a completed American feature with no prior arrangement with the producer: a true independent film. Such was the case in 1925. Joseph von Sternberg had immigrated to New York from Austria as a child. He made training films for the Army during World War I and worked as an assistant to various East Coast directors. In 1924 he moved to Los Angeles, hoping to direct. He had a screenplay. George K. Arthur was a British thespian who'd come to California to act. He had $5,000. The two joined forces, and von Sternberg shot his own script around the docks of San Pedro Bay. Arthur acted along with other unknowns.

The Salvation Hunters is a simple, downbeat drama about a poor, unambitious couple, The Boy (Arthur) and The Girl (Georgia Hale), who live with The Child in a battered boat. They accept a room in exchange for The Girl's sexual services. Only when The Brute (Olaf Hytten) mistreats The Child does The Boy summon enough pride to face him. The strength of *The Salvation Hunters* is its harbor-dredge symbolism and picturesque, shadowy evocation of despair. It was considered quite "European" (i.e. artistic) in 1925.

Von Sternberg persuaded Chaplin, Fairbanks, and Pickford to screen the film. Impressed, they bought the $5,000 movie for $6,000 and released it through UA, hailing it as a work of new cinematic genius. Critics had their reservations. Calling early reports overly generous, *Variety* stated (with a jab at the director's heritage): "*The Salvation Hunters* is nothing more nor less than another short cast picture to express an apparently Teutonic theory of fatalism."[19]

But Hollywood was abuzz. Von Sternberg was suddenly thrust into studio meetings. He went on to virtually invent the modern gangster movie with Paramount's *Underworld* (1927), and he crafted seven stylish Marlene Dietrich features, including *The Scarlet Empress* (1934). George Arthur starred in a few forgotten comedies and later produced and distributed a few forgotten independents. United Artists galloped on towards the dawn of talking pictures, unaware of the winding road ahead.

Avant-garde

The avant-garde film movement began in Germany and France shortly after World War I and spread during the silent era to the Soviet Union and Great Britain. European intellectuals gravitated to the exciting new medium of moving pictures. Major artists—including Salvador Dali, Man Ray, Jean Cocteau, and Hans Richter—explored the limits of film. Influenced by Sigmund Freud's theories of the subconscious, these films were part of the surrealist art movement. They explored the imagery of dreams, often cutting together conflicting and sometimes shocking images. Sexual themes were addressed through allegories.

The experiment was slower to develop in America. In 1921, Charles Sheeler and photographer/future documentarian Paul Strand created a short, abstract, visual poem about New York City called *Manhatta*. But it wasn't until the final years of the Roaring Twenties that the European movement impacted stateside. American enthusiasts gathered in cafes or art galleries to watch what was then called the "little cinema." Some wrote about such films in obscure journals, others picked up 16mm cameras and made celluloid experiments. The motion picture medium was being democratized.

The Life and Death of 9413—A Hollywood Extra (1927) was a one-reel dream film. Directed by Robert Florey, it was the first movie shot by the legendary Gregg Toland (then twenty-three), one of three cinematographers who worked on it. *The Life and Death of 9413* features stark sets by art designer/coeditor/cocinematographer Slavko Vorkapich, who was clearly influenced by German expressionism. The film features an extra (Jules Rancort), who has the numbers "9413" stamped on his forehead and who dreams of being branded a "star." While climbing the stairs to "SUCCESS," a destiny spelled out in electric lights, he falls. He then rides a bike to Heaven (a machine shop) and rubs away "9413." An accompanying program claimed *The Life and Death of 9413* was made for $97.50.

Slavko Vorkapich went on to become a studio art director and montage expert. Robert Florey crafted three additional experimental shorts—*The Loves of Zero, Skyscraper Symphony*, and *Johann the Coffin Maker* (all around 1928)—before directing more than sixty features for Hollywood studios between 1929 and 1950. Gregg Toland revolutionized cinematography with his monumental camerawork in *Citizen Kane* (1941) and other classics.

One of the most intriguing experimental features of the silent era was scripted, directed, and edited by a research scientist and sometimes professional boxer from Budapest, Hungary. After studying for a medical degree, fighting in World War I, and painting movie sets, Paul Fejos (1897–1963) immigrated to the United States in 1924. A bacteriology technician, he wanted to break into directing features but was repeatedly rebuffed. Finally, one of his ideas sparked some interest: in the split second before a man drowns himself, his entire life flashes before his eyes. He pitched the idea to would-be producer Edward Spitz, who loved it.

Fejos directed from his own script, and Spitz produced *The Last Moment* for a measly $13,000, in true independent style. Spitz convinced Danish-born actor Otto Matieson ("The Man" in *The Salvation Hunters*) to star for free and the young cinematographer Leon Shamroy to shoot (some say essentially direct) for next to nothing. He convinced a studio to let him rent space for a nominal fee during odd hours, and he bought film stock on credit. With shots picked up at odd moments whenever a stage and actors were available, production took three months.

Lost and Found

> WITH EVERY FOOT OF FILM THAT IS LOST, WE LOSE A LINK TO OUR CULTURE, TO THE WORLD AROUND US, TO EACH OTHER, AND TO OURSELVES.
>
> —Martin Scorsese

Before 1951, films were made on nitrate film stock, and, in less than perfect conditions, nitrate deteriorates rapidly until it turns to dust. It's also highly flammable. Of the American features made with nitrate (or pre-nitrate) fewer than half survive today. Less than 20% of the U.S. features from the 1920s are known to exist, and the numbers are much lower for earlier years. Independent movies, which were rarely stored in vaults, have fared the worst.

continued

Lost and Found

continued

Among the countless lost independents are *Purity, The Jungle, The Lost Moment,* Walt Disney's *Little Red Riding Hood* (1922), and the early work of directors like Alice Guy Blaché, King Vidor, and Oscar Micheaux. The vast majority of race pictures no longer exist.

The only good news is that previously lost films are occasionally found. Several Micheaux features have been rescued. In 1996 two very significant films surfaced: *When Bearcat Went Dry* (1919) and *Richard III* (1912); both are independents. In the first, Lon Chaney stars as a villain. The second is the oldest surviving feature film (it was retrieved in near mint condition).

Meanwhile, preservationists are working against time to transfer nitrate film to safety stock. Because even safety stock slowly deteriorates and because even movies from recent decades have faded, digital technology may provide the ultimate solution. Such important independents as *Nanook of the North, Intolerance, White Zombie,* and the surviving cartoons of Winsor McCay have been lovingly remastered and released on DVD, often with enhancements such as additional footage and new orchestral scores.

■   ■   ■   ■   ■   ■   ■   ■

Unfortunately, *The Last Moment* (1928) is now lost. Though an "art picture" told from the lead's point of view without intertitles, it was never as marginal as the more self-consciously abstruse avant-garde films. It begins with a man (Matieson) drowning in a pond, followed by expressionist images of death: double and triple exposures, faces, lights, spinning wheels, a shower of stars, an explosion. Then it traces the man's life from childhood to running away on a ship to getting hit by a car to marrying a nurse to divorce to war to love again and to the death of his second wife. Walking home, he sees his reflection in a pond, walks in, and drowns himself. The end.

Spitz screened the completed feature for critic Welford Beaton of *The Film Spectator*, who wrote in a headline, "Introducing you to Mr. Paul Fejos, Genius." Beaton went on to call *The Last Moment* "one of the most outstanding works of cinematic art that was ever brought to the screen."[20] Charlie Chaplin arranged for United Artists to acquire and distribute it. Reviews praised *The Last Moment*'s daring and imagination, though some critics were put off by its impersonal style. *Film Daily* said it "goes in heavily for unique camera angles. Parts of the production are extremely interesting; parts are not. An intelligent experiment."[21] *Variety* called it "a picture for the Greenwich Village faddists to chew over . . . [an] interesting, freaky, and slightly morbid arty picture."[22]

Riding the Hollywood waves generated by *The Last Moment*, Fejos signed a contract at Universal. He directed *Lonesome* (1928), which is now heralded as a pioneering example of *cinema verité* and neorealism. He is credited, along with cinematographer Hal Mohr, with inventing the modern camera crane they used to make *Broadway* (1929). In the thirties in Europe, Fejos made adventurous documentaries. He eventually returned to a career in scientific research. Leon Shamroy felt his contributions to *The Last Moment* were overlooked, though it wouldn't be long before he would be recognized. Over the next four decades, Shamroy was exalted as one of Hollywood's top cinematographers, winning four Academy Awards and receiving eighteen nominations.

Sexploitation

Exploitation pictures continued to find their audience during the age of Prohibition. Most played at big-city grind houses (old nickelodeons or unsuccessful first-run theaters) which often changed pictures daily and rarely closed. Grind-house flicks were not necessarily sordid, but nearly all of them were bad. Unable to find distribution elsewhere, they went to dingy dives and received a tiny fee, a sensational title, and usually a very short run.

One notable exception was a 1928 movie directed by Norton Parker that was shot for $2,500 in ten days and went on to gross more than $2.5 million. *The Road to Ruin* follows a teenage girl who, neglected by her parents, takes up smoking and drinking and engages in a series of affairs with older men. Apprehended by police during a strip poker game, the teen is sent home, only to discover she's pregnant. After an illegal abortion, the phrase "THE WAGES OF SIN IS DEATH" appears over her bed in fire. As if that's not enough, she dies of shock when paired off with her father in a house of ill repute.

The Road to Ruin was very popular on the roadshow circuit, advertised with lurid billboards emphasizing "No one under 16 admitted." It was also sponsored by juvenile authorities and shown as a cautionary tale in high schools. *The Road to Ruin* was remade with sound in

1933, codirected by none other than Mrs. Wallace Reid. The sound version replaced the original in grind houses, where its notoriety pulled in curious customers for two decades.

Walt Disney

Once upon a time, a commercial artist from Kansas City started as an independent filmmaker and grew into the ruler of the world's largest entertainment empire. In 1920, the teenaged Walt Disney (1901–1966) began producing cartoons. Less than two years later he incorporated Laugh-O-gram Films. The animated shorts made it into theaters, but little profit made it back to Disney, and Laugh-O-gram soon went bankrupt. At his lowest, Disney was reduced to a diet of bread and beans and to trading drawings for a haircut.[23] In 1923 he sold his only valuable possession, his movie camera, to pay off debts. He moved to Los Angeles for a fresh start.

Walt and his business-oriented brother Roy, joined shortly by animator Ub Iwerks, produced a series of cliché-ridden shorts called *Alice Comedies*. They began to turn a profit. Business was booming by the time Disney started a new series in 1927 called *Oswald the Lucky Rabbit*. But it all came crumbling down when his distributor stole away his animation staff. Disney scrambled for a new vehicle and came up with an anthropomorphic rodent called Mortimer.

Depending on which story one believes, either Disney's wife or an early distributor suggested a name change for Mort. Mickey Mouse was born. First drawn with sharp teeth, the character was cocky and cruel—a real rat. A survivor amidst creative catastrophes, Mickey's initial starring roles were mute: *Plane Crazy* and The *Gallopin' Gaucho* (both 1928). In October 1927, Warner Bros. premiered *The Jazz Singer*, the first major talkie, and suddenly sound was all the rage. Disney, a technical perfectionist, wanted audio.

Iwerks drew a new cartoon, *Steamboat Willie*. In it, a more innocent Mickey Mouse steers an elastic boat and rescues Minnie Mouse from the villainous Pete. In September of 1928, Disney traveled with film prints and audio notes to New York City. After acquiring the appropriate sound (not easy in an age when audio technology was patented and monopolized), Disney arranged to have *Steamboat Willie* play in a Manhattan theater. The press raved. Audiences were awed. With its music and effects synchronized to the on-screen action (at one point Mickey plays a concert with the anatomies of barnyard animals),

A star is born: Mickey with music in *Steamboat Willie*.
© Disney Enterprises, Inc.

Steamboat Willie represents the first genuinely artful use of sound in cinema.

Still, Disney could not get the distribution deal he wanted. He settled for a standard state's-rights arrangement that paid him 10 percent of the gross, and he gave *Plane Crazy* and *The Gallopin' Gaucho* musical scores. In early 1929, Disney created a new Mickey Mouse sound picture, *The Opry House*, and he set out to generate a movie without mice. It became the delightfully macabre *The Skeleton Dance*, the first of the *Silly Symphony* series in which action on-screen was created to match prerecorded classical music instead of the other way around.

The shorts were widely seen and quickly assimilated into popular culture. Disney signed a distribution contract with Columbia in 1930 and a more lucrative one with United Artists in 1932, while expanding his roster of celluloid characters and production staff. Soon he was incorporating color. Meanwhile, Mickey Mouse became a marketing maestro, selling chalkboards, handkerchiefs, and baby bottles.

Disney's company was a full-fledged studio when it released a feature in 1937, the hugely successful *Snow White and the Seven Dwarfs*. And it grew and grew and grew.

By the end of 1928 silent movies were obsolete. The studios had taught their films to talk, leaving many established actors and directors behind. Most independent companies were wiped out by the high cost of audio technology. And the Great Depression took care of the rest. Disney picked a good time to become a Hollywood mogul. The last decade of cinematic silence was a period of remarkable innovation, but as the movies found their voice and the studio walls grew ever higher, innocence ended. The future for mavericks looked bleak.

Notes

1 Flaherty, Robert J. with Frances Flaherty, *My Eskimo Friends* (New York: Doubleday, 1924), 47.
2 Sanderson, Lennox, Jr., "The Black in Silent Film," *Magill's Survey of Cinema: Silent Films, Vol. 1*, ed. Frank N. Magill (Englewood Cliffs, NJ: Salem Press, 1982), 21.
3 Sanderson, 21–22.
4 *Variety*, 2 Sept. 1921.
5 *Photoplay*, Nov. 1921, 64.
6 Vidor, King, *A Tree is a Tree* (New York: Harcourt Brace, 1953), 46.
7 *Variety*, 9 May 1919.
8 *Daily Worker*, 10 May 1927.
9 *Variety*, 13 April 1917.
10 Brownlow, Kevin, *Behind the Mask of Innocence* (NY: Alfred A. Knopf, 1990), 50.
11 *Photoplay*, June 1915, 42.
12 Kozarski, Richard, "The Years Have Not Been Kind to Lois Weber," *Village Voice*, 10 November 1975.
13 Carter, Aline, "Muse of the Reel," *Motion Picture Magazine*, March 1921.
14 *Variety*, 3 Feb. 1926.
15 *Motion Picture News*, 2 Dec. 1922.
16 *BBC Talk* (radio broadcast), London, 14 & 24 June, 1949.
17 Roger, Manvell, ed., "Robert Flaherty Talking," *The Cinema*,

1950 (Hadmondsworth, England: Penguin, 1950), 12.

[18] *Variety*, 4 May 1927.

[19] *Variety*, 4 Feb. 1925.

[20] *Film Spectator*, 26 Nov. 1927.

[21] *Film Daily*, 11 March 1928.

[22] *Variety*, 14 March 1928.

[23] Schickel, Richard, *The Disney Version: The Life, Times, Art and Commerce of Walt Disney*, rev. ed. (New York: Simon & Schuster, 1985), 80.

1929-1944

OUTSIDE THE WALLS

Having exhausted the supply of big companies, I
was left with one alternative: to raise the money
and make the picture myself.

—KING VIDOR[1]

*Saturday Sinners and Sunday Saints Clash in the
Battle of Good Against Evil!*
—ADVERTISING SLOGAN FOR *GO DOWN, DEATH*

They were dumps. They were dingy dives with hard wooden seats
and water-stained screens and rickety projectors. Pallid film prints
drifted in and out of focus. Tinny speakers crackled. In the first years
of the Great Depression most nonstudio films were relegated to the
grind houses of Times Square and similar urban districts. As a result,
the word "independent" became synonymous with something less
than trash.

Debased as independent films were, their producers had competition. Poverty Row studios sprouted up to fill the least desirable
screens and the bottom (B movie) rungs of double bills, which were
nearly universal by the mid-thirties. Meanwhile, the big studios grew
even bigger, monopolizing the best venues and serving up their own
B material.

Silent flicks could still play at grind houses in 1929, but by the following year the only mute movies were travelogues. Because they

could be produced without synchronized sound equipment, there were more than twenty travel documentaries and animal hunt pictures released in 1930. Many were screened with phonograph narration called disc lectures. The market fizzled fast. The added expense and technical concerns of audio recording caused most independent producers to look for other work. Those that remained in the business were debilitated by the aftereffects of the stock market crash of October 29, 1929.

The studios, too, were hit hard by the Depression. While buoyed by the novelty of talkies in 1930, attendance and admission prices dropped dramatically in the following years, reaching a nadir in 1933, when a third of all theaters closed. But the downward spiral would be short-lived. The industry soon bounced back, and the Big Five —Warner Bros., Paramount, MGM, Twentieth-Century Fox, and RKO—and, to a lesser degree, Universal and Columbia (which did not own their own theater chains)—began an expansion of popularity in 1934 that peaked in 1946 (after the war and just before television) with an all-time high in movie attendance.[2]

During those dozen years, the Big Five solidified their monopolies over production, distribution, and exhibition. All of the largest studios owned their own film exchanges and theater chains. They also effectively owned their own producers, directors, writers, actors, editors, and all the other carefully compartmental-

---

■ ■ ■ ■ ■ ■ ■ ■ ■

Studio Ten

Some movies that seem characteristically independent were produced by major studios. In chronological order, these are ten of the most significant.

Traffic in Souls. Universal's wildly successful exploitation picture.

Freaks. Tod Browning's controversial gothic about the love lives of circus freaks was prematurely shelved by MGM and it was banned from Great Britain. It later became a hit at revival houses.

Lady in the Lake. A rare Hollywood experiment. MGM's 1946 mystery is presented entirely in second person with the camera showing only what a private eye sees.

Psycho. It's hard to fathom how tawdry and shocking Alfred Hitchcock's low-budget classic was in 1960. It revolutionized the horror genre, paving the way for realistic, independent horrors.

continued

Studio Ten

continued

Husbands. Vintage Cassavetes—as raw as his rawest indies.

Harold and Maude. Anti-establishment cult comedy about a morbid young man liberated by a life-loving old woman.

Hearts and Minds. This anti-Vietnam War documentary was financed by Columbia, but that studio refused to release such a political tract. Distributed by Warner Bros., it won the 1974 documentary Oscar.

The Rocky Horror Picture Show. Campy, pansexual, horror musical. The ultimate cult movie.

Interiors. Woody Allen's humorless family drama, influenced by Ingmar Bergman. Allen has had the most idiosyncratic career of any studio director. Among his other "art films": *Stardust Memories, September, Husbands and Wives.*

Repo Man. Alex Cox received a throwaway budget (by studio standards) of $1.5 million to make this 1984 punk/sci-fi cult flick.

Ten Honorable Mentions: *Gun Crazy; Where's Poppa?; Midnight Cowboy; Five Easy Pieces; Shaft; Up in Smoke; Personal Best; Silent Night, Deadly Night; Do the Right Thing; Natural Born Killers.*

■   ■   ■   ■   ■   ■   ■   ■

ized workers in the assembly line who churned out movies like so many sausages. It must be noted that they often churned out damn good sausages. The five years between 1939 and 1944—when the studio system was at its peak—spawned such cinematic landmarks as *Citizen Kane, The Wizard of Oz, Casablanca, Gone With the Wind, How Green Was My Valley, Fantasia, Double Indemnity, Mr. Smith Goes to Washington, Sullivan's Travels,* and *The Grapes of Wrath*—a pretty good all-time top ten list. But the dream factories didn't leave much room for those who dared to work outside their system.

By the mid-thirties, United Artists—the antistudio—had fallen on rough times. The film careers of three of its partners—Fairbanks, Pickford, and Griffith —were over, done in by substandard productions and changing public tastes; and the fourth, Chaplin, would produce a mere six motion pictures over the next three decades. Griffith opted out of UA in 1932. Fairbanks died in 1939. Pickford and Chaplin weren't speaking to each other. Key producers Goldwyn and Zanuck left the fold, and Zanuck made Schenck the new chairman of Fox. Suffering from a management and talent deficit, UA limped through the thirties and forties. It still distributed high-quality productions like John Ford's seminal semi-indie western, *Stagecoach* (1939), and several great features from producer David O. Selznick, but, with Hollywood's best talent almost always under someone else's contract, United Artists was forced to fill out its release schedules with mediocre British imports and less-than-mediocre B westerns.

The term "Poverty Row" originated in the twenties to describe an area of central Hollywood where various fly-by-night producers gathered to make fast and cheap formulaic flicks. They rented studio space by the day and distributed via state's-rights, churning out mostly westerns. (A more specific location around Gower Street was called "Gower Gulch" because of all the cowboys on horses who waited there for movie work.) Soon the term "Poverty Row" came to be applied disparagingly to any minor film company. Formed in 1924, Columbia Pictures was a Poverty Row graduate that grew into a major studio in the thirties. It was the only such success story.

The bigger Poverty Row companies were semi-indie studios. After Columbia moved up, Monogram (founded in 1930) and Republic (founded in 1935) were the largest movie factories on Poverty Row. For their assembly-line westerns (known disparagingly as "oaters"), they employed such legends as John Wayne, Tex Ritter, Roy Rogers, Raoul Walsh, and John Ford. Most flicks were shot in ten days or less with budgets between $30,000 and $60,000. (In the late forties, Republic moved into bigger-budgeted "premiere" pictures and made several true classics.) Specializing in melodramas and comedies, Producers Releasing Corporation (PRC), founded in 1940, infamously cranked out pictures even faster and more cheaply. Smaller dumps came and went within a few years, including Tiffany, Majestic, Chesterfield, and Grand National.

The Poverty Row companies struggled to survive in the dank alley between major studio B units and true independents. Their mission was not to make quality motion pictures. They served only to fill up screens with vapid serials and singing cowboys, and in the process, they crowded the entryway for genuine mavericks. Some independent filmmakers tried to squeeze in amongst the B movie clutter, but to truly thrive during these unforgiving years one needed to blaze an entirely different path.

Victor Halperin

A former stage actor and director, Victor Halperin dove into the B market. He began directing, sometimes writing, and, with his brother Edward, coproducing undistinguished independent movies in the mid-twenties. He made six such silent features, all with exploitation elements, and with the coming of sound kept right on going. In 1930, the Halperin brothers made a sensationalistic melodrama called *Party Girls* about the lives of $100-a-night escorts. Douglas Fairbanks, Jr. (following in his father's large footsteps) headlined with silent star Marie Prevost. *Variety* wrote: "One of the scenes the censor went near-sighted over. You see the masseuse doing the slapping with Miss Prevost just showing enough of herself to let you know she has a lot."[3] Viewed today, *Party Girls* is tame and tedious, and, like many early sound pictures, everyone seems to be aiming their dialogue towards a microphone.

Then in 1932, Victor Halperin directed and, with brother Edward, coproduced a minimasterpiece. *White Zombie* was shot for $50,000 raised through a New York securities firm. The brothers rented stages at

In *White Zombie*, Bela Lugosi (with outstretched arm) puts a spell on Robert Frazer.

Universal and RKO and recycled impressive sets from *Dracula* (1931). Dracula himself, Bela Lugosi, stars in perhaps his finest role as Murder Legendre, an evil witch doctor in rural Haiti. Universal's legendary makeup wizard Jack Pierce powdered the creepy undead.

Written by Garnett Weston and based on a popular play, *White Zombie* unfurls like a dark fairy tale. Plantation owner Beaumont (Robert Frazer) asks zombie master Legendre to help him win Madeline (silent star Madge Bellamy). Placed under a spell with a poisoned rose, she's turned into a zombie, silently roaming Legendre's castle with others similarly afflicted. Disheartened by her emotionless gaze, Beaumont tells undead Madeline, "I must take you back." "Back to the grave, monsieur?" Legendre snarls. Beaumont: "Anything's better than that awful expression. You must put the light back into her eyes and bring laughter to her lips." Before he can revive her, Beaumont himself is placed under the voodoo master's control, and it's up to Madeline's husband (John Harron) to sneak into the castle and rouse the walking dead.

White Zombie's dark castle by the sea, expansive sets, and murky forests are beautifully evocative, as is the nighttime cinematography of Arthur Martinelli. Utilizing poetic nonverbal passages, Halperin avoids the common pitfall of the early sound era: too much stationary talking. There's a splendid *Metropolis*like scene in which zombies silently toil in a sugar mill like cogs in a machine, the only sound coming from the moan of the large wooden gears. In an emotional vignette, Neil is alone at a cafe while behind him giant shadows of blissful couples are projected onto a corrugated tin wall. Also great is the dialogue-free sequence where Madeline, under Legendre's grip, attempts to stab Neil. *White Zombie* soars with inventive direction, romantic dialogue, and Lugosi's sinister presence.

At the time of its release by United Artists, *White Zombie*'s enslaved workers—once secure citizens no longer controlling their destinies—became a metaphor for the horrors of the Depression and its ubiquitous breadlines. *White Zombie* was advertised with the sentence "Unusual Times Demand Unusual Pictures." Though it was a commercial success, reviewers were largely blind to its elegiac pleasures. But the years have been kind and, seen today, *White Zombie* remains a gothic gem that more than holds its own against the studio horror classics of the era (*Frankenstein, Dracula, King Kong*).

Halperin followed with an intriguing choice, *Supernatural* (1933), starring the legendary Carole Lombard and future western icon Randolph Scott. A doctor (Scott), researching the paranormal, learns that a dead murderess has transferred her criminal personality to an innocent woman (Lombard). Unfortunately, *Supernatural* runs out of thrills early.

Halperin sometimes aimed a little higher than the typical formula, but he still made B movies. *I Conquer the Sea* (1936) is a tedious ocean adventure set in Portugal. Authentic whaling footage is poorly incorporated. In *Revolt of the Zombies* (1936) a World War I French combat unit is unbeatable because it's undead. After the war an expedition is sent to Cambodia to eliminate the pesky ghouls. A great setup turns dull with no scares and little characterization. *Nation Aflame* (1937) was an undistinguished organized crime picture. *Torture Ship* (1939), based on a Jack London story, is a very bad ocean adventure combined with a zombielike experiment. Halperin helmed his final film, *Girls Town* (1942), for PRC. The director of a truly great movie who was never invited through the studio gates, Victor Halperin has been virtually forgotten.

B Movies

A unique and tragic exploitation picture surfaced in 1931, though most of the drama occurred behind the camera. The plot of *The Viking* is a boring Nordic love story written by Garnett Wilson (of *White Zombie* fame). Shooting took place in the subarctic of Newfoundland, Canada. Leaving the cast behind, adventurous producer/director Varick Frissell and twenty others took an old sealing ship, *The Viking*, out to capture extra footage of an iceberg on March 16, 1931. *The Viking* exploded when the TNT onboard detonated, and Frissell and the crew perished.

Veteran George Melford took over direction. The film's title was changed to *The Viking* to take advantage of the hype from the accident, and Sir William Greenfell provides an on-screen eulogy for Frissell and crew. Shots of dynamite blasting ice out of the ship's path take on new meaning, but the real thrill is seeing hundreds of men perilously walk on undulating ice cakes, leaping from one block to another. The adventure is great. The acting, dialogue, plot, and sound quality are not. Advertising tried to exploit Frissell's death, but *The Viking* quickly sank.

By 1932, crime and gangster tales were all the rage. United Artists

released the classic *Scarface* that year, and a host of independent producers turned out their own hard-boiled flicks. Audiences cheered
gunmen at a time when Prohibition (in its final days) had made criminals out of tens of millions and when the Depression was making
lawlessness more tempting than usual. *Cross-Examination* was one of
the eleven features the notoriously prolific Richard Thorpe helmed in
1932. Set in a courtroom, it tells an engaging murder case through the
words of opposing counsels and witnesses, using flashbacks to highlight violent portions of the testimony. Based on a popular play, *The
Last Mile* (1932) was directed by Sam Bischoff and features Preston
Foster as killer Mears, a prisoner who leads the takeover of a death
row cell block. The stark, atmospheric cinematography was by the
great Arthur Edeson (*Casablanca*). Other 1932 crime indies include the
Barbary Coast gangster tale *The Docks of San Francisco* and the gangland melodrama *Exposed*. By the end of 1933, the short spurt of
Hollywood thuggery was arrested by order of the censors. Celluloid
criminals, though, would return with a vengeance.

Among the other independents of the early thirties were the ocean-
faring World War I action picture *The Sea Ghost* (1931), the pro-
Prohibition melodrama *Ten Nights in a Bar-Room* (1931), a courtroom
drama called *No Living Witness* (1932), and the boxing picture *The Big
Chance* (1933), featuring thirteen-year-old Mickey Rooney. Traditional
B movie indies were few and far between for the next two decades.

Most such releases came from tiny Poverty Row companies that
tried to hit but missed. John Wayne, between stints at Warner Bros.
and Monogram, made sixteen westerns for Lone Star Productions
from its founding in 1933 until it merged with Republic two years
later. Each was shot in a ridiculously brief four days with a tiny
$10,000 budget. The first, *Riders of Destiny* (1933), is infamous for
being Wayne's only crooning cowboy "oater." He plays Singin' Sandy
Saunders and periodically moves his lips while Smith Ballew serenades. Wayne also stars as a playboy in the melodrama *His Private
Secretary* (1933), released on a state's-rights basis.

Wanting to fully cash in on MGM's Tarzan craze of the thirties, the
Lord of the Jungle's author, Edgar Rice Burroughs, launched his own
production company. Burroughs produced a twelve-part serial, *The
New Adventures of Tarzan* (1935), shot in Guatemala with Olympic
shot-putter Bruce Bennett (then billed as Herman Brix) in the lead
role. He also financed a documentary entitled *Tundra* (1936) and made

a couple of lame Tarzan features with footage from the serial. Debts forced Burroughs out of business in 1938.

Fanchon Royer was one of the few female producers of the thirties. She oversaw numerous B movies for Poverty Row studios before forming her own company in 1937. Fanchon Royer Features made dramas on a shoestring and released most of them via state's-rights. Her best known is *A Million to One* (1938), a stale Olympics story directed by Lynn Shores and featuring twenty-year-old Joan Fontaine. *Religious Racketeers* (1938), written and directed by Frank O'Connor, is a fictional exposé of corrupt spiritualists. It features the frail widow of Harry Houdini speaking as herself. Elmer Clifton (*Down to the Sea in Ships*) helmed the unthrilling auto race yarn *10 Laps to Go* (1938). During the late thirties, Royer's company was prolific but not successful. She changed the name to Way of Life Films and produced and distributed Catholic-themed pictures throughout the early forties.

More than ever, it was up to the truly independent filmmakers to pursue the types of movies that even the Poverty Row factories wouldn't touch. One such maverick was Bud Pollard, who wrote, directed, produced, edited, and sometimes acted in his own features. In rapid succession, Pollard covered a wide array of genres: silent melodrama (*The Danger Man*, 1930), exploitation (*Girls for Sale!*, 1930), fantasy (*Alice in Wonderland*, 1931), Italian-language (*O Festino o la Legge*, 1932), African-American (*The Black King*, 1932), monster (*The Horror*, 1932), Jewish-themed (*Victims of Persecution*, 1933), and war documentary (*The Dead March*, 1937). Few of Pollard's films survived, and even fewer were well-reviewed. Pollard settled on black-cast movies in the mid-forties.

King Vidor

King Vidor, enjoying the financial security of studio paychecks, made an easy transition to sound with the groundbreaking all-black musical *Hallelujah* (1929). He received an Oscar nomination for it and another for *The Champ* (1931). Vidor was at the top of his profession in 1933 when he proposed a sound sequel to one of his silent classics. As the country strained under the weight of the Depression, Vidor felt the timing was perfect for him to "corral this nationwide unrest and tragedy into a film. I wanted to take my two protagonists from *The Crowd* and follow them through the struggles of a typical young American couple in this most difficult period."[4]

The exuberant ditch-digging scene in *Our Daily Bread*. Tom Keene gives directions.

Vidor followed John and Mary of *The Crowd* (1928) onto a cooperative farm. That the idealistic Vidor would see a co-op as a better home for them is not surprising, as his earlier MGM movie paints a cynical portrait of an idealistic man stripped of his dreams by modern society. *The Crowd* was a critical success, receiving two Academy Award nominations, but was a box office dud. Audiences didn't want to see their quiet desperation on-screen. They wanted to escape.

Vidor's idea for the sequel, *Our Daily Bread*, presented an escape route, though it wasn't one the studios were comfortable with. Despite Vidor's stellar reputation, every Hollywood house passed on the project. New kid RKO picked it up for a moment but quickly dropped it. A tale about unemployed workers forming a farming commune did not appeal to the conservative Hollywood moguls. Communes sounded like communism. And with fields turning to dust and farmers joining soup lines, audiences weren't yearning for farms. These were years of escapism: musicals, monsters, and the Marx Brothers.

But King Vidor's vision was unshakable. His heart was set on *Our Daily Bread* and he would get it made—even if he had to do it alone. Vidor formed Viking Productions in February 1934 with himself as president and sole stockholder. Just as today, in order to get bank financing, a filmmaker back then needed a signed agreement with a distributor. Vidor showed his script (cowritten with Elizabeth Hill and noted director/screenwriter Joseph Mankiewicz) to Charlie Chaplin; United Artists provided a tentative distribution agreement. Still, when bankers read the screenplay about a potential utopia without capitalism, Vidor endured another stream of rejection letters.

Vidor started casting anyway. His first impulse was to have *The Crowd*'s James Murray play John again, but Murray had slipped into alcoholism (he would jump or fall to his death in 1936). Instead, he cast Tom Keene, who would prove ineffective in the role. Vidor had married and divorced the original Mary, Eleanor Boardman, so he cast Karen Morley in the role. He would marry and later divorce this Mary, too. Vidor put up his own $90,000 and began production on an abandoned golf course and at Edgar Rice Burroughs's 160-acre ranch in Tarzana. Several weeks into the shoot, a bank loan of $125,000 came through.

Our Daily Bread premiered at the Chicago World's Fair in 1934. It played for President Roosevelt at a special White House screening. Released by United Artists, the completed feature drew all the controversy the studios and bankers feared it would. Indignation bubbled when it won second prize at the Moscow Film Festival. Hearst's *Los Angeles Examiner* called it "pinko." The *Los Angeles Times* refused to run ads. But others praised it. *The New York Times* called it "momentous . . . the most significant cinema event of the year."[5] The film was a modest success, and Vidor broke even.

In reality, the problem with *Our Daily Bread* is not that it's too political—it's that it's not political enough. It sets up an idyllic commune of excessively virtuous characters while ignoring pressing issues. Only in Hollywood can an unemployed violinist be taken in as a member who contributes to the co-op by giving fiddle lessons. The slim conflicts emerge through contrived bitterness towards John and the suspicions of a platinum tart (Barbara Pepper) who wanders onto the farm for no other reason than to raise suspicion. None of the tension rings true.

More importantly, the people don't seem real. When asked to throw their possessions on a common pile, they comply like Halperin zombies. Conflict should have been born out of the very concept of cooperative living and its departures from capitalism. Instead, economics is never an issue. The only attempt at a political dialogue occurs during a silly campfire meeting in which socialism and republicanism are mentioned, causing the Swedish foreman (John Qualen) to scratch his head and say, "I don't know them fancy words, but we need a strong boss." Earnest John is thus elected benevolent authority. End of political debate.

The plot is simplistic, but *Our Daily Bread* is no less subversive for lack of complexity. It does present a way of life opposed to most American institutions. If *The Crowd* presents a man broken down by the free enterprise system, *Our Daily Bread* shows him finding the ultimate fulfillment through the strength of a collectivist group. No individual wealth. No structured government. No profit motive.

The real strength of *Our Daily Bread* is its visuals (cinematography by Robert Planck) and editing (by Lloyd Nosner). Influenced by the cutting of Russian filmmakers, the drought montage is memorable and the irrigation-ditch-digging conclusion, which took ten days to stage and shoot, is brilliant. Vidor did away with sound equipment and used a metronome and the pounding of a bass drum to make the picks and shovels move in exact 4/4 time.[6] Set to music, the rhythmic results are truly rousing. When the farmers successfully irrigate the fields it is one of the most joyous scenes in cinema. Despite the corny story and poor acting, *Our Daily Bread*'s glorification of common people working together still holds the power to move.

Vidor wrote: "Independent producers by their very nature must be more daring than their brothers in the big factories. They have less to lose and more to gain by taking a big gamble. Since they lack the big stars to give their projects big box office insurance, they must produce films that are daring, startling, or different . . ."[7] King Vidor took a huge gamble with *Our Daily Bread* and produced one of the most subversive American feature films of all time.

Vidor's relationship with the studios following *Our Daily Bread* was a rocky one. He quit *The Wizard of Oz* (1939) after three weeks and *Duel in the Sun* (1946) before editing. Branded a communist for *Our Daily Bread*, Vidor later directed Ayn Rand's libertarian/right-wing *The Fountainhead* (1949) and helped found the Motion Picture Alliance, a conservative group that sided with the House Committee on Un-American Activities (HUAC) against Hollywood leftists.

Though he veered from left to right, Vidor remained a populist and a dreamer who wanted what was best for the common man, regardless of ideology. Most importantly, when circumstances demanded it, King Vidor was daring enough to put his money and his reputation on the line to tell the socially significant stories big movie factories wouldn't touch.

Sexploitation

In 1922, in the midst of the Arbuckle manslaughter scandal, Hollywood moguls formed the Motion Picture Producers and Distributors of America (MPPDA), a calculated attempt to clean up the industry's image through self-censorship. Former Republican party chairman and US Postmaster General William Hays was appointed chairman, a powerful title which he weilded for two decades. The MPPDA became known as the Hays Office. In 1930 it drafted a strict set of "good taste" rules and standards that was effectively ignored while gangsters and harlots promenaded across the screen. But in 1934, the new National Legion of Decency threatened a wide Catholic boycott of any work that didn't meet its approval. Movie producers buckled, and, beginning in July 1934, the Hays Code was enforced with a vengeance.

The Code's three overriding principles were: (1) The audience's sympathy must never be thrown to the side of crime, wrongdoing, evil, or sin. (2) Only correct standards of life shall be presented. (3) No natural or human laws shall be ridiculed. These seem vague enough to dance around, but the devil, so to speak, was in the details. The Hays Code specifically outlawed such things as revenge, detailed presentations of crime, illegal drug trafficking, inessential scenes of passion, suggestive postures and gestures, rape, profanity, the mention of sex hygiene or venereal disease, the comic use of religion, even the mere suggestion of interracial copulation, and any "indecent exposure." This allowed for plenty of good old American gunplay, but it virtually eliminated any hint of S-E-X (Mae West would soon push the envelope with her arsenal of double entendres).

The Hays Code had a chilling effect on American cinema for the next three decades, stifling creative freedom. All producers belonging to the MPPDA (which was at least every producer working for or with a studio) were obligated to submit scripts and completed films for an official Production Code Seal. Screenplays or prints that weren't approved were forced to make the necessary cuts. Because it was nearly impossible to secure proper advertising or respectable theaters without a seal, most nonstudio features were also voluntarily submitted for approval.

But not all of them. Exploitation was a mainstay of grind houses before and after the Code. There were lines around the block for a 300-seat Times Square dump screening *This Nude World* (1933), even though the flesh scenes are in long-shot from behind. There were protests and calls for censorship wherever it played. That same year, *Damaged Lives* oozed onto the scene. Directed by the prolific Edgar Ulmer (much more to follow) and supposedly sponsored by something called the "American Social Hygiene Association," it's a sixty-minute drama about venereal disease with a thirty-minute VD lecture tacked on. *Damaged Lives* is tame and lame, though it raked in nearly $2 million when it was released by Columbia, made the Legion of Decency's first "Condemned List," and helped to usher in enforcement of the Production Code.

And after the Code the exploitation kept on coming. Such flicks were not advertised in major newspapers or screened in "legitimate" theaters, so they didn't need any censor's stamp of approval. Sparked by the success of *Damaged Lives, Damaged Goods* (1937) is one of many VD knockoffs. It's *Citizen Kane* when compared to some of the other sensationalized dreck of the era. *Child Bride* (1937) follows a teacher as she tries to stamp out underage sex in the Ozarks. *Unashamed* (1938) is a nudist musical about a stenographer (without much nudity or music . . . or stenography). *The Terror of Tiny Town* (1938) was billed as an "all-midget western." *Life Returns* (1939) depicts a supposedly real experiment where a dead log is brought back to life. (Note: Watching a "dead" log is even more boring than it sounds!) And *Kidnaping Gorillas* and *Bride of Buddha* (both 1941) are exploitation documentaries that combine nearly nude natives with animal violence.

Exploitation soon blossomed into its own genre with its own sub-categories and rules. There were VD flicks: melodramatic tales that included a "clap reel" (sold by medical supply companies) of diseased private parts. There were birth flicks: melodramatic tales that included an actual human "birth reel" (also bought from medical supply companies). There was the overwrought WARNING! propaganda about the evils of drugs or promiscuity, which often included tacked-on clap or birth reels. There were nudism romps, which seldom had any nudity. There were exploitation documentaries with topless natives. And there was sideshow schlock involving human oddities, cruelly racist caricatures, and/or atrocities. Virtually all such celluloid purported to be about education and, therefore, usually featured some tacked-on cautionary message.

Outside the big cites, such exploitation entertainment toured via roadshows. Like revivalist preachers and carnival barkers, roadshow promoters would blow into town, lease a theater, post sensational fliers, draw a quick and lucrative payoff, and move on before things got too hot. At most screenings someone (often an actual carnival barker) would lecture or sermonize in order to "square up" (slap on a moral message) and hawk merchandise. Pamphlets were the real moneymakers of these enterprises, and they were typically sold for more than the price of admission. Such publications covered the film's purported topic while offering—under the guise of science or religion—the promise of even more lurid details. Pitchmen often played on viewers' guilt to peddle overpriced Bibles.

For these and a hundred other scams, the various roadshow producers and promoters were affectionately known as the Forty Thieves. They included Louis Sonney, maker of hundreds of sexy shorts, S. S. (Steamship) Millard, and Pappy Goldin. J. D. Kendis oversaw a few dozen flicks in the thirties and forties in the vein of *Gambling With Souls* (1936), about prostitution, and *Secrets of a Model* (1939), in which a country girl is tricked down to her underwear. The first was directed by the busy maverick Elmer Clifton, who made six pictures for Kendis; the second was one of the more than 140 features helmed by B-movie titan Sam Newfield. Future distinguished director and Hollywood Ten member Edward Dmytryk debuted with an "oater" for Kendis called *The Hawk* (1935).

Dwain Esper (1893–1982), one of the Forty Thieves, was a great promoter but one of the worst directors in the history of cinema. His first production, *The Seventh Commandment* (1932), directed by James Hogan, is a cautionary tale about a young woman who contracts syphilis. Like future exploitation celluloid, it features a birth reel; unlike future flicks, the birth is by cesarean section. *Modern Motherhood* (1934), produced and directed by Esper, delivered what it promised: a vaginal birth, the depiction of which caused much controversy.

Esper formed Road Show Attractions and traveled the country with his motion pictures. In small towns his movies were shown at midnight marquees; in cities they played in burlesque houses. His wife lectured and pitched merchandise at the screenings. In 1934, in order to fill out his trash roster, Esper produced an antidrug flick, *Narcotic*; a savage tribe "documentary," *Forbidden Adventure*; and a shlockfest called *Maniac*. The latter, also helmed by Esper and written by his wife, is among the worst movies ever made. It features corpse stealing, a doctor squeezing out and eating a cat's eye, nudity, rape, a climactic fight between two women with hypodermic needles, sublimely horrendous acting, and periodic on-screen text describing various mental illnesses! Tasteless and ridiculous throughout, *Maniac* is so bad it's great.

Esper next directed *Marihuana, the Weed with Roots in Hell* (1936). The title tells it all. *Marihuana* was revived for a few laughs in the seventies with the even more hysterical *Reefer Madness* (1936), another independent. Esper's short *How to Undress in Front of Your Husband* (1937) failed to deliver on its promise of nudity. He also acquired *Angkor* (1937), a sordid "documentary" about half-naked Cambodians supposedly mating with apes. Esper roadshowed his pictures for years. In 1948, he bought the rights to Tod Browning's controversial classic *Freaks*, which he distributed under various titles for a decade. A horrendous filmmaker but a master Thief, Dwain Esper retired to work on improving motion picture technology and expanding his collection of World War II footage.

Documentary

At the other end of the talent spectrum, F. W. (Frederick William) Murnau was one of the greatest directors of the German silent era, helming the masterpieces *Nosferatu* (1922) and *The Last Laugh* (1924). In 1926 he arrived in Hollywood, signed a five-picture deal with Fox, and created the visually dazzling *Sunrise* (1927), which was a huge success critically but not commercially. His next movie flopped, and he was replaced by hacks on his third. With the advent of sound, Fox dropped the German artist. Meanwhile, Robert Flaherty's brief Hollywood romance was over. The documentarian had bought a yacht, with plans to return to the South Seas. In 1930, the two rebel filmmakers met. It was then that Murnau and Flaherty, unconventional giants of silent film, agreed to join and make a motion picture outside the Hollywood studios.

The formation of Murnau-Flaherty Productions caused quite a stir.

Murnau's technical expertise and Flaherty's ability to dramatically portray native people quickly drew capital to the project. Before long the codirectors and their crew were on a ship bound for Tahiti. When funding failed, Murnau agreed to finance production on a tight budget. Flaherty wanted to shoot a nonfiction narrative about how Tahitians were exploited by white traders and explorers. Murnau sought a traditional parable and found it in the Polynesian legend of a pearl fisherman in love with a maiden who is consecrated to the gods and taboo to all men. For the role of the virgin, Murnau chose seventeen-year-old Anna Chevalier, a novice he spotted in a local tavern.

Flaherty had little interest in the tale. He set up his customary developing lab in a shed, but as production progressed he withdrew from the process. Contrary to reports, Flaherty stayed on the island until production wrapped but by then had sold his share in the company back to Murnau. Though Flaherty is credited as codirector, he had very little to do with production and nothing to do with editing.

The completed docudrama, *Tabu: A Story of the South Seas* (1931), is Murnau's. It's silent, though the musical soundtrack is crucial. The plot occasionally creaks, but the mysticism is enchanting and the visuals are dazzling. Cinematographer Floyd Crosby deservedly won an Oscar. Crosby went on to shoot other documentaries and dozens of films for Roger Corman.

Fleeing the Depression, Flaherty and family were in Europe when *Tabu* opened. With British backing, Flaherty shot the nonfiction short *Industrial Britain* (1931) and the documentary features *Man of Aran* (1934) and *Elephant Boy* (1937). He did not return to America until 1939, when Britain entered World War II. F. W. Murnau also missed the premiere of *Tabu*. One week before the picture opened, Murnau, at the age of forty-two, died in an automobile crash in California. *Tabu* was a huge commercial success.

Pare Lorentz (1905–1992), a former journalist and movie critic, was appointed film advisor to President Roosevelt's US Resettlement Administration. While holding that position, he made the twenty-one-minute documentary *The Plow That Broke the Plains* (1936), which addresses the soil erosion mismanagement that led to the Dust Bowl of the Great Depression. This short played in commercial theaters (which rented it for free), was seen by a wide audience, and had a great influence on nonfiction cinema. Shot by future documentarians Leo Hurwitz, Ralph Steiner, and Paul Strand, *The Plow That Broke the*

Plains is a subtle political movie, precisely shot, carefully edited, and brought to life with a manipulative musical score. Lorentz said of his film, "It is a melodrama of nature, the tragedy of turning grass into dust, a melodrama that only Carl Sandburg or Willa Cather perhaps could tell as it should be told."[8]

His next prettified picture, the thirty-two-minute *The River* (1937), expands upon his first. It traces the history of the Mississippi River, documents its misuse, and hails conservation and the Tennessee Valley Authority. This is accomplished with a sense of operatic poetry, melding music and visuals, fact and drama. The splendid cinematography is by Floyd Crosby, Stacey Woodard, and future documentarian Willard Van Dyke. The Hollywood studios complained about their "government-sponsored competition," but *The River*, too, was widely seen and influential.

With many more social issues to tackle, the Roosevelt administration created the US Film Service in 1938 and named Pare Lorentz administrator. Lorentz helmed the feature-length *The Fight for Life* (1940), which used actors and a script to propagandize for better pre- and postnatal health care in urban areas. Its staged scenes lack the power of his two earlier pictures, though the photography by Floyd Crosby is again stellar. *The Fight for Life* paved the way for the gritty docudramas of the fifties.

In 1939, Lorentz convinced Robert Flaherty to make a film for the US Department of Agriculture. *The Land* (1941) is Flaherty's most traditional movie. With vivid images and simple narration, it explains soil erosion and how it can be prevented. By blaming government for much of the current problem, *The Land* was deemed politically embarrassing to the Roosevelt administration, which financed it, and was thus not widely shown.

By the time *The Land* was released, the new Republican Congress had disbanded the US Film Service, believing it to be politically biased. Pare Lorentz went on to make shorts for RKO as well as for the military during World War II. He later produced commercial and industrial movies. His contributions to political documentary and social docudrama had far-reaching effects.

Though the Film Service had been squelched, there were still plenty of true rebels willing to make more polemical cinema. In 1931, the New York Film and Photo League was formed; its members included Herbert Kline, Elia Kazan, Leo Hurwitz, and Ralph Steiner. With disorganized branches throughout the country, the NYFPL spawned progressive newsreels and documentary shorts, agitated for left-wing causes, and published an obscure magazine. None of its films played to more than limited groups of committed radicals. In 1937 the group essentially morphed into Frontier Films, a collective of documentarians. Financed by leftists (including composer Aaron Copland and writers Clifford Odets, Lillian Hellman, and John Dos Passos), Frontier was committed to bringing socially relevant documentaries to a wide audience.

Ralph Steiner and Willard Van Dyke left Frontier and made *The City* (1939), a visual essay that uses a clash of images to advocate careful urban planning. Chicago native Herbert Kline helmed Frontier's first documentary, *Heart of Spain* (1937), an account of the Spanish Civil War. Kline also codirected *Return to Life* (1938), a collection of Spanish loyalist newsreels, and he captured the outbreak of World War II in *Crisis* (1938) and *Lights Out in Europe* (1940). Outside of Frontier, Kline then teamed up with one of America's greatest authors to forge a classic docudrama of social concern.

"This is the story of the little pueblo of Santiago on the skirts of a hill in the mountains of Mexico. And this is the story of the boy Juan Diego and of his family and of his people, who live in the long moment when the past slips reluctantly into the future." So begins the narration to *The Forgotten Village* (1941), spoken by Burgess Meredith and penned by novelist John Steinbeck, whose legendary tale of the Depression, *The Grapes of Wrath*, was then a critical and commercial sensation. Steinbeck wrote the script for *The Forgotten Village*; Herbert Kline followed it closely. For ten months Kline and crew lived among the peasants of a poor Mexican village, detailing birth, sickness, and death through staged events, using a documentary approach. As with most nonfiction productions of this era, they shot without sound.

The Forgotten Village suffered threats of censorship over an offscreen childbirth, but it won the cases on appeal. Its message in support of birth control also angered many. Reviews were mostly favorable. The *Los Angeles Daily News* said, "As a social document, it achieves importance, depicting as it does the triumph of modern medicine over superstition and ignorance."[9] Herbert Kline went on to direct several features, most notably the Israeli documentary *My Father's House* (1947) and Hollywood's *The Fighter* (1952).

In *Native Land*, a farmer (Fred Johnson) fears for his life after speaking up for justice at a meeting. Courtesy of the Academy of Motion Picture Arts and Sciences.

Meanwhile, Frontier Film's few works of propaganda culminated in the legendary docudrama *Native Land* (1942). Directed by New York natives Leo Hurwitz (also editor) and Paul Strand (also cinematographer), authored by famed screenwriter Ben Maddow (under a pseudonym), narrated by Paul Robeson, and acted by members of the left-leaning Group Theatre, *Native Land* comprises a virtual "Who's Who" of artists who would be blacklisted as "communist subversives" in a few short years.

The completed feature is not overtly socialist, but it is critical of unrestrained capitalism. Maddow utilized 1938 Congressional testimony regarding corporate violations of the Bill of Rights. In a series of reenactments interspersed with documentary footage, a case is built that "a handful of fascist-minded corporations" are conspiring to undermine unionism through spying, thuggery, and murder. As the title suggests, *Native Land* is also proudly (and carefully) American, arguing that labor organization is even more necessary to quickly build munitions for World War II.

And yet the war stifled its circulation. Unions that contributed to *Native Land* withdrew support after the attack on Pearl Harbor on December 7, 1941. They feared the movie was too divisive for wartime. *Native Land* virtually disappeared upon initial release. Sparked by HUAC, however, it has grown through the decades into a proudly progressive memorial. Its legend exceeds its artistry, but the force of the vignettes and Strand's dark and restless photographic style remain compelling.

Native Land's directors were soon blacklisted from Hollywood. Paul Strand, who contributed to many of the most important nonfiction films for two decades, returned full-time to his first love, the still camera, securing his status as a world-famous realistic photographer. Leo Hurwitz directed (mostly uncredited) documentaries for television and a few independent features—most notably the four-hour visual elegy to his wife, *Dialogue With a Woman Departed* (1981). With the outbreak of World War II and the poor distribution of *Native Land*, Frontier Films disbanded.

Yiddish and Edgar Ulmer

Yiddish cinema during this period was developing into a unique worldwide genre. Because the language was the same and because themes and Old World settings were similar, a film produced in

Russia or Poland could be as successful in Manhattan as one shot in Brooklyn. And a Bronx-made flick could be a hit in Austria. Like the race pictures, Yiddish movies provided Orthodox Jews with a representation of their own customs, legends, and language, which Hollywood ignored. Yet even more than black-cast movies, Jewish-American films were marginalized into a very few (mostly lower Manhattan) theaters, making it especially difficult to realize a profit or raise a substantial budget.

The first American-made Yiddish talkies were produced in the early thirties by Judea Pictures and its president, Joseph Seiden. These shorts were budgeted at less than $3,000 and shot with stationary cameras. They suffer for their poverty, but they do feature some of New York's best cantors and Yiddish theatrical legends.

Traditional Jewish cinema reached its worldwide peak in the mid-thirties. The most famous Yiddish feature, Poland's *Yidl with a Fiddle*, a musical, was a minor worldwide hit in mainstream theaters in 1936. Sparked by *Yild*'s success, American producer Roman Rebush wanted to create Yiddish motion pictures that could draw both gentiles and Jews. Ashamed of the minuscule production values and technical inadequacy of previous efforts, he hired a genuine Hollywood director.

Well, sort of genuine . . . and sort of Hollywood. Maverick extraordinaire Edgar Ulmer (1904–1972) helmed he best and most successful American-Yiddish features, but he did much more than that. No one in the history of cinema has a low-budget résumé as expansive as Ulmer's. In addition to Yiddish and English, he also directed films in German, Spanish, Czech, Hungarian, Slovak, Italian, and Ukranian (most of which were shot in America). He made a picture with an all-black cast. He helmed the aforementioned exploitation blockbuster as well as one of the best studio B movies and some of the greatest Poverty Row pictures. Over a six-decade career, Ulmer worked in virtually every genre of low-budget cinema. Others would claim the crown, but Edgar Ulmer was the true King of the Bs.

Ulmer was born in Austria and, after an early start in theater, worked in the art department of legendary German features including *Golem* (1919; he was fifteen), *The Last Laugh*, and *Metropolis* (1926). The young, wavy-haired Ulmer then came to America, called the shots on a few quickie "oaters," and assisted on substantial features, including Murnau's *Sunrise* and *Tabu*. Returning to Germany, he codi-

rected *People on Sunday* (1929) a documentary notable for the crew
members who immigrated to America and became Hollywood legends: Robert and Curt Siodmark, Eugene Schüfftan, Fred Zinnemann,
and Billy Wilder. (In various categories, they went on to collect thirteen Academy Awards and thirty-one nominations. Ulmer was never
nominated.) In 1933, back in America again, Ulmer helmed the very
successful VD melodrama *Damaged Lives*. His name doesn't appear on
the Poverty Row westerns he shot in five days for a fee of $300 each.

The delectably macabre horror classic *The Black Cat* (1934), directed
for Universal's B division, would by itself be reason to celebrate
Edgar Ulmer. He made two additional Bs for Universal under the
pseudonym "John Warner," but the moralistic Ulmer, with brooding
moods and a headstrong will, could never be just another part of
what he called the "hash machine." In fact, for the next three decades
Ulmer would toil as far away from the major studios as possible.

Between the dawn of the sound era and the first Yankee shots in
World War II, there was a thriving American market for movies in the
native languages of recent immigrants. Theaters in ethnic neighborhoods imported and screened entertainment from the motherland
without dubbing or subtitles, a practice that still occurs in some communities. In New York City in 1939 there were twenty-five venues
playing motion pictures in the following nine languages: French,
German, Polish, Italian, Russian, Yiddish, Greek, Hungarian, and
Chinese, as well as one that specialized in Irish imports.[10]

A few theater owners and enterprising producers decided to make
such foreign-language features domestically. Because the exhibition
prospects were meager (often limited to only the producer's theater),
the budgets were minute. Companies didn't stay in business long.
Still, that didn't discourage Edgar Ulmer from accepting directing
gigs. He made a Ukranian movie in 1937 and another in 1939 (both
shot in New York), and numerous other foreign-language pictures
uncredited or with pseudonyms. And he helmed Yiddish features.

For $300, Ulmer directed the Yiddish-language, Roman Rebush
production *Green Fields* (1937), shot in eight days for $8,000. Because
he spoke little Yiddish, Ulmer had codirector Jacob Ben-Ami handle
the dialogue. *Green Fields* is a lyrical, slow-moving tale of a wandering scholar in search of a meaningful life. It played at the same New
York theater for twenty weeks and was a hit abroad; French critics
named it the Best Foreign Picture of 1938.

Next, Ulmer called the shots on *The Singing Blacksmith* (1938), an unoriginal period piece with an interesting production story. Searching for a site to double as medieval Europe, Ulmer found an old Catholic monastery in New Jersey. The monks let him shoot on the grounds, but the location had a couple of unusual neighbors. On one side was a nudist camp. On the other was a German-American bund (a pro-Nazi sympathizers group). As Ulmer recounts, "So that nothing could happen to the sets as we built them, the [Jewish] academicians and their pupils stood at night with guns, so the Bund couldn't do anything to our construction."[11] Jewish scholars, monks, nudists, and Nazis in New Jersey. Now that's independent filmmaking!

The King of the Bs directed two additional Yiddish features, *The Light Ahead* (1939) and *American Matchmaker* (1940). Set in nineteenth-century Russia, the first is a romance about a young couple aided by a wise bookseller. The second is a modern comedy, a consciously light picture for increasingly dark times.

As war brewed in Europe, the Father of Yiddish Cinema, Sidney Goldin, returned to America. He began helming *The Cantor's Son* (1937) but died before it was completed; Ilya Moteleff finished directing. It's the story of legendary cantor Moishe Oysher, who plays himself. Oysher also stars in *The Vilner Cantor* (1939, aka *Overture to Glory*), the tale of another Yiddish singing legend. Directed by Max Nosseck (*Dillinger*) and sporting elegant sets and costumes, *The Vilner Cantor* was meant to make a mainstream splash, but events in Germany shifted the focus.

World War II and the Holocaust ended European-Yiddish cinema, and although there were scattered efforts throughout the forties, the American-Yiddish industry effectively died as well, hastened by the increasing assimilation of American Jews.

Edgar Ulmer continued making movies without money. The all-African-American *Moon Over Harlem* (1939) was shot in four days with short ends (leftover scraps from the film rolls of other productions). The nightclub scenes were picked up in a Harlem club after its 2:00 A.M. closing, and the more than fifty singers received 25 cents each for a day's work.

During the forties, Ulmer worked for the most impoverished of the Poverty Row Studios. He made ten features for PRC, including the impressionistic *Bluebeard* (1944) and the legendary *Detour* (1946). Most of Ulmer's PRC features were filmed in one fast week or less and at a lightning pace of more than eighty camera setups daily. By this time the Austrian immigrant had a reputation for turning straw into gold. Edgar Ulmer kept receiving—and often soliciting—straw, forever spinning.

African-American

The sound era ushered in major studio, black-cast films. In 1929 there were two musicals, Fox's *Hearts in Dixie* and MGM's popular *Hallelujah*. Both clung to shuffling stereotypes, as did, to an even greater degree, the most popular radio show of the era, "Amos 'n' Andy," where blacks were played by whites. "Amos 'n' Andy" was such a phenomenon in the thirties that, rather than trying to compete, some movie theaters shut down their projectors when it was broadcast and played the fifteen-minute program for the audience.

In 1933, the first widely released independent black-themed film was distributed by United Artists. *The Emperor Jones* was directed by Dudley Murphy and written by DuBose Heyward (based on a play by Eugene O'Neill). The cinematographer was Ernest Haller (Academy Award winner for *Gone With The Wind*). Frank Wilson, Fredi Washington, and Moms Mabley are featured.

The star of *The Emperor Jones* was appearing in only his second motion picture (the first being Micheaux's *Body and Soul*), but by this time Paul Robeson was a major stage figure. Earlier, Eugene O'Neill had persuaded Robeson to postpone a law career and star in the writer's Broadway shows *All God's Chillun Got Wings* and *The Emperor Jones*. When the film's casting began, Robeson was the natural choice to repeat his role of the defiant and proud leader.

Religious but hypocritical, Brutus Jones (Robeson) kills a man in a gambling brawl and is sentenced to work on a chain gang. He escapes from the shackles to a Caribbean island, where he works for a white trader (Dudley Digges) and maneuvers his way into power. Upon seizing the island's throne by seeming immortal, he admires himself in a mirror and pronounces, "Mr. President. No." Pause. "King Brutus. No. Somehow that don't make enough noise." He then commands the white trader to light his cigarette. "You have just had an audience with the Emperor Jones!" Brutus rules ruthlessly until he's brought down by a native rebellion.

Because of its bold plot and Robeson's strong presence, *The Emperor Jones* retains much of its dynamism today. During 1933 and

Poster for *The Emperor Jones*. Paul Robeson is depicted as servant, rebel, schemer, ruler, and brute.

for decades later, the movie, the character, and the star were held up as symbols of black power. Brutus Jones is an intelligent, defiant, and mostly dignified (if arrogant) African-American who outsmarts his white oppressors. He is killed in the end—hunted in the jungle like a savage, crawling and moaning as drums beat relentlessly—but the memory of the first hour cannot be erased. Emperor Jones was so unlike Hollywood's servile black caricatures that African-Americans couldn't help but cheer.

Meanwhile, the race picture industry sputtered through the Depression. Almost alone during the early years of sound, Oscar Micheaux kept right on making movies. He turned out the part-talkie *Daughter of the Congo* in 1930 and followed with the first sound race feature, *The Exile* (1931), financed by the white owner of Harlem's Apollo Theater.

If anything, Micheaux's pictures decreased in quality with the addition of an audio track. He continued to pound them out in a week or so for $15,000 or less at essentially one location (usually the home or office of a friend) and with two takes or less per shot. The difference was that now actors clearly read longer passages from cue cards, their flubbed lines were often kept in the final print, and half-hearted attempts were made at wretched musical numbers. Micheaux sometimes seemed not to care about the microphone. In *The Girl from Chicago* (1932) he can be heard on the soundtrack guiding performances and calling for silence.

Micheaux the homesteader continued to tour the country, personally promoting his creations. Because black film venues were virtually nonexistent during the early thirties, he convinced white theater owners to show his movies during "colored matinees." His and the few similar flicks also played at midnight screenings for white audiences in search of the "exotic." For this reason, Micheaux inserted cabaret sequences in his films and gave them titles like *Darktown Revue* (1931) and *Harlem after Midnight* (1934). Economics forced him to abandon the social themes of his silent pictures.

By the time black theaters began to open again in the mid-thirties, Micheaux had weathered some lean years. He was creating content that his white financiers could approve. Meanwhile, he was increasingly criticized by the black press for his bourgeois ideology and for favoring light-skinned black characters over those of darker hues. A call for African-Americans to return to farms, *God's Stepchildren* (1939) includes harsh comments about darker skin and the work ethic of some of his race. It was protested by African-Americans and withdrawn from some theaters. Micheaux felt that he was misunderstood, that he was merely telling the truth to best help his race. He made sixteen features between 1930 and 1940. In the forties, he returned to writing novels, though Oscar Micheaux wasn't quite through with film production.

As the Depression eased, the race film market was resuscitated by *Dark Manhattan* (1937). Scripted and produced by George Randol and helmed by Henry Fraser, it features Ralph Cooper as a gangster who rises to the top of the Harlem numbers racket. *Variety* said the "film is [the] best technically ever made with complete colored cast."[12] It was certainly one of the most successful. *Dark Manhattan* opened in Los Angeles and quickly spread to other major cities. More than a dozen independently made black gangster flicks followed in rapid succession.

With the help of white backers, *Dark Manhattan*'s Ralph Cooper organized Million Dollar Pictures, which made some of the most significant race pictures of the era, including *The Duke Is Tops* (1938), marking the debut of Lena Horne; *One Dark Night* (1939), starring Mantan Moreland; and *Reform School* (1939), with Louise Beavers. During these years, actors like Horne, Moreland, and Beavers would shift between starring roles in independent race pictures and supporting (and often demeaning) characters in mainstream Hollywood features.

In addition to those three, the list of notable African-Americans who appeared in nonstudio black-cast cinema is impressive: Paul Robeson; Spencer Williams; boxer Joe Louis; dancer/actor Bill "Bojangles" Robinson; singers Nat King Cole, Dinah Washington, and Josephine Baker; actresses Dorothy Dandridge, Nina Mae McKinney, and Ruby Dee; agriculturist George Washington Carver; jazzman and singing cowboy Herbert Jeffrey; rodeo star Bill Pickett; comics Moms Mabley, Stepin Fetchit, Dewey "Pigmeat" Markam, Slick and Slack, and John "Rastus" Murray; and actors Eddie Anderson ("Rochester" to Jack Benny), Lorenzo Tucker, and Clarence Muse.

Such movies were of poor quality, crippled by technical inadequacy and the slimmest of budgets. They also slipped into a creative rut of simply copying popular Hollywood genres, grinding out crime dramas and musicals and domestic comedies that were doomed in comparison by their poverty. Most were produced and directed by whites for white-owned companies and screened in freezing-in-the-winter, sweltering-in-the-summer white-owned theaters in black ghettoes.

The most significant black filmmaker of the forties was Spencer Williams (1893–1969), who had been a prolific and popular star in (and occasional writer of) race pictures in the thirties. In 1941, the plump Williams teamed with Alfred Sack of Dallas's prolific Sack Amusement Enterprises (a white backer of Oscar Micheaux). As long as he turned a profit, Sack allowed Williams to write, direct, and act in whatever stories he chose. So Williams tried something different, a melodrama about the African-American religious experience called *The Blood of Jesus* (1941). Good and evil fight for the soul of a woman (Cathryn Caviness) who was accidently shot by her husband (Williams). In this case, the tiny budget gives the heavenly visuals a folk art feeling. The film is also buoyed by nearly continuous music, mostly classic spirituals. In the small world of black theaters, *The Blood of Jesus* was a hit.

Williams followed with two additional religious features, *Brother Martin* (1942) and *Go Down, Death!* (1944), and a pair of serious dramas, *Marchin' On* (1943) and *Of One Blood* (1944). They were less successful, and the slim profit margin of race pictures caught up with Williams, who was forced to turn to suggestive topics like *Dirty Gertie from Harlem, U.S.A.* (1946) and *Beale Street Mama* (1946). He directed his final feature, *Juke Joint*, in 1947. Strapped with budgets of less than $15,000, Spencer Williams tried to present socially significant stories but ended up showing a Dirtie Gertie striptease. His early films are compelling when not technically inept. For better and for worse, Williams was the Oscar Micheaux of the forties. He went on to his greatest fame as costar Andy Brown on the "Amos and Andy" TV series.

Independent black-cast features lurched into the postwar years. The market seemed as strong as it was at the end of the silent era, but, as always, the foundation was precariously fragile: simple stories, meager budgets, disorganized distribution, and a few hundred decrepit theaters in poor neighborhoods. Any significant change could bring it all tumbling down.

Douglas Sirk

In the late thirties, with fascism in Europe, numerous filmmakers left the Continent for California. Danish-born Douglas Sirk (1900–1987) was among them. He directed movies in Germany before fleeing Nazism and then suffered through several years of aborted projects with American studios. To eke out a living, he farmed chickens and avocados. One person who knew Sirk's reputation was Seymour Nebenzal, an ocean-hopping American who had produced *M* (1931) and other German classics. Nebenzal had the perfect idea for Sirk's American directing debut: *Hitler's Madman* (1943). It had a $300,000 budget, three credited writers, and uncredited help from Edgar Ulmer. Among the German immigrants in the crew was legendary cinematographer Eugene Schüfftan, also making his American debut. Based on well-publicized events occurring just five months before production, *Hitler's Madman* is a sensationalistic saga about the Czech villages brutally destroyed by Nazis after German commandant Heydrich (John Carradine) is assassinated. Twenty-one-year-old Ava Gardner has a small role. *Hitler's Madman* sold to MGM, but was overshadowed in 1943 by the work of another director who fled Germany, Fritz Lang's *Hangmen Also Die*, a film about the same events.

Nebenzal, Sirk, and Schüfftan teamed up again on *Summer Storm* (1944), based on Chekhov's play *The Shooting Party*. Set evocatively in prerevolutionary Russia, married Olga (Linda Darnell) seduces a count and a judge, bringing tragedy to all involved. Sirk next made semi-indies released by United Artists. In the fifties, he went under contract with Universal, crafting such celebrated melodramas as *Magnificent Obsession* (1954), *All That Heaven Allows* (1955), and *Imitation of Life* (1959), now seen as highly stylized and ironic.

Avant-garde

A hand reaches down to leave a flower on a road. A sultry young woman picks up the flower and walks along the road and into a house. She sees a shrouded figure with a mirrored face disappearing around the bend ahead of her. This is the opening of the ground-breaking trance experiment *Meshes of the Afternoon* (1943). The sultry young woman is the movie's director, Maya Deren. Over the next nearly two decades, she inspired and led the American avant-garde into something resembling a movement.

The sound era of experimental film began with silent cinematic poems. Herman Weinberg created *City Symphony* (1929) and *Autumn Fire* (1930), which use montage to make rhythmic visual correlations. At the same time, photographer and future documentarian Ralph

Steiner crafted two short studies of water patterns, H^2O (1929) and *Surf and Seaweed* (1930). Steiner was assisted by future directing legend Elia Kazan on *Pie in the Sky* (1934), shot in a junkyard.

Others explored different avenues. James Watson and Melville Webber teamed up again for the stylized Biblical allegory *Lot in Sodom* (1933). Mary Ellen Bute devised pioneering experimental animation in shorts like *Anitra's Dance* (1936) and *Toccata and Fugue* (1940). And Joseph Cornell assembled the first crucial collage film, *Rose Hobart* (1937). A surreal tribute of sorts to the actress of the same name, it utilizes images clipped and rearranged from a lame jungle melodrama in which Hobart starred (*East of Borneo*, 1931). *Rose Hobart* was at least two decades ahead of its time.

Meanwhile, the broader base for artistic cinema grew. In 1931 the first international film festival was born in Venice, Italy. In 1932 both the Film Forum (in New York) and the New York Film Society were launched, the former to show mostly leftist pictures, the latter to screen primarily foreign fare. New York's recently founded Museum of Modern Art established a film collection in 1935 and began regularly scheduled public screenings there in 1939. Los Angeles was then and is now the worldwide center for film as commerce, but the center for film as art was then and, to a large degree, is now the Upper West Side of Manhattan.

Maya Deren (1917–1961) was born in Russia and immigrated to New York as a child. She studied journalism, literature, and dance. In 1942 the exotic beauty married her second husband, Czech filmmaker Alexander Hammid (he worked on numerous features, including *The Forgotten Village*). Together they shot *Meshes of the Afternoon* in their own home with primitive 16mm equipment. The fourteen-minute film feels like a dream as a woman (Deren) repeatedly chases a figure and the figure chases her in an endless escalating cycle with changing perspectives, much symbolism, and a seemingly tragic ending. In dramatizing a woman's sexual attraction and fear, Maya Deren said her film "externalizes an inner world to the point where it is confounded with the external one."[13]

Deren expanded upon the techniques of *Meshes* in her trance movie *At Land* (1944), and she combined their ideas with her interest in dance in *Choreography for the Camera* (1945) and *Ritual in Transfigured Time* (1946). But her greatest accomplishment was that she liberated the American avant-garde from Greenwich Village cafes. It's a story for the next chapter, but, for now, know that Maya Deren brought experimental film to universities and film societies and popular theaters. She proselytized for the cinema of personal expression whenever she wrote and wherever she went.

16mm

Through the decades, most avant-garde movies have been shot and projected in 16mm, but virtually all commercially distributed films are projected in 35mm. 35mm has remained the industry standard since the earliest days. And yet the film stock and lab costs are much cheaper when a movie is shot in 16mm; the equipment is lighter and more mobile (thus a smaller crew can be used), making it attractive to financially strapped independents.

A key factor in the growth of independent motion pictures was the boom in 16mm equipment after the war. During World War II, the troops watched training demonstrations as well as the latest Hollywood features via thousands of 16mm projectors. As the war ended, there was a surplus of such equipment, and it found its way into schools, film societies, and museums, where its influence was wide. The Museum of Modern Art circulated 16mm prints of classic features, documentaries, and experimental work. Suddenly, 16mm didn't just mean a reel on foot fungus.

In 1944, H. V. George independently produced and financed a typical bargain-basement "oater" that he hoped would be the start of a series. He hired established western director Lambert Hillyer and established actors Russell Wade, Andy Clyde, and Jack Kirby. The feature, *Sundown Riders*, was shot in eight days for $30,000, paying all necessary guild and union fees. What makes *Sundown Riders* unique is that it was captured in color 16mm and sold in color 16mm to the home and institutional markets. All owners of projectors could screen it themselves. It was, in a figurative sense, the first direct-to-video movie.

An apprehensive Hollywood watched from the sidelines. The experiment was not a success, and there would be no *Sundown* series. Still, it demonstrated the expanded opportunities available with cheaper stock and equipment. Such openings would prove fruitful in coming decades when 16mm could be optically blown up to make a 35mm release print (a relatively common occurrence in the modern independent scene). [14] George's gamble didn't pay off, but when the studios had production, distribution, and exhibition monopolized, as they did between the birth of sound and the end of the war, the most daunting challenge for maverick production companies was finding theaters to screen their movies.

Soon independent filmmakers wouldn't have to try the *Sundown Riders* trail. Forces were at work in 1944 that would set free a whole slew of screens and eventually break down the vaunted studio system. Forces were at work that would do nothing less than completely alter the path of American cinema.

Notes

[1] Vidor, 222.

[2] Balio, Tino, *The American Film Industry* (Madison: Univ. Of Wisconsin, 1976), 225. Weekly ticket sales reached ninety million in 1946. Combined domestic box office grosses for the eight majors (the Big Five and Universal, Columbia, and United Artists) leaped from $193 million in 1939 to $332 million in 1946.

[3] *Variety*, 8 Jan. 1930.

[4] Vidor, 221.

[5] *New York Times*, 7 Oct. 1934.

[6] Vidor, 225.

[7] Vidor, 222.

[8] Snyder, Robert L., *Pare Lorentz and the Documentary Film* (Norman: Oklahoma Univ., 1968), 37.

[9] *Los Angeles Daily News*, 2 Feb. 1942.

[10] Gomery, Douglas, *Shared Pleasures: A History of Movie Presentation in the United States* (Madison: Univ. of Wisconsin, 1992), 178.

[11] Bogdanovich, Peter, "An Interview: Edgar G. Ulmer." *Film Culture* 58-59-60 (1974), 216.

[12] *Variety*, 17 March 1937.

[13] Deren, Maya, "Notes, Letters, Essays," *Film Culture* 39 (Winter 1965), 31.

[14] Independent filmmakers, including John Cassavetes, John Waters, and Spike Lee, have shot and edited in 16mm (or the more rectangular format, Super 16) before obtaining distribu-

tion. The distributor then absorbed the lab costs of optically doubling the release prints to 35mm. The image quality is not ideal—often appearing somewhat grainy when projected—but it has allowed modern movies to be made for less than $150,000.

1945-1952

SYSTEM BREAKDOWN

Sometimes when you can't afford it, you improvise,
and it comes off better.

—SAM FULLER

We independent producers must continue to
explore new themes, try new ideas, discover new
creative talents in all departments.

—IDA LUPINO AND COLLIER YOUNG
"DECLARATION OF INDEPENDENCE"[1]

Questions as to whether or not the major studios constituted a monopoly loomed over Hollywood for decades. They began back in 1921 when the Federal Trade Commission issued its first complaint but became decidedly more serious when the United States Justice Department filed suit in July 1938. Certainly the studios took notice, but the glacial progress of litigation lulled many into complacency. The suit wouldn't be settled until July 1949, and the studios and theaters wouldn't be in full compliance until 1957.

The Paramount consent decrees helped bring down the studio system, slowly grinding it to a halt from the mid-forties to the mid-fifties. Just as in the dying days of the Trust four decades earlier, when the film factories suffered losses, independent producers made gains. When the system began to break down, new opportunities arose.

It was called the Paramount case because Paramount was the largest defendant, but all of the Big Five (Paramount, RKO,

Twentieth-Century Fox, Warner Bros., and MGM) were named, and the Little Three (Columbia, Universal, and United Artists) were dragged in as coconspirators. The case stemmed from charges that the studios constituted a monopoly. Because they owned the vast majority of first-run venues, the case went, they strangled independent theaters and theater chains with such practices as block booking (forcing venues to rent groups of movies), blind booking (forcing venues to rent movies sight unseen), and the fixing of admission prices.

Compromises were reached in 1940, but nothing about movie exhibition really changed. In 1944 the Justice Department renewed its antitrust suit and the case began its crawl through the legal system. When the New York District Court ruled in 1946, the decision was appealed to the Supreme Court. The Court announced its first decision in 1949: the studios must divest from their theater chains. Even then, the Big Five tried to finesse their way around the law by splitting themselves into separate divisions for production and exhibition. Legal delays continued through the early fifties.

It is easy to overstate the effects of the Paramount consent decrees on exhibition. In actuality, the major studios have always maintained an effective monopoly of the best venues, if only because they consistently generate movies with the greatest potential for ticket sales. Furthermore, by the time independent theaters could book the feature of their choice, thousands of them were already out of business, strangled by a changing marketplace that included the proliferation of television sets and suburban drive-ins.

The Paramount decision's greater effect was to hasten the death of the studio production system. From the beginning of sound until the end of World War II, American filmmaking was dominated by wholly contained and compartmentalized factories. During the mid-forties, this system began to break down.

The seeds of destruction were sown in 1941 with the Revenue Act, which raised taxes to astronomical levels in an effort to finance America's wartime defense buildup. The top bracket was lowered to $200,000 and taxed at a rate of 90 percent. This meant Hollywood's elite took home 10 percent of their salary (minus their agent's share, their lawyer's share, and their accountant's share). Suddenly, no one wanted a long-term contract or a substantial wage. Movie stars and moviemakers wanted one-picture deals and profit participation (preferably with a "guaranteed profit"), wherein their return would be taxed only at the capital gains rate of 25 percent. Short-term contracts led to more freedom and mobility.

One by-product of this trend was the proliferation of semi-indie production companies. David O. Selznick (*Gone With The Wind*) had been an "independent" producer for most of the Roosevelt era, but he was essentially a two-legged studio, perpetuating the rules of the system. Stanley Kramer was the first modern semi-indie. After World War II, his company produced such critically acclaimed features as *Home of the Brave* (1949), *High Noon* (1952), and *The Wild One* (1954). Most of Kramer's movies were released by United Artists. Between 1952 and 1967, Kramer was nominated for an amazing nine Academy Awards as producer ("Best Picture") or director; he won none.

In 1943, United Artists had only sixteen semi-indie producers under contract. They generated few movies. But when talent was no longer bound by contracts, when a few semi-indies collected Oscars, and when production company ownership provided a substantial tax shelter, setting up shop quickly became the "in" thing to do. Burt Lancaster (with Harold Hecht) and Kirk Douglas were among the first, but by the time Hecht/Lancaster won an Academy Award for *Marty* in 1955 the list of legends with their own enterprises was long: Robert Mitchum, Gregory Peck, Frank Sinatra, Billy Wilder, George Stevens, John Houston, Alfred Hitchcock, Marlon Brando, and many more. In the previous two decades United Artists had been hurt by its lack of contract talent. Now it was helped. By 1958, UA had signed more than fifty semi-indie producers. The studio's profits soared. Year after year it took home more Academy Awards than any other Hollywood house.

The broader semi-indie system spread to all the studios. In 1945 there were forty "independent" production companies. Two years later there were ninety. By 1957 there were 170. Conversely, the number of actors, screenwriters, and directors under contract shrank from nearly 1,500 in the mid-forties to just 355 ten years later . . . and that list would continue to dwindle.[2]

The semi-indie system persists to this day. The degree of creative and financial autonomy in such productions was then and is now somewhere between slim and none. To truly gain freedom, filmmakers must completely disassociate themselves from the studios until their vision is put on film: no financing, no presigned distribution agreement, no help, no interference. In the Truman years there were still precious few rebels desperate or courageous enough to grab the bar without a safety net beneath them. But that number would grow.

After the War

In 1945 the country celebrated the end of the war. This was the beginning of both an economic boom and a baby boom (in a world that now literally could go "boom"). In the halcyon days before television, fully half of America went to movie every week.

In this climate, a group of ex-servicemen produced their own feature. Directed by Irving Allen (in the middle of a mediocre B career) and starring Eddie Albert in an early role, *Strange Voyage* (1945) is a leisurely search for buried treasure in Southern California.

West Point's two all-American football greats "Doc" Blanchard and Glenn Davis could have resigned their commissions in 1947 and joined the National Football League. Instead, they became naval officers. During the sixty-day furlough between graduation and active duty, they starred in their own story, *The Spirit of West Point* (1947), directed by B specialist Ralph Murphy. Newsreel clips and stock footage are mixed poorly with clichés and bad acting.

Another maverick made something a cut above. Italian-American composer Gian-Carlo Menotti adopted his hit opera *The Medium* for the big screen in 1951. Saddled with a slim budget, his direction still shows flair. Shot on location in Italy, the dialogue is sung in English. Marie Powers and Leo Coleman repeat their Broadway roles, accompanied by the Symphony Orchestra of Rome. *The Medium* tells a creepy tale of a crooked spiritualist (Powers), her daughter (Maria Alberghetti), and a mute gypsy (Coleman). This remains a truly original movie that effectively captures the mood of the Italian slums. Menotti's music was nominated for an Academy Award.

Sexploitation

Meanwhile, in a Main Street theater in a small town in middle America, a man who renamed himself after a grocery store chain was hawking the most successful roadshow picture in history. He went by the unlikely name of Kroger Babb (1907–1980), and his film had the innocent yet slyly suggestive title of *Mom and Dad* (1945).

Previously, Babb and two partners toured the South and Midwest exploiting *Dust to Dust* (1944). When Babb wanted to make his own cautionary tale on teenage pregnancy, his partners opted out. So he raised money from exhibitors, his future wife wrote the script, and he came to Hollywood and hired the prolific director William Beaudine. Babb's Hygienic Productions shot *Mom and Dad* on the Monogram lot.

Mom and Dad is a typical cautionary melodrama. It opens with the National Anthem and the proclamation that this is a "vital educational production, appealing to all true Americans." A high school girl's parents avoid lecturing her on the birds and the bees. She gets pregnant, her boyfriend dies before they can marry, and a sincere teacher advocates sex ed in schools. It's all subdued and silly. Controversy was drummed up, as it was with many such roadshow features, by screening it with a medical birth reel. Sometimes a clap reel was thrown in, too.

Kroger Babb perfected the pitch. *Mom and Dad* screenings were segregated for men and women. At the midpoint, the film stopped and Babb appeared as "eminent hygiene commentator, Mr. Elliot Forbes." For legal reasons, he was careful not to call himself a professor or a doctor. "Mr. Elliot Forbes" wove his spell, explaining the basics of birth control and hawking two pamphlets—from the "Women's Research Guild"—called *Secrets of Sensible Sex*. A buck for one or two bucks for both. Who could go another day without such secrets? Kroger Babb often sold both pamphlets to every member of the audience.

During the first years of the baby boom, controversy followed *Mom and Dad* across the country, and the outcry was often initiated by Babb himself. He was chased out of one town and into another. If he needed to turn up the heat, he'd distribute "SHOCKING TRUTH" fliers. If he needed to cool things off, he'd prescreen *Mom and Dad* without the birth reel for school boards and police chiefs. Smooth-talking Babb could almost always gain the necessary approval. He kept a file with hundreds of authentic letters of recommendation from public officials and doctors—all snookered by the master.

Kroger Babb changed his pitch in 1949, when he produced *The Prince of Peace*, a passion play shot in Oklahoma. During the accompanying lecture, "Alexander Hayes" (or whatever euphonious name Babb was using that night) hawked religious pamphlets and Bibles just as easily as "Elliot Forbes" sold sex secrets. By the early fifties, Babb's Hallmark Productions was an established—if not respected—distributor of exploitation flicks. It produced or acquired numerous minor vehicles over the next three decades, releasing them via roadshows and state's-rights.

In 1950, a couple of ex-GIs, Richard Kay and Harry Rybnick, used their own $6,000 to slap together some clips of strippers and called the resulting movie *International Burlesque*. Offering an unfulfilled promise of nudity, it was a surprise success. Similar flicks flooded the market, playing in the least desirable theaters or between acts in burlesque houses. They were inoffensive, monotonous, and fraudulent.

There were always 16mm stag films playing somewhere that delivered the pornographic goods, but those not invited to the parties were growing weary of being suckered with a sensational pitch. Audiences wanted to view more than they could see in the local burlesque joint, and—thanks but no thanks, Mr. Elliot Forbes—a little less than they would see in a VD clinic or a maternity ward.

Edgar Ulmer

Whether he was on a cramped Poverty Row stage or stealing shots in a one-way street, Edgar Ulmer kept right on making B movies. One never knew where his name would appear, but wherever it did, chances were he had directed the movie more cheaply and better than the next guy could.

Trying to jump-start a floundering career by playing exotic beauty roles, German-born actress Hedy Lamarr purchased the rights to a best-selling trashy novel, hired Edgar Ulmer, and assembled the closest thing the King of the Bs ever had to an A-level cast: Lamarr, Louis Hayward, George Sanders, and Gene Lockhart. The result was *The Strange Woman* (1946), an independent released through United Artists that features Ms. Lamarr stalking various men and conspiring to kill her husband. Ulmer's directing is intense and features some vibrant camera moves that show he could do more with a bigger budget.

Next came Ulmer's second stab at an A production. It was also an independent released by United Artists. *Carnegie Hall* (1947) is a tedious story of a pianist (William Prince) groping toward stardom. The concert performances from several giants of classical music, including pianist Arthur Rubinstein, violinist Jascha Heifetz, and soprano Lily Pons, are the only reason to see it.

Between a feature in Italy and several for United Artists, Ulmer made one of his best for the Poverty Row house Eagle-Lion: the Southern drama *Ruthless* (1949).

Robert Clarke wrestles with the alien in *The Man from Planet X*.

UFO intrigue was the new rage in this period, and Edgar Ulmer and writers/producers Aubrey Wisberg and Jack Pollenflex competed with Hollywood to create an alien visitation picture, *The Man from Planet X*. In 1951, it narrowly beat two studio classics, *The Day the Earth Stood Still* and *The Thing*. (An earlier independent, *The Flying Saucer*, 1950, was not about actual space visitors.) Hobbled by a budget of only $38,000, Ulmer and company rented gothic sets left over from *Joan of Arc* and worked a foggy Moorish setting into the sci-fi plot. Two scientists, the daughter of one, and a newspaperman go to a Scottish island to observe a planet hurtling toward Earth. An expressionless humanoid alien shows up. When the bad scientist tries to use the extraterrestrial for evil, the alien resists and instead forces the humans to work as slaves. The dialogue is stilted, but *The Man from Planet X* is notable for its fast pace, energetic camerawork by John Russell (*Psycho*), and eerie atmosphere.

Ulmer continued to work wherever he could through the mid-sixties, generating pictures for Allied Artists (formerly Monogram), AIP, and others in America, Italy, and Germany. He directed the independent crime drama *The Naked Dawn* (1955), starring Arthur Kennedy. Shot in ten days in color, it's an effective little robbery caper.

Edgar Ulmer directed more than 120 films. He preferred to work in the low-budget arena because it provided the most creative freedom. He was able to bring his German expressionist influences and art design background to even the silliest clichéd story shot with the slimmest possible schedule. Edgar Ulmer and Sam Fuller were the best when it came to consistently crafting something worthwhile in two weeks or less. The last lines of *Ruthless* are a fitting eulogy for Edgar Ulmer: "He wasn't just a man. He was a way of life."

African-American

Pioneer Oscar Micheaux made his final film in 1948, directing, scripting, and producing the black-cast drama *The Betrayal*. He envisioned the film, over three hours in length and covering a variety of socially relevant topics, as the epic culmination of his filmmaking career. It was released with atypical fanfare by Astor Pictures (a Poverty Row distributor best known for reissuing major studio flicks). Opening in a "white" theater, it was reviewed in the mainstream press. Unfortunately, *The Betrayal* is one of the worst Micheaux movies. Full of stationary dialogue scenes and wooden acting, it was justifiably panned. *Variety* patronizingly pronounced, "Its amateurishness limits its appeal to Negro centers."[3] It flopped everywhere.

Oscar Micheaux died in 1951. Fittingly, he was on a promotional tour. Unfittingly, his death went virtually unnoticed. In the years since, several of his lost films have been discovered. Micheaux left behind a complex legacy. The movies he made rarely approach the level of art, and sometimes they're awful. Yet in the long history of American commercial cinema, Micheaux was among the most prolific mavericks. He

was a self-taught rancher, novelist, filmmaker, and motion picture distributor. As a black man in a segregated country, Micheaux created
forty-six black-cast, black-story feature films over thirty years, bridg-
ing silence to sound, without ever once stepping foot inside the mono-
lithic studios. For that alone he deserves to be celebrated. In 1987,
Oscar Micheaux received a star on the Hollywood Walk of Fame.

By 1946, the number of theaters specializing in black-cast films
had again grown to more than six hundred. Simultaneously, the
number of black-cast features addressing serious issues had dwin-
dled to virtually none. By the late forties, most independent race pictures (virtually all of which were produced, directed, and distributed
by whites) fit into one of two categories: (1) broad, lightweight comedies wherein performers like Mantan Moreland and Stepin Fetchit
stand on a sparse set and crack tired jokes, and (2) musical revues
where the slimmest of plots are mere excuses for lively musical numbers from legends like Louis Jordan, Cab Calloway, Duke Ellington,
and Count Basie.

Independent African-American cinema was finally killed in the
early fifties. Due to the rising cost of film production, the always slim
profit margin, and the cultural blinders of their white filmmakers and
financiers, race pictures stopped taking even the slim chances they
took in the early forties. Black audiences increasingly turned to other
forms of entertainment, especially television.

The death blow, however, was integration. Just as Jackie Robinson
breaking the color barrier of major league baseball signaled the end of
the Negro League, black actors and themes in prestigious Hollywood
productions doomed race pictures. Studio features had always played
in and around black neighborhoods, and as a whole they were preferred by African-Americans—far more blacks saw *Gone With The
Wind* than ever heard of *Dirty Gertie From Harlem, U.S.A.* Throughout
the forties, blacks in the North increasingly attended traditionally
"white" movie palaces to see the latest from Hollywood. Recognizing
a profitable market, the majors began producing their own "colored"
musical revues for the bottom rungs of urban double and triple bills.
Such films featured top names like Louis Armstrong, Pearl Bailey, and
the Mills Brothers.

Then 1949 rocked the crumbling African-American movie houses
with a windfall of major studio, black-themed dramas, most notably
Home of the Brave, Pinky, and *Intruder in the Dust.* (For more than a

decade after blacklisting began in 1947, racism was the one issue progressive filmmakers could safely tackle.) With Hollywood generating quality features about people of color, the low-rent, plotless race pictures became superfluous almost overnight.

The independent black film industry came tumbling down—just as it had when sound technology and the Depression rocked it two decades earlier. Only this time there was no Oscar Micheaux around to revive it. By the time Sidney Poitier became a major movie star in the fifties, the race picture business was history and most of the old theaters were demolished. Generating more than 500 independent features, a separate cinema had been necessary for decades, but at the dawn of the second half of the twentieth century it was time to bid it farewell. The broader independent community would now have to pick up where Hollywood left off. Future nonstudio black-cast movies would not be part of an industry unto itself. They would play in integrated theaters and often be marketed to all potential viewers, regardless of race.

Neorealism in *The Quiet One*.
Courtesy of the Academy of Motion Picture Arts and Sciences.

In fact, it was already happening. In that same landmark year of 1949, along came two independents, *The Quiet One* (discussed with documentaries) and *Lost Boundaries*. The latter was produced by Louis de Rochemont and directed by Alfred Werker. The script (credited to four writers) was based on a *Reader's Digest* account of a black family that lived as whites in New England for twenty years. Shooting took place in Portsmouth, New Hampshire with a cast of then unknowns.

Unable to find employment at either black or white hospitals, light-skinned Dr. Carter (white Mel Ferrer) moves his light-skinned wife (white Beatrice Pearson) to New Hampshire, where they simply stop telling people what race they are. They have children. The family fits in well in the white community—until the deception unravels. "Why didn't you tell me I was Negro!" wails son Howie (white Richard Hylton). The town turns against the Carters, but a concluding sermon brings everyone together.

Lost Boundaries was both a critical and a commercial success. *The New York Times* named it the fourth best film of the year. Although it was banned in Atlanta for being "contrary to the public good," it was well received in most communities, even in the segregated South. Today, individual sequences feel preachy (the concluding sermon) or overwrought (Howie searching for his roots in Harlem), and some viewers find the use of white actors to play blacks off-putting. First-rate performances are mostly lost in the melodrama. Still, as its title suggested, *Lost Boundaries* began to erase some cinematic barriers and point the way toward an integrated future.

Avant-garde

After World War II, foreign cinema invaded America. Two major international film festivals began, Cannes (in 1947) and Berlin (in 1950). Movies that stirred up interest there and at the Venice Film Festival made their way across the Atlantic. Italian neorealism followed this route, bringing its low-budget, socially conscious tales with natural settings and working-class characters to American shores. The first of these bleak poems, Roberto Rossellini's *Open City* (1945) and *Paisan* (1946) both made $1 million at American box offices and generated much publicity. Neorealism reverberated through independent film for the next decade and can be seen in such American films as *The Quiet One* and *On the Bowery*.

In the next few years, theaters in urban centers began to specialize in foreign features, screening now legendary pictures like Italy's *The Bicycle Thief* (1949) and Japan's *Rashoman* (1951). The art house was born. Walter Reade, Jr. owned several such theaters in New York, and in 1953 he began opening them in other American cities. Local film societies and universities also began to show foreign works. The proliferation of such venues laid the foundation for a still larger wave of international cinema in the late fifties and, eventually, for artistic American independents.

For the time being, however, American art films were limited to the purview of the avant-garde. Experimental cinema began a period of growth and increased visibility that lasted two decades. When Maya Deren started screening her works and lecturing at universities in 1945, she found an audience eager for more challenging moving pictures. Deren's theoretical writing on visionary cinema was circulated among the growing underground, and her films became a staple at the Provincetown Playhouse in Greenwich Village. In 1946, the busy Deren was awarded the first Guggenheim Fellowship ever granted a filmmaker. She went to Haiti to shoot a documentary on rituals and dance, work that eventually resulted in a book but no motion picture.

Two people who attended a Maya Deren screening at the Provincetown Playhouse were

■ ■ ■ ■ ■ ■ ■ ■

Foreign Ten

In chronological order, these are ten of the foreign films that had the greatest impact on American independent cinema.

Un Chien Andalou. (France) Classic 1928 avant-garde short by Luis Buñuel and Salvador Dali. It famously begins with an eyeball being slashed by a razor.

Man with a Movie Camera. (Russia) This 1929 feature combines documentary and experimental techniques.

The Bicycle Thief. (Italy) Definitive neorealist film. Simple masterpiece of a poor father and son searching Rome for a stolen bike.

Breathless. (France) Definitive French New Wave film. Romantic crime classic breaks cinematic rules with jump-cut editing and a seemingly improvisational style.

Hiroshima, Mon Amour. (France) Another New Wave landmark. Nonlinear segments, jump cuts, and documentary

continued

Foreign Ten

continued

footage are incorporated into a psycho-logical tale of interracial romance.

Blow-Up. (Italy/Britain) Michelangelo Antonioni's exploration of illusion and reality in swinging London was a much-debated art-house smash in 1966.

I Am Curious—Yellow. (Sweden) A political drama with nearly explicit sex. Its censor-ship victories paved the way for hardcore pornography.

A Room with a View. (Britain) The first of Merchant and Ivory's elegant period pieces to break out of cinematheques. Spearheaded the gentility genre of quiet adult dramas.

La Femme Nikita. (France) Luc Besson's highly stylized action-thriller became a sub-titled hit with the MTV generation in 1991. Also notable: Hong Kong's *Hard-Boiled.*

The Crying Game. (Britain) Neil Jordan's jarringly original thriller with a love story with a twist became a sensation.

Ten Honorable Mentions: *Tokyo Story; And God Created Woman; Chronicle of a Summer; Shoot the Piano Player; Persona; King of Hearts; Last Tango in Paris; La Cage Aux Folles; 28 Up; Like Water for Chocolate.*

Amos Vogel and his wife Marcia. Inspired, they began their own Manhattan screening society in 1947 called Cinema 16. For the next sixteen years, Cinema 16 educated and entertained a generation of cinéastes while premiering most of America's crucial avant-garde movies. The Vogels also distributed experimental work throughout the world and collaborated with Maya Deren to honor exceptional independent films.

Meanwhile, the West Coast had opened its own prestigious vanguard venue. In 1945, the San Francisco Museum of Art launched the Art in Cinema screening series, which within two years became dedicated almost exclusively to the avant-garde. Until it began to turn away from such work in the mid-fifties, it was the premiere site west of Manhattan. Word of what was happening in New York and San Francisco spread to intellectuals throughout America, and hundreds of museums and universities began to screen experimental motion pictures.

One film that was shown in 1946 at both Cinema 16 and Art in Cinema was *Dreams That Money Can Buy.* Conceived and scripted by Dadaist painter and European avant-garde film pioneer Hans Richter (who immigrated to America from Germany in 1941), it's an ambitious feature about a young man who sells his dreams to others. Each of the trance sequences is directed by a different artist: Richter, Man Ray, Max Ernst, Fernand Léger, Marcel Duchamp, and Alexander Calder. Richter said of the completed film, "We created as an artist does, for his own responsibility and not for the audience. . . . You don't have to understand it to enjoy it."[4] The result is unenjoyable not because it is cryptic, but because the dreams are neither as imaginative nor as skillfully rendered as expected. *Dreams That Money Can Buy* found its way into some commercial theaters.

Kenneth Anger (1927–) grew up in Hollywood, acted in *A Midsummer Night's Dream* (1935) when he was eight, and made his first short film when he was nine. In 1947, at the ripe old age of twenty, he spawned the short *Fireworks*. In it, Anger plays a guilt-ridden homosexual who dreams of being beaten by sailors. This leads to sexual fulfillment (a penis becomes a Roman candle). In the film's prologue, narrator Anger tells us, "In *Fireworks* I released all the explosive pyrotechnics of a dream." It was an auspicious and daring debut.

Curtis Harrington (1928–) also started early in Los Angeles. He made short experimental flicks in his early teens. Harrington was eighteen when he created *Fragments of Seeking* (1946), a trance movie of some renown. Others followed. Finding it impossible to earn a living as a vanguard filmmaker, Harrington would eventually move towards the mainstream.

For a decade after World War II, dreams remained the most popular subject of the avant-garde, but artists were also exploring the very medium of moving pictures, working with stop-motion animation and image collages. Those who made a significant impact include Norman McLaren (*Begone Dull Care*, 1950), Dorsey Alexander (*Dime Store*, 1949), and Art in Cinema founder Frank Stauffacher (*Zigzag*, 1950).

By the early fifties, the beatnik culture of poetry, jazz, and improvisation was centered primarily in Greenwich Village, San Francisco, and the beach communities of Los Angeles. The quest for something new and something shocking attracted more and more way hip cats to experimental film screenings. Some of these nonconformists in a conformist age would decide to make their own movies. Avant-garde cinema would continue to grow along with interest in foreign fare, forming a solid base for art houses to build on.

Documentary

The term "docudrama," a fictionalized account of actual events or circumstances, is now chiefly applied to the sort of TV movies-of-the-week where somebody dies of a terminal disease or falls down a well. In fact, the docudrama form has a grand tradition, dating back to such films as *Tabu*, *The Fight for Life*, and *Native Land*. With a story line and characters, such films weren't so far removed from Hollywood productions and could therefore attain wider commercial distribution than typical documentaries could. In the late forties and throughout the fifties, docudramas dominated nonfiction cinema.

Robert Flaherty received an offer from the Standard Oil Company to make a docudrama set in a Louisiana bayou about the hard work a petroleum company does before striking oil. The company would finance the film with $175,000 (which would later balloon to nearly $260,000). Flaherty would have full artistic control, be the sole owner of the film, and would not be required to make reference to Standard Oil in the titles.

Flaherty began work in 1946 with a cast of nonprofessional actors and a crew headed by debuting cinematographer and future documentarian Richard Leacock. The completed feature, *Louisiana Story* (1948), was widely proclaimed as Flaherty's masterpiece. Every ten years *Sight and Sound* magazine polls international film critics to determine "The Ten Greatest Films of All Time." On the inaugural list in 1952, *Louisiana Story* tied for fifth place with Griffith's *Intolerance*.[5]

Louisiana Story tells the simple story of a Cajun boy (Joseph Boudreaux) who enjoys exploring the outdoors. When an oil company comes to drill, he watches them work. There is much exquisite photography of the swamps and the oil derrick and some thrilling moments with an angry alligator, but how this "screenplay" (by Flaherty and wife Frances) was nominated for an Academy Award is a mystery. Because Flaherty was that rarest of documentarians—one with little interest in politics—*Louisiana Story* maintains his objective gaze and ignores even the most basic questions about environmentalism and economics. It's a good film that had a wide influence, but *Nanook of the North* is Flaherty's masterpiece.

Flaherty never fit into the world of commercial cinema. He was a generous man and a reckless spender, a combination that often left him nearly broke. In 1951, while waiting for government funding for a documentary about Hawaii, he accepted a job offer to shoot a

Cinerama newsreel about General MacArthur returning from Korea. Flaherty did it out of economic necessity. He hated everything about the oversized political event and the oversized Cinerama equipment. While stressed out in Chicago, he contracted pneumonia. Sixty-seven-year-old Robert Flaherty died of complications shortly thereafter.

After seeing *Louisiana Story*, cinematic legends Charlie Chaplin, Jean Renoir, and Dudley Murphy sent Flaherty a cable: "Do this again and you will be immortal and excommunicated from Hollywood which is a good fate."[6] Of course, the joke was that Robert Flaherty had effectively excommunicated himself from Hollywood two decades earlier. Hollywood knew this. The documentarian's death was commemorated with a mere three-line notice buried on page 5 of *The Hollywood Reporter*. Flaherty despised the studios, but studio artists had no reason to dislike Robert Flaherty. He was a prospector with a camera, a filmmaking giant who could turn fact into poetry, and a pioneer who invented the documentary feature as a means of interpreting human life.

Like *Louisiana Story*, *The Quiet One* (1949) is a docudrama about the experiences of a boy. It presents a ten-year-old African-American youth (Donald Thompson) under psychiatric care at a boys' school. His history is traced through flashbacks to his loveless home in the Harlem slums. The project was conceived by Film Documents, formed two years earlier by Janice Loeb, William and Helen Levitt, and the film's director, former concert violinist and military documentarian Sidney Meyers.

Producer Janice Loeb explains, "We started by buying a camera and taking pictures in East Harlem. We shot some pictures in the streets, then suddenly thought we should photograph a child."[7] The filmmakers prepared an original story after consulting with psychiatrists at the Wiltwych School for Boys in upstate New York. Legendary writer James Agee penned the narration (delivered by Gary Merrill), which dominates the soundtrack. When the filmmakers scouted kids in Harlem, twelve-year-old Donald Thompson stood out. His dad agreed to let him act as long as he didn't miss school, so shooting took place after 3:00 PM and on weekends, in real homes in Harlem and at the Wiltwych School. The budget was a mere $28,000.

The Quiet One won the prestigious International Award at the 1949 Venice Film Festival. In a glowing review *The New York Times* pointed to the film's neorealism, stating, "In several respects this hour-long picture, shaped from the stuff of modern life is comparable to those stark film dramas which have come from Italy since the war. . . . In a sense, it might be reckoned the *Shoeshine* of American urban life . . ."[8] *The Quiet One* retains much of its power today. It represents the rare ability of a motion picture to compassionately capture childhood in all its complexity.

Navajo (1952) is yet another sensitive docudrama about a non-Anglo boy, this time a seven-year-old Native American named "Son of the Hunter" (novice Francis Kee Teller) who speaks no English and lives happily on a reservation. When the authorities place him in a white public school, he flees into the Arizona wilderness. *Navajo* was produced and written by Hall Bartlett (who also plays the school counselor) and directed by the prolific Norman Foster. Shot over three months in Northern Arizona, the beautiful scenery is captured in black-and-white by cinematographer Virgil E. Miller.

The New York Times wrote: "Although it is an indirect plea for understanding—on both sides—*Navajo* is no preachment. It is basically—from its simple but poetic narration to its panoramic vistas of the rugged Southwest—an unusual picturesque and convincing look at the Red Man."[9] Insensitive language aside, this assessment remains true. Though in 1952 it might have been enough merely to show the concerns of an Indian child, *Navajo* would benefit from more conflict and a deeper examination of the issues surrounding forced integration.

The following year, *Navajo*'s Hall Bartlett wrote and produced another nonstudio feature about a Native American. *Crazylegs* (1953), directed by Francis Lyon, stars football legend Elroy "Crazylegs" Hirsch in an unimpressive gloss of his own story.

Ida Lupino

The daughter of successful acting parents, Ida Lupino (1918–1995) was born and raised in London, England. At the age of fifteen, she accompanied her mother on an audition for the British film *Her First Affair* (1932). The director deemed mom too old, but spotted her daughter offstage, and Ida Lupino got the role. After appearing in several British features in 1933, Lupino moved to Hollywood, signed a Paramount contract, and promptly dropped her English accent.

After a plethora of minor ingenue roles, Lupino drew attention in *The Light That Failed* (1939). In the early forties, she signed with Warner Bros. and came into her own, playing ambitious headstrong dames in hard-boiled plots. Calling herself "the poor man's Bette Davis," the whiskey-voiced actress shines in movies like *They*

Ida Lupino.

Drive By Night (1940) and *High Sierra* (1941). Plum acting roles came less frequently after the war. She let her Warners contract expire. In 1948, Italian neorealist director Roberto Rossellini said to Lupino, "In Hollywood movies, the star is going crazy, or drinks too much, or he wants to kill his wife. When are you going to make pictures about ordinary people in ordinary situations?"[10]

Lupino and her new (second) husband, producer Collier Young, came up with an idea for a film about illegitimate births. When studios turned it down, they went to a fledgling independent, Emerald. There, Lupino coproduced and cowrote *Not Wanted* (1949), a compassionate but dramatically limp tale of unwed mothers. Veteran maverick Elmer Clifton was enlisted as director. When Clifton had a heart attack after three days of production (he subsequently died of complications), Lupino stepped in as the uncredited director. Ads read, "Ida Lupino Presents *Not Wanted*" and then proclaimed, "A Frank Story As Bold As The Screen Has Ever Told." *Not Wanted* was an unexpected success. It electrified Hollywood with its truly independent production and the vibrant young female force behind it.

In rapid succession, Lupino and Young set up their own production company, Filmakers, and announced their divorce. They were married less than two years, but their filmmaking relationship lasted four more. Young produced the films that Lupino wrote and directed. Lupino loved her new occupation. She handled her male crews with matronly coaxing and became known for her quick pace and velvety touch with actors. On the set she liked to be referred to as "mother." She was the second woman admitted into the Director's Guild of America, and, incredibly, the only working female of its 1,300 members.[11]

Lupino invested her own savings in Filmakers' first production, *Never Fear* (1950), shot in fifteen days for $150,000. It's an earnest but dated drama about polio victims. The highlight is a wheelchair dance. Before *Never Fear*'s premiere, Filmakers signed a three-picture financing/distrib-

■ ■ ■ ■ ■ ■ ■ ■

Women

Motion picture directing has always been a nearly exclusive male club. There have been many years in which not a single feature film was helmed by a female, and no American woman has ever been nominated for a directing Academy Award. The situation was actually better for women in the teens and twenties than it was for a long time following. In those years, there were several female directors working in and out of the studios, including independents Alice Guy Blaché, Lois Weber, and Natacha Rambova. Nearly one-fourth of Hollywood's working writers in 1928 were women.

continued

ution deal with RKO. Shortly thereafter, the couple published their own "Declaration of Independence" in the industry papers, championing the "new power and excitement" of independent producers and encouraging others to blaze a trail.[12]

At RKO, Young and Lupino talked up the exploitable aspects of their scripts while making earnest social dramas about the new suburban landscape. Their movies combined claustrophobic emotionalism with blunt neorealism. *Outrage* (1950) is a courageous movie about a woman who is raped and then further traumatized by gossipy neighbors. It crumbles around its own contrivances, but the sensational topic made *Outrage* RKO's most profitable release of the year. Despite its sexy title, *Hard, Fast and Beautiful* (1951) is a standard melodrama about a domineering mom forcing her daughter to endure the rigors of competitive tennis. Lupino wanted to make

Women *continued*

There followed a period of five decades in which, with rare exceptions, the studios simply refused to advance women into the roles of director, producer, or executive. The number of female writers was perpetually below ten percent. Though there were lean years in nonstudio production as well, independence has always provided the greatest opportunities—especially after the women's liberation movement of the seventies. Among the females who launched their careers (and, more often than not, maintained their careers) in the independent arena are: Maya Deren, Ida Lupino, Shirley Clarke, Doris Wishman, Barbara Kopple, Joan Silver, Debra Hill, Claudia Weill, Lizzie Borden, Susan Seidelman, Penelope Spheeris, Nancy Savoca, Christine Vachon, and Allison Anders.

pictures on racism and atomic disaster, but tycoon Howard Hughes (who bought RKO in 1948) nixed such plans. She instead helmed *The Hitch-Hiker* (1953), a taut seventy-one-minute car ride through the Mexican wilderness with a murderous hitcher. Lupino correctly proclaimed it her best film.

Filmakers was gathering much critical acclaim, but RKO was reaping most of the profits. When their contract expired, the divorced duo decided to produce and distribute outside the studios. They attracted investors and lined up four films, each budgeted at $125,000. The first, *The Bigamist* (1953), is interesting because Young's new wife, Joan

Fontaine, stars with his ex-wife, Lupino. Young wrote and produced; Lupino directed. Edmund O'Brien is a guilt-ridden salesman in love with both his infertile, gently emasculating wife (Fontaine) and a wry, vivacious waitress (Lupino). Though the story is sluggish, the acting is first-rate. The powerhouse cast, which also includes Jane Darwell and Edmund Gwenn, had profit participation in lieu of salaries. After mixed reviews and a struggle to attain bookings, there were no profits. The studios still cast long shadows.

Filmakers completed three other independent features, but none were directed by Lupino. (Without Lupino in the chair, Filmakers earlier made the unimpressive semi-indies *The Vicious Years* [1950], *On the Loose* [1951], and *Beware My Lovely* [1952]. The last stars Lupino.) *Mad at the World* (1955) is a mediocre drama about revenge. *Crashout* (1955), a prison-break story starring William Bendix and Arthur Kennedy, is entertaining. And the hard-nosed crime drama *Private Hell 36* (1954), about cops who keep stolen loot, has its atmospheric moments, though the film's production meetings were undoubtedly more fun. It was directed by Don Siegel, who went on to helm such classics as *Invasion of the Body Snatchers* (1956); the dialogue director was the great Sam Peckinpah (his debut); the cinematographer was two-time-Oscar-winner Burnett Guffey; the writers were Young and Lupino. Young produced. Lupino starred. Lupino's new husband, Howard Duff, is featured, and Dorothy Malone plays Duff's wife. According to participants, Lupino repeatedly clashed with Siegel.

Ida Lupino would only helm one additional feature film, the non-independent *The Trouble With Angels* (1966). She continued to act, however, and she was a true female pioneer as a television director, helming more than one hundred episodes for such series as "The Twilight Zone" and "The Untouchables."

The Hitch-Hiker is timeless, but most of Lupino's movies are rooted in the fifties and now show their age. Still, Lupino should be commemorated for going against the grain to tell serious, realistic tales about important topics of her time, unburdened by ideological piety or pat solutions. She rejected the term "feminist" and preferred to work with men, yet "mother" followed the barely traveled path of Lois Weber in addressing issues of female sexuality and independence. She retraced Weber and Vidor's trail of social-themed nonstudio film production, leading the way for many others. With a nod to Gertrude Stein, Lupino's director's chair read "The Mother of All of Us."

Sam Fuller

If Lupino is the mother, then Sam Fuller (1911–1997) is the father—and what wondrous war stories the old man told. Fuller was a weaver of barbarous, no-budget B movies with sentimental souls. Critic Andrew Sarris labeled him "an authentic American primitive." The man and the legend are intertwined as one, but both were born in Massachusetts, grew up on the brick streets of Prohibition Gotham, and came of age clutching a rifle on Omaha Beach. Fuller's two main formative influences were tabloid journalism and World War II. He started as a copyboy at age twelve and was soon a crime reporter for New York City's most lurid tabloid, the *Graphic* (dubbed the *Porno-Graphic*), chasing down grisly stories and following the principle of "creative exaggeration."

In the mid-thirties, he wrote pulp novels and screenplays, selling eight scripts for small checks. After Pearl Harbor, Fuller enlisted in the Army and served in the 1st Infantry Division, which stormed the beach on D day. The average age of soldiers was nineteen; Fuller was thirty-one. The first footage he ever shot was of the horrors of a Czechoslovakian death camp. When he returned to America, the short, cigar-puffing Fuller wrote a successful novel about the newspaper business, *The Dark Page*, that sold to director Howard Hawks. (Hawks later sold it to Columbia, where it became *Scandal Sheet* [1952].)

Frustrated with trying to break in at the studios, Sam Fuller hooked up with independent producer Robert Lippert. A theater owner who turned to production, Lippert executive-produced more than 300 low-budget movies between 1944 and 1966. Many were released through his own company, Lippert Pictures. He allowed Fuller to direct his own scripts, but the producer provided precious little financing. Fuller had only ten days to shoot his debut. He gave it a tabloid-style moniker, *I Shot Jesse James* (1949).

As Sam Fuller recalls after twenty-three films, "I didn't really know anything about directing, but I think any writer who describes anything that has any emotional impact has an ability to direct a picture."[13] Capturing the action, Fuller focused on emotions for the next four decades.

I Shot Jesse James is a psychological study of Robert Ford (John Ireland), the man who killed Jesse James. Fuller frames him in close-up much of the time. A perfectly staged highlight is the scene in

A Korean orphan (William Chun) points to Gene Evans's
lucky bullet hole in *The Steel Helmet*.
© 1956 Deputy Corporation.

which a troubadour sings of Ford's cowardice to his face. Though it trots
slowly for stretches, *I Shot Jesse James* remains an effective antiwestern.
The writing and directing shine. *I Shot Jesse James* turned a modest profit for tiny Lippert.

The next time Fuller had a fifteen-day schedule and the services of
legendary cinematographer James Wong Howe and actor Vincent
Price. Based on fact, *The Baron of Arizona* (1950) tells a fascinating yarn
about a land office clerk (Price) in the Old West who schemes to gain
possession of Arizona. He forges documents which state that an
orphan girl is the Spanish heir to the territory. When the girl reaches
adulthood (Ellen Drew), Price marries her and his plan actually starts
to work. Landowners are enraged. With clandestine scenes in a can-
dlelit Spanish monastery, Price's regal presence, the emphasis on a
fraud investigation, and a tabloid love story, this is anything but a
typical western.

Fuller was back to a ten-day schedule and a $100,000 budget for
The Steel Helmet (1950). It's one of his best movies, and one of the

greatest no-budget flicks ever made. *The Steel Helmet* was the first American feature set in the Korean War—though it was shot entirely in Los Angeles's Griffith Park. The locations are sparse. Gene Evans stars effectively as the gruff Sergeant Zack. Helped by a South Korean orphan, he takes up with a platoon and kills a communist prisoner in a moment of rage. "A dead man's nothin' but a corpse," is Zack's earlier epitaph for a fallen comrade. *The Steel Helmet* is a tense, unglamorous portrait of war. The acting and screenplay are first-rate.

The Steel Helmet's depiction of an American killing an unarmed North Korean stirred up controversy. From local newspaper editorialists all the way to President Truman, "patriots" railed against it. Fuller was branded a communist. Later in his career he would be called a fascist. He was neither. When the publicity and the film's timely topic made it an unexpected hit, no one was happier than Sam Fuller. He had a whopping one-third share of the profits.

Fuller finally garnered studio attention. He signed with Twentieth-Century Fox, for which he wrote and helmed *Fixed Bayonets* (1951), another Korean War drama. Next, he turned from war to his other passion, penning a script about the nineteenth-century tabloid business in New York. The problem was that Fox chairman Darryl Zanuck wanted the film to be a color musical, not the gritty drama Fuller imagined.

So Fuller financed *Park Row* (1952) entirely with his own money (all of his *Steel Helmet* profits and then some), also scripting, directing, and producing it. Most of his funds went into an elaborate four-story set that recreates 1886 Park Row down to the slightest detail. Gene Evans stars again, this time as an editor launching his own tabloid to challenge the dominant paper of a news magnate (Mary Welch). A tough, entertaining picture, *Park Row* never made a dime.

Broke, Fuller went back to work for Fox, writing and directing two of his best features, *Pickup on South Street* (1953) and *House of Bamboo* (1955), and one not so great, *Hell and High Water* (1954). Fox's Darryl Zanuck was always amused by the theatrical pulp artist. Fuller carried a real gun and he would sometimes shoot it to start a take, causing the crew to scurry for cover. He once fired it in a concrete screening room to show Zanuck it worked; the bullet ricocheted off walls and over heads. Another time, screenwriter Philip Dunne remembers a huge explosion: "Darryl [Zanuck] looked off into the distance and smiled and just said, 'That's Sammy Fuller blowing the ass out of Stage 16.' "[14] Always a maverick, Fuller would return to independent cinema again, firing more ricocheting shots and setting off bigger bombs.

Hugo Haas

If Lupino and Fuller are the parents of the modern independent film, then Hugo Haas (1903–1968) is the forgotten uncle. His name doesn't appear in most cinema guides, yet Haas made (usually producing, writing, directing, and starring in) fifteen independent features. They just weren't very good.

Born and raised in Czechoslovakia, Haas worked in the theater. Between 1925 and 1938, he acted in thirty-eight Czech films, several of which he wrote, five of which he directed. Fleeing the Nazis, Haas made and starred in French movies before arriving in America in 1942. Hollywood saw the stout, droopy-eyed foreigner, heard his thick accent, and stuck him in numerous minor character roles during the forties.

But Hugo Haas was a proud man. He came to America with the rights to *Watchman 47*, a Czech novel that he wanted to direct, but the studios wouldn't even schedule a meeting to discuss it. So Haas took his life savings, money from friends, and credit (for a total of $85,000) and cowrote (with Arnold Phillips), coproduced, directed, designed, edited, and starred in *Pickup* (1951), based on *Watchman 47*. It was shot in a scant eleven days. *Pickup* is the ironic tale of a lonely railroad dispatcher (Haas) who comes to town to buy a puppy and ends up with a larcenous floozy (Beverly Michaels). She marries him for the few dollars he's tucked away and then plots to eliminate him. Tables turn. In the end the dispatcher is lonely again—except he has a puppy.

The acting and script are weak, but the production created a buzz in Hollywood. Columbia picked up *Pickup* for $125,000. Before his American debut was released, Haas said, "Frankly, if someone offered me bigger money to make bigger pictures, I wouldn't accept. I want to stay in this category of pictures and make adult movies."[15]

His next feature was *The Girl on the Bridge* (1951), a twelve-day shoot with Haas again wearing most of the hats. He plays a jeweler who talks an unwed mother (the ineffectual Beverly Michaels again) out of jumping from a bridge. Eventually he marries her. When her old boyfriend shows up, the jeweler kills a man in self-defense.

Guilt-ridden, the jeweler leaps from the bridge. Haas compared *The Girl on the Bridge* to Dostoevsky; no one else did. In *Strange Fascination* (1952) a concert pianist (Haas) sees his character and career disintegrate after he marries a blond bimbo (Cleo Moore). It's corny and ineptly executed.

The New York Times wrote: "Not even discounting Orson Welles, something new under the Hollywood sun has emerged in the past year in the form of a one-man picture production company."[16] Hugo Haas was no Orson Welles. The quality of his films remained adequate at best. He specialized in the sort of somber, one-note melodramas that went out of style in the Jazz Age. Still, despite bad reviews and meager circulation efforts, Hugo Haas didn't stop making motion pictures. For the rest of the fifties, when most independent efforts were aimed at bringing teens to drive-ins, Haas kept right on concocting bleak morality plays.

Novelty Exhibition

Regular television broadcasts began after World War II, though by 1948 there were fewer than 200,000 sets in America. Then the boom began. Variety shows. Game shows. Uncle Miltie. Everyone loved Lucy. In 1950 there were four million sets, and just four years later the number soared to thirty-two million. The entire film industry was rocked. As Samuel Goldwyn asked, "Why should people go out and see bad pictures when they can stay at home and see them for nothing?" That was the key question, and, as usual, it was those outside the studios who came up with the most creative answers.

Michael Todd was a former Broadway producer who turned to film production in the mid-forties. He became obsessed with extremely large screens as a means of countering small TV tubes and their static-frosted shades of gray. Todd was one of the original partners in Cinerama, a process that utilizes three cameras simultaneously during production and three projectors simultaneously in order to show a moving picture on a huge curved screen. It was developed by Paramount special effects wiz Fred Waller and introduced at the 1939 World's Fair using eleven projectors.

The first Cinerama release was the expensive, independently produced *This Is Cinerama* (1952), a thrill-filled travelogue that most famously features a front-seat view of a roller-coaster ride. Business maneuvers forced Michael Todd out of the company before the premiere, but *This Is Cinerama* utilized Todd's marketing strategy of heavily promoted roadshows, advance (and expensive) ticket sales, and an intermission. The traveling event played in only seventeen theaters worldwide (thirteen in America), but it became the third-highest grossing film in history. More Cinerama travelogues followed, but the fad faded quicker than the hula hoop. MGM shot a version of its fictional epic *How the West Was Won* (1962) in Cinerama, but by that time the often jarring and blurry technique was no longer novel.

Meanwhile, Todd started his own production company, adopting a process utilizing a single camera with four lenses that is screened with one 70mm projector. He named the company and the process Todd-AO. The musicals *Oklahoma!* (1955), *Around the World in 80 Days* (1956), and *South Pacific* (1958) adopted the process, as did *Cleopatra* (1963). Because 70mm projectors were scarce, movies were shot in both Todd-AO and standard 35mm and were usually screened in the latter format.

Master showman Michael Todd (married to Elizabeth Taylor at the time) died in a plane crash in 1958. By then, CinemaScope and other wide-screen processes were everywhere: Cinemiracle, Quadravision, Wonderama, Thrillerama, VistaVision, and on and on. No matter how lame the content, every movie was suddenly sold as a miracle of technology and an unparalleled visual phenomenon.

Three-D was another such "wonder" unveiled to counter television. Methods for producing and projecting films to make them appear three-dimensional originated in the silent era, but in the fifties 3-D was suddenly fresh and amazing. Audiences gawked at screens through tinted glasses. *Bwana Devil* (1952) was the first widely released 3-D feature. An independent production, it was helmed, produced, and scripted by Arch Oboler, a long-time radio writer with a spotty cinematic career. Robert Stack and Nigel Bruce star. Based on fact, the story (retold in the 1996 *The Ghost and the Darkness*) is centered around two hungry lions halting construction of a railroad in British East Africa. The completed color film chugs like a broken locomotive, and it's unlikely that seeing it in an added dimension could make this bad movie good. According to reports, the much publicized 3-D shot of a lion "leaping" from the screen was a yawn, but other 3-D gimmicks such as a native throwing a spear caused audiences to gasp and duck. *Bwana Devil* was a big hit.

On *Bwana*'s heels, the 3-D *House of Wax* (1953) garnered Warner Bros. even greater success. The minicraze was on, and more indies jumped into the fray. Actor John Ireland and Oscar-winning cinematographer Lee Garmes codirected *Hannah Lee* (1953, aka *Outlaw Territory*), a mediocre color western that barely takes advantage of its third dimension. *Cat Woman of the Moon* (1953), directed by famed editor Arthur Hilton, tells of . . . well, cat women on the moon. In black-and-white, it too failed to exploit its added visual depth. By the end of 1954, unable to live up to its promotional push, the 3-D fad was already over.

Drive-in theaters were a more enduring novelty. The number of drive-ins grew from 300 in 1946 to over four thousand by 1957 (and shrank back to a few hundred by the eighties). Giant outdoor screens viewed through car windows didn't lend themselves to intimate dramas, but they were ideal for flying saucers and beach parties and drag-racing juvenile delinquents. Drive-ins became an integral part of the growing youth market.

As television reduced the overall movie audience in the fifties, the importance of nonadults to the motion picture industry expanded. Most of the country might have slunk in their couches, hypnotized by "The Honeymooners" and "I Love Lucy," but teens still went to the movies hand-in-hand on Friday nights, and preteens still squirmed through matinee double features on Saturdays, jumbo popcorn at their sides. Now, more than ever, Hollywood targeted young Americans.

The changing marketplace presented a clear opportunity for mavericks. Some autonomous filmmakers would go after the same youthful ticket buyers as the studios. Others, attempting to circumvent the movie factories, would focus on attracting the kids' overlooked parents. Either way, the market was opening. Bug-eyed monsters, bouncing nudists, gritty docudramas—there was no telling what independent cinema would unleash on Eisenhower's America.

Notes

1 *Variety*, 20 Feb. 1950.
2 MacGowan, Kenneth, 318.
3 *Variety*, 30 June 1948.
4 *Variety*, 28 April 1948.

[5] Neither film has appeared on subsequent lists. *The Bicycle Thief* was number one in 1952. *Citizen Kane* has occupied the top position on every subsequent list. *Intolerance* and *Louisiana Story* are the only American indies to appear.

[6] Rotha, Paul, *Robert Flaherty: A Biography* (Philadelphia: Univ. of Pennsylvania, 1983), 260.

[7] *Los Angles Times*, 4 April 1949.

[8] *New York Times*, 14 Feb. 1949.

[9] *New York Times*, 2 Feb. 1952.

[10] *San Diego Tribune*, 2 Feb. 1949.

[11] Then called Screen Directors Incorporated, The Directors Guild of America began in 1936. The first woman admitted was Dorothy Arzner who directed between 1927 and 1943.

[12] *Variety*, 20 Feb. 1950.

[13] Server, Lee, *Sam Fuller: Film is a Battleground* (Jefferson, NC:McFarland & Company, 1994), 25.

[14] Server, 5–6.

[15] *L.A. Daily News*, 16 Nov. 1950.

[16] *New York Times*, 2 Sept. 1951.

OPPORTUNITY KNOCKS

My first project was to be called "It Stalked the Ocean Floor." The title was changed because the distributors felt it was too cerebral.

—ROGER CORMAN[1]

By the early 1950s, the term "independent film" was still a grindhouse epithet. "Art films" had their hip fans, but most Americans expected subtitles and obliqueness. The studio system was dying, but the major movie factories still reigned supreme, controlling the best talent and the best theaters. And in a few short years, television had established itself as an essential household appliance. Into such a climate a few brave rebels trod.

Roger Corman

In the history of youth flicks and B movies, one extraordinary man of ordinary talent towers above all others. Since 1954, he has directed more than fifty feature films and produced and/or distributed more than 260 more. He has also discovered and employed many of the most important cinematic figures of the last four decades, including Martin Scorsese, Francis Ford Coppola, Jack Nicholson, Robert

Towne, James Cameron, Tommy Lee Jones, John Sayles, Peter Bogdanovich, and Jonathan Demme.

He is the Drive-In Deity, Roger Corman (1926–). A shy man with an engineering degree from Stanford, Corman seemed miscast as the ultimate low-budget movie mogul. But temperaments, like appearances, can be deceiving. Though most of his movies fall far short of art, Roger Corman knows the low-budget film business as well as anyone, before or after.

After a stint in the Navy and three boring days as an engineer, he gave up the career he had spent four years studying for and headed for Hollywood. Corman started at the bottom, as a messenger for Twentieth-Century Fox, and he climbed his way up to the $32.50 per week position of story analyst (script reader). Still too far removed from the actual filmmaking work he craved, Corman left the country and, courtesy of the GI Bill, studied postgraduate literature at Oxford.

Upon return, Roger Corman sold a screenplay called "The House By The Sea" to Allied Artists. With a nod towards the popular TV series "Dragnet," the title for his mediocre crime drama was changed to *Highway Dragnet* (1954). Corman received cowriter and associate producer credits but had no creative control. By the time Allied Artists finished its alterations to his script, Corman had the same plan as virtually every frustrated film professional since Edwin Porter.

The difference—especially in the fifties—between the Drive-In Deity and most dreamers is that Corman actually did it. He did it before *Highway Dragnet* even hit the screens. He made his own movie with his own money. With the $3,500 he earned for *Highway Dragnet*, he formed Palo Alto Productions (named after Stanford's home) and peddled shares to friends. Wyott Ordung, an occasional actor who had recently sold a script, contributed the final $2,000 of the $11,000 budget on condition that he be allowed to direct.

The Monster from the Ocean Floor (1954) was filmed in six days in Malibu with a skeleton (but union) crew. Corman served as producer, grip, and driver. The cinematographer was Floyd Crosby (*Tabu*), who would shoot several Corman flicks. The completed feature is terrible, too boring for even a few campy laughs. The pathetic giant squid monster is actually a puppet shot through a cloudy fish tank! Still, Corman was about to formulate his most important rule of filmmaking: when you make a movie for nearly nothing, it's easy to turn a profit. *The Monster from the Ocean Floor* sold to Lippert Pictures for a

$60,000 advance; it eventually returned $110,000 to Palo Alto Productions. Even in the fifties, these were paltry sums by Hollywood standards, but Corman, a trained engineer, could do the math. His business had just made an incredible ten times its outlay. He remembers, "I took the money from that movie and made another one. I've never stopped."[2]

Corman wrote and produced *The Fast and the Furious* (1954), a hohum fugitive tale set in the world of auto racing. With a $50,000 budget, he hired established actors John Ireland and Dorothy Malone for less than their usual fees. Ireland agreed to star only if allowed to direct (he split the credit with Edward Sampson). Six weeks after beginning the nine-day shoot, there was a completed print. Offers came from Republic, Columbia, and Allied Artists, but Corman decided to sign with old friend Jim Nicholson, who was then starting a tiny film company with a lawyer named Samuel Z. Arkoff.

When Nicholson and Arkoff slated *The Fast and the Furious* as their first release, their company was American Releasing Corporation, but they changed the name to American International Pictures (AIP) two years later. AIP was the right company at the right time. It started with mostly monster and hotrod movies, added a series of classier Edgar Alan Poe horror pictures in the early sixties (directed by Corman), and then switched to beach blanket nonsense and hippie flicks. With cheaply produced popcorn fodder, AIP rode the youth market to tremendous profits.

Roger Corman worked hand in hand with AIP through the years. Sometimes he produced and financed films that the ministudio released. Sometimes he directed for AIP for a fee. On still other occasions he made AIP-style movies for himself or other companies. When Corman signed over *The Fast and the Furious* in 1954, it was as part of a three-picture deal, with the future American International Pictures agreeing to release his next two. After letting a pair of neophytes call the shots, Corman was itching to take control.

Roger Corman's directorial training consisted of one day at the beach with a key grip shooting a five-page script in 16 mm. When he saw the footage at the lab, it looked so awful that he decided it was beyond editing. The Drive-In Deity was ready to go.

Corman cowrote, directed, and produced *Five Guns West* (1955), a lackluster Civil War–era western about five criminals sent on a violent mission for the Confederacy. It features John Lund, Dorothy Malone, and plenty of stock shots of rampaging Indians. Shot in nine days for $60,000 in color, it turned a profit for AIP, as did Corman's color, $80,000 follow-up, *Apache Woman* (1955), which loses an intriguing pro-Native American message among tedious scenes and risible dialogue. Lloyd Bridges headlined, and drive-in mainstay Dick Miller made his acting debut.

Roger Corman next called the shots on a feature for Southern state's-rights distributors, the Woolner brothers (never to be confused with Warner Bros.). In addition to its campy title, *Swamp Women* (1955) has a campy premise: a New Orleans policewoman (Carole Matthews) infiltrates the all-women Nardo Gang in search of stolen diamonds. Unfortunately, *Swamp Women* is too slow to be much campy fun. Like most of Corman's features, it suffers from a lack of detail in production design, cinematography, sound, etc. The small things (which together can have a big effect) were generally considered unnecessary expenses in a Corman budget.

Meanwhile, Arkoff and Nicholson had an idea for boosting the low fees their B pictures commanded. AIP would distribute their movies in pairs as ready-made double features, an A and a B. The inaugural "A picture," and the first of many monster movies the Drive-In Deity directed, was *The Day the World Ended* (1956). It's one of Corman's best. On Destruction Day 1970, seven people isolated in a mountain valley house survive a nuclear holocaust. In the woods is at least one radioactive mutant. *The Day the World Ended* is imbued with a creepy atmosphere and has a few good scares. Arkoff and Nicholson teamed it with an awful acquired indie, *The Phantom from 10,000 Leagues*. Other Poverty Row companies quickly adopted the strategy, and prepackaged double bills swept into theaters across the nation.

Motion pictures—big, colorful, and full of action—survived the worst of TV's initial assault and, in mid-1956, exhibitors even announced a product shortage, calling for more youth movies. Happy to oblige, independent companies churned out lame quickies like *Mesa of Lost Women*, *Man-Beast*, and *The Flaming Teen-Age* to fill the void. Two of the campiest arrived in 1958. In *The Brain from Planet Arous*, an evil floating mind inhabits the body of John Agar as it attempts to control Earth, but a benevolent brain hides in Agar's dog waiting for the right moment to save the day. *My World Dies Screaming* is a haunted house tale featuring Cathy O'Donnell and a lot of hokum about the subconscious. The prologue announces, "Not

EVERY MAN ITS PRISONER...EVERY WOMAN ITS SLAVE!

IT CONQUERED THE WORLD

PETER GRAVES · BEVERLY GARLAND · LEE VAN CLEEF

Lobby card for *It Conquered the World*.

only will the picture communicate with you visually, but subconsciously through your brain." Your brain will think it's terrible, but it's good for a few laughs.

The no-budget dreck came fast and furious during these years. Smaller and more exploitive versions of AIP popped up and made half a dozen quickies with monster makeup and stock footage. One studio that stayed longer was producer/director Jerry Warren's Associated Distributors Productions. Warren ground out flicks like *Teenage Zombies* (1958), which has no underage undead despite its catchy AIP-style title. Another indie, Ray Kellogg, directed two Texas flicks that are utterly ridiculous, *The Killer Shrews* and *The Giant Gila Monster* (both 1959). Close-ups of animals are cut with long-shots of people to supposedly make rodents and lizards look huge. They don't.

The Angry Red Planet (1959) is a cheesy independent effort worth noting. Its Martian footage is shot in "Cinemagic," an optical effect that makes everything (including astronauts) appear as though literally viewed through rose-tinted glasses. The giant spider/crab/rat and the ship-absorbing amoeba monster are especially amusing. *The*

Angry Red Planet was directed by writer Ib Melchior and shot by the great cinematographer Stanley Cortez (*The Magnificent Ambersons*). Cortez often worked on impoverished productions, feeling they allowed for more experimentation.

The prolific Roger Corman, doing his part to help out exhibitors, directed and produced twelve movies in 1956 and 1957, including *It Conquered the World* with its infamous cucumberman monster, the above-average alien vampire flick *Not of this Earth*, and *Attack of the Crab Monsters*, the first Corman project to gross more than $1 million. The keys to success with monster movies were a sensational title, a shocking trailer, and a freakish lobby poster. Quality was a bonus. "The whole idea was to tell an interesting, visually entertaining story that would draw young people to the drive-ins and hardtop theaters, and not take yourself too seriously along the way,"[3] Corman once said.

The Drive-In Deity produced and directed *Bucket of Blood* in five days in 1959. A delightfully dark spoof of beatnik pretensions and wax museum horrors, it serves as the perfect prelude to his next feature. By the time 1960 rolled around, Corman had his own production/distribution company, Filmgroup, and he shifted his focus between there and the bigger-budgeted gothic Poe flicks for AIP. In the first two years of the next decade, Roger Corman would make his most intriguing movies, both indies. The first he shot in a mere two days to break his *Bucket of Blood* record. The second, an underappreciated gem, was the dearest to his heart; he called it his "art film." After seventeen financial successes, it would be his first flop.

The Blacklist

Searching for communists in the film industry, the House Un-American Activities Committee of the US Congress first held closed hearings in Los Angeles in May 1947. The event moved to Washington, DC in the fall of that year when ten screenwriters and directors refused to answer questions and were held in contempt. The so-called Hollywood Ten were sentenced to six to twelve months in prison. Simultaneously, they were blacklisted from the entertainment industry. It was only the beginning. The HUAC hearings continued through 1953. During that time dozens of artists were banned from Hollywood employment. Motion picture guilds and unions demanded that their members sign loyalty oaths to the government.

Entertainers apologized for their progressive beliefs. Meanwhile, in the Senate, Joseph McCarthy searched for Reds at every government water cooler.

In this atomic climate, members of Congress, the FBI, the INS, law officers, and hundreds of local residents tried to stop one low-budget independent film from being produced. Though they failed, *Salt of the Earth* (1954) would not be commercially distributed in America for more than a decade. The film was the only blacklisted work of art of the McCarthy era.

The docudrama *Salt of the Earth* was made by a group of ostracized filmmakers: director Herbert Biberman (one of the Hollywood Ten), producer Paul Jarrico, Academy Award–winning screenwriter Michael Wilson, cinematographers Leonard Stark and Stanley Meredith, composer Sol Kaplan, and actor Will Greer. Those involved who weren't banned would be when news of *Salt of the Earth* hit Hollywood. The principals formed the Independent Productions Corporation in 1951 with plans for several political movies. There would be only one.

Salt of the Earth tells the true story of a year-long strike at a zinc mine in New Mexico. The walkout is won when the miners' wives take over the picket line after the workers are prevented from demonstrating. The focus is on a Mexican-American family whose patriarch (Juan Chacon, a real striking miner) must come to terms with the political awakening of his wife (Rosaura Revueltas), who protests all day while he does the housework and child-rearing.

The film tackles women's liberation, racism, and union solidarity against oppressors. Those themes, coupled with *Salt of the Earth*'s ostracized crew and the many striking miners in the cast, made it a magnet for controversy. As it went into production, news hit the US capital. Representatives on the House floor denounced *Salt of the Earth* as a communist tool. HUAC and the FBI began surveillance. On February 26, 1953, the film's female lead, Rosaura Revueltas, who was Mexican, was arrested by the INS for having entered the country illegally. A crew member wrote in his diary, "Immigration agents arrested Rosaura last night. As they led her off, we all stood around feeling angry and helpless . . . but today we all worked harder than ever with a new zest and new grimness . . . the bond between the crew members and the union cast is stronger than ever . . . nothing can stop us now from finishing this film."[4]

On March 2, fifty local residents ran a camera crew out of tiny Central, New Mexico. On March 3, in Silver City, 150 angry citizens surrounded the film crew, instigated mild violence, and issued an Old West warning: "Get out of town by noon tomorrow or go out in a black box."[5] On March 4, fifty state and local cops armed with shotguns kept order as a mile-long line of protestors threatened the production. Filmmakers needed only a few additional shots of Revueltas but were able to make do without them. *Salt of the Earth* wrapped on March 7, the same day Revueltas was set free to return to Mexico.

But making *Salt of the Earth* was only the first battle. The projectionists union blacklisted it. *Salt of the Earth* played publicly at a single theater in New York City in March of 1954. Some reviewers praised its artistry. Others condemned its progressive themes. Most never got a chance to see it. The *Hollywood Citizen News* wrote: "It has a worthy cause to plea, but it loads the dice so heavily all chance of sympathy is lost. The film is unlikely to draw much of an audience in the U.S. but, crude though it be, it may become effective anti-American propaganda in Latin American countries."[6]

That review was certainly correct about an American audience; *Salt of the Earth* wouldn't play at a second commercial theater in the United States for another decade. It was, however, shown at underground screenings and achieved great success in the Soviet Union, China, and European countries. The French Motion Picture Academy voted *Salt of the Earth* 1954's best picture, and it won the grand prize at the Prague Film Festival, fueling its critics' contention that it was communist propaganda. In 1956, *Salt of the Earth*'s producers sued the studios, theater chains, and what seemed like the entire entertainment industry (there were 110 defendants) for $7.5 million, claiming their film was prevented from attaining proper domestic distribution. The suit was dismissed in 1959, then reinstated and dismissed again in 1964. Fueled by the controversy, *Salt of the Earth* finally went into a general but limited release in America in 1965.

Though *Salt of the Earth* is sometimes overly pedagogic, it has many qualities to recommend: dirty-faced neorealism; dynamic characters, including a strong female lead; a taut pace; jarringly emotional scenes; and, not least of all, its place in history as a battle-scarred, long classified document from the darkest days of the Cold War.

In 1954, the same year that *Salt of the Earth* should have been released, the studio feature *On the Waterfront* deservedly won eight

Oscars, including director, writer, and picture. Director Elia Kazan and writer Budd Schulberg made this allegory as a stinging defense of their controversial compliance with HUAC.

It wasn't until 1960, when semi-indie producers Otto Preminger and Kirk Douglas openly employed suspected ex-communists, that the Hollywood blacklist effectively ended. In the face of HUAC and *Salt of the Earth*'s suppression, progressive filmmakers shied away from overtly political themes for a decade. Finally, in 1964, *Dr. Strangelove* lampooned the lunacy of the Cold War and *Point of Order* (more to follow) savaged McCarthy with his own words.

Avant-garde

The literary and artistic underground came aboveground in Manhattan in the fifties. Jack Kerouac and other beat writers penned influential works. *The Village Voice*, the king of weekly alternative papers, was founded in 1955. And avant-garde cinema flourished under the guidance of Maya Deren, Cinema 16, and a new and even more tireless cheerleader from Lithuania.

Maya Deren did very little filmmaking in the fifties, but she persisted in agitating for the cause. She founded the Film Artists Society in 1953 (subsequently named the Independent Film Makers Association), and in 1955 she formed the Creative Film Foundation to offer financial support to makers of abstract movies. Meanwhile, her theoretical tracts—no matter how abstruse their prose or obscure their publication—continued to find an audience.

One such publication that had a huge impact on cinema scholarship was *Film Culture*. It quickly adopted the subheading "America's Independent Motion Picture Magazine," marking a change in the traditionally derogatory use of the word "independent." The magazine was founded in 1955 by Jonas Mekas (1922–) and his brother Adolfas, who had immigrated to New York City from Lithuania five years earlier. The premiere copy included an article by Hans Richter (the Mekas brothers' film teacher at City College of New York) that affirmed the avant-garde. However, in the third issue, Jonas Mekas let loose a blazing editorial entitled "The Experimental Film in America." Subheadings tell the tale: "The Adolescent Character of the American Film Poem," "The Conspiracy of Homosexuality," and "The Lack of Creative Inspiration: Technical Crudity and Thematic Narrowness."[7]

Filmmakers named in the essay attended an emergency meeting

called by Maya Deren to discuss a possible lawsuit. All was eventually forgiven. Mekas later called this his "Saint-Augustine-before-con-
version-piece," and by 1958 he was the avant-garde's most vocal and
least critical supporter. That year his weekly column "Movie Journal"
first appeared in *The Village Voice*, informing a wide intellectual audience about the latest happenings in the celluloid underground. He
wrote in an early *Voice* column: "Every breaking away from the conventional, dead, official cinema is a healthy sign. We need less perfect
but more free films. If only our youngest film-makers—I have no
hopes for the old generation—would really break loose, completely
loose, out of themselves, wildly, anarchically! There is no other way to
break the frozen cinematic conventions than through a complete
derangement of the official cinematic senses."[8]

Bruce Conner (1933–) seems to have followed this advice with his
movie entitled, simply, *A Movie* (1958). Without permission, Conner
assembled what he called "found images"—sections of celluloid culled
from newsreels and assorted old flicks. He intercuts shots of bliss with
those of destruction, and he leaves in blank frames and stray titles such
as "The End" near the beginning. With *A Movie*, Bruce Conner perfected the collage film. *A Movie* would reverberate through the decades,
and an indirect influence can be seen in today's music videos.

Kenneth Anger crafted two additional dream films, *Eaux D'Artifice*
(1953), a hypnotic poem about a water fairy, and *Inauguration of the
Pleasure Dome* (1954), a tour de force mythological ballad. He then
dedicated himself to penning the book *Hollywood Babylon*, a lurid collection of silent-movieland scandals. Published in France in 1958 and
America in 1960, it was a cult sensation.

Robert Frank and Alfred Leslie oversaw the ultimate Beat flick,
Pull My Daisy (1959). Scripted by author Jack Kerouac, *Pull My Daisy*
features poet Allen Ginsburg, painter Larry Rivers, and others in a
weird story of a religious meeting at Neal Cassady's house. It was
shot silent with way hip bebop narration from Kerouac. *Pull My Daisy*
was essential viewing for the Greenwich Village coffeehouse crowd
and remains an amusing curio.

Others mapping new territory include James Davis, who explored
two key ingredients of filmmaking—light and mirrors—in short films
like *Through the Looking Glass* and *Analogies* (both 1955), and Robert
Breer, who developed the cinematic equivalent of cubism in
Jamestown Baloos (1957) and *Eyewash* (1959). Avant-garde films played

to receptive audiences at the thriving Cinema 16 and similar urban venues. In retrospect, it was the quiet before the storm. The stage was set for the sixties and true cinematic anarchy.

Hugo Haas

Hugo Haas kept right on churning out independent melodramas, usually as writer, director, producer, and star. Strapped with meager production values, he brought his Eastern European sensibility to simple plots with improvised dialogue.

Thy Neighbor's Wife (1953) and *Bait* (1954) are period morality plays, the first set in nineteenth-century Moravia, the second in a mining camp. *One Girl's Confession* (1953) and *Hold Back Tomorrow* (1955) try to put a new spin on prison dramatics. The title character of *The Other Woman* (1954), set in the film industry, plots revenge on her former boss. *Tender Hearts* (1955) and *Edge of Hell* (1956) are pure syrup, the first about an ex-circus clown (Haas) who lives in a cellar, the second about a pauper (Haas), a dog, and a small boy. And *Hit and Run* (1957) has an exploitable plot in which Haas's character attempts to eliminate his young wife's boyfriend. In most of these films Cleo Moore, Haas's mainstay, acts as stiff as a board.

Lizzie (1957) was Haas's most ambitious picture yet. For the first time, he worked for another company with a script by someone else— Mel Dinelli (adapting a story by Shirley Jackson). Elizabeth (Eleanor Parker) has three personalities: the "good" Beth, the coarse, aggressive Lizzie, and her shy, neurotic norm. This presents a challenge for her dedicated psychiatrist (Richard Boone). Joan Blondell as drunken Aunt Morgan and Haas as a meddling neighbor are featured effectively, and Johnny Mathis pops up to croon a couple of hit tunes in a nightclub. This is Haas's best feature, though it was rightfully overshadowed by the film it rushed to beat to theaters, Fox's blockbuster Oscar-winner *The Three Faces of Eve* (1957).

Again working on assignment with a bigger budget (allowing him to film in CinemaScope), Haas helmed *Night of the Quarter Moon* (1959), a dated melodrama about a white man (John Barrymore, Jr.) who marries a woman of mixed race (Julie London). The cast includes familiar names: Nat King Cole (who sings on-screen), Agnes Moorehead, and Jackie Coogan. Haas also made the independent *Born to Be Loved* in 1959; it may be his worst film. Universal bought this tired romance set in phony tenements.

Haas's final film, *Paradise Alley* (1961, aka *Stars in the Back Yard*), was his most personal. Haas headlines as a once famous filmmaker who moves to the slums and cheers everyone up by pretending to shoot a movie about them. *Paradise Alley* is corny but offbeat, a fitting conclusion to a unique career. Hugo Haas was a limited screenwriter and competent director who forged melodramas with impoverished budgets. An optimistic immigrant, he stuck to his dream, though the audience for such simple tales had long since faded into history.

Morris Engel and Ruth Orkin

New Yorkers Morris Engel (1918–1986) and Ruth Orkin (1923–1985) were a husband-and-wife team of still photographers who turned to independent filmmaking. In conjunction with fellow rookie Ray Ashley, they divided the screen credits on the lyrical low-budget gem, *The Little Fugitive* (1953). A seven-year-old boy (Richie Andrusco) mistakenly thinks he's killed his older brother. He runs away to Coney Island. Enjoying the day, he shows no remorse.

Variety wrote, "This lays bare the child mentality, self-sufficiency and cold logic which borders on cruelty."[9] Despite the fittingly bleak cinematography and harmonica-heavy score, *The Little Fugitive* is never leaden. Effectively directed, acted, and edited, it was the surprise hit at the 1953 Venice Film Festival and became a minor sensation stateside.[10] The screenplay was nominated for an Academy Award. *The Little Fugitive*'s publicized success led future American renegades to stir up attention and secure distribution through foreign film festivals.

Engel and Orkin were back at the Venice Festival in 1955 with *Lovers and Lollipops*. Again they share directing, producing, and, with Mary Madeleine Lanphier, screenwriting credits; they split cinematography (Engel) and editing (Orkin). *Lovers and Lollipops* is a modest story about a young widow (Lori March) whose new marriage is disrupted by her six-year-old daughter (Cathy Dunn). As in *The Little Fugitive*, this film is carried by its black-and-white New York visuals and its compelling presentation of a child's point of view.

Engel and Orkin journeyed once more to the Venice festival with *Weddings and Babies* (1958). This time Engel assumed most of the behind-the-camera roles; Orkin is not credited. Again it is a simple tale: a photographer (John Myhers) and a model (Viveca Lindfors) in

New York contemplate marriage. The film's strength is its realism: intimate acting, authentic "Little Italy" locations, and natural, black-and-white cinematography. It was shot with a portable synchronous sound camera designed by Engel.

As accomplished photographers, Morris Engel and Ruth Orkin used vivid cinematography to portray urban dramas. Engel made one unreleased feature film in the eighties. The couple returned to still photography in later years.

Robert Aldrich

The grandson of a four-term US Senator and the cousin of New York governor (and eventual US Vice-President) Nelson Rockefeller, Robert Aldrich (1918–1983) was a born leader. He grew up in Rhode Island surrounded by Republican wealth, but the liberal Aldrich turned away from financial and political career paths. Unable to serve in the military because of a college football injury, Aldrich—with his combed-back hair, stout shape, and ever-present black-rimmed glasses—came to Hollywood in 1941 and found his own route to power and prestige. Starting as a clerk at RKO, Aldrich worked his way up the studio ladder. In the early fifties he directed television episodes. The baseball tale *Big Leaguer* (1953) marked his big-screen directing debut, and other studio features followed in rapid succession.

In twenty-one days in 1955, Aldrich produced and directed a semi-indie for Parklane Productions. United Artists provided the $400,000 budget. The film was only a modest domestic success for UA at the time, but the French championed its dazzling pace, stylized camerawork, and combustible attitude. *Kiss Me Deadly* was a major influence on the French New Wave, which in turn was a major influence on American independent film. *Kiss Me Deadly* would eventually be rightly celebrated as a pulp masterpiece.

The studio bosses still viewed directors as little more than assembly-line personnel, frequently allowing them no control over such crucial matters as casting and editing. Aldrich hated the compartmentalized studio system and its stifling effects on individuality. He set up his own company, Associates and Aldrich. Though he and his wife owned 80 percent, Aldrich, in his customary unassuming manner, gave the associates (his manager, lawyer, etc.) top billing.

Aldrich produced and directed *The Big Knife* (1955), a scathing

The independent star (Jack Palance, second from right) confronts the studio "suits" in *The Big Knife*. Rod Steiger is on the right. © 1955 Associates and Aldrich Co., Inc.

attack on the Hollywood factories and their system. It includes allusions to real-life moguls Jack Warner (Warner Bros.) and Harry Cohn (Columbia). James Poe adapted a play by famed playwright/screenwriter Clifford Odets. Jack Palance does a great job as Charles Castle, a troubled movie star who wants out of his contract. Rod Steiger steals the show as the slimy, oh-so-cool, and a little psycho studio executive who won't let him go. The knife digs deep. Ida Lupino (as the estranged wife of Charles), Shelley Winters, and Wendell Corey have supporting roles.

Virtually all of *The Big Knife* takes place on the Castle property, primarily in the living room/bar with its rock walls and playboy pad decor. Because of its limited settings, melodramatic dialogue, and energetic acting, it sometimes feels like the filmed stage play it is, and yet *The Big Knife* is never dull. From the opening Bel-Air flyover to the tragic offscreen conclusion, you can see Aldrich's talent in every creatively framed shot and hear it in the skilled use of sound and silence.

The Big Knife was a hit at the 1955 Venice Film Festival. Predictably, United Artists was the one studio willing to distribute it. It lost money. Working for the hand he just bit, Aldrich helmed *Autumn Leaves* (1956) for Columbia.

Robert Aldrich went completely independent again with the brutal antiwar picture *Attack!* (1956). Screenwriter James Poe again adapted from a play (*The Fragile Fox* by Norman Brooks). Jack Palance again stars, this time as the hardened and heroic leader of a platoon in World War II's Battle of the Bulge. He growls to a cowardly officer, "I'll shove a grenade down your throat and pull the pin." Lee Marvin, Buddy Epson, and Eddie Albert are among the chiseled faces in the excellent cast. Joseph Biroc provided the crisp black-and-white cinematography.

Violence, pain, and fear pervade *Attack!* The Germans make formidable villains, but *Attack!* is more frightening when it portrays American soldiers as victims of an incompetent bureaucracy. After reading the script, the Army refused to lend technical support or equipment, forcing Aldrich to tighten up the $800,000 budget. He cut battle scenes in order to afford props and settings. *Attack!* won the grand prize at the 1956 Venice Film Festival and was well reviewed stateside. *Variety* said, "Pic gains realism through depicting Army brass and GIs as humans with different reactions to the reality of combat. It's an effective psychological study, picking up impact from the performances."[11] The years have been kind to *Attack!* It remains fresh, virtually cliché-free, and worthy of its exclamation point.

With two good but financially disappointing indies behind him, Robert Aldrich was forced to return to the studios and their dreaded contracts. He was fired from *The Garment Jungle* (1957) after refusing to soften the script. Creatively stifled and suffering tax troubles, he worked in Europe for years. Aldrich returned to Hollywood to helm a few notable films, including the campy thrillers *What Ever Happened to Baby Jane?* (1962) and *Hush . . . Hush, Sweet Charlotte* (1965).

After directing the hugely popular World War II epic *The Dirty Dozen* (1967) for MGM, Aldrich took his substantial share of the profits and resuscitated Associates and Aldrich. The optimistic leader bought studio space in Hollywood and crafted several semi-indies, most notably *The Killing of Sister George* (1968). All were financial failures. Aldrich sold his studio in 1971. Back working for the Hollywood majors, he directed some good films (*Ulzana's Raid*, [1972], *The Longest Yard* [1974]) and some not so good. Robert Aldrich, a man of substantial talents and a stubborn but generous nature, directed thirty features. His two true independents and many of his later works deal with the struggle to overcome institutional oppression, a theme dear to his heart during his forty years in and out of the Hollywood studios.

Directing Debuts

Prolific studio director Irving Pichel died during the shooting of the nonstudio *Day of Triumph* (1954). His thirty-sixth picture is a moving color version of Christ's death and resurrection starring Robert Wilson as the Messiah and Lee J. Cobb as a Zealot. Studio director Peter Godfrey's last of twenty-four pictures was also an independent, *Please Murder Me* (1956), an inventive courtroom thriller with Angela Lansbury as an accused killer and Raymond Burr as her attorney. Pichel and Godfrey were rare Hollywood veterans who sampled the indie route when their studio contracts expired.

Raised in Kansas City, Missouri and a bomber pilot in World War II, Robert Altman (1925–) was rebuked by Hollywood after selling a script. He returned to Kansas City and worked on industrial films for a decade. Then Altman wrote, directed, and produced an independent feature. *The Delinquents* (1957) is a dull, wayward-youth melodrama about a good teen (nineteen-year-old Tom Laughlin) who goes bad when he joins a street gang. Catching the juvenile delinquent and rock-and-roll craze, it was a minor hit for United Artists. With George W. George, Altman also made *The James Dean Story* (1957), a documentary about the film icon who died two years earlier. Altman went on to become a seminal Hollywood director of the seventies and a key figure in the indie scene of the eighties and nineties.

Stanley Kubrick (1928–1999) also started with tiny budgets and meager distribution, and he also went on to become one of the most celebrated filmmakers in the world. Kubrick took up still photography as a child, and by the time he was seventeen he was a staff photographer at *Look*. Five years later he quit his day job to make movies, creating three short documentaries that sold to RKO. The precocious twenty-four-year-old then set his sights on crafting a feature film.

Kubrick raised the $10,000 budget for the film from his father and uncle (it cost another $20,000 in postproduction). With a script from poet Howard O. Sackler, he directed and shot *Fear and Desire* (1953) in the mountains of Southern California. Four World War II soldiers are stranded behind enemy lines. One of the GIs is played by future screenwriter/director Paul Mazursky. Kubrick's versatile camerawork almost overcomes the limited settings, poor sound, and overwrought dialogue. *Fear and Desire* squeezed its way into some theaters, but, despite its tiny budget, never turned a profit. In later years, the director called his debut "undramatic and embarrassingly pretentious."[12]

Going independent again, Kubrick raised $40,000 from his friends and family and directed, coproduced, shot, edited, and wrote *Killer's Kiss* (1955). A struggling boxer (Jamie Smith) falls for a dancer (Irene Kane). He comes to her aid when she's imperiled by her gangster ex-boss (Frank Silvera). The story is standard pulp, and the acting is barely adequate. What sets *Killer's Kiss* soaring for stretches is Kubrick's visual flair. He gives New York a dreary, noir atmosphere and makes great use of locations such as a festive Times Square and a misty Brooklyn Bridge. The brutal, stylized boxing scene is bested in cinema only by *Raging Bull*—which it influenced. The climactic joust where store mannequins get dismembered is also a tour de force. United Artists picked up *Killer's Kiss*, imposed a happy ending, and distributed it worldwide. The making of the film inspired Matthew Chapman's independent feature *Strangers Kiss* (1984).

Stanley Kubrick cowrote and directed the semi-indie *The Killing (1955)*, a taut, inventively structured tale about a daring racetrack robbery. In exchange for a percentage of the profits, Kubrick took no salary, but *The Killing* remained in the red. He had the same deal on the stunning World War I semi-indie *Paths of Glory* (1957). Again, the film was successful critically

■ ■ ■ ■ ■ ■ ■ ■

War and Peace

World War I. US engaged: April 1917 to Nov. 1918. This was the first major war since the invention of the movie camera, and the government made certain all films were suitably patriotic until years after the armistice. *The Sinking of the Lusitania* was a rare independent about the events. WWI veterans include Paul Fejos, Hans Richter, Ernest Schoedsack, and Merian Cooper.

World War II. US engaged: Dec. 1941 to Sept. 1945. The second global war had profound effects on the movie industry. Film stock was rationed; European filmmakers and actors immigrated to America; and the Office of War Information previewed films for any unpatriotic content. The only war-

continued

War and Peace *continued*

themed indies during these years were documentaries like *Lights Out in Europe*. Later fictional efforts include *Fear and Desire* and *Attack!* Sam Fuller, Robert Altman, Russ Meyer, and Albert and David Maysles were WWII veterans.

Korean War. US engaged: June 1950 to July 1953. Fuller's *The Steel Helmet* was the singular film about this conflict released while it was in progress. Frank Perry served in the war.

Vietnam War. US engaged: May 1965 to Jan. 1973. This prolonged effort mobilized many independent filmmakers in opposition. Jon Jost spent two years in prison rather than serve. The documentary *In the Year of the Pig* was the earliest big-screen condemnation of the war, followed by *Winter Soldier*. They were required viewing among war protestors. Films like *Medium Cool* and *Greetings* sided with draft resistors. Later war-themed indies include *Streamers* and *84 Charlie Miopic*.

■ ■ ■ ■ ■ ■ ■ ■

but not commercially.

Kubrick's faltering career was resurrected in big-budget Technicolor with *Spartacus* (1960). The epic was a box-office sensation that thrust its still young and forever headstrong director into studio meetings and story conferences. That's when Stanley Kubrick said goodbye. He moved to England in 1961, and in the subsequent four decades made only eight feature films (most with American studios). All of them are ambitious and stylistically distinctive, including the classics *Dr. Strangelove* (1964), *2001: A Space Odyssey* (1968), and *The Shining* (1980).

Dreck

Phil Tucker was a very bad director. His *Dance Hall Racket* (1952), an inferior exploitation flick about vice, was written by legendary underground comic Lenny Bruce and features Bruce (as a hoodlum), his wife, and his mom. *Robot Monster* (1953), shot in 3-D for $20,000, is one of the worst movies ever made as well as one of the most unintentionally laughable. It features a lumbering alien in a gorilla suit with a diver's helmet for a head. Surprisingly, the musical score was an early effort of future composing great Elmer Bernstein. (Everyone has to start somewhere: Bernstein next scored *Cat Women of the Moon*.)

But as bad as Phil Tucker was, no one compares with the infamous Ed Wood, Jr. (1924–1978). A former Marine and an unapologetic transvestite, Wood's initial writing/directing efforts went unreleased.

Thankfully for bad film lovers everywhere, his paean to cross-dressing, *Glen or Glenda?* (1953), made it onto a few big screens. It features low-budget veteran Lyle Talbot as a policeman, Wood (under the pseudonym "Daniel Davis") as a heterosexual cross-dresser, an absurdly ranting Bela Lugosi ("Bevare!") as a narrator in a haunted house, mismatched stock footage, surreal dream sequences, and the regular Ed Wood assortment of bad acting, camerawork, editing, music, production design, and on and on.

Glen or Glenda? has a simple earnestness. With a dramatic topic that was a virtual atomic bomb in the Eisenhower era, Wood did not consciously make an exploitation flick. He merely advanced a premise—acceptance of transvestites—that was dear to his heart. In fact, some involved with production insist he was trying to create an art film (which would almost explain the hodgepodge of dreams and unrelated stock footage) to convert beatnik audiences to his liberated worldview. Released without so much as a nod from the Breen Office (formerly the Hays Office), the ridiculous *Glen or Glenda?* (under various titles) had scattered showings via state's-rights. It failed to recoup its $26,000 cost, but failure would not deter Ed Wood.

He next scrounged together $22,000 and made *Jail Bait*. Despite a highly exploitable title, this is a standard melodrama about a criminal who forces a plastic surgeon to give him a new face. Future Hercules Steve Reeves is miscast as a detective. Technically, *Jail Bait* is as awful as any Ed Wood movie, but the script and acting fail to provide the usual quota of unintentional laughs, making this bad movie just bad.

On the other hand, *Bride of the Monster* (1955) is delightfully atrocious. In his last speaking role, Bela Lugosi stars as a mad scientist trying to create supermen via injections of atomic energy. Scary-looking pro wrestler Tor Johnson lumbers around as Lugosi's silent assistant. The producer's son has a key role and acts as bad as everyone else. Lugosi pretending to grapple with the (obviously rubber) octopus he keeps in his backyard (!) is hilarious.

When it comes to sheer idiocy and incompetence, no motion picture ever made is as much fun as *Plan 9 From Outer Space* (1956). Wood wrote, directed, produced, and edited. Conspiracy theorists take note: Both *Plan 9 From Outer Space* and one of the few flicks that compares, *Maniac*, were shot more than two decades apart by the same man—William Thompson. Most of *Plan 9*'s slim budget came from ministers who insisted that the movie's principals, including Wood, be baptized in a Beverly Hills

Tor Johnson on the "spaceship" in *Plan 9 From Outer Space*.

swimming pool. Shooting lasted only four or six days, depending on the legend.

Battling morphine addiction, Bela Lugosi headlines, but he actually died before *Plan 9* was produced. No such minor inconvenience would deter Ed Wood. He inserted footage of the horror icon shuffling around his actual home. For the rest of the movie, Lugosi's character is played silently by Wood's wife's chiropractor (noticeably taller than Lugosi) with a cape pulled over his face. The cast consists of the usual collection of misfits: Tor Johnson (in an unfortunate speaking role) as a police inspector who becomes a ghoul; TV horror movie hostess Vampira, who merely wanders around with her arms outstretched; and the psychic Criswell, who tells us, "Future events like these will affect you in the future." In his final role, Tom Keene, star of *Our Daily Bread*, plays the Air Force colonel.

As expected, the plot of *Plan 9*—something about grave-robbing space aliens—makes no sense. The real fun is in the inane dialogue, pathetic acting, continuity errors, and bargain-basement production values. An airplane cockpit is merely two folding chairs, a shower curtain, and a round thermometer on the wall. The flying saucers look like paper plates, but they're actually Cadillac hubcaps. The command center of a spaceship is a ham radio on a wooden desk with curtains for walls. Day shots are cut with night shots. Cars race in the wrong direction. Straight-faced lines include: "Inspector Clay's dead. Murdered. And somebody's responsible." And on and on. It's a classic.

Wood next made *Night of the Ghouls* (1958, aka *Revenge of the Dead*) with Tor Johnson, Criswell, something resembling a story about ghosts and clairvoyants, and the usual assortment of bad dialogue, acting, production design, editing . . . you name it. Criswell asks, "How many of you know the horror, the terror, I will now reveal to you?" Anyone who's seen an Ed Wood flick has a pretty good idea. Further evidence is *The Sinister Urge* (1960), which tries to explain how photos of scantily clad women will draw boys into juvenile delinquency. *The Sinister Urge* was advertised as "A SMUT PICTURE!"

Wood wrote some wretched screenplays produced by others, and he made a few industrial films, but *The Sinister Urge* aimed him toward his further descent. He made smut. The innocence of *Glen or Glenda?* vanished. Between 1963 and his death in 1978, Wood (often using pseudonyms) knocked off more than seventy-five ultratrashy novels and fetishism "studies." Because he was a rapid-fire typist and never made revisions, some of the 200-page books were actually authored in one booze-filled day! They read like it. A total of twenty-two were published in the months of September and October 1968. Titles such as *The Love of the Dead*, *Raped in the Grass*, and *Sex, Shrouds and Caskets* hint at their depravity. In the late sixties and early seventies, Wood also made pornographic films, including a series of "sex education" loops, and the notorious *Necromania* (1971), which combines horror with fornication and features sex in Criswell's coffin. Wood even appears in some X-rated features—fully clothed, if sometimes in women's garments.

Ed Wood received a mere $300 to $500 per smut book; porno screenwriting and directing fees were even lower. Wracked by alcoholism and poverty, he died two years before the 1980 book *The Golden Turkey Awards* named him the worst director of all time and *Plan 9 From Outer Space* the worst movie ever made.[13] Wood would've loved the fame. In 1994, Tim Burton directed *Ed Wood*, an affectionate black-and-white biopic about the legend. In it, Wood (played by

Johnny Depp) says of *Plan 9*, "This is the one. This is the one I'll be remembered for." Indeed.

Sexploitation

In May 1952, the United States Supreme Court ruled against censoring Roberto Rossellini's *The Miracle*, an Italian import that New York officials had deemed sacrilegious. In so doing, the Court held for the first time that motion pictures are protected under the First Amendment. (Previously, movies were held to be merely commercial enterprises and not subject to the standards of speech or press.) It was a swift and crippling blow to censorship boards. Coupled with subsequent decisions, only obscenity would remain as a legitimate reason for governmental prior restraint. This ruling would have far-reaching effects on American cinema.

Of course, the Production Code and its myriad restrictive rules still stood between objectionable material and innocent eyes, but the Code also suffered a debilitating defeat. In 1953, Otto Preminger refused a request of the Breen Office to edit his semi-indie *The Moon Is Blue* in order to remove words like "virgin" and "pregnant" and a reference to a character being both immoral and likeable. To its credit, United Artists released *The Moon Is Blue* without Code approval. Fueled by the controversy, the romantic comedy grossed more than $6 million and was nominated for three Academy Awards. The theory that a film couldn't thrive without an MPAA (formerly MPPDA) seal was smashed. In the coming decade, others—independent or not—followed *The Moon*. The Code remained, but it would never again be as feared. (The Code was revised in 1956, allowing the previously taboo topics of prostitution, narcotics use, and miscegenation.)

Shortly thereafter, an otherwise insignificant French picture starring the bodacious Brigitte Bardot, . . . *And God Created Woman* (1956), achieved great fortune and fame for its fleeting nudity. Suddenly the term "European" became synonymous with "naked dames," and "art film" with "smut." It certainly brought a lot of men into cinematheques in the late fifties.

The easing of restrictions was felt most directly in "grind houses," a term that by this time applied almost exclusively to theaters specializing in the titillating and the terrifying. In the last half of the fifties, they became windows into the liberating sport of nude volleyball. The same year that *Playboy* hit the stands, the first color fleshfest, *Garden of Eden* (1954), was released. It was made by B specialist Max Nosseck (*The Vilner Cantor*) at a Tampa nudist camp and photographed by Boris Kaufman the same year in which he won the Academy Award for his cinematography in *On the Waterfront*. The greatest distinction of *Garden of Eden* is that after it was banned by the New York censorship board as obscene, the decision was overturned in 1957 by the New York Court of Appeals. The winning argument was that nudism is merely a lifestyle choice.

Suddenly the gates were opened for "nudies" to play in many more theaters than the Forty Thieves roadshow circuit. Staged nudist camp romps flooded the market. They invaded burlesque and grind houses. On screen, naked men and women went to great lengths to hide their crotches behind towels, volleyballs, and shrubbery. (No genitalia was shown in above-ground nudies.)

Exploitation producer David Friedman remembers the epidermis epidemic: "We all started making the volleyball epics. Living in Chicago, you want to get out for the winter, so we always wanted to go to Miami to make pictures. We get to the nudist colony down there, and they want us to take off all our clothes. Fine. I look around for all the gorgeous blondes, and—Jesus Christ!—they look like they've been rotting in cold storage. . . . All these old geezers with missing teeth . . . so we had to salt the mines." [14] Friedman and company brought in strippers and models to play the family nudists.

David Friedman's director/partner Herschell Gordon Lewis shot *The Adventures of Lucky Pierre* (1959) in four days. The duo followed with *Daughter of the Sun* (1960) and a barrage of similar skin-dependents. They were a small part of the breast avalanche of the early sixties. But that's a tale for the next chapter.

Garden of Eden had been a legal and promotional success, but it had not been a box-office breakthrough. The man who truly put soft-core pornography on the map was an easygoing *Playboy* photographer named Russ Meyer (1922–). He grew up in Oakland, where at fourteen his devoted mother (who married six times) pawned an engagement ring to buy him an 8mm movie camera. He was a combat photographer in World War II and claims to have lost his virginity during the war on a brothel excursion financed by Ernest Hemingway. Meyer remembers returning home unsure what to do with his life. A friend asked, " 'Why don't you start shooting girls?' And so I did, and I dug

Russ Meyer.

it, I really dug it. I had kind of a bombastic style, very mild by what's considered strong today, but I got into it hammer and sickle."[15] Meyer also worked on industrial films and a burlesque picture, and he was the cinematographer of *The Desperate Women* (1954), an exploitation flick with an anti–(illegal)-abortion message.

In the late fifties, Meyer was approached by Pete DeCenzie, owner of an Oakland burlesque theater, to make a nudist camp movie. Inspired by the bumbling title character of the French film *Mr. Hulot's Holiday* (1953), Meyer had an idea for something different. Producer DeCenzie put up most of the $24,000 budget; the rest was raised from Meyer's old army buddies, one of whom, Bill Teas, plays the title character. Meyer also made use of a friend's well-lit dentist's office, making Mr. Teas a deliveryman of false teeth. Much of the rest he winged as he went along. Thirty-seven-year-old rookie Russ Meyer was writer, director, cinematographer, camera operator, and editor. He shot the sixty-three-minute feature in four days without sound.

The completed film, *The Immoral Mr. Teas* (1959), does away with the nudist camp pretense and follows a polite bachelor who gains the unexplained ability to see through women's clothing. From the beginning, Meyer was a perfectionist, and his debut is remarkably well made, with crisp color photography and fast-paced editing. Laughs are provided by the running voice-over commentary, which sounds as earnest and good-natured as an educational film on woodland birds. *Mr. Teas* otherwise plays like a silent comedy. Accordion music adds to the mirth. Today, the partial nudity seems almost innocent, but upon release the film was seized in San Diego. Its legend quickly spread. *The Immoral Mr. Teas* grossed more than $1 million on its initial run.

Mr. Teas was the first movie to bring laughter to grind houses, thus defusing the embarrassment of audiences viewing topless women on-screen, probably for the first time. It was also the inaugural skin flick to play mainstream venues, though such bookings were still limited. Most importantly, it invented a genre, the nudie-cutie. Nudie-cuties combine bare breasts and buns with harmless jokes and slapstick, often at the expense of their bumbling male antihero; most were in color and utilized voice-over narration in lieu of dialogue. There would be more than 150 nudie-cuties (all independents) released during the first three years of the sixties, but *The Immoral Mr. Teas* is the greatest. Russ Meyer was on his way to becoming one of the most important independent filmmakers in history.

Novelty Exhibition

In the tradition of Cinerama and 3-D, one man waged a personal battle with complacent television viewing. By combining the showmanship of exploitation roadshows with the youth appeal of horror pictures, William Castle (1914–1977) became the King of the Movie Gimmicks. Still, most of his prolific career had nothing to do with scheming. He started in the late thirties as an actor and became a director of minor studio flicks. Castle had helmed more than forty mostly undistinguished features (eight were released in 1954 alone!) and was producing for television when he set out to finally make something that would get noticed.

Screenwriter Robb White teamed up with Castle, penning both the script and a check for most of the $150,000 budget. In nine days, Castle produced and directed the small-town thriller *Macabre* (1958), starring William Prince and Jim Backus. The black-and-white film has some surprisingly gruesome effects, but it's not well made and not particularly scary. What *Macabre* needed was a gimmick, and William Castle dreamed up a classic: he convinced Lloyd's of London to insure anyone who saw *Macabre* for $1,000 against "death by fright."

"Of course, it would be an awful thing if somebody did die in the theater," Castle told White, adding, "The publicity would be terrific though."[16] A thousand-dollar death would have bought a few hundred times that much publicity. Nobody died, but Castle milked the insurance policy stunt wherever *Macabre* played, inserting copies of the warranty into advertising, conspicuously parking hearses outside theaters, and hiring bogus nurses to stand in lobbies. It all worked. *Macabre* was a box-office success.

Castle as director/producer and White as writer followed quickly with *The House on Haunted Hill* (1958). In this campy horror gem, a tycoon (perfectly played by Vincent Price) offers a group of people $10,000 each if they can spend a night in his creepy mansion. The gimmick is that *The House on Haunted Hill* was supposedly shot in an amazing new screen process called "Emergo." At the proper moment during the screening, a luminous plastic skeleton was rigged to pop out and fly over the audience with ropes. "Emergo" was prone to failure, and it wasn't exactly an amazing process under the best of circumstances, but, as always with exploitation, it was all about the promise, not the delivery.

William Castle kept right on promising. As a semi-indie, he made his most famous picture, *The Tingler* (1959), for which theater seats were rigged to provide mild electric shocks at appropriate times in the horror film. *Thirteen Ghosts* (1960) utilized 3-D-style glasses allowing audiences to see phantasms. *Homicidal* (1961) included a "Fright Break" during which audience members could get a refund if they were too scared and they were willing to be humiliated in a "Coward's Corner." And *Mr. Sardonicus* (1961) supposedly allowed the audience to pick the movie's ending, though only one was really shot. Castle's later films were gimmick free. He produced the horror classic *Rosemary's Baby* (1968) for Paramount. William Castle was working on his 107th motion picture when he died at the age of sixty-three. He is fondly remembered for bringing carnival showmanship to Saturday matinees.

Documentary

In addition to *The Quiet One, Navajo,* and *Salt of the Earth,* the fifties provided other seminal docudramas: gritty, hard-hitting, and distinctly urban. *Crowded Paradise* (1956) is more melodrama than docudrama. Helmed by Fred Pressburger, it tells a contrived tale of Puerto Ricans in Manhattan. The acting by veterans Hume Cronyn and Nancy Kelly (as tenement superintendents) is stellar, as are performances by newcomers Mario Alcade and Enid Rudd (as an engaged Puerto Rican couple). The black-and-white location cinematography by Boris Kaufmann is also captivating. But *Crowded Paradise* crumbles around its patronizing message about the "Puerto Rican problem."

Yale chemistry graduate Lionel Rogosin (1924–) was a wealthy executive in his father's thriving textile business when he became troubled by the poverty near his Greenwich Village home and decided to do something about it. Rogosin used his own money to produce and direct *On the Bowery* (1956), a neorealist view of New York's skid row as seen by three male residents. Bowery homeless men play themselves in a tale of alcoholism and despair. Both real and staged footage is expertly shot in alleyways and pawnshops by Richard Bagley, who, with Rogosin, wrote the scripted material.

On the Bowery was a minor critical sensation that won the

Documentary Prize at the 1956 Venice Film Festival and was nominated for an Oscar the following year. It remains a provocative record of New York's mean streets and the bottom spirals of alcoholism. Leading man Ray Salyer was offered a studio contract after *On the Bowery* hit Hollywood. He declined. He just wanted to be left alone, saying, "There's nothing else in life but the booze."

Rogosin next helmed *Come Back, Africa* (1959), a docudrama about a black man struggling to make a living in South Africa at the height of apartheid. The Zulu man and his family are exploited and tormented by racist whites and a senseless bureaucracy. Rogosin shot some of the footage with a hidden camera, then smuggled exposed film out of the country to avoid the authorities. The completed feature played at the Cannes Film Festival in 1959, where it was hailed as a political landmark.

Come Back, Africa was at first unable to secure American distribution, so Rogosin, the committed liberal with both a big heart and a big wallet, launched his own exhibition space. He bought and renovated a Greenwich Village theater, renaming it the Bleecker Street Cinema. The Bleecker became a popular venue for independent movies in the sixties and seventies, and Rogosin became a fixture of the New York indie scene. He continued to make social documentaries—such as *Good Times, Wonderful Times* (1966), about the futility of war, and *Black Roots* (1970) and *Black Fantasy* (1972), both about racism—but they were little seen outside his own theater. He finished his final feature, *Arab Israeli Dialogue*, in 1974, the same year he sold the Bleecker Street Theater.

A soothing oasis among urban docudramas is Bert Stern's *Jazz on a Summer Day* (1959). Shot in color at and around the Newport Jazz Festival of 1958, this is the first great musical concert film. By concentrating as much on the audience, children playing, and the nearby America's Cup yacht race as on the stage, Stern captures the happy, laid-back feel of optimistic America at the height of the postwar boom. Legendary performers include Louie Armstrong, Chuck Berry, Dinah Washington, Thelonious Monk, and Mahalia Jackson.

Not nearly so optimistic, *The Savage Eye* (1959) was a long-range project jointly scripted, directed, and produced by three men: Hollywood screenwriter Ben Maddow (*Native Land*); Sidney Meyers, director of *The Quiet One;* and documentarian Joseph Strick. Four years of weekends were required to capture and assemble *The Savage*

Eye with a budget of $65,000. The list of cameramen is long and includes Haskell Wexler in one of his earliest jobs.

Meyers described *The Savage Eyes* as "the story of an American woman's journey through one year of divorce and her discovery of love amid the violence and splendor of a modern city."[17] The divorced woman is played by Barbara Baxley. *The Savage Eye* is a *Lolita*like travelogue of the seedy side of mid-century urban America: boxing and wrestling matches, saloons, strip joints, faith healing. Everywhere are unfriendly faces lined with despair. Some of the footage was shot with a hidden camera. There is no dialogue, but the narrator, called "The Poet" (Gary Merrill), serves up a stream of hard-boiled voice-over: "The slime of loveless love, masturbation by proxy." "[A divorcee] living on bourbon, cottage cheese, and alimony." In the end, after an affair and a nervous breakdown, the woman begins to connect with people again, gaining, as The Poet says, "the courage to say no to nothingness."

The Savage Eye hit Hollywood like a brass-knuckled sucker punch to the crotch. Reviews were often fawning. *The New York Times* was more reserved: "Although it is clouded by an overabundantly lush, consciously poetic narration and it is as cold as a scalpel in its dissection, this dramatized documentary of a year in the life and thoughts of a young divorcee is obviously a labor of love and a forceful display of cinematic pyrotechnics."[18] Somewhere between exploitation and art, fact and fiction, *The Savage Eye* had trouble finding an audience, but its black-and-white neorealism was a cinematographer's dream, reverberating throughout the entertainment industry. Style is sometimes enough.

By the end of the fifties, the motion picture studios had made peace with the small screen, selling or leasing their movies to networks and producing their own TV programs. Republic and RKO were out of business. Exploitation specialist Crown International was formed. Though autonomy during these years was mostly fueled by youth pictures and soft-core pornography, art houses were about to be rocked to their very foundations.

A coup d'état was coming, the instigators of which were a group of French cinéastes who put down the film journals they wrote for and grabbed 16-mm cameras. Their movies would have a lasting and significant impact on nonstudio film worldwide. Rebels in America would carry the cause to cities big and small. Anything seemed possible. For independent cinema, the first seven years of the sixties would be both the innocent days of Camelot and an exhilarating underground uprising building towards revolution.

Notes

---

1. Naha, Ed, *The Films of Roger Corman: Brilliance on a Budget* (New York: Arco Publishing, Inc. 1982), 94.
2. Naha, Ed, 8.
3. Corman, Roger, and Jim Jerome, *How I made a Hundred Movies in Hollywood and Never Lost a Dime* (New York: Random House, 1990), 33.
4. "From a Crew Member's Diary." *California Quarterly* (Summer 1953), 68.
5. *Los Angeles Times*, 4 March 1953.
6. *Hollywood Citizens News*, 15 March 1954.
7. *Film Culture* (May–June 1955), 15–20.
8. *Village Voice*, 4 Feb. 1959.
9. *Variety*, 23 Sept. 1953.
10. With *Louisiana Story, The Quiet One, Navajo,* and *The Little Fugitive* released between 1948 and 1953, realistic adult dramas with grade school children as protagonists proved to be a unique, critically and commercially successful independent genre. Foreign films have presented such stories (Francois Truffaut named *The Little Fugitive* as an influence on his *The 400 Blows*), but there have been almost no similar American features before or since.
11. *Variety*, 12 Sept. 1956.
12. Walker, Alexander, *Stanley Kubrick Directs* (New York: Harcourt Brace Jovanovich, 1971), 17.
13. Medved, Harry and Michael, *The Golden Turkey Awards* (New York: Perigee, 1980), 176–181, 204–208. The other three nominated directors for "worst of all time" are Phil Tucker, William Beaudine, and Herschell Gordon Lewis—all celluloid mavericks.
14. Friedman, David, interviewed by David Chute, "Wages of Sin," *Film Comment* 22 #4 (July/Aug. 1986), 46.
15. Turan, Kenneth, and Stephen F. Zito, *Sinema: American*

Pornographic Films and the People Who Make Them (New York: Praeger Publishers, 1974), 31.

[16] McGee, Mark Thomas, "King of the Gimmicks," *Fangoria* 12 (1981), 35.

[17] *New York Times*, 23 Aug. 1959.

[18] *New York Times*, 30 June 1960.

1960-1967

AHEAD OF THE CURVE

Art may be indefinable, but for me it is important to do something significant. The form must grow from the subject matter and from our times. The artist must be engaged in his times in the strongest way possible.

—LIONEL ROGOSIN[1]

I immediately made another film with a lot of nudity and big tits and all that stuff. I copied myself maybe ten, eleven more times.

—RUSS MEYER[2]

What would become one of the most influential movements in the history of film originated in the small French film journal *Cahiers du Cinéma*. Its writers included François Truffaut, Eric Rohmer, Jean-Luc Godard, and André Bazin. In the fifties, the magazine embraced the auteur theory—the concept of director as author—arguing for the critical ascendancy of filmmakers who imprinted their personality on film. Some of the auteurs advanced were then unheralded mavericks, including Robert Aldrich, Sam Fuller, and Edgar Ulmer. Throughout the sixties, this theory rewrote film history and criticism worldwide. Equally important, the *Cahiers* critics attacked the stale "tradition of quality" and argued in favor of a freer style: more location shooting, looser writing and acting, and consciously cinematic camera movement and editing. In essence, though it championed directors who made personal movies within the system, *Cahiers du Cinéma* was for independence.

The theories only had great impact because *Cahiers* critics applied their ideas in a real way by scripting and directing low-budget films. In 1959, Truffaut made *The 400 Blows*, Godard created *Breathless*, and Alain Resnais crafted *Hiroshima, Mon Amour*. Stylistically, they were startling. When the French swept into Cannes that year, the world took notice. What became known as the *Nouvelle Vague*, or the French New Wave, continued through the early sixties. Meanwhile, the refreshing films of 1959 hit the rest of the world the following year.

The French New Wave impacted American independent films through such techniques as improvised dialogue, handheld camerawork, and deliberately rough editing, but its more important legacy was to put into practice the philosophy of "Do your own thing." For decades the idealized *Nouvelle Vague* has served as a rallying cry, encouraging students, critics, and fans to grab a camera and tell their own stories their own way.

Another important consequence of the French New Wave stateside was that it broadened the already burgeoning audience for foreign fare, and such viewers would be the natural fan base for domestic art movies. Fueled by both an increased interest in cinema and the increased odds of seeing bare breasts, the exhibition of international cinema mushroomed in the fifties. In 1945 in America there were twelve art houses; by 1960 there were approximately 550.[3] Unfortunately, in the Kennedy years the system of dispersal to cinematheques was disorganized at best. In 1963 there were approximately eighty distributors of art-house fare, but such companies were often in debt or inept.

United Artists was not the solution—if it ever was. UA was now owned by lawyers, not artists. It was also a major Hollywood player, sweeping eleven Academy Awards in 1960 and winning five Best Picture Oscars during the sixties. With more semi-indie producers under contract than ever before, UA seldom picked up legitimate independents. However, in 1959, the studio bought Lopert Films as an autonomous distributor of foreign (especially British) pictures and, on occasion, domestic indies.

It was the cinematheques themselves that formed the crucial distribution infrastructure. Don Rugoff owned the popular New York City art houses Cinema 1 and Cinema 2, and he booked several others. In 1963, he launched a company called Cinema 5 to release foreign films and American indies. Cinema 5 expertly circulated such key off-Hollywood features as *The Cool World; One Potato, Two Potato; Putney Swope;* and *Harlan County, U.S.A.* In the late sixties, the term "Cinema 5" became synonymous with "art film."

Dan Talbot opened the New Yorker Theater in Manhattan in 1960, showcasing quality foreign and domestic features. When he learned that the only way he could screen the Italian *Before the Revolution* (1964) was to acquire the US rights, Talbot became a distributor by proxy. New Yorker Films was a dispenser of quality cinema through the early eighties. Meanwhile, Walter Reade, Jr. continued to expand his chain of art houses (there were more than seventy by 1970) while moving into distribution via Continental Distributing.

Festivals also blossomed. The San Francisco International Film Festival started in 1957; the New York Film Festival was launched in 1962. They were the first major cinema showcases outside of Europe, and though they would eventually become crucial proving grounds for key American-made indies, their programs were filled with mostly foreign works. The chief early legacy of the New York festival was that it brought quality non-Hollywood cinema to the influential Manhattan media, thus furthering the cause of art houses. Still, throughout the sixties, the big events in Venice and Cannes remained the best venues for Americans to stir up attention and secure circulation.

The fragile infrastructure was laid (though most of it would be replaced within two decades). Now there were places to see artistic independent films, companies to distribute them, and critics to champion them. All that was missing was the American auteurs to seize the day.

John Cassavetes

John Cassavetes (1929–1989) was born the son of Greek immigrants in New York City and grew up on Long Island just outside of Queens. Though he became a successful Hollywood actor, he never really left the middle-class neighborhoods, the personal struggle for self-worth (his father had made and lost a fortune), or the melting (and boiling) pot of ethnicities. He studied English and theater. In the fifties, he played mostly frustrated James Dean types on stage, television, and in films. He starred on the TV series "Johnny Staccato." In 1956, the tousle-haired leading man began a "method" workshop for unemployed actors. While discussing this group on a radio talk

John Cassavetes.

show he mentioned the possibility of turning an improvisation into a movie. Much to his surprise, $20,000 in contributions poured in from listeners.

So Cassavetes became a filmmaker. He matched the donations with another $20,000 from himself and his showbiz friends, and he began to shoot a 16mm, black-and-white, unscripted story about an interracial love affair. Produced (and coedited) by Maurice McEndree, the intermittent production took two years, shooting in the Times Square area of Manhattan. Most of the actors were inexperienced. They improvised. Cassavetes explained that the scenes "were predicated on people having problems that were overcome with other problems."[4]

The actors share their names with their characters, adding to the documentary feel. Lelia (Lelia Goldini), a light-skinned black woman, lives with her two brothers, tortured jazz musician Hugh (Hugh Hurd) and outwardly happy Benny (Ben Carruthers). Tension with her brothers develops when Lelia and hip, white Tony (Anthony Ray), fall in love. As in virtually all such interracial stories of this and earlier eras, the white man jilts the black woman when he discovers her true race.

Shadows captures the bohemian subculture of Manhattan in the late fifties. The film, like a jazz improvisation, pulsates to the vibrant music of Charles Mingus. The shaky handheld camera, mixed with jarring close-ups, has the feel of a home movie. But despite a stellar soundtrack, *Shadows* lacks a coherent theme, and performances sometimes strike the wrong notes. Individual stanzas impress, as in the confused anxiety the virginal Lelia feels when being courted by urbane Tony, but the elements fail to meld into a satisfying whole. It feels amateurish.

But amateurish wasn't necessarily an insult at the time of the film's release. After all, the impetus of the New Wave was a rejection of polished studio quality. Throughout his long career, Cassavetes would cling to the title "amateur director," along with "professional actor."

Shadows was first screened at Cinema 16 in late 1959. After a second show, Jonas Mekas wrote, "Rightly understood and properly presented, it could influence and change the tone, subject matter, and style of the entire independent American cinema. And it is already beginning to do so."[5] *Shadows* won acclaim at the 1960 Cannes Film Festival.

Due partly to Cassavetes's celebrity status and partly to timing, when *Shadows* finally received a relatively wide domestic release in 1961, it was elevated as nothing less than the precursor to an American cinematic revolution. The American New Wave was still a few years off, but when it came, Cassavetes would be at the front of it. What is patently false is to hold *Shadows* up as the genesis of American independent cinema. If this book does nothing else, let it smash this myth once and for all.

Shadows was simply the right movie at the right time with the right press-savvy director behind it. Art cinema lovers wanted to believe that Americans could create raw, rebellious films as vibrant as those of the French critics. They proclaimed John Cassavetes their chosen auteur, their savior from the rigid Hollywood style on the one side and the ponderous avant-garde on the other.

Cassavetes directed two Hollywood features, *Too Late Blues* (1961) and *A Child Is Waiting* (1962). Both were commercial and artistic disappointments. A year after his debut, the rebellious filmmaker was already weary of studio interference. Cassavetes returned to acting in such notables as *The Killers* (1964), *The Dirty Dozen* (1967), and *Rosemary's Baby* (1968). During these years—despite an Academy Award nomination and worldwide fame—the "professional actor" was merely biding time until he could be an "amateur director" again, longing to fulfill his promise.

Shirley Clarke

Raised in Park Avenue wealth, Shirley Clarke (1925–1997) was a dance prodigy. She presented her first choreographed work at seventeen and became president of the National Dance Association at the age of twenty-one. In the mid-fifties, Clarke's exploration of movement led her to make short dance films and the documentary *Bullfight* (1955). She codirected the twenty-minute documentary *Skyscraper* (1959), nominated for an Academy Award. Around this time, she attended a popular off-Broadway play called *The Connection*, about junkies waiting to score heroin. Clarke remembers, "I watched this play fascinated and it struck me that the camera could come in on these guys—these dope addicts—and you'd believe them. I've always been intrigued with what is cinematic and to me, the most important thing is audience identification with our camera."[6]

After eight short films, Clarke made a feature. The $150,000 budget was raised through small investments. Playwright Jack Gelber adapted his work for the big screen, making crucial changes, and Clarke assembled a stellar crew, including cinematographer Arthur Ornitz. The cast was mostly unknowns who stayed that way, Roscoe Lee Browne (debuting) excepted. Shooting took place on one grimy set.

An interracial group of irritated or lethargic jazz musicians and others wait in the apartment of Leach (Warren Finnerty) for a man to show up with their heroin fix. *The Connection* (1961) is about addiction and abandoned dreams, but it's also about filmmaking and the relationship of artists to their subjects. Amongst the junkies in the New York City flat is a fictional documentary director (William Redfield) and his cameraman. The director himself tries heroin.

Because the dialogue includes a few utterances of the word "shit" (heroin), there was a minor outcry. *The Connection* was banned in New York state (the ruling was later overturned), which helped elevate Clarke's feature as the hip flick to see. The underground press loved it; most mainstream critics had the opposite reaction. Brendan Gill in *The New Yorker* pronounced it "a stunt that doesn't work . . . and radically unpleasant to watch. I felt like a medical student making his first plunge into the peritoneal cavity."[7]

The years have sanded away the edges that once made *The Connection* "radically unpleasant." Subsequent television and film documentaries have shown us real junkies. The discussion of "shit" and the one on-screen injection in the film no longer shock. And although some performances feel weighted down by their theatrical origins, *The Connection* soars. Much of the acting is excellent, the setting is evocative, and it all throbs with a terrific jazz score by Freddie Redd (who plays a junkie piano player) and *cinema verité* photography.

In the early sixties, Shirley Clarke joined with Jonas Mekas to help organize and support independent filmmakers. She brought together the often territorial genres of artistic nonstudio cinema: avant-garde, documentary, and festival-bound fiction. After a personal request from President Kennedy, Clarke directed the documentary *Robert Frost: A Lover's Quarrel With the World* (1963); it won an Academy Award.

Clarke's next feature was produced by future *cinema verité* documentarian Frederick Wiseman. *The Cool World* (1964) is a brutally honest docudrama about African-American youth gangs in Harlem. It follows teenage Priest (Carl Lee, who, with Clarke, adapted the script from a book and a play) as he tries to obtain a gun. Gloria Foster and Clarence Williams III stand out in a cast that includes many amateurs. The gritty black-and-white New York photography by Baird Bryant is intoxicating, as is the jazz and rock-and-roll score. Depicting an urban reality of crime, drugs, anger, and hopelessness, *The Cool World* was truly a groundbreaking portrait of inner city life. It plays like an updated sequel to *The Quiet One* or the angry flip side of the blockbuster *West Side Story* (1961).

Clarke's *Portrait of Jason* (1967) is a controversial documentary portrait of black homosexual hustler Jason Holliday. He simply talks to
the camera for an hour and forty-five minutes. "This has all been a
waste," Jason says of his life. "Because white people are fascinating.
They think you're just a dumb, stupid little colored boy. You're trying
to get a few dollars, and they're gonna use you as a joke. It gets to be
a joke sometimes, as to who's using who." The raw monologue
repulsed many American critics, but it was well received in Europe.
Swedish cinema legend Ingmar Bergman called *Portrait of Jason* "the
most fascinating film I've ever seen."

In the late sixties, Hollywood beckoned. Shirley Clarke tried to
initiate a studio movie (written by Shelley Winters), but it never
materialized. A true maverick, she always regretted the attempt. In
the seventies, she taught film at UCLA and created avant-garde
videos. Clarke fashioned the acclaimed documentary *Ornette—Made
in America* (1985), about jazz innovator Ornette Coleman.

Devoid of liberal guilt or white patronization, Clarke made elo-
quent social critiques with mostly black characters. She said in 1992,
"I never felt that anything about my own life was going to interest
anyone else, so I chose surrogates—underdogs, outsiders—whom I
identified with."[8] A daring filmmaker, Shirley Clarke was committed
to telling the honest tales that others either ignored or shielded their
eyes from.

Directing Debuts

Hollywood notables continued to make their directorial debuts
outside the studio walls. While still in his early twenties, Tom
Laughlin (*Billy Jack*) wrote, directed, and starred in a couple of high-
school tales—*The Proper Time* (1960) and *Like Father, Like Son* (1961)—
that were barely released. Sam Peckinpah (*The Wild Bunch*) first
helmed the mediocre western *The Deadly Companions* (1961) for an
independent company. Philip Kaufman (*The Right Stuff*) and
Benjamin Manaster wrote and directed the religious satire *Goldstein*
(1965), which won an award at Cannes. And Richard Rush (*The Stunt
Man*) called the shots on the drive-in hit *Hell's Angels on Wheels* (1967),
starring Jack Nicholson.

No outsider in the early sixties made a greater initial splash than
Frank Perry. It was the kind of story Hollywood loves. A man who'd
never before shot so much as a home movie and his wife who'd never

before written a script made their own feature film. It became a substantial success with critics and ticket buyers. A few months later, in a classic Hollywood ending, husband and wife were nominated for directing (his) and screenwriting (hers) Academy Awards.

Frank Perry (1930–1995) began working in Connecticut theater as a teenager. By the late fifties, after years of stage-managing and assisting on movies and a stint in the Korean War, Perry was an occasional producer of plays and nonfiction TV. His interest in cinema was growing, as was his frustration with having no creative control. Meanwhile, Perry's playwright wife Eleanor read a book called *David and Lisa*, authored by psychiatrist Theodore Rubin, M.D. She turned it into a screenplay.

Because the story is set almost entirely at one location—a mental hospital—shooting could be accomplished cheaply. Still, raising the meager budget proved difficult for rookie producer Paul Heller and director Frank Perry. More than a thousand potential investors said no. A hundred or so said yes. Through selling small shares, they slowly raised the needed $150,000 budget. They cast Janet Margolin to play Lisa, and—after the first choice pulled out one week before shooting—Keir Dullea as David. It was Margolin's first film, Dullea's second. Shooting took place on an old estate in Pennsylvania. Corners were cut everywhere (one-fourth of the script was never shot). After wrapping, Perry bought champagne to celebrate, though he was certain he'd made a bomb.

He was wrong. *David and Lisa* (1962) tells the story of David, a young adult brought to a mental home because he cannot stand to be touched. He's fascinated by Lisa, a schizophrenic who talks backwards in rhymes and thinks she's two people. When Lisa runs away, David follows and takes the first steps towards feeling something. Much of *David and Lisa* is stiff and stagy, with sparse production design and a hollow soundtrack, but the sensitive and unique story captivated viewers and won many fans in 1962. *David and Lisa* was a hit at the Venice Film Festival and a surprise critical and commercial success in America. The Perrys spent a nervous night at the Oscars.

Riding high, Frank and Eleanor signed with United Artists and made *Ladybug, Ladybug* (1963). Working mostly in New York, Frank Perry remained a proud outsider, even as he cashed studio checks, for the next two decades. He helmed (and often produced) distinctly original and consciously adult stories, including *The Swimmer*

(1968); *Diary of a Mad Housewife* (1970), written by Eleanor shortly before she and Frank divorced; and *Mommie Dearest* (1981). Diagnosed with inoperable prostate cancer in 1990, Perry made an autobiographical documentary entitled *On the Bridge* (1992), which explores his various medical treatments. Frank Perry's distinguished career, in which he directed seventeen features, has been largely underappreciated.

Stage and TV scribe Leslie Stevens wrote and directed a lurid little picture called *Private Property* (1960). His agent, Stanley Colbert, produced. Respected cinematographer Ted McCord (*Treasure of the Sierra Madre*) was behind the camera. With a $60,000 budget, they shot for ten days in and around Stevens' Beverly Hills home (publicity claimed the prop budget was 97 cents).

Private Property tells a highly exploitive tale of delinquent Duke (Corey Allen), who schemes to help dim-witted Boots (Warren Oates) lose his virginity. They stalk and spy on a sexually frustrated Hollywood Hills housewife (Kate Manx). Duke seduces her. When he hands her over to Boots, violence erupts. At the conclusion, after the housewife has been stalked, raped, and nearly killed, her square husband asks, "Anna, are you alright?" She answers, "I wasn't, but I am now."

Private Property predated Russ Meyer's roughies, and it was denied a Production Code seal. With the *Nouvelle Vague* all the rage, Stevens stated that his picture represented the "American New Wave." He didn't fool many critics, but such billing did manage to sneak *Private Property* into art houses, where it stirred up controversy just by being there. Stevens went on to create and executive-produce the classic science-fiction television series "The Outer Limits."

Curtis Harrington says, "The human spirit, to me, is much more important and interesting than corporeal reality—I've always just tried to plunge in and film that."[9] Harrington was the avant-garde prodigy of the forties and fifties who went Hollywood. In the late sixties and early seventies, working for a variety of studios, he specialized in low-budget psychological horror flicks and TV movies. In between, Harrington made a transitional film.

Written and directed by Harrington, *Night Tide* is the story of lonely sailor Johnny Drake (Dennis Hopper) who falls in love with a peculiar woman named Mora (Linda Lawson). She works as a mermaid at a pier amusement park near Los Angeles, and she may or may not be an actual sea nymph. Mora fears that if they make love Johnny will drown like two of her previous lovers. The sailor is trapped somewhere between hallucination and reality.

Though it's underwritten with a sappy orchestral score, Harrington's crisp direction, the mythic characters, and Hopper's sad gaze allow this pensive saga to burrow under your skin. *Night Tide* was praised when it played at the 1961 Venice Film Festival, but it wasn't picked up and released by Universal until 1963. Difficult to categorize, it slipped through the cracks upon initial release and was later mistakenly pushed as a horror flick instead of a love story. The hypnotic *Night Tide* is a clear extension of Harrington's personal vision, for he had been filming dreams for two decades.

Roger Corman

Roger Corman continued to pump out drive-in double bills for AIP and for his own production company. Most of them had nothing to do with "art" or a new wave and they assiduously avoided politics. But in 1960, Corman was still only thirty-four, still just five years beyond his directing debut, and he still felt the heady rush of independence. Not having experienced the sting of a financial flop, he may also have felt almost invincible in the low-budget arena. He was willing to experiment.

On the heels of the five-day shoot for *Bucket of Blood*, Corman challenged himself and his crew to shoot a feature in only two days. Writer Charles Griffith (who penned *Bucket of Blood* and numerous Corman pictures for two decades) dreamed up an ingenious screenplay that combines monster movie elements with dark humor. The script includes impoverished settings, Jewish caricatures, a dead-on "Dragnet" parody, and a wealth of perverse dialogue (prostitute: "How's the rain on the rhubarb?"). Griffith also directed the exteriors and appears as the holdup man and as an extra.

The Little Shop of Horrors (1960) follows a schlemiel named Seymour (Jonathan Haze) who works in a skid-row flower shop in Los Angeles (though it feels like New York). Audry (Jackie Joseph) is his coworker and eventual girlfriend. Seymour discovers a new plant, Audry Jr., that craves blood, grows to enormous size, and talks (Griffith is the voice). He procures it human food and, in the suitably perverse conclusion, becomes part of the plant. The most famous scene features a young Jack Nicholson as a gleeful, squeaky-voiced masochist who reaches sexual ecstacy during a painful visit to the dentist.

Principal photography of the $27,000 *Little Shop* was indeed completed on a stage in two very long days, utilizing two cameras and prelit sets (similar to those of a TV sitcom), though there were four additional days of exterior photography. Jonathan Haze received a mere $400 for his starring performance. According to Griffith, real skid-row homeless people were paid 10 cents to appear on-screen.[10] The movie's amazingly short and cheap production, coupled with its utterly original script, allowed it to be specially screened out of competition at the 1960 Cannes Film Festival. *Little Shop* was distributed by AIP on a double bill with Corman's far inferior *The Last Woman on Earth*. It was a moderate success.

But its legend grew like Audry, Jr. *The Little Shop of Horrors* was reincarnated as a popular musical in the early eighties, and that version was the basis for an enjoyable movie in 1986. The comical songs of the colorful remake by Frank Oz led many to believe it's a spoof of a pathetic B picture. In fact, it's a loving tribute to a small classic. The original, darker *Little Shop* stands on its own as Corman's most enjoyable motion picture. It's a black comedy groundbreaker and one of the best movies ever made in less than two weeks, let alone two days.

The Drive-In Deity produced and directed six films in 1960 and five in 1961 and was in the midst of crafting his popular Poe series of bigger-budgeted gothic horrors for AIP. He wanted to do something different, something artful, something meaningful. So Corman acquired the rights to the fact-based novel *The Intruder* by Charles Beaumont, and Beaumont adapted it (and appears on-screen as the tolerant principal). The story follows Yankee bigot Adam Cramer (William Shatner), who goes to a Southern town simmering over the integration of its high school. He manipulates and inflames the already dangerously racist white locals into violence against the black community but is ultimately exposed as an immoral agitator and coward.

The most likely supporters of the film, AIP, Allied Artists, and United Artists, wouldn't touch the controversial, epithet-filled script during those years of freedom rides and fire-bombings. So Corman financed *The Intruder* (1961) through his own Filmgroup. Wanting to get into production and distribution, Pathé Labs fronted some of the costs. *The Intruder* was produced on location in a small all-white town in the southeastern corner or Missouri, forty miles from the Arkansas border, a little more than three years after the tumultuous school desegregation crisis in Little Rock. Some local residents were none too happy about a bunch of Hollywood types making a movie about racism on their public property. The concluding lynch mob sequence was shot in three different schoolyards because the local sheriff kept chasing the crew away. Location shooting paid off however, because locales such as a diner, a street of crumbling shacks, and a plantation estate are evocative.

The Intruder was admitted to both the Cannes and the Venice Film Festivals, but it was withdrawn from Cannes when tensions around desegregation swelled in the South. Pathé pulled out of distribution, fearing riots. Released by Filmgroup and barely promoted, *The Intruder* died at the box office.

The Intruder is an immensely powerful tale, very relevant to its time and place. Unlike other movies with this theme, *The Intruder* avoids sermonizing and theatrics. It follows the villain (the most interesting character) more closely than the heroes and martyrs, and then-unknown William Shatner is surprisingly effective as the sly, egomaniacal Adam. The writing, acting, and directing are first-rate. Only the inexplicable ignorance of a white girl manipulated into setting up a black boy mars the fast-moving plot. The roaming camerawork (by Taylor Byars) is spiked with low-angle close-ups. The quick editing and rousing music are equally inspired. A night scene where Adam and hooded KKK figures haul a cross in an auto caravan through the black section of town is truly horrifying—reminiscent of *The Birth of a Nation*. Corman's courageous "art film" was his first to lose money. True to form, the Drive-In Deity later rereleased *The Intruder* under the titles *Shame* (the video uses this name) and the highly exploitable *I Hate Your Guts!* Well, a guy's gotta make a buck.

An inveterate tightwad, Corman states that "after *The Intruder* I was obviously not particularly eager to take risks and set myself up for another beating."[11] Instead, throughout the sixties he churned out low-budget, drive-in flicks for his own Filmgroup and slightly bigger-budgeted features for AIP. Still, Corman's influence on independent cinema was far from over. Since the sixties he has been primarily a producer and in 1970 he founded his own studio, New World, a creator of routine low-budget fare and a distributor of some of the most important foreign films (and a few American indies) of the seventies.

Theater

Eugene O'Neill's play *Long Day's Journey Into Night* follows the emotional disintegration of the Tyrone family during one tumultuous day and night in 1912. O'Neill never allowed his autobiographical work to be performed during his lifetime, but after his death in 1953 it became a Broadway hit. Sidney Lumet was a television director before he successfully made the leap to film with *12 Angry Men* (1957). In the early sixties, he teamed up with TV producer Ely Landau to bring O'Neill's play to the big screen.

They would create it apart from the studios, small in scope, faithful to O'Neill's words and stage direction. The cast and crew were convinced to work for tiny fractions of their usual salaries. Spencer Tracy was Lumet's first choice for the role of the Tyrone family patriarch, but he requested a typical salary of $500,000. Because the entire production cost $400,000, Ralph Richardson got the role, joined in the cast by Katharine Hepburn, Jason Robards, and Dean Stockwell. The crew included such heavyweights as cinematographer Boris Kaufman and composer Andre Previn.

Long Day's Journey Into Night (1962) is one of cinema's best adaptations of a play. The acting is universally excellent; the tension is strong. It was both a critical and a commercial hit. Katherine Hepburn was nominated for an Academy Award. Sidney Lumet went on to make such studio classics as *Dog Day Afternoon* (1975), *Network* (1976), and *The Verdict* (1982).

Another independent adaptation of a play fell just short of Lumet's low-budget sensation. *The Balcony* (1963) has a cast of notables— Shelley Winters, Peter Falk, Lee Grant, Ruby Dee—who give superb performances, and it benefits from stellar black-and-white cinematography by George Folsey, who was nominated for an Academy Award.[12] Though Joseph Strick's (*The Savage Eye*) direction is too restrained, the strong elements of French legend Jean Genet's play pack a wallop. *The Balcony* is a surreal political fable about a brothel during a revolution. It scathingly satirizes religion and government. Joseph Strick would continue to make challenging fiction and nonfiction movies, including adaptations of seemingly unadaptable novels by James Joyce and Henry Miller.

Sam Fuller

After his three films for Fox in the mid-fifties, Sam Fuller formed his own semi-indie production company, Globe Enterprises (named for the newspaper in *Park Row*). He wrote, directed, and produced six semi-indies in four years. In *Run of the Arrow* (1957), a Confederate soldier aligns himself with Indians rather than accept surrender. *China Gate* (1957) was the first motion picture to deal with the Vietnam War (then being fought by the French). A compelling western starring Barbara Stanwyck, *Forty Guns* (1957), illustrates the pitfalls of being only *semi*-independent during these years: Fox forced Fuller to alter the ending so that Stanwyck lives. In *Verboten* (1959), an American GI falls for a German girl during World War II. The forward-thinking *The Crimson Kimono* (1959) tracks the murder of a stripper while highlighting a clash of cultures. And the visually impressive *Underworld U.S.A.* (1960) features a gritty crime plot. Fuller also made *Merrill's Marauders* (1962) for Warner Bros. Tired of constraints and studio meetings, he yearned for the total freedom he had known a decade earlier.

When he was fully liberated, Fuller went onto create his two most jarring and daring pulp movies, a pair of features that exist somewhere between all-out trash and the art of a mad genius. The first, *Shock Corridor* (1963), follows self-serving crime reporter Johnny Barratt (Peter Breck), who gets himself committed to an insane asylum so he can talk to the three witnesses of a murder: a turncoat GI who now thinks he's a Confederate soldier, a black man who tried to integrate a school and now thinks he's in the KKK, and a onetime atomic genius who now thinks like a child. Johnny solves the murder, but by the time he wins a Pulitzer Prize and is able to leave the premises, the pain of the inmates has driven him insane.

Shock Corridor was shot by legendary cinematographer Stanley Cortez, always up for the challenge of something unusual. He and Fuller wanted to make the visuals even more surreal, but they ran out of financing. As it is, *Shock Corridor* is plenty weird, with jarring camera angles, bizarre hallucinations, sinister sounds, and a general aura of sleaziness. In the most perverse but exciting scene, Johnny is attacked by a fierce gang of attractive nymphomaniacs. During shots of the title corridor, Cortez placed dwarves at the end so the hall would appear longer than it really was. On the last day of shooting, the crew flooded the soundstage for an imaginary rainstorm inside the hospital corridor (intercut with scenes of Niagara Falls). Other hallucinations (in color in this otherwise black-and-white flick) were actually Fuller's 16mm home movies from a trip to Brazil and from his *House of Bamboo* production in Japan. The shots are inappropriate, yet with all the other weirdness going on they almost fit in.

Shock Corridor was dismissed as B movie trash upon its initial domestic release (because of its title, it was sometimes promoted as a horror picture). *Variety* felt Fuller was trying to say something about American values, "but the melodrama in which he has chosen to house those ideas is so grotesque, so grueling, so shallow and so shoddily sensationalistic that his message is devastated."[13] And yet, across the Atlantic, Fuller's latest was virtually worshiped. It played at one Paris theater for five years. It was usually joined on European double bills by its melodramatic twin, *The Naked Kiss*. Shot six months apart, both were financed by Leon Fromkess (producer of *Bluebeard*, *Detour*, and dozens of others for PRC) and Sam Firks.

Sam Fuller directs Constance Towers and children in *The Naked Kiss*
© 1964 Allied Artists Pictures. Courtesy of the Academy of Motion Picture Arts and Sciences.

The Naked Kiss begins without a fade-in, precredits, before audiences have even settled into their seats, with one of the most startling first scenes in the history of cinema. Kelly the prostitute (Constance Towers) is savagely beating up her pimp. (The camera was strapped to the chest of the actor playing the pimp, so we feel the blows.) Kelly's wig is pulled off, revealing her bald head. As the procurer lies battered and drunk, Kelly takes the $75 he owes her and, while gazing into the camera like a mirror, fixes her makeup.

The Naked Kiss follows tough, intelligent Kelly as she attempts to go straight in a small town. She's a nurse's aide to handicapped children and accepts a marriage proposal from handsome millionaire Grant (Michael Dante), who knows her past. Everything is going great until she discovers Grant is a pedophile who wants to marry her only because as an "abnormal" former hooker she will understand his perversion. She kills him. No one believes her story. Finally the molested girl tells all, but by this time Kelly is disillusioned with the hypocritical "normal" people. In an ending as bold and raw as the beginning, Kelly rejects the town's apologies and walks away, presumedly to return to prostitution.

Sam Fuller remembers, "The original impression I wanted was of a wonderful, almost dull, very, very ordinary love story: the poor girl from the wrong side of the tracks, the rich man who falls in love with her. Well, I hate those kinds of stories. So I knew I was going to have fun the minute she finds him molesting the child."[14]

The Naked Kiss was again shot by Stanley Cortez, though with less flair than *Shock Corridor*. It again includes Fuller's home movies (a gondola ride in Venice). In addition to the opening, the scene where Kelly—carrying her wedding dress—discovers Grant with the girl is marvelously staged, shot, and edited. As Kelly clubs him to death with a telephone, her wedding veil covers his face.

Like *Shock Corridor*, *The Naked Kiss* was celebrated in Europe but virtually ignored upon release in America. Both films remain neglected in their auteur's native land. Unfortunately, these startling features marked the end of Sam Fuller's true independence. In subsequent years, he made several movies with European companies and two with American studios, *The Big Red One* (1980), a World War II yarn, and *White Dog* (1982), which was shelved after being erroneously charged with racism. Fuller lived his final fifteen years in Paris, where he was correctly hailed as a cinematic genius. He acted in European productions, usually portraying a variation of his own hard-boiled, cigar-chomping persona.

Samuel Fuller made twenty-three films in forty years. Most of them were shot in two weeks or less. All of them—even *The Big Red One*, which concentrates on the soldiers, not the spectacle—were essentially B movies. But the majority of them were also something more than B movies. His best work transcends hackneyed genre convictions and slim production values through its creator's sheer audacity. Fuller's pulp pictures batter bigotry, they praise individualism, they brutalize stoolies and wimps, and they honor working-class stiffs (even whores) with strong convictions. No matter what odd angle or jarring close-up Fuller's camera rubs your face in, it mirrors the organic (and sometimes messy) excitement or confusion of real life. In Jean-Luc Godard's *Pierre le Fou* (1965), Sam Fuller plays himself at a party, dressed in a dark suit, with dark shades and his ever-present cigar. Asked to define a movie, he responds, "Well, a film is like a battleground: Love. Hate. Action. Death. In one word—emotions."

Monte Hellman

Like Fuller, Monte Hellman (1932–) crafted marginalized, masculine movies. After studying drama and film, he began his career, like so many others, working for Roger Corman. Corman's Filmgroup produced Hellman's directorial debut, *The Beast from Haunted Cave* (1959), a bargain-basement effort in which fleeing robbers tangle with a spiderlike monster. A few years later, the frizzy-haired Hellman began collaborating with another Corman veteran, Jack Nicholson. Nicholson stars in the mediocre World War II thriller, *Back Door to Hell* (1964), which Hellman made in the Philippines with the even less interesting adventure flick *Flight to Fury* (1964).

With Nicholson collaborating and slim financing from Corman, Hellman directed two enigmatic "art westerns" that were never given proper domestic releases but went on to become cult favorites. Both *The Shooting* and *Ride in the Whirlwind* were shot in an ugly Utah desert in the summer of 1965; Corman provided $160,000 for both. Nicholson wrote, coproduced, and stars in *Ride in the Whirlwind*, in which cowboys (Nicholson, Cameron Mitchell, and Tom Filer) are pursued by a hanging posse for a crime they didn't commit. In the end, not much is resolved. Millie Perkins and Harry Dean Stanton have supporting roles. Nicholson also coproduced *The Shooting*, written by Adrien Joyce, and he again stars in this metaphysical tale about identity and fate. A mysterious woman (Millie Perkins) hires two bounty hunters (Warren Oates and Will Hutchins) for an unspecified mission. They're eventually joined by a villainous gunslinger (Nicholson) as their trek takes them deeper and deeper into unforgiving wasteland. The ending supplies a dramatic twist.

Neither *Ride in the Whirlwind* nor *The Shooting* resembled traditional westerns (which were all but dead by the mid-sixties), and certainly they were nothing like the typical Corman flick that could slip onto a double bill and entertain the kids. After they were well received at festivals, the Walter Reade Organization picked up the domestic rights to both. But Reade was scared of opening cowboy pictures—even solemn, enigmatic ones—in art houses, so he sold them directly to television, where they've seldom been screened. Meanwhile, the French company that bought the foreign rights went bankrupt. In 1968 *Ride in the Whirlwind* and *The Shooting* were finally able to play on the big screen—in Paris, where they were hailed as works of genius.

Through the years, the reputation of these two modern "lost" films grew. In 1972, Hellman's bleak westerns received limited theatrical distribution in America, and they've played at revivals ever since. As with most discovered films, they don't quite live up to their legends, but despite (and sometimes because of) muddled sound, visuals, and plots, both *Ride in the Whirlwind* and *The Shooting* are a pair of oddly captivating motion pictures.

Though Hellman's Utah productions secured his reputation (mostly in Europe) as a cult auteur, they did little to bolster his career prospects. He made the existential road picture *Two-Lane Blacktop* (1971) for Universal. It flopped, though it also became a cult favorite. Since then, Hellman has worked as a film editor as well as a director of marginal movies (often with foreign financing) such as *Cockfighter* (1974); *China 9, Liberty 37* (1978); and *Iguana* (1989). He was an executive producer of *Reservoir Dogs* (1992).

African-American

Nineteen sixty-four was the year after the March of Washington, the year of the Civil Rights Act and the year Martin Luther King, Jr. was awarded the Nobel Peace Prize. On the heels of *Shadows*, 1964 served up three dramatic independent features about black citizens in an integrating society. The first, *The Cool World*, was discussed previously.

Unlike other films about doomed interracial romances, *One Potato, Two Potato* was the first to bring its couple to the altar. White Julie (Barbara Barrie), with a six-year-old daughter, weds black Frank (Bernie Hamilton), her coworker at a factory in a Midwestern town. Complications with Frank's parents are ironed out, but those with Julie's white ex-husband boil over. He sues for custody of the child and wins.

One Potato, Two Potato marked the film debut of TV director Larry Peerce. The film was scripted by Raphael Hayes and Orville Hampton (based on Hampton's play); the screenplay was nominated for an Academy Award. Shooting took place in Painesville, Ohio, with a budget of $230,000 raised from forty-three individuals. As the South battled desegregation, the American selection committee rejected *One Potato, Two Potato* for the Cannes Film Festival. The French let it in anyway. This daring film with a somber, documentary feel was a hit at Cannes, earning standing ovations and a best actress award for Barbara Barrie. Cinema 5 released it domestically.

The critical reception was almost universally positive. *The New York Times* named *One Potato, Two Potato* one of the ten best films of 1964 and stated: "It does not soar on wings of artistry in keeping with its strong subject. But it speaks out resolutely on a generally shunned social theme that is a credit to the courage of its producers and the team that made it."[15] And that is its true merit. At the height of the struggle for civil rights, the filmmakers dared to tell a subdued story of interracial marriage. Hollywood studios finally mustered up some courage with *Guess Who's Coming to Dinner* (1967). Nominated for ten Academy Awards (winner of two), that glossy Stanley Kramer drama thoroughly eclipsed *One Potato, Two Potato* in popularity. Still, it was a little independent movie that blazed the trail.

Nothing but a Man was the third racial trailblazer of 1964. In this deceptively simple story of poor African-Americans in the Deep South, Duff (Ivan Dixon) is a railroad worker and a father. He falls in love with a preacher's daughter (jazz singer Abbey Lincoln) and, against her parents' wishes, they marry. Trapped in a life of near-poverty with outside forces pressing in, Duff battles feelings of inadequacy. He struggles to accept his wife's love and extend love to his own son.

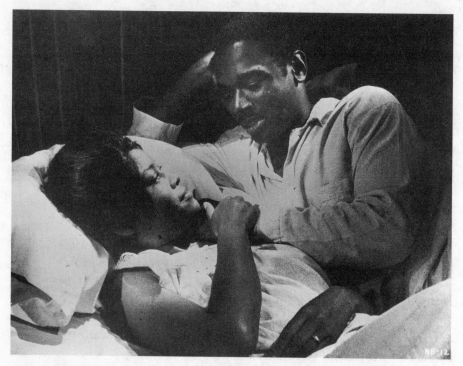

Abbey Lincoln and Ivan Dixon in *Nothing But a Man*.
© 1964 Cinema V. Courtesy of the Academy of Motion Picture Arts and Sciences.

Although virtually ignored when released, *Nothing But a Man*'s reputation has grown, and deservedly so. It's a powerful motion picture that presents complex, real-life problems and courageously avoids easy resolutions. The stellar cast includes Yaphet Kotto, Moses Gunn, and Esther Rolle. *Nothing But a Man* was helmed by Michael Roemer with cinematography by Robert Young. Both are credited as producers with Robert Rubin and as writers of the excellent script. Until 1964, Roemer and Young were primarily documentarians, and their nonfiction backgrounds are clearly felt in the realistic acting, photography, and settings.

Robert Young previously wrote and directed the psychological thriller *Trauma* (1963), a $70,000 independent about an amnesiac witness to murder. As shall be seen, he went on to have a varied career forging socially conscious features in and out of the studios.

Michael Roemer wrote and directed another independent film (co-produced with Young), but it was unable to secure distribution for twenty years. *The Plot Against Harry*, a mild-mannered comedy about a Jewish racketeer (Martin Priest), was produced in 1969. It sat on a shelf for two decades until Roemer dusted it off and submitted it to a few festivals. Adopted by critics, the movie received a commercial release and positive reviews in 1989. Like Hellman's rediscovered westerns, *The Plot Against Harry* doesn't merit overflowing praise, but it is more amusing than most movies dutifully distributed.

Horror

In 1962, a creepy little shocker drifted onto a few drive-in screens. It was made for a mere $33,000 and filmed mostly in Lawrence, Kansas entirely by rookies. The producer/director was an industrial filmmaker; the cast and crew were unknown locals. The movie played mostly rural areas and disappeared fast. But it wouldn't die. It haunted the dusty reaches of late-night TV, plaguing the dreams of those who stumbled across it. And its legend grew. In 1989, it was resurrected and nine minutes that had been excised by the distributor without the director's permission were restored. Finally, in art houses around the country, it was championed as the inventive, eerie, minimasterpiece of horror that it is.

The movie is *Carnival of Souls* (1962). Its producer/director was Harold ("Herk") Harvey. Its writer was John Clifford. *Carnival of Souls* is the shiver-inducing story of organist Mary Henry (Candace Hilligoss), who is the lone survivor when a car plunges into a river. It seems to take her hours to surface, and she remembers nothing. Mary takes a job as a church organist in Salt Lake City. While driving there, she is haunted by a cadaverous man (Harvey). There are consistently creepy moments when ghosts seem to be calling Mary home, until the journey ends at a deserted carnival.

Carnival of Souls presents a woman who was never really alive—no lover, no friends, no religion—and thus cannot even recognize her own death. Special effects are minimal. Instead, *Carnival of Souls* relies on Maurice Prather's crisp cinematography, Harvey's effective pacing, and Clifford's clever plot. Crudely poetic, the completed film plays like Val Lewton overseeing an episode of "The Twilight Zone." Some lines and line readings fall flat, but *Carnival of Souls* is a true hair-raiser.

The creator of another little shocker did not have the luxury of a clever concept. The twenty-four-year-old had been recording sound for Roger Corman and while in Great Britain, pitched an idea to the

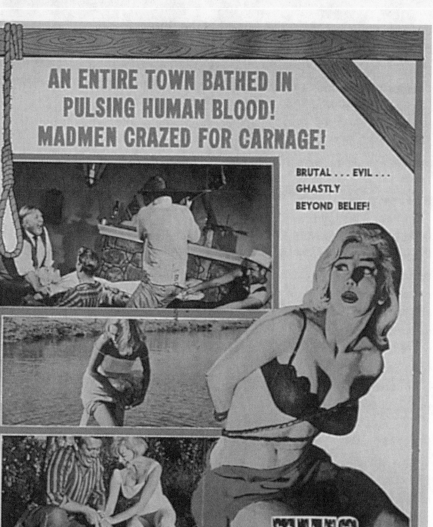

Highly exploitive poster for *Two Thousand Maniacs!*

Drive-In Deity: "A man goes to a pond and takes off his clothes, picks up these dolls, ties them together, goes under the water, dives down . . . And Roger says, 'Change the man to a woman, and you can do it.' "[16] With $20,000 from Roger Corman and another $20,000 from a British producer, he shot *Dementia 13* (1963) in two weeks in Ireland. It's a derivative psychological horror flick with a few shocks and some inventive camerawork. What makes it most notable is that its writer/director/producer was Francis Ford Coppola, who, in the next decade helmed such classics as *The Godfather* (1972), *The Godfather Part II* (1974), and *Apocalypse Now* (1979). *Dementia 13* was Coppola's second movie. He debuted as director, producer, and cowriter with *Tonight for Sure* (1961), a nudie-cutie.

Meanwhile, around the time of *Dementia 13*, producer David Friedman and director Herschell Gordon Lewis were turning out topless romps that got lost in the flesh explosion of the early sixties. They needed something to stand out, and they came up with a new genre to play in grind houses, something as exploitable as nudity but much more shocking: gore. If sex doesn't sell, try blood.

Lewis shot *Blood Feast* (1963) in five days in Miami for $24,000. It's a terrible movie about a homicidal maniac who mutilates young women. The horrendous acting and incompetent camerawork are punctuated with the ripping out of a tongue and the scooping out of a brain and the splashing of buckets of crimson blood.

The ads for *Blood Feast* screamed: "NOTHING SO APPALLING IN THE ANNALS OF HORROR! You'll Recoil and Shudder as You Witness the Slaughter and Mutilation of Nubile Young Girls in a Weird and Horrendous Ancient Rite! MORE GRISLY THAN EVER IN BLOOD COLOR!" It was a big hit on the Southern drive-in circuit. Spotting their target audience, Friedman and Lewis set their next gorefest, *Two Thousand Maniacs!* (1964), in the rural South. Yankee tourists are gruesomely slaughtered by ghosts of the Confederacy masquerading as friendly townspeople. The final installment in Friedman and Lewis's "Blood Trilogy" is *Color Me Blood Red* (1965). An artist discovers he can paint only with blood, with predictably violent results when he runs out of supplies.

Friedman and Lewis went their separate ways after *Color Me Blood Red*, but they both kept pumping out exploitation. David Friedman produced and distributed increasingly risqué soft-core pornography like *Thar She Blows* (1969) and *Trader Hornee* (1970). He eventually crossed over to hard-core. In addition to gorefests and nudies, Herschell Gordon Lewis called the shots on no-budget biker, hillbilly, juvenile delinquent, and monster flicks. All this from a man who started as an English professor. Though he was versed in classic literature, Lewis was a thoroughly inept filmmaker. He fittingly concluded his directing career with a trash opus of both blood and nudity, *The Gore-Gore Girls* (1972, aka *Blood Orgy*). It was his forty-ninth film (pseudonyms were sometimes used). Living in Chicago, Lewis later owned movie theaters and an advertising agency.

There were several *Blood Feast* imitators in the sixties, but the real impact of its standard-setting ugliness was not absorbed until the seventies. Meanwhile, for drive-ins and double features, all manner of independently made no-budget horror and fantasy dreck would slither to the screen. A few titles tell the story: *Eegah!* (1963), *They Saved Hitler's Brain* (1963), *The Naked Witch* (1964), *The Creeping Terror* (1964), *Santa Claus Conquers the Martians* (1964), *Monster a Go-Go* (1965), and *The Incredibly Strange Creatures Who Stopped Living and Became Mixed-Up Zombies* (1965). They were sold mostly via outrageous titles, a SHOCKING! poster, and a sensational preview reel. Most came and went quickly only to reemerge a couple years later at midnight on TV creature feature shows. Monster movies never die.

Sexploitation

The nudie-cutie market mushroomed: *B-O-I-N-N-G!* (1962), *Goldilocks and the Three Bares* (1963), *Naked as Nature Intended* (1963), *Take Your Clothes Off and Live* (1964), *My Tale Is Hot!* (1964), *SINderella and the Golden Bra* (1964), and on and on. Hundreds of motion pictures were given the "Approved by the American Sunbathing Association" stamp. Because it was not legally prudent to show physical contact, voyeurism reigned. By 1963, even with the minuscule budgets of topless comedies, it became increasingly difficult to make a buck. There were just too many nude volleyball games.

Russ Meyer, the man who brought laughs to skin theaters with *The Immortal Mr. Teas*, made five additional nudie-cuties: *Eve and the Handyman* (1960), starring his wife; *Erotica* (1961); *Wild Gals of the Naked West* (1961), an effective western spoof; *Europe in the Raw* (1963); and *Heavenly Bodies!* (1963). Like others, Meyer struggled to attract attention in the crowded topless market. So, following the lead of *Private Property* and pictures like *Poor White Trash* (1961), *The*

Animal (1963), and David Friedman and Herschell Gordon Lewis's *Scum of the Earth* (1963), Meyer spawned something in black-and-white, with rural settings and a mixture of suggested sex and violence—the roughie.

Meyer's first roughie was *Lorna* (1964). He directed, produced, shot, and edited, utilizing his customary tight and tiny crew (often as small as three people; actors doubled as sound technicians) and his biggest budget yet, $60,000. James Griffith penned the script and is featured. *Lorna* tells of the sexually frustrated title character (Lorna Maitland) who lives in a backwoods shack with her husband. An escaped convict spies on her as she swims nude and sexually assaults her; Lorna gets turned on. They go back to the shack, but her husband comes home early and wreaks vengeance.

Lorna introduced a key Meyer plot device: the insatiable, voluptuous woman coveted by a dim-witted brute. The film's action is motivated entirely by lust. Despite its reprehensible rape-as-a-turn-on element, the mild nudity of *Lorna* allowed it to be screened at more theaters than nudie-cuties. It was a huge success, especially in the South. Free publicity came when the censorship board of Maryland banned *Lorna*, stating it was that "exceptional motion picture which not

Exploitation Marketing

"SCOOP!! WAKE UP MR. AND MRS. AMERICA. SEE THE PICTURE THAT EXPOSES THE NAKED TRUTH ABOUT THE NATIONS [sic] MOST VITAL PROBLEM."
—*Skid Row* (1938).

How do you sell an awful movie with no known actors? Sometimes a roadshow maven stirred up editorials. Most of the time, exploitation relied on sensational posters and trailers. Hundreds of films were advertised as the most shocking or daring ever made. Like carnival freak shows, anything was said on the outside to lure ticket buyers in.

"SHOCK-FILM OF THE CENTURY!"
—*Tortured Females* (1965)

In the exploitation explosion of the sixties, outrageous lobby posters were remarkably similar. Screaming headlines and nubile, barely clothed women adorned both horror and sex posters. On the former, the female is cowering or tied up; on the latter,

continued

Exploitation Marketing
continued

she's lounging or standing with spread legs. The "ADULTS ONLY" warning was a crucial attention-grabber. Trailers were a tease, cutting away just before the sins and promising to show all in the feature film. Such previews were especially valuable because they played only before similar flicks, thus pitching the target audience.

"SADISM WAS JUST AN APPETIZER FOR THE *BLOODTHIRSTY BUTCHERS!*"

(1970)

By the seventies, when horror was as gruesome as promised and pornography went all the way, it became harder to sell exploitation with a sensational pitch. Instead, a few producers thrived on genuine controversy—even if they created it. Not only did the distributor of *Snuff* start a rumor that the movie contained a real murder, he hired people to picket theaters and he sent fake FBI agents to question those attending.

"FORBIDDEN BY LAW! FORBIDDEN BY SOCIETY! FORBIDDEN BY COMMON DECENCY!"

—*The Forbidden* (1966)

■ ■ ■ ■ ■ ■ ■ ■

only speaks for itself but screams for all to hear that it is obscene."[17] Russ Meyer had his new formula.

The title of Meyer's next film, *Mudhoney* (1965), is followed by the line "leaves a taste of evil!" Written by George Costello and Raymond Friday Locke, it depicts a small Missouri town in the early thirties where a combination of dense men and balloon-breasted women are involved in sins. A Northern stranger (John Furlong) wanders in and becomes entangled in the schemes of an evil drunk (the excellent Hal Hopper), who lies, cheats, rapes, and kills. Lorna Maitland and Rena Horton are featured as prostituting sisters. Meyer made German newcomer Horton a deaf mute because of her thick accent. *Mudhoney* thrives on a cast of rural caricatures, evocative black-and-white cinematography, and the sense of a mythic, Southern-gothic locale. Blink a few times and you'll miss the nudity. *Mudhoney* is Meyer's best film, but it was not a big commercial success.

Meyer followed with a pair of disappointing features. Shot in Germany for prolific producer Albert Zugsmith, *Fanny Hill: Memoirs of a Woman of Pleasure* (1964) is a tame adaptation of the bawdy novel set in an eighteenth-century London brothel. In *Motor Psycho* (1965), a vengeance-seeking couple tangle with a brutal motorcycle gang, but the trip isn't as much fun as it should be.

Then came what filmmaker John Waters has called "beyond a doubt, the best movie ever made. It is possibly better than any film that will be made in the future."[18] *Faster, Pussycat! Kill! Kill!* (1966) is a camp trash classic. "Ladies and gentlemen, welcome to violence: the word and the act. While violence cloaks itself in a plethora of disguises, its favorite mantle still remains: sex." So begins the film, which serves up three typically voluptuous and atypically tough females: Varla (Tura Satana), Rosie (Haji), and Billie (Lori Williams). After a drag race, Varla karate chops a young man to death, and the three go-go dancers kidnap his girlfriend. They spend the remainder of the movie scheming to take money from a paraplegic rancher and his two sons while their perpetually crying captive tries to break free. Murder catches up with the pussycats.

In order to play at all drive-ins, *Faster, Pussycat! Kill! Kill!* contains no nudity (today it would be rated PG-13). Meyer and writer Jack Moran compensated by exaggerating the sexual innuendo, violence, and action. Exotic Varla provides much of all three. She is the ultimate

The bountiful femme fatales of *Faster, Pussycat! Kill! Kill!*
(l-r) Haji, Lori Williams, Tura Satana.
RM Films International, Inc.

amoral, ball-busting dominatrix, brutalizing the entire cast with a wicked tongue and lethal hands. Varla's cracks, Meyer's editing and direction, and the bachelor-pad jazzy score give the picture real zip. As the poster said, "GO-GO For A WILD RIDE With The ACTION GIRLS!"

Russ Meyer assembled a $12,000 color collage of bare-breasted footage played with a soundtrack of stripper interviews and named this "sociological document" *Mondo Topless* (1966). A sweaty saga about the lustful happenings at an out-of-the-way inn, *Common Law Cabin* (1967) is sort of a color roughie. The three lead actresses supposedly had identical measurements of 44-24-34 and were advertised as the "Big 6." The inferior *Good Morning and Goodbye!* (1967) was made around the same time and dealt with similar concerns.

Sexploitation was an easy route into motion picture production. If you had $30,000, something resembling a script, and two weeks to shoot, you could slap together a flick that could turn a profit. Starting with the nudie-cutie *Kiss Me Quick* (1964), Harry Novak and his Box Office International produced and/or released more than 200 soft-core, horror, hillbilly, and other exploitable pictures through the mid-seventies. After eight nudie-cuties like *Nude on the Moon* (1961), the Queen of Sexploitation, Doris Wishman, made the delectable roughie *Bad Girls Go To Hell* (1965). Radley Metzger crafted a rough little exploiter about prostitution, *The Dirty Girls* (1965), before moving on to increasingly better produced soft-core fantasies, starting with *Carmen, Baby* (1967). And a film called *This Picture Is Censored* (1966), produced and directed by Barry Mahon, presented the sex, nudity, and violence censored out of other movies. Predictably, it was banned in some communities, which only fueled its publicity.

By the end of 1967, there was a thriving sexploitation industry with specialized distributors and theaters. In addition to grind-house devotees, better venues had a growing middle-class clientele. The barriers around what was permissible were expanding all the time, attracting news stories and curious ticket buyers.

Avant-Garde

Andy Warhol and John Palmer shot the Empire State Building with an unmoving camera, without sound, from 8:00 PM until dawn on July 30, 1964, stopping only long enough to load new rolls of 16mm film. The completed film lasted eight hours. The closest thing to excitement that occurred was when the sun came up. When *Empire* premiered at the Film-Makers' Cinematheque a few months later, the audience hated it. They booed. They threw stuff at the screen. They left in droves. They demanded a refund and threatened to pummel theater personnel.

It was left to Jonas Mekas to sing its praise. Mekas was then firmly ensconced as the leader and principal advocate of the avant-garde. The previous holder of that title, Maya Deren, passed the torch by guest-writing Mekas's *Village Voice* column shortly before her death from a brain hemorrhage in 1961. She was forty-four.

At the height of its influence, Mekas's *Film Culture* was on-par with France's *Cahiers du Cinéma*. Respected critics such as Andrew Sarris (one of its editors), Pauline Kael, and future director Peter Bogdanovich wrote for the magazine, as did dozens of filmmakers, including Jean-Luc Godard, Stan Brakhage, and John Cassavetes. In 1962 and 1963 *Film Culture* published articles by Sarris that officially brought the auteur theory to America. *Film Culture* ceased regular publication in 1966.

In 1960 Mekas called together a group of independent filmmakers, including Shirley Clarke, Gregory Rogosin, and Emile de Antonio. In their "First Statement" in *Film Culture*, they pronounced the "decay of the Product film" and committed themselves to a cinema of "personal expression" with plans for grants, a festival, and a cooperative circulation center.[19] Formed in 1962, the Film-Makers' Cooperative was an idea that worked. It accepted all 16mm experimental movies regardless of quality and distributed them to whoever was willing to pay. Seventy-five percent of the rental fees were returned to the filmmakers, with the other one-fourth covering costs. The Film-Makers' Co-op has stayed in nonprofit business through the decades. Its present catalogue lists more than 4,000 titles by more than 700 filmmakers. It rents movies to museums, universities, media centers, corporations, and individuals. Mekas also organized a nonprofit venue, the Film-Makers' Cinematheque, which opened in New York in 1964.

Jonas Mekas also made movies. He created the beatnik vanguard picture *Guns in the Trees* (1960), and he turned out a stream of challenging cinematic work, including documentaries. Mekas shot *The Brig* (1964), a harrowing adaptation of a stage work by Kenneth Brown, in one night with a handheld camera. Though the film is fiction, Venice Film Festival jurors thought he had captured a live play and voted it best documentary.

Jonas's brother, Adolfas Mekas, also crafted experimental films. Most famous is the improvisational comedic feature, *Hallelujah the Hills* (1963), which played some commercial theaters. With Adolfas and his friends romping around outdoors mocking movies, *Hallelujah the Hills* could easily have been an embarrassment. Instead, it remains light and mostly fun, filled with visual gags, continuity breaks, and the subversion of cinematic assumptions.

In the first seven years of the sixties—an age that began with beatniks and ended with hippies—the audience for the new cinema blossomed. Vanguard flicks were called "underground movies," and they were the hip thing to see. New works (mostly shorts) were screened each week in cramped venues. Evaluating movies that are often purposely confusing and sloppy can be difficult, but a few films and filmmakers clearly left significant legacies.

Bruce Connor continued his collage experiments. A wide variety of quick, mostly military "found images" are used in *Cosmic Ray* (1962) to mimic a sexual experience. *Report* (1965) is Connor's collage meditation on the Kennedy assassination. Jack Smith made the murky, mythic *Flaming Creatures* (1963), which stirred up controversy for its sexual content. Michael Snow shot *Wavelength* (1967), a continuous forty-five-minute circular pan and zoom that became a film-school staple. And Gregory Markopoulos (who started making experimental shorts in the late forties) crafted movies like *Twice a Man* (1963), which trod on Kenneth Anger's terrain of homosexuality and mythology.

Anger himself forged his most influential motion picture, *Scorpio Rising* (1964), which takes thirteen popular songs from the early sixties and juxtaposes them with different homoerotic motorcycle gang fantasies and assorted masculine images (Hitler, Christ, Brando). Along with Bruce Connor's collages, *Scorpio Rising* charted the territory that music videos would later occupy. Among those who sued over this contentious work were the American Nazi Party (for "desecrating the swastika") and representatives of the Rondells and Bobby Vinton (for failure to obtain music rights). Anger's sly sense of humor was evident as he dedicated the film to the Hell's Angels. He went on to make more polemical movies, most especially *Lucifer Rising* (1973, revised 1980), a worldwide paean to occultism.

Since creating his first short, *Interim* (1951), as a foster teen, Stan Brakhage (1933–) has been one of the most prolific and inventive artists of noncommercial cinema. He has crafted more than 200

Advertising for a Kenneth Anger screening in 1964.

hours. Several unique motion pictures were constructed without a camera by pasting materials or created images directly onto film stock. The most famous is *Mothlight* (1963), which Brakhage fashioned by running moth wings through an optical printer.

Brakhage's *Dog Star Man* (1965) is an underground epic, feature-length, silent, and consistently hypnotic. (It was originally shown as five separate shorts between 1959 and 1964.) The completed feature utilizes a variety of free-form techniques to contemplate such things as the birth of consciousness, the four seasons, the struggle with nature, and the magic of sexuality. *Dog Star Man* predated the full flowering of the psychedelic movement, but its legend as a head trip grew through the late sixties and early seventies.

Always innovative, Brakhage would continue to create a wide variety of experimental films, including *Lovemaking* (1968), *The Act of Seeing With One's Own Eyes* (1971), and *The Text of Light* (1974). He regularly lectured on vanguard cinema and authored the seminal 1963 book *Metaphors of Vision*.

Chappaqua (1966) was not a formal experiment, but it found a home in the growing underground. Conrad Rooks financed, produced, directed, wrote, starred in, and released this feature, none of which he did particularly well. However, the cinematography by the legendary Eugene Schüfftan and Robert Frank is often remarkable, as is the editing. *Chappaqua* tells the confused story of an alcoholic heroin addict (Rooks) searching for a cure in Paris. The slim plot is merely an excuse to show a steady stream of hallucinations: flashbacks to childhood, contrasting styles and colors, and figures like William Burroughs, Allen Ginsburg as the messiah, Ornette Coleman, Dracula, Ravi Shankar and his Eastern music (composer Philip Glass also contributed), and a mishmash of assorted oddities. Viewed without chemical accompaniments, *Chappaqua*, like most head trips, grows tiresome fast. It marks the point where the underground began to turn away from formal experimentation and towards drug-fueled outrageousness.

The shy, insecure son of Czech immigrants, Andy Warhol (1928–1987) grew up in Pittsburgh and later moved to New York City, where his silk-screened images of Campbell's Soup cans, Coca-Cola bottles, and iconic celebrities earned him worldwide notoriety in the early sixties. The blank-faced Warhol, with his white fright wig and laconic monotone, loved the fame. He became the informal CEO of his own Factory, a loft that served as a magnet for New York's underground artists, the hip, the beautiful, the stoned, the lost. Through the years, in addition to painting, Andy Warhol was involved in publishing, writing, photography, music, and television. One of the first and most significant areas he branched into was cinema. He bought a 16mm camera in 1963. Telling friends that he had no idea how to load or focus it, the pop artist said, "I'm going to make bad films."[20]

Andy Warhol was a man of his word. Four hours a night for several nights, he filmed his sleeping friend John Giorno. The camera didn't move; Giorno moved just a little. Warhol cut the footage into a six-hour silent epic called, appropriately, *Sleep* (1963). The result was a movie that very few people saw and even fewer sat through until the end, yet the controversy it stirred brought new and wider attention to vanguard film. What were people to make of a six-hour motion picture in which virtually nothing happens? Mainstream critics dismissed it, but some hip New Yorkers read it as a test of patience or were drawn to it as a focus for meditation.

Warhol followed *Sleep* with a series of silent, static, one-subject movies. He shot them day and night at the Factory, utilizing whoever was hanging around. The camera, like Warhol, adopted the pose of detached and bored observer. Titles include *Haircut* (one man cutting another's hair), *Eat* (a man taking thirty-three minutes to eat a mushroom), *Empire* (an eight-hour continuous view of the Empire State Building), *Drunk* (seventy minutes of independent filmmaker Emile de Antonio downing a quart of whiskey), and *Taylor Mead's Ass* (a seventy-minute examination of . . . well, you get the idea). Warhol said of this 1963–1964 period: "I made my earliest films using, for several hours, just one actor on the screen doing the same thing; eating or sleeping or smoking; I did this because people usually just go to the movies to see only the star, to eat him up, so here at least is a chance to look only at the star for as long as you like, no matter what he does, and to eat him up all you want. It was also easier to make."[21]

Most of these flicks played only at the Factory. In 1965, the pop artist began creating sound films starring the Factory's drugged-out Edie Sedgwick. Such movies were usually senseless conversations, sometimes interrupted by senseless violence. Paul Morrissey (1939–), a social worker from the Bronx, showed up at the Factory around this time and recorded the sound for *My Hustler* (1965), the first Warhol movie in which the camera moves. It was also the first to turn a profit.

Between June and September of 1966, Warhol shot numerous one- and two-reel motion pictures at the Factory, in various apartments, and at Manhattan's Chelsea Hotel. The shorts present raw confessions, spontaneous violence, drug-taking, and "real emotions"; they blur the line between acting and reality, gay and straight. When Jonas Mekas prodded the pop artist for a feature to show at Cinematheque, Warhol and Morrissey edited the vignettes together so that two shorts ran side-by-side simultaneously, mixing action and conversation, color and black-and-white, sound and silence (the audio for only one side of the split screen plays at a time).

The completed three-and-a-half-hour mishmash of footage is *Chelsea Girls* (1966). After two sold-out months at Cinematheque, it moved into more mainstream theaters and emerged as the first underground movie to creep aboveground. *Chelsea Girls* was invited to the Cannes Film Festival, but it was denied an official presentation after French critics walked out en masse. Its legend only grew. In America, the film captured the curiosity of intellectuals as much as it did underground trippers. Shocking when not banal (but mostly banal), *Chelsea Girls* was championed by some mainstream critics. *The New York Times* gave it a mixed review, calling it "a travelogue of hell—a grotesque menagerie of lost souls whimpering in a psyche-delic moonscape . . ."[22]

Warhol made a few improvisational movies in 1967 (the year of the "Summer of Love") that were barely shown. One of them, *I, A Man*, featured a wannabe screenwriter and radical feminist named Valerie Solanas. In June of 1968 (the year of assassinations), she fired three bullets at close range into Andy Warhol's chest and abdomen, nearly killing him in an act that symbolized the end of innocence for the avant-garde. (The event and its preceding days were recreated in Mary Harron's semi-indie *I Shot Andy Warhol*, 1996.) The under-ground was becoming less about formal experimentation and more about outrageousness, about pandering to youthful rebellion and the drug culture. And it worked. The new cinema was about to reach astonishing heights in popularity.

Feeling the power of the surging youth movement, middle-aged Jonas Mekas addressed his comments to the film establishment in December 1966: "This is what I have to tell the old croaks: Give up the fort, we're climbing up the walls, we are climbing up the gate—we'll scalp you by dawn. You know, by now, that you can't beat us, so why don't you join us? But before you join us, leave your tastes outside, by the door. We want your unconditional surrender! This is an ultima-tum from the underground!"[23]

Documentary

Cinema verité developed simultaneously on both sides of the Atlantic. The concept of direct cinema had actually been around since Lumière and Edison captured everyday activities. After World War II, the bleak location shooting of neorealism was a great influence. In America, independent films like *The Little Fugitive, On the Bowery, Jazz on a Summer's Day*, and *Shadows* were clearly experimenting with what would be called *cinema verité* techniques. Then D. A. Pennebaker and Richard Leacock made a pioneering direct cinema TV movie called *Primary* (1960), which covered, without comment, the 1960 Democratic Presidential primary between John F. Kennedy and

Hubert Humphrey. It was the first of a series of television documentaries that featured raw footage instead of the typical polished interviews, voice-over commentary, and archival material.

Cinema verité at its purest is unfiltered and unreconstructed—just turn the camera on and watch people. The possibility for such freedom increased in the Kennedy age with new, portable, synch-sound equipment. Suddenly cameramen could easily capture action, be it real or staged. Movies could be made faster with smaller crews, and they could be made cheaper, leading to more opportunities for independent filmmakers.

An engineering graduate of Yale and MIT, D. A. (Don Alan) Pennebaker (1925–) moved from electronics to advertising to documentaries. It was in the latter that he found his calling, crafting nonfiction flicks in the fifties. In 1959, he entered into a cooperative agreement with fellow *verité* advocates Richard Leacock, Shirley Clarke, Willard Van Dyke, and Albert Maysles. The group, called Filmakers (not to be confused with Lupino and Young's production company), shared equipment and worked jointly on projects. Alone or in tandem, Pennebaker directed groundbreaking television programming.

An inherent risk of direct cinema is that without the usual commentary and archival material the subject will not prove interesting enough to carry a film. Some of Pennebaker's early work suffers this fate. In 1965, however, he caught the right person at the right time when he and his three-man crew shot Bob Dylan (then twenty-four) touring England at his musical peak. Captured with a handheld camera in grainy, often poorly lit black-and-white, with less-than-ideal sound quality, *Don't Look Back* (1967) has the feel of fly-on-the-wall authenticity, even though Dylan seems aware of the lens during candid moments. Though Dylan comes off as an egotistical jerk in the many interviews, the high points are the classic songs. The movie's first sequence in which Dylan holds up cue cards with words from "Subterranean Homesick Blues" and drops each at the appropriate time in the song is terrific music video; MTV played it frequently in the early eighties. When no distributor would touch it, Pennebaker distributed *Don't Look Back* himself. He went on to specialize in music documentaries.

Emile de Antonio (1920–1989) grew up in a wealthy family and was educated at Harvard. After a series of occupations (longshoreman, barge captain, book editor, teacher), he turned his leftist political philosophy towards the big screen. De Antonio constructed his first feature, *Point of Order* (1964), from television footage of the Army-McCarthy hearings of 1954. This mesmerizing historical document presents Senator Joseph McCarthy and his aide Roy Cohn as they entangle themselves in a web of their own making. You can see the end of McCarthyism etched into the Senator's face as charges of a wide network of communists in the federal government repeatedly go unsubstantiated while evidence of his unethical tactics mounts. Joseph McCarthy was censored and effectively silenced after these hearings (he died in 1957).

De Antonio was never silenced. He made *That's Where the Action Is* (1965), about New York City's mayoral campaign, and *Rush to Judgement* (1967), about the JFK assassination. In the coming years— as a war raged in Vietnam and Richard Nixon sat in the Oval Office— Emile de Antonio's documentaries would grow even more radical.

In the late fifties, law professor Frederick Wiseman (1930–) took his students into the Bridgewater (Massachusetts) Hospital for the Criminally Insane to encourage compassion for society's less fortunate. In the next decade, recognizing the power of cinema, Wiseman turned away from legal briefs and towards independent film. He produced Shirley Clarke's *The Cool World*, on which he lost money. Later, still haunted by the horrifying images of life in the state mental hospital, he obtained permission to shoot inside Bridgewater from Massachusetts Attorney General Edward Brooks and Lieutenant Governor Elliot Richardson (who later served in Nixon's cabinet). The resulting *verité* documentary, *Titicut Follies* (1967), so-named for a play the inmates perform, generated more legal controversy than any film since *The Birth of a Nation*. It is the only motion picture banned in America for reasons other than obscenity; the exhibition of it was suppressed for twenty-four years.

Titicut Follies is difficult to watch and impossible to forget. Shot in 16mm black-and-white, without narration, it presents a world where abuse is routine. The male inmates of Bridgewater are stripped of their humanity. They are herded around naked, mocked, insulted, injured, and ignored by the guards. One is brutally cut while being shaved. Another is callously force-fed through a tube in his nose (neglected, he later dies). These supposed patients are seen as they really are: victims of a dangerously cruel institution.

Titicut Follies premiered at the 1967 New York Film Festival. No one who saw it was unmoved, but critics split over its shocking content. *The New York Times* called it "an extraordinarily candid picture of a modern Bedlam, where the horrors are composed of indifference and patronizing concern."[24] Brendan Gill wrote in *The New Yorker*, "It is a sickening picture from start to finish. . . . It has no justification for existing except to the extent that it is intended to have legislative and other non-aesthetic consequences."[25]

Massachusetts officials saw the horrors of *Titicut Follies* as clearly as every other viewer, but they had a different response. Elliot Richardson was elected Attorney General of Massachusetts at approximately the same time as Wiseman's documentary played the New York Film Festival. Richardson instituted a successful legal challenge to prevent the movie from being commercially screened. His argument was that because the inmates (many of whom are seen fully nude) had not given proper permission to be viewed on public screens, *Titicut Follies* was an invasion of their privacy. Wiseman countered that he had such permission, and that it was always obtained in the presence of a guard.

Whatever their motivations, the opponents of *Titicut Follies* raised valid questions about the responsibility of documentarians to their subjects. Did all the dozens of men seen exposed and suffering know what they were giving permission for? Could the movie have been shot so as not to infringe upon people's basic level of privacy or was such footage necessary to fully document the state's abuses? In this case, Wiseman clearly felt it was better to show the naked truth than temper it, even though it prevented his movie from being theatrically distributed. Wiseman says, "Rather than launching an investigation into conditions in our mental institutions, the state went after my film. I suppose it was a case of wanting to kill the messenger."[26] Some officials suppressed the message, but the conditions exposed in *Titicut Follies* were not ignored. The movie generated much controversy and editorializing. After a special screening, the Massachusetts legislature launched investigations into mental facilities and made improvements in Bridgewater. (The hospital continued to be plagued by further scandals in subsequent years.)

It was the Massachusetts Supreme Court that kept *Titicut Follies* from commercial theaters. For more than two decades, the groundbreaking *cinema verité* documentary could be shown only to professionals and students involved in mental health issues. Ironically, the

Bridgewater Hospital screened it annually for its employees—as a training film on what not to do. In 1969, a $5 million civil lawsuit for breach of privacy was brought against Frederick Wiseman by thirty-five inmates; the suit was rejected in 1972. With the argument that enough time had passed to negate privacy rights, *Titicut Follies* was finally set free by the Massachusetts Supreme Court in 1991. It was first shown on PBS later that year, with some controversy over its male nudity. Though it was not released for twenty-four years, the martyred *Titicut Follies*—with its *verité* style, bold content, and sociological purpose—anticipated a true independent film revolution.

Two other films stirred up even greater attention. The biggest commercial hit of 1967 was *The Graduate*, from the semi-indie Avco-Embassy. *The Graduate* emphasizes the then much discussed generation gap. It champions impulsive youth while ridiculing the values of financially successful adults. The other key film of 1967 was Hollywood's *Bonnie and Clyde*, which turns murderous outlaws into heroes and, for the mainstream, spilled a trailblazing quantity of blood. Highlighting *Bonnie and Clyde*, the December 8, 1967 issue of *Time* magazine announced in a cover story: "The New Cinema: Violence . . . Sex . . . Art." It sounded like a formula. It was the beginning of a wave.

The next wave would consist of an explosion of renegade activity, the charge of zealous troops fresh out of film schools, and, above all else, a willingness to shatter old barriers, disregard moral judgements and genre conventions, and explore uncharted and previously taboo territory. Watch out, old croaks. The next few years would be nothing less than the most exciting time in the history of cinema.

Notes

[1] Mekas, Jonas, "The New American Cinema," *Film Culture* (Spring 1962), 7.

[2] Turan, Kenneth and Stephen F. Zito, 31.

[3] Gomery, Douglas, 193.

[4] Jacobs, Diane, *Hollywood Renaissance* (New York: Delta, 1977), 31.

[5] Mekas, Jonas, *Village Voice*, 27 Jan. 1960.

6   Thompson, Howard, "On Making a Movie 'Connection.' " *New York Times*, 6 Nov. 1960.
7   *New Yorker*, 17 Nov. 1962.
8   *Pacific Film Archives*, Sept./Oct. 1992.
9   *LA Weekly*, Feb. 7–13, 1997.
10 Fischer, Dennis, "Roger Corman's Little Shop of Horrors," *Cinefantastique 17*, 1 (Jan. 1987), 30.
11 Corman, Roger, with Jim Jerome, 104.
12 During his fifty-seven year career, Folsey was nominated thirteen times for a cinematography Academy Award; he never won.
13 *Variety*, 10 July 1963.
14 Sherman, Eric and Martin Rubin, *The Director's Event: Interviews With Five American Film-Makers* (New York: Atheneum, 1970), 174.
15 *New York Times*, 30 July 1964.
16 Cowie, Peter, *Coppola* (New York: Charles Scribner's Sons, 1989), 27.
17 de Grazia, Edward, and Roger K. Newman, *Banned Films: Movies, Censors & the First Amendment* (New York: R. R. Bowker, 1982), 276.
18 Waters, John, *Shock Value: A Tasteful Book About Bad Taste* (New York: Delta, 1981), 192.
19 *Film Culture* 22–23 (1961), 131.
20 Bockris, Victor, *The Life and Death of Andy Warhol* (New York: Bantam, 1989), 133.
21 Berg, Gretchen, "Andy Warhol: My True Story," *Los Angeles Free Press 6*, 11 (1967).
22 *New York Times*, 2 Dec. 1966.
23 *Village Voice*, 1 Dec. 1966.
24 *New York Times*, 4 Oct. 1967.
25 *New Yorker*, 28 Oct. 1967.
26 *Los Angeles Times*, 14 Oct. 1991.

1968-1974

PUSHING THE ENVELOPE

Who will survive—and what will be left of them?
—ADVERTISING SLOGAN FOR *THE TEXAS
CHAINSAW MASSACRE*

I hate entertainment.—JOHN CASSAVETES[1]

It was marked by the assassinations of Martin Luther King, Jr. and Robert Kennedy at the beginning and the resignation of Richard Nixon at the end. During the years between, war raged in Vietnam, protesters marched on campuses, drug use accelerated, sexual mores relaxed, and Watergate wracked the nation. Disregard for authority grew.

Independent film both led and followed the revolution. While Hollywood stayed on the sidelines and waited for something to be popular, nonstudio cinema plunged right in. There were no rules anymore. Horror flicks explored the boundaries of blood, sexploitation pictures were usurped by hard-core pornography, and underground movies went to shocking extremes. Whether as an artistic choice or out of economic necessity, *cinema verité* techniques—especially shaky handheld cameras and natural lighting—lent many independent films an anticorporate legitimacy.

This was also the time when Martin Scorsese, George Lucas, Brian De Palma, Oliver Stone, and Steven Spielberg launched their directing careers. Prospective directors were now coming out of film schools—steeped in foreign classics and the auteur theory—and many sprinted off to make independent movies instead of climbing the traditionally slow ascent up the Hollywood ladder.

In these years of marijuana smoke and protest chants, the most important single event for the future of outlaw cinema took place in a room filled with middle-aged men in gray suits. When producers were unable to obtain Code approval for a few quality features, the Motion Picture Association of America finally ended its opposition to age classifications. In the hope of averting increasingly frequent censorship battles, the MPAA instituted the modern ratings system in November 1968. With this, the Production Code was swiftly killed, thirty-eight years after its birth. In its place was a voluntary procedure to which, like the Code, virtually every nonexploitation producer agreed. Movies would be rated "G" (general audience), "PG" (parental guidance suggested; originally called "GP"), "R" (restricted; no one under seventeen admitted unless accompanied by parent or guardian), and "X" (adults only; usually set at under-eighteen not admitted. "PG-13" (parents strongly cautioned) and "NC-17" (no one under seventeen admitted) were instituted in 1984 and 1990, respectively.

At first, adult dramas and comedies were released with X ratings (most notably the mainstream success *Midnight Cowboy*, 1969), but the X label (or XXX) was quickly appropriated by the flourishing pornography industry. Blue movies wore their scarlet X (without actual MPAA disapproval) as a badge of honor. Whatever the intention, the ratings system created a home for sexually explicit movies and helped shelter them from censorship. After all, the argument followed, since all motion pictures are now clearly labeled, shouldn't informed adults be allowed to view whatever entertainment they desire? It made it difficult for any remaining censors to win a battle, even on grounds of obscenity. At the same time, the R rating separated the adult from the ADULT!!! This led to a marked increase in mainstream movies in which profanity, sex, and violence were integral to the story.

The censors were effectively silenced at the same time that rebels were pushing the barriers. Add to this mix the volatile culture of the Nixon era—along with a legion of talented young artists, a few wily veterans, and some courageous gamblers—and you had a cinematic revolution, the American New Wave. Though the studios quickly absorbed many of the auteurs and ideas of this movement, the American New Wave was born in the cameras of low-budget visionaries struggling to make a statement, make art, and make a living in the scorned, abused, and sometimes transcendent world of independent film.

Revolution Now

Nineteen sixty-nine was the year half a million people gathered at Woodstock for three days of peace, love, and music; ten thousand young Americans died in Vietnam; two marches on Washington, DC each drew more than a quarter of a million war protestors; and, in December, three hundred thousand people attended a rock concert at Altamont Speedway, where a black man was stomped to death by Hell's Angels, symbolically bringing to an end the peace and love of the Age of Aquarius. And yet 1969 was a year like any other for the studios. The biggest moneymaker—and winner of four Academy Awards—was Twentieth-Century Fox's *Butch Cassidy and the Sundance Kid*, a likeable western with two wisecracking criminals and a bicycle-riding interlude to the tune of "Raindrops Keeping Falling on My Head."

Meanwhile, on a Southwestern highway, Wyatt (as in Wyatt Earp) and Billy (as in Billy the Kid), two long-haired, dope-smoking rebels, roared by on psychedelic choppers as "Born To Be Wild" wailed. It was an independent event that spoke to a generation and young adults went to this "western" over and over. *Easy Rider* (1969) opened in the summer of Woodstock and by the end of the year was the most successful nonstudio motion picture since D. W. Griffith wrote history with lightning.

The idea for a different kind of biker flick originated in the recorded mutterings of Peter Fonda, the thirty-year-old son of legendary actor Henry Fonda, brother of Jane Fonda and father of Bridget Fonda. Of his few minor acting credits, most notable were two starring turns for Roger Corman, the successful pot-smoking biker romp *The Wild Angels* (1966), and the LSD fantasy *The Trip* (1967). The latter was scripted by Jack Nicholson and costarred Dennis Hopper. Thirty-three-year-old Hopper had begun earning a living as an actor in *Rebel Without a Cause* (1955); wallowing in booze and drugs, he had failed to break through.

Now Fonda as producer and Hopper as director took the idea for *Easy Rider* (then called *The Loners*) to AIP, the roadhouse of biker flicks. AIP expressed interest but was not eager to let the volatile Hopper direct. So Fonda pitched it to producer Bert Schneider, cocreator of "The Monkees" TV series. With his sense for the youth market, Schneider saw potential. He provided the $360,000 budget (eventually $500,000). They would make it themselves. Fonda, Hopper, legendary screenwriter/novelist Terry Southern, and (uncredited) Nicholson fleshed out a screenplay. Who did how much writing is disputed. Hopper was director and starred in the role of Billy. Fonda produced and costarred as Wyatt (aka "Captain America" for his flaglike gas tank and helmet). Jack Nicholson, thirty-two, had also been on-screen for more than a decade, mostly in forgotten Corman productions like the Hellman "lost" westerns. He too seem destined for the sidelines of stardom. Now he accepted the role of alcoholic lawyer George Hanson when Rip Torn backed out.[2]

Shooting in 16mm took place in the Southwest and South. Many of the locals who appear are authentic, as are their reactions to the two flamboyant longhairs on wild choppers. Every joint smoked on-screen was real, supposedly for reasons of authenticity (and fun), but it seems to further anesthetize the already laid-back performances of Fonda and Hopper. Nicholson, however, is electric. According to legend, generous amounts of LSD and cocaine were used by the cast and crew. The friendship of Fonda and Hopper was severed during the volatile production. As their director was deluded by chemicals and megalomania, cinematographer Laszlo Kovacs and editor Donn Cambern strived to cover up Hopper's excesses and technical sloppiness.

Easy Rider begins with Wyatt and Billy selling Mexican cocaine to an American dealer (music producer Phil Spector). They buy fancy motorcycles, hide their money in the gas tanks, and begin a road trip to New Orleans. Along the way they smoke dope by a campfire, stay on a ranch, smoke more dope by a campfire, stay on a hippie commune, and say a lot of groovy things that are supposed to be profound. *Easy Rider* doesn't really kick in until Wyatt and Billy meet George. They expose the lawyer to the freedom of choppers and smoking dope by campfires ("Lord have mercy, is that what I think it is?" George asks). It was a star-making performance by Nicholson, even though his character is doomed, beaten to death by rednecks.

Wyatt and Billy continue to New Orleans and Mardi Gras, where they drop LSD with two hookers (Toni Basil and Karen Black) in a cemetery. After they're rich with drug money, Wyatt tells Billy, "We blew it, man." Because of the spiritual costs of their journey? Because they've bought into the American dream? (Fonda's stated motivation was that the director—the tyrannical, drug-fueled Hopper—had blown their chance for success.) The pair ride down another country road only to be shot dead by unknown locals in a pickup truck.

The term "easy rider" is slang for men who live off the wages of women, and it can be seen as a metaphor for the fatuous materialism of America. Still, contrary to its reputation, *Easy Rider* has almost nothing to do with radical politics or hippie enlightenment. It's closer to the Hell's Angels than Abbie Hoffman. Furthermore, it seems frequently to be mocking its heroes and, in a broader sense, institutions of the counterculture. Whether or not this was the filmmakers' aim is up for debate. Fonda says it was; Hopper disagrees. Regardless, young people recognized something fresh and liberating in *Easy Rider*. They responded to its positive depiction of drugs, its rock-and-roll soundtrack, and its sense of abandon.

The shocking conclusion hit hard. For some it hit too hard—Bob Dylan pleaded with the filmmakers to change it. It solidified Billy and Wyatt as martyrs. It also confirmed what most longhairs felt squares thought of them (before pulling the trigger, the hillbilly asks the then familiar question, "Why don't you get a haircut?"). Along with the assassinations of King and Kennedy the year before and the upcoming murder at Altamont, the sudden violence symbolized an end to youthful idealism.

Easy Rider had its mainstream supporters upon release. Though aware of its contradictions, critic Pauline Kael grasped its appeal, how it "attracts a new kind of 'inside' audience, whose members enjoy tuning in together to a whole complex of shared signals and attitudes . . . the movie obviously rings true to the audience's vision. It's cool to feel that you can't win, and that it's rigged and hopeless. It's even cool to believe in purity and sacrifice."[3]

Released by stodgy Columbia, *Easy Rider* grossed more than $40 million worldwide at a time when tickets sold for $2.50 or less. Fonda (15½ percent) and Hopper (11 percent) received substantial shares of the profits (Hopper later sued for a bigger slice; he lost). With Terry Southern, they were nominated for screenwriting Academy Awards.

(Southern received only $3,500 for his work on *Easy Rider*, despite credible evidence that he did virtually all of the writing. He was broke at the time and in debt when he died in 1995.) The two long-haired rebels were suddenly the hot outsiders who showed the Hollywood suits how to reach the youth culture. Predictably, the studios came calling. Fonda directed and starred in an offbeat western, *The Hired Hand* (1971); it flopped. He soon returned to a stream of forgettable acting roles. Hopper directed, wrote, and starred in a pretentious tragedy, *The Last Movie* (1971); it flopped. He spent many years in a drug haze, but recovered in the mid-eighties. Since then he has been a captivating actor and less-successful director. Nicholson pocketed only a tiny slice of *Easy Rider*'s immense profits, but the movie made his career. He was nominated for a supporting actor Academy Award—his first of eleven nominations so far (he's won three). He would, of course, go on to much bigger paydays.

The shotgun blasts at the end of *Easy Rider* reverberated throughout Hollywood. The studios scrambled to attract the counterculture. In the early seventies, traditionally cautious corporations churned out road pictures and drug pictures and sensitive-loner pictures, all hoping to duplicate *Easy Rider*'s box-office numbers. Most didn't come close—though a few are artistically superior. The real legacy of *Easy Rider* is that it officially ushered in the American New Wave of small, personal, frequently challenging movies.

While *Easy Rider* was attracting the long-haired hippies, another off-Hollywood movie drew the smaller constituency of short-haired leftists. *Medium Cool* (1969) was everything *Easy Rider* wasn't: fiercely political, precisely constructed and shot, and authentic to a fault. Influenced by the films of Jean-Luc Godard as well as Marshall McLuhan's media theories (from which the title was appropriated), Haskell Wexler (1926–) set out to craft a motion picture that would weave fact with fiction. He would succeed to an extent he never anticipated. Wexler was already an Academy Award–winning cinematographer by the time he wrote, directed, shot, and coproduced *Medium Cool*. He was also a committed leftist, concerned about the injustices of modern America. He had previously made the political documentary *The Bus* (1965), about the March on Washington.

Medium Cool was conceived as an ironic parable about a passive Chicago reporter (Robert Forster) who becomes increasingly drawn into the political and sociological ramifications of the stories he covers.

The detached observer. Robert Forster shoots tragedy in *Medium Cool*.
Copyright © 1969 Paramount Pictures. Courtesy of Paramount Pictures.

He has an affair with a poor widow (Verna Bloom), befriends her son,
and quits his job when he learns that his television network is handing
his tapes over to the FBI. Real footage and amateur performers mix
with staged scenes and professional actors. As in *Easy Rider*, the main
characters meet a violent end. When their car explodes in a park, people snap photos and the camera pans to reveal Haskell Wexler shooting with his camera. Wexler then pans to the audience watching him,
implicating the viewer as an idle voyeur in the preceding events.

Medium Cool is a unique intellectual exercise from start to finish,
but what really sets it apart is that much of its footage was shot in
Chicago at the 1968 Democratic Convention. As Chicago's Mayor
Daily ruled inside the amphitheater, hundreds of Vietnam War protestors were beaten by police in Grant Park and surrounding streets
as the world watched. Wexler, a native Chicagoan, had had a hunch
that there would be trouble, and he plunges us right into the thick of
it. At times actors from the "fictional" film are on-camera amidst real

rioting. During a violent sequence, someone in the actual film crew can be heard shouting, "Watch out, Haskell! It's real!"

In 1968, *Medium Cool* was considered a revolutionary document. Paramount picked it up but kept it on a shelf for more than a year. Wexler later learned through the Freedom of Information Act that *Medium Cool* was under surveillance from at least four federal agencies and that the government tried to convince Gulf-Western (Paramount's parent company) not to distribute it. Paramount released *Medium Cool* only after *Easy Rider*'s tremendous antiestablishment success and as eight— soon to be seven—alleged instigators of the Chicago protests went to trial. Even then, Wexler had to delete provocations ("Let's get the fuckers") uttered by the police and add provocations ("Pigs eat shit") from the protestors. The movie was given an X rating by the MPAA board, officially because of frontal nudity, but mostly because of politics. Fiercely intellectual, *Medium Cool* was a critical but not a commercial success.

Haskell Wexler went on to make such political documentaries as *Brazil: A Report on Torture* (1971, with Saul Landau); *Interviews with My Lai Veterans* (1971, with Joseph Strick); and *Introduction to the Enemy* (1974, with Jane Fonda, Tom Hayden, and Bill Yahrans). Wexler has also shot various indies, fact and fiction, while maintaining his status as one of Hollywood's elite cinematographers. *Medium Cool* echoes throughout his work.

John Cassavetes

John Cassavetes leaped back into independent filmmaking, adapting an unproduced play he had written called "The Marriage." Actors—all friends of Cassavetes—performed most of the technical duties. Stop-and-start shooting took eight months; stop-and-start editing lasted two years. The completed feature, blandly entitled *Faces* (1968), is the rawest of Cassavetes's pictures. In the black-and-white, *verité* style of *Shadows*, with poor lighting and sound and no musical soundtrack, *Faces* lays bare a failed upper-middle-class marriage. Shot almost entirely in houses and bars, it has an alcohol-addled, claustrophobic feel. Unlike *Shadows*, *Faces* was thoroughly scripted, although, as always, Cassavetes gave his actors a green light to improvise.

"What the hell are we talking about?" Dick (John Marley) asks at a drunken gathering. "Who cares!" comes the reply. Exactly. After an opening scene which assails the movie studios, aging Dick has an after-work rendezvous with call girl Jeannie (Cassavetes's wife, Gena Rowlands). The film concludes the next day with Dick's wife Maria (Lynn Carlin) saying to him, "I hate my life. I just don't love you." In between are hollow trysts between Dick and Jeannie and Maria and Chet (Seymour Cassel). A fourteen-year marriage implodes, and the pain is intense.

Faces is itself a painful moviegoing experience, loaded with shrill laughter but no humor, nonsensical conversations, and a barrage of self-hating bitterness. It is jarring (if not boring) because it plays in virtual real time, not the increased tempo of most other non-avant-garde films. To watch *Faces* is to be stuck for two hours with a drunken husband and wife revealing their anxieties. Actors are brutalized with close-ups (shot from across the room with a long lens) to emphasize the rugged terrain of skin under a microscope. *Faces* is almost never enjoyable. Still, two years after the similarly themed Oscar-winner *Who's Afraid of Virginia Woolf?*, many adults found in Cassavetes's psychological drama an honest portrait of real emotions. For these viewers, the discomfort they experienced watching *Faces* merely confirmed its raw honesty, so unlike the sugary emotions served up by Hollywood.

Telling the kind of small, personal stories the studios wouldn't touch was always Cassavetes's goal. And in this case he stumbled onto a formula that a sizeable portion of the general public and the Hollywood community applauded. Though reviews were split, *Faces* was a surprise box-office success. In the same year in which Cassavetes starred in *Rosemary's Baby*, *Faces* earned him an Academy Award nomination for screenwriting. Lynn Carlin and Seymour Cassel were nominated for supporting actress and actor.

Written and directed for Columbia, *Husbands* (1970) is filled with raw emotions, middle-aged angst, and stumbling improvisations. It is the most "independent" studio film of the American New Wave. Cassavetes also turned out an implausible romance for Universal, *Minnie and Moskowitz* (1971).

Then he began a two-year, start-and-stop journey to make his masterpiece. As usual, the cast and crew worked for no up-front pay. Cassavetes and Peter Falk financed the film out of their bank accounts. When the money ran out, Cassavetes mortgaged his house to keep rolling. It was the only American motion picture to play at the

1974 New York Film Festival, and it was well received, but after the losses incurred by *Husbands* and *Minnie and Moskowitz*, no distributor would touch a John Cassavetes movie.

A Woman Under the Influence (1974) is a two-hour-and-thirty-five-minute acting tour de force. Mabel (Gena Rowlands), housewife and mother, loves her blue-collar husband, Nick (Peter Falk), and he loves her, but he has trouble understanding her and she increasingly has trouble communicating. Mabel grows insecure around her own children, behaving like a child herself. Eventually, under pressure from his mother (Katherine Cassavetes, the director's mom), Nick has Mabel committed to a mental asylum. When she returns, the couple is determined to succeed, but the situation seems just as hopeless—though as loving—as before she left.

Rowlands's performance as the vulnerable, volatile Mabel Longhetti is spellbinding; she deservedly received a Best Actress Oscar nomination. Cassavetes was also rightly nominated for his surprisingly precise directing; he always finds an interesting place for the camera. The kitchen confrontation between Nick, Mabel, and a doctor is unforgettable for its passion, but the scene where Nick rides with his young kids on the back of a truck, lets them drink beer, and gently caresses his daughter's face is equally memorable for its special calm. When Nick invites his hard-hat coworkers in and Mabel serves up spaghetti, the festering tension of a woman trying to hold herself together is almost unbearable. As its very title implies, *A Woman Under the Influence* brings up intriguing questions about the role of women in a changing society. In the feminist rhetoric of the era, it showcases the "housewife in bondage" struggling to find fulfillment. It also represents the full fruition of Cassavetes's non-Hollywood style.

When all the established companies passed on releasing his best movie, Cassavetes set up his own distribution company, Faces International, in order to distribute it himself. As *A Woman Under the Influence* was booked into theaters, Cassavetes, Falk, and Rowlands toured the country promoting it. The critical reception and two Oscar nominations helped the film get noticed. It earned more than $6 million in North America, a respectable showing. Few who saw *A Woman Under the Influence* forgot it. Through the years, even with its scarce availability on videotape and television, its reputation has grown. In a 1996 poll, *Filmmaker* magazine named *A Woman Under the Influence* the most important independent film of all time.[4] Though perhaps

Gena Rowlands in *A Woman Under the Influence*.
© 1974 Faces Distribution Corporation.

that's an overstatement, *A Woman Under the Influence* is a fiercely emotional movie from a fiercely autonomous director and the quintessen-
tial motion picture of the American New Wave.

Peter Bogdanovich

Robert Altman, Hal Ashby, Bob Rafelson, Mike Nichols, and Francis Ford Coppola are crucial members of the American New Wave who did not helm a single independent feature during this period (though Altman would specialize in indies and semi-indies in the future). They made their small, distinct features with the blessing and financing of the studios. In the wake of *Easy Rider*, as the majors backed unconventional movies like *Five Easy Pieces* (1970) and *Harold and Maude* (1971), there was a blurring in artistic content between studio and independent films. This forced true outsiders to be even more creative and/or outrageous in order to get noticed in the changing marketplace.

The American New Wave, like its earlier French counterpart, was fueled by energetic rookies. One traveled the same route as his *Cahiers du Cinéma* cousins; he actually wrote for that publication. Peter Bogdanovich (1939–) had also been a writer for *Film Culture*, a programmer of films at the New Yorker Theater and the Museum of Modern Art, and an occasional director of off-Broadway plays. Then, in 1965, his life was changed, like many others, by the Drive-In Deity. Movie nerd Bogdanovich first worked on *The Wild Angels*, and he was assigned

■ ■ ■ ■ ■ ■ ■ ■

Below-the-Line

In movie budget language, actors, directors, producers, and screenwriters are "above-the-line" and receive the biggest salaries and credits. However, the following "below-the-line" categories can be just as crucial.

CINEMATOGRAPHY. A scarcity of time and money often limits lighting and camera choices, and yet cinematographers have distinguished themselves with low budgets. Twelve Oscar-winners have shot independent films, including Gregg Toland, Leon Shamroy, James Wong Howe, and Haskell Wexler. Among the best photographed indies: *Tabu, Badlands, Let's Get Lost, Ulee's Gold.*

EDITING. Most non-studio movies are cut according to the rules of cinematic grammar. Still, the underground and *cinéma vérité* impacted independent editing in the sixties and seventies via such techniques as jump cuts and real-time pacing (see *Greetings* and *Faces*). Furthermore, there has always been more experimentation away from Hollywood. Notable indies: *The*

continued

Below-the-Line *continued*

Plow That Broke the Plains; Mean Streets; El Mariachi; fast, cheap & out of control.

PRODUCTION DESIGN. With slim design budgets, sets and props are often current and ordinary. That said, some nonstudio features have created distinctive designs. Notable indies: *Phantom of the Paradise, Hester Street, Eraserhead, Nowhere.*

MUSICAL SCORE. Music is an important but underappreciated component of filmmaking. It conveys information, establishes moods, and maintains continuity. As with production design, skimping in this category harms many low-budget films. *Easy Rider, Reservoir Dogs*, and others make good use of popular songs. Those with effective original scores include *Sisters, Halloween*, and *Safe*.

SOUND. Modern studio films almost never have poor audio, yet murky dialogue and hollow soundtracks have long plagued independents, mostly because of inexperienced crews. *The Honeymoon Killers* and *Straight Out of Brooklyn* are among the many low-budget films with noticeably flawed sound. Indies with praiseworthy audio: *Eraserhead, Blood Simple, The Thin Blue Line.*

to insert "girl footage" in a lame Russian picture that Corman bought and retitled *Gill Women of Venus* (1967). Bogdanovich learned fast in Roger Corman's film school. He would soon graduate to his big break.

Horror icon Boris Karloff still contractually owed Corman a few days of work after Corman's quickie thriller *The Terror* (1963) came in under-schedule. With help from Sam Fuller and Fritz Lang, Bogdanovich dashed off a screenplay to utilize Karloff. The plot was inspired by Charles Whitman, who in 1966 murdered his mother and wife before shooting forty-six people, fourteen fatally, from a tower at the University of Texas. Corman agreed to foot the $130,000 bill. Bogdanovich produced, directed, and edited *Targets* (1968). Future *Easy Rider* cinematographer Laszlo Kovacs is responsible for the superb color photography.

In *Targets*, horror veteran Byron Orlok (Karloff) refuses to act in the movie of director Sammy Michaels (Bogdanovich). Orlok claims that horror flicks are no longer scary when compared with real life. He does, however, agree to go to the premiere of Sammy's new feature. Meanwhile, Bobby Thompson (Tim O'Kelly) loves guns. One day he calmly snaps. He fatally shoots his wife, mother, and a delivery boy. Heavily armed, Bobby climbs on top of an oil refinery and—in a truly chilling scene—lines up speeding cars in the crosshairs and shoots people driving on a Los Angeles freeway. The police chase him into the drive-in theater showing Sammy's horror flick (Corman's *The Terror*). When Bobby shoots more people through a hole in the screen, he demonstrates that "real life" *is* scarier than movies. Orlok disarms the gunman. As he is ushered off to jail, Bobby boasts, "I hardly ever missed, did I?"

A unique amalgamation of styles, *Targets* had ample chances to fail. Instead, it soars. The script is clever, the staging and camerawork are assured (with nods to Bogdanovich favorites Alfred Hitchcock and Howard Hawks), and the tension is great when we are forced to watch innocent victims through Bobby's gunsight. *Targets* is a tribute to movies (and Karloff's career), a playful swipe at complacent Hollywood, and a riveting suspense thriller.

Bogdanovich the critic felt his debut would get better press if it wasn't released by AIP, so he convinced Corman to let him shop around. He screened it for some of his friends, including Peter Fonda, Dennis Hopper, and Jack Nicholson. Their reaction was subdued, though they would soon hire most of the *Targets* crew to make *Easy Rider*. Bogdanovich's screening for the industry trade papers was more successful. Both *The Hollywood Reporter* and *Variety* published mildly favorable reviews, allowing the film to secure a distribution deal with Paramount (for $150,000—a $20,000 profit for Corman).

Targets was released in August 1968, two months after the assassination of Robert Kennedy, four months after the assassination of Martin Luther King, Jr. In such a climate the movie became a rallying cry for gun control; a brief plea for legislation was added to film prints, though Bogdanovich denies he set out to make a message movie. *Targets* was Boris Karloff's favorite film. Before his death in 1969, he finally played the unarmed hero conquering the human "monster." Peter Bogdanovich went on to craft such studio features as *The Last Picture Show* (1971), *Paper Moon* (1973), and *Mask* (1985).

Brian De Palma

With seven independent features (and one with a studio) released between 1967 and 1974, Brian De Palma (1940–) was the preeminent director of the American New Wave. He grew up in Philadelphia the son of a surgeon, later joking that his father's occupation led to his high tolerance for on-screen blood. De Palma started as a physics major at Columbia but found himself drawn to drama. He began making short films in New York in the early sixties.

De Palma spent the years 1964–1966 on a stop-and-start collaborative effort to create a feature film. Wilford Leach, Cynthia Monroe, and De Palma share writing, directing, and producing credits on what eventually became *The Wedding Party*. De Palma did all of the camera placement and editing; Leach handled the actors; Munroe put up the $100,000 budget. The result is a stale, corny movie about a nervous bride and a reluctant groom (the ineffective Charles Pfluger). De Palma tried to spice up the conventional plot with visual flair, but it doesn't help. *The Wedding Party* is most notable for marking the debuts of Robert De Niro (twenty-one in 1964; the credits read "Robert DeNero") and Jill Clayburgh (twenty; she plays the bride). The filmmakers organized screenings but were unable to win circulation. So they put *The Wedding Party* on a shelf. In 1969, when De Palma had achieved some fame, he and his partners financed a limited release.

Collaborating with two college roommates, De Palma next wrote and directed an erotic thriller and *Rashomon*like exercise, *Murder A La Mod* (1967), which shows the same killing from three points of view: a soap opera, a Hitchcocklike episode, and a burlesque comedy. The result is visually inventive, but the script is confusing and often vapid. *Murder A La Mod* played two weeks in New York City and then disappeared.

Even with two undistributed films to his credit, headstrong Brian De Palma was undeterred. He hooked up with young wannabe producer Charles Hirsch, and the two wrote a counterculture comedy. Hirsch raised $15,000 from his parents and two investors; the rest of the $43,000 budget came via credit. *Greetings* (1968) is a tawdry comedy about three obsessed young men in Vietnam-era New York. Jon (Robert De Niro) is a voyeur who gets women to strip for his camera. Awaiting his draft notice, Paul (Jonathan Warden) is preoccupied with sex arranged through computer dating. Lloyd (Gerrit Graham) is consumed by the Kennedy assassination and spends his time trying to prove a conspiracy. Paul avoids the draft and becomes a porno actor. Lloyd is assassinated. Jon is sent to Vietnam, where he convinces Vietcong women to pose nude.

Greetings is an absurdly comic movie about pornography and politics and the nature of cameras and filmmaking, some of De Palma's
personal fixations. *Greetings* is sometimes sloppy and self-congratula-
tory; other times it's as self-assured as the work of De Palma's idols
(the influences of Jean-Luc Godard and Michelangelo Antonioni are
evident). The editing is fast and often bypasses rules of continuity.
Throughout, *Greetings* showcases the courage Hollywood hadn't yet
mustered by taking on specific political targets: the Vietnam War,
Lyndon Johnson, and the Warren Commission Report.

Greetings was picked up by a tiny distributor (Sigma III). Because
of nudity, it earned the distinction of being the first motion picture to
receive an X rating. It was sold as a "sex protest film." A mixed review
in *The New York Times* stated: "Most of it is strained and unfunny, with
some generous nudity for nudity's sake and a hip sprinkling of four
letter words. . . . De Palma shows talent and the inclination of an original style in his handling of actors and the ingenuity of his framing."[5]
Greetings connected with the counterculture it was made for and
became a surprise hit, grossing more than $1 million on its initial run
(80 percent of the profits went to Sigma III).

In the controversial Greenwich Village play *Dionysus in '69*, audience
members were encouraged to strip naked and perform with the cast. De
Palma filmed a performance. He shot the stage and his two codirectors
shot the audience. The three views are laid side by side in a triple-screen
motion picture, *Dionysius in '69* (1969), that was barely released.

De Palma next wrote and directed a sequel to *Greetings*. Entitled *Hi,
Mom!* (1970), it follows the voyeur Jon (Robert De Niro), who returns
from Vietnam determined to earn a living from his obsessions. He
makes candid porno films of his neighbors. Jon becomes involved in
a theater troupe of black militants who appear in whiteface and paint
the white audience black. When the troupe tires of theatrics, they take
up revolutionary actions.

Hi, Mom! is a warped, vaudeville-style look at Vietnam-era
America. The "Be Black Baby" play (a black-and-white sequence in the
color film) is raw and in-your-face. It feels misplaced, even in this odd
movie. *Hi, Mom!* is often amusing. Though well reviewed, it had trouble finding an audience, even in 1970. The title certainly didn't help.
(*Hi, Mom!* was also released under the porno-style monikers
Confessions of a Peeping John and *Blue Manhattan*.)

With five features to his credit before his thirtieth birthday, it was time for De Palma, the leading New York independent film-maker, to head for Hollywood. He went on to shoot a comedy for Warner Bros. starring Tommy Smothers and Orson Welles, but the precocious director clashed with the West Coast stars and was fired near the end of the shoot. The movie was edited without him, shelved for two years, and released as *Get To Know Your Rabbit* in 1972. It bombed.

Meanwhile, producer Ed Pressman and director Paul Williams (not the composer) teamed up to make three independent youth films. *Out Of It* (1969) is an underrated high-school comedy starring Jon Voight. *The Revolutionary* (1970) is a taut political fantasy about a college stu-dent who becomes an anarchist. It benefits from a strong cast: Robert Duvall, Jon Voight, Seymour Cassel, Jennifer Salt. *Dealing: Or the Berkeley-to-Boston Forty-Brick Lost-Bag Blues* (1972), based on a Michael Crichton novel, features Barbara Hershey and John Lithgow in a dated tale of pot-pushing at Harvard. All three movies tanked at the box office. (Paul Williams was perhaps the most promising director of

Margot Kidder and the mad doctor (William Finley) in *Sisters*.
© 1973 American International.

the era but failed to break through.) Pressman/Williams desperately needed a hit.

So Williams folded up his directing chair for a few years, and Pressman/Williams produced a thriller directed and cowritten (with Louisa Rose) by Brian De Palma. *Sisters* (1973) is a twisted tale of a model (Margot Kidder) separated from her Siamese twin. Her personality splits into bad and good. When somebody is killed, a reporter/neighbor (Jennifer Salt) and a private detective (Charles Durning) investigate.

The bloody murder and its cleanup are brilliantly staged, the atmosphere is creepy, and the self-conscious musical score by composing legend Bernard Hermann is superb. Still, *Sisters* stumbles after the first half hour. As a psychological thriller, the plot lacks the requisite number of twists and scares. *Sisters* represents De Palma's first complete homage to Alfred Hitchcock, borrowing from *Rear Window* (1954) and *Vertigo* (1958). The film includes another voyeuristic parody—a game show called "Peeping Tom"—and some of De Palma's trademark split-screen effects. *Sisters* played favorably at a couple of American film festivals. Distributed by AIP, it was a moderate success.

With a profitable movie to their credit, Pressman/Williams pursued a feature that De Palma had been trying to get off the ground for five years, a rock-and-roll parody of *The Phantom of the Opera*. They shopped the idea to studios, but no one bit. Finally they took the script to the other Paul Williams (the composer), then at the height of his career, who agreed to star and compose the score. His enthusiasm helped secure the appropriate financing.

With Pressman producing and De Palma writing and directing, *Phantom of the Paradise* tells the musical story of composer Winslow (William Finley), who is framed by Swan (Williams), the head of Death Records. Swan has sold his soul to the devil for eternal youth. After escaping from prison, Winslow destroys Swan's studio, but his face gets maimed in a record presser and he becomes the melancholy Phantom. He haunts Swan's palace, the Paradise, hoping to help Phoenix (Jessica Harper) and defeat Swan and his glam groups.

Part horror flick, part musical, part comedy, a mixture of *Faust*, Hitchcock, *The Cabinet of Dr. Caligari*, and a few dozen other influences, it's a wicked satire of seventies glitter rock and a tribute to the joys of cinema. Though the film sets its sights unattainably high and falls short of greatness, it brims over with a contagious exuberance and stylized wit. Williams's lyrics are fun and his score with George Tipton was nominated for an Academy Award. The camerawork by Larry Pizer and production design by Jack Fisk are first-rate.

Before *Phantom of the Paradise* was finished, Universal (owner of *Phantom of the Opera*) sued over the rights to its property; the case was settled out of court. A record label also threatened a suit when its name was unintentionally used. Because reshooting was impractical, De Palma was forced to optically change the label name wherever it appeared in the finished print (the mat effect is noticeable).

Phantom of the Paradise sold to Fox for $2 million, but the studio didn't know what to do with it so it was marketed halfheartedly as a horror spoof during the same year in which *Young Frankenstein* was a hit. *Phantom of the Paradise* bombed, though it became a cult favorite, consistently shown at cinematheques in Europe. Like *Hi, Mom!*, *Phantom of the Paradise* is a movie that was both of its era and years ahead of its time.

De Palma went on to helm studio thrillers—*Obsession* (1976), *Carrie* (1976), *The Fury* (1978)—which finally established him as a mainstream director. But he returned to independence again, this time while teaching a college filmmaking course. He figured the students could best learn how to create a feature by doing it. So he put up his own money, got his colleagues to invest (including Steven Spielberg and George Lucas), and convinced friends, including Kirk Douglas and Nancy Allen (then De Palma's wife), to act. Students were involved in directing (though De Palma alone is credited), writing, and producing *Home Movies* (1979). This unfunny comedy about the border of film and reality was barely released (the video is entitled *The Maestro*). De Palma has made strictly studio pictures since, including such big-budget, glossy events as *Scarface* (1983), *The Untouchables* (1987), and *Mission Impossible* (1996).

Martin Scorsese

As an asthmatic youth growing up amidst nuns and gangsters in New York's Little Italy, Martin Scorsese (1942–) developed a lifelong love affair with the movies. After a stint in the seminary, he earned degrees in film from New York University. In school, Scorsese's short movies won awards, but his first stab at a feature, *I Call First*, was not well received. He stayed on as an instructor at NYU, and, with encouragement and financing from the head of the film department, the exuberant Scorsese set out to remake *I Call First*.

A principal problem with the student production was its amateurish acting. Only one lead from the original appears in the new and improved version, *Who's That Knocking at My Door* (1968, aka *J. R.*). The debuting actor, then working as a court stenographer during the day, remembers, "I always knew *Who's That Knocking* would get done because Marty had that passion. We made the film for an entire winter on weekends, because we all had to earn money weekdays to buy food and pay the rent. After I saw the first rushes, the scene inside the church, where the song 'Who's That Knocking at My Door?' is playing, I knew that I was with somebody special."[6] The actor was Harvey Keitel, and he and that special director have maintained a working relationship ever since. Scorsese also teamed up with a young editor from school, Thelma Schoonmaker, who through the decades has cut many of his best films.

Who's That Knocking at My Door follows J. R. (Keitel), an aimless young Catholic, as he hangs out with his friends and courts a more educated woman (Zina Bethune), whose name is never mentioned. J. R. categorizes single women as broads you have sex with and virgins you can marry. He wants "the Girl" to remain chaste until their wedding night, and he is outraged when he learns that she has lost her virginity through rape. J. R.'s emotions swirl.

Captivating if uneven, *Who's That Knocking at My Door* is the jagged work of an experimenting young auteur. It contains great moments: the title sequence rock-and-roll rumble, the *Rio Bravo* photo montage, the love scene shot in extreme facial close-ups, the music gone awry during the rape flashback. The influences of Cassavetes and the *Nouvelle Vague* are clear. We also see the beginnings of Scorsese's preoccupations and style: Catholic guilt and idolatry, Italian characters, a New York setting, a classic rock-and-roll soundtrack, masculine bravado, and a highly mobile camera.

The completed black-and-white feature (still entitled *I Call First*) debuted at the Chicago Film Festival of 1967 and received a rave notice from a young Roger Ebert. However, a movie addressing Catholic values was a tough sell during the liberated late sixties, and Scorsese could attain distribution only by adding a sex montage scene. Four years after it began as a student project, the mistitled

Who's That Knocking at My Door was released by a company that specialized in pornography. It disappeared fast.

After his sometimes dazzling debut went virtually unnoticed, Scorsese worked various motion picture jobs. He taught at NYU until 1970, ever expanding his encyclopedic knowledge of cinema. He supervised *Street Scenes*, an unreleased documentary on campus war protests. He was an assistant director and editor on the hugely successful concert film *Woodstock* (1970). And he went through Roger Corman's graduate course in low-budget moviemaking when he helmed *Boxcar Bertha* (1972), a standard robbers-on-the-run effort, produced by Corman and starring Barbara Hershey.

In 1972, the almost-thirty-year-old Scorsese was living in Hollywood and worried that his current path was not leading to the promised land. He remembers a conversation with the father of the American New Wave: "After he saw a rough cut of *Boxcar Bertha*, John Cassavetes told me it was nice for what it was, but warned me not to get hooked up in it again. . . . He asked me if I didn't have something I really wanted to do. I told him I had this script called 'Season of the Witch,' but that it needed work, rewriting. He said, 'So do it.' "[7]

That script (originally penned in 1966 with Mardik Martin) turned into the movie *Mean Streets* (1973), and it made Martin Scorsese's career. Corman offered $150,000 in financing if it was rewritten as a blaxploitation picture. Scorsese balked. After trying for years, the writer/director finally got it off the ground when he hooked up with the road manager for The Band, Jonathan Taplin, who raised the $350,000 budget and served as producer. *Mean Streets* also marked the first of Scorsese's many electrifying collaborations with Robert De Niro, a gifted actor on the brink of superstardom. Though *Mean Streets* is set in New York's Little Italy, to save money it was shot primarily in Los Angeles and used much of the crew from *Boxcar Bertha*.

Mean Streets tells a loosely structured, seemingly spontaneous tale of four young men on the outskirts of the Mafia. Charlie (Harvey Keitel) is a guilty Catholic who wants his small-time gangster uncle to let him take over a bankrupt restaurant. Between routine hustles and skirmishes, he tests himself, passing his hand through flames, pondering the fires of Hell. Johnny Boy (De Niro) is an unpredictable hood, prone to setting off bombs for kicks and borrowing money he never intends to repay. Michael (Richard Romanus) is a loan shark with whom Johnny Boy has racked up a debt. Tony (David Proval) owns the bar where everyone congregates. Budding saint Charlie attempts to save Johnny Boy, but they're steering towards a violent conclusion.

Mean Streets feels both as free as a joyride and as preordained as a Catholic mass. It pulsates with visually dazzling camerawork, a restless editing pace, a score of classic sixties pop songs, and spellbinding acting. Violence always threatens to explode. Individual sequences stand out: the camera following Charlie through Tony's red lit club; a roving rumble in a pool hall, instigated when Johnny Boy is called a "mook," though no one is sure what it means; the playful lovemaking between Charlie and Teresa (Amy Robinson); and Johnny Boy stretched out on a grave as he and Charlie hide in a cemetery. *Mean Streets* is a movie of mesmerizing scenes, some of which were improvised.

Not every critic believed the exceptional pieces fit together to form a great film, but for the many who missed *Who's That Knocking*, *Mean Streets* heralded the arrival of an important director and at least one magnetic actor. When it opened at the 1973 New York Film Festival, *Variety* criticized the lack of a tightly structured story, but then announced: "There is much evidence here of a potentially extraordinary filmmaking talent. Scorsese may not always manage to clarify his characters' interiors, but he is exceptionally good at guiding his largely unknown cast to near-flawless recreations of type. Outstanding in this regard is De Niro, who should finally move out of the 'promising' category. . . ."[8] Harvey Keitel is equally compelling.

Warner Bros. released *Mean Streets* (acquired for $750,000) at the same time as the blockbuster *The Way We Were* and just before its own megahit *The Exorcist*. Scorsese's slice-of-urban-life did fine in New York, but elsewhere it slipped in and out of theaters fast. The slim box-office receipts didn't really matter in the long run, however. Hollywood now knew Martin Scorsese. In time, *Mean Streets* would be championed as an independent classic, inspiring a generation of movie mavericks. It made several lists for "Ten Best of the Decade," including *The New York Times*'s. Robert De Niro was voted 1973's best supporting actor by the National Society of Film Critics. Martin Scorsese went on to become one of the world's most accomplished filmmakers. A virtuoso visual stylist, he has crafted such studio masterworks as *Taxi Driver* (1976), *Raging Bull* (1980), *The King of Comedy* (1983), and *Goodfellas* (1990).

African-American

The early seventies saw more features produced for an African-American audience than at any time since the death of the race picture industry. Virtually all of them were low-budget; many of them were independent. People who lived through this era of Afros and platform shoes tend to remember the blaxploitation flicks: the pimps and super studs, the action heroes and buxom babes who never answered to the Man and always moved to a funky beat. But there was also a miniexplosion of virtually unnoticed nonstudio black-themed dramas. Though it never quite developed into the African-American New Wave, the legacy of black-themed movies in the first half of the seventies cannot be dismissed as mere exploitation.

Melvin Van Peebles (1932–) traveled the world as a young man. Born in Chicago and educated in Delaware and West Virginia, he served in the Air Force and then eked out a living as a portrait painter in Mexico. Van Peebles shot his first short films in 1958 while employed at a San Francisco post office. Unable to break into Hollywood, he moved to Holland and then France, where he lived for ten years, working as a crime reporter and authoring French-language novels.

Van Peebles's first feature is an adaptation of one of his books, *The Story of a Three Day Pass* (1967), which he shot in Paris. This romance of a black American soldier falling for a white French girl is clumsy, but it played in America and generated positive reviews. Courted by Hollywood, Van Peebles next called the shots on Columbia's *Watermelon Man* (1970), about a white bigot (black actor Godfrey Cambridge) who suddenly wakes up black. Both of Van Peebles's initial features had a strong sociological edge, but neither can compare to the raw radical rage of his third.

The film was "Dedicated to all the Brothers and Sisters who had enough of the Man," and it captured the fire of the then raging Black Power movement. No Hollywood studio wanted to finance an incendiary work like *Sweet Sweetback's Baadasssss Song* (1971). So Van Peebles raised the $500,000 budget himself from the African-American community (including $50,000 from Bill Cosby). In addition to playing the title character, Van Peebles wrote, produced, directed, composed, and edited. Before he began the script, he made a note of seven "givens" for a viable film project. Number 1 was "NO COP OUT." Number 3 was "ENTERTAINMENTWISE. A MOTHER FUCKER."

Promotional shot of Melvin Van Peebles from *Sweet Sweetback's Baadasssss Song*.
Courtesy of Melvin Van Peebles.

Sweetback (Van Peebles) works as a sexual performer in a brothel. When two white cops brutalize a black man, Sweetback smashes their heads with his handcuffs. He then runs, aided by "The Black Community" (as the credits read). After killing another pair of white cops, he keeps on running, bedding women along the way. In the end, Sweetback is running in Mexico, but a title warns white America to "WATCH OUT" because he's "coming back to collect some dues."

Sweet Sweetback's Baadasssss Song fails to articulate everything it wants to say. Most scenes consist of Sweetback running or people talking about him running. "Given" number 3 is clearly violated. Still, this was a startlingly powerful movie. As a hymn of pain and transcendence, it was firmly in the tradition of African-American songs and literature, yet it was groundbreaking as a First World film. *Sweetback* appropriated traditionally racist stereotypes (the stud, the violent criminal, the whore) while maintaining an angry, uncompromising defiance throughout. Van Peebles never once changes his expression. Stoic and nearly mute, Sweetback meets violence with violence. He is a man of the streets who takes us to the crumbling ghettoes traditionally overlooked by Hollywood. The movie is technically crude, yet its murky zoom photography, repetitive porno-jazz score, and head-trip editing (superimpositions, split screens, repetitions of shots, etc.) add to its underground ambience. Black Panther leader Huey Newton called it "a great revolutionary document."

Sweetback was given an X rating for its mild sexual content (Van Peebles used the catchy marketing line "Rated X by an all-white jury"). When no distributor would touch his film, Van Peebles booked it into a couple of theaters himself and handed out flyers on street corners. As its notoriety grew, tiny Cinemation picked it up (it was rereleased by New World in 1974). *Sweet Sweetback's Baadasssss Song* became a national sensation. Most white reviewers were either outraged or dismissive, though some complimented Van Peebles's audacity. Most black writers either cheered its in-your-face bravado or condemned its elevation of an apolitical criminal. A master promoter, Van Peebles was always willing to weigh in on the topic. He told *Time* in 1971, "Of all the ways we've been exploited by the Man, the most damaging is the way he destroyed our self-image. The message of *Sweetback* is that if you can get it together and stand up to the Man, you can win."[9] Sweetback, the sexist, superstud, killer-on-the-run, isn't much of a role model, but, as with *The Emperor Jones* four decades earlier, it was exciting for a sizable number of blacks (and some whites) in 1971 to see any African-American fighting back.

Everyone heard about Van Peebles's movie. *Sweet Sweetback* grossed $15 million. There was a *Sweetback* book and a *Sweetback* album, and there were T-shirts, posters, even nightgowns. Van Peebles, who owned all the rights, made a fortune. He also became something of a folk hero in the black community: the uncompromising expatriate who stuck it to the Man. He hasn't directed a significant movie since, but he has acted in numerous films, penned screenplays, books, and plays, and become a renowned stock trader. His son, Mario Van Peebles, an actor and filmmaker, debuted in his father's controversial feature at age thirteen as the childhood Sweetback having sex with an adult woman.

As *Sweet Sweetback's Baadasssss Song* invigorated urban audiences, a little studio film called *Shaft* stirred up even more business, and together they ushered in the blaxploitation movement of cheaply made black-themed action pictures. *Shaft* was directed by Renaissance man Gordon Parks. In turn, his son, Gordon Parks, Jr., helmed the independent *Super Fly* (1972). Scripted by Phillip Fenty, *Super Fly* is the tale of Youngblood Priest (Ron O'Neal), an ultracool coke dealer with a trademark fedora, long pimp-style coats, and a chromed-out Cadillac. Youngblood wants to score a big deal before leaving the dope business for good, which he does by defeating the white crime bosses. Like *Sweetback*, the movie's $500,000 budget came from African-American businessmen, who made it back with interest when *Super Fly* grossed millions. And like *Sweetback*, the movie they invested in stirred up controversy in the black community.

Super Fly was condemned by the NAACP and some African-American journalists for glorifying a drug dealer, but it was embraced by urban audiences, who thrilled to its portrait of a bold black man living on his own terms. After Youngblood tells his friend Eddie (Carl Lee) he's thinking of leaving the drug business, Eddie responds, "You gonna give all this up? Eight track stereo, color TV in every room, and can snort a half a piece a dope every day. That's the American dream ... Well, ain't it? ... I know it's a rotten game, but it's the only one the Man left us to play, and that's the stone cold truth." *Super Fly* has some awkward moments, but it also includes the classic soul/funk music of Curtis Mayfield (who appears in a nightclub to sing the title song), great gritty Harlem photography (including a still photo/split-screen drug-deal sequence), and the perpetually cool performance of Ron O'Neal. It was an auspicious debut from Gordon Parks, Jr., a still photographer who went on to helm three more blaxploitation pictures, most notably *Three the Hard Way* (1975). Scouting a movie, the junior Parks died in a plane crash in Kenya in 1979 at the age of forty-four.

During the proliferation of blaxploitation films, there was no discernible difference between those ground out at the studios and those—such as *Detroit 9000* (1973) and *The Black Godfather* (1974)—produced independently. Virtually all of them were technically inept, thematically weak action flicks with flamboyant heroes. Harkening back to the race pictures of the forties, many were merely ebony versions of mainstream Hollywood movies, doomed to the margins by comparison. And as in days gone by, a bottleneck developed as these interchangeable flicks vied for a limited audience.

Blaxploitation screeched to a halt in 1975, when urban ticket buyers, tired of the same cheap formulas, went to *Jaws* three times instead. Before then, in 1972, the studios served up two popular black-cast dramas, *Sounder* and *Lady Sings the Blues*; together they received nine Oscar nominations (and won none). Renegades also crafted serious fare, but these films received much less attention.

In 1970, D. A. Pennebaker and Richard Leacock produced and Herbert Danska directed the first "rap picture," *Right On!* It's a filmed record of The Original Last Poets (Felipe Luciano, Gylan Kain, David Nelson) reciting their guerilla poetry on the streets and rooftops of New York City. *Right On!* never made it above the underground, but it remains a fascinating cultural curio.

Honky (1971), on the other hand, is a cheap exploitation flick pretending to be something more. It mangles a high-school romance between a black girl (Brenda Sykes) and a white boy (John Nielson) and throws in a pot-selling subplot. The prolific William Graham directed. The fine score by Quincy Jones is wasted.

Ossie Davis, a veteran stage and film performer, called the shots on the studio feature *Cotton Comes to Harlem* (1970) and followed with *Kongi's Harvest* (1971), a US/Nigerian drama shot in Nigeria. J. E. Franklin then adapted her play *Black Girl* to screen (1972), and Davis directed. A rare dramatic work about African-American females, this emotional tale follows a young woman (Peggy Pettit) who wants to escape the ghetto and become a dancer. Her mother is blind to her own mistakes; her grandmother is painfully aware of them. Another young woman (Leslie Uggams) represents the black bourgeoisie. *Black Girl*'s theatrical roots sometimes entangle its progress, but the acting is strong. Unfortunately, as with other African-American indie dramas during these years, the distributor was unsure how to market *Black Girl*. Sold as a work of explosive rage, it went to the same urban theaters that specialized in blaxploitation and kung fu, where it disappeared quietly. Davis returned to Nigeria to direct and star (with his wife, Ruby Dee) in *Countdown at Kusini* (1976), a tepid liberation tale financed by the black sorority Delta Sigma Theta.

Cinerama, *Black Girl*'s distributor, did only slightly better releasing another 1972 drama about an African-American woman. The screenplay for *Georgia, Georgia* (1972) was authored by acclaimed poet Maya Angelou. Shot on location in Sweden with Swedish director Stig Björkman and an American cast, it's a melodramatic tale of a black songstress, Georgia (Diane Sands), on tour in Europe. Her relationship with a white photographer (Dirk Benedict) stirs up controversy. *Variety* said, "Maya Angelou has packed her first script with just about as many clichés as it will stand, than [sic] the producers added a few of their own . . . the overall impression is that of an amateurish, poorly-written, poorly-directed and mostly ineptly-played film."[10]

In the tradition of *The Crimson Skull* and company, it was again up to the independent arena to educate America on the neglected history of blacks in the Old West. Bill Cosby executive-produced and stars in *Man and Boy* (1972), directed by E. W. Swackhamer. Cosby plays a quiet Civil War veteran who homesteads the Arizona prairie with his family. He and his son go on a journey to recover a stolen horse from a thief. *Man and Boy* is a slow, simple drama and a good-hearted family film.

One of cinema's most intriguing black-themed independents is the little seen *Ganja & Hess* (1973), written and directed by Bill Gunn (1929–1989). Before scripting *The Landlord* (1970), Gunn was an actor, playwright, and novelist. After Gordon Parks, he tied with Ossie Davis as the second African-American to direct a studio production, helming *Stop!* in 1970. A jungle exploration tale told from the perspective of black natives, *Stop!* was stopped before release and placed in a vault by Warner Bros. The only surviving print (a rough cut) was publicly screened (at the Whitney Museum) only after Gunn's death. Reaction was mixed. *Ganja & Hess* would follow a similar path.

Kelly-Jordan Enterprises, the small New York company behind *Georgia, Georgia*, hired Gunn and provided the $300,000 budget for *Ganja & Hess*. The executive producers wanted a frightful blaxploitation picture like AIP's popular *Blacula* (1972). Gunn later claimed he inserted typical horror genre subterfuge in his script to appease the moneymen, only to remove such elements in postproduction. The word "vampire" is never uttered in *Ganja & Hess*, and none of the typical bloodsucker clichés are in evidence. Shooting took place in upstate New York.

Stuffy Egyptologist Dr. Hess Green (Duane Jones) is stabbed with an ancient African dagger by research assistant George Meda (Gunn). Hess comes under a curse that makes him crave blood. After Meda kills himself, Hess takes up with the widow, beautiful, aloof Ganja (Marlene Clark). They marry. Ganja and Hess seek to quench their blood lust and break the curse. Hess is saved in a church and dies under a cross—a vampire suicide. Ganja will continue her fleshly addiction.

Ganja & Hess has nudity, sweaty eroticism, and puddles of blood, but it's not exploitation. Gunn's movie is about addiction (to power, money, sex, drugs, blood), about cultural assimilation, about the black bourgeoisie feeding on the lower class, and about Christianity in modern society. The work of cinematic visionaries is evident throughout in the sumptuous costumes, the varied musical score (by Sam Waymon), the acting of Gunn and Clarke, which included lengthy improvisations, and the smoldering, highly stylized cinematography of James E. Hinton. There's a terrific scene where the controlling Ganja coyly berates Hess's butler (Leonard Jackson), whose head is blocked by the top of the frame as though she sees him as mere meat. Also inspired are the cries of a baby during a tilted shot of a poor mother Hess has seduced and killed, the legendary African queen surreally standing in the background at Ganja and Hess's wedding, and the slow-motion footage of Hess running through a field accompanied by raw gospel music after he has been spiritually saved in a *verité*-style sequence.

Ganja & Hess opened in New York City in April 1973. It was negatively reviewed (*Variety* called it "a sex film with blood"[11]) and sparsely advertised. Strapped by debt, Kelly-Jordan promptly pulled it. Convinced he had made an important motion picture, Gunn took *Ganja & Hess* to Cannes in May, where it won a standing ovation and was lavished with praise by French critics. The director knew his movie needed to be nurtured in art houses, but it was too late for Kelly-Jordan. They sold *Ganja & Hess* to Heritage Enterprises, which reedited it, excised thirty minutes, inserted Gunn outtakes, and replaced the musical score.[12] In 1975, a very different *Ganja & Hess* was rereleased as a standard horror flick under the titles *Blood Couple* and *Double Possession* (director: the pseudonymous "F. H. Novikov"); it bombed again. The legal rights became entangled. Until his death in 1989, Bill Gunn went about his life as a writer and occasional TV director and actor. He would occasionally screen the one deteriorating print he had, which he stored in a vault at the Museum of Modern Art. Meanwhile, cheap public-domain videos of the severely edited version leaked out under various titles. For fifteen years, *Ganja & Hess* remained a nearly lost classic. Struck from a previously unknown print, the original director's cut finally found its way to the home market (on DVD) in 1998, twenty-five years later.

With dense visual allegories, poetic monologues, and raw blood, sweat, and lust, *Ganja & Hess* is a self-indulgent original, one of American cinema's most potent ethnic features. James Monaco called it the "great underground classic of Black film and, I think, the most complicated, intriguing, subtle, sophisticated, and passionate Black film of the Seventies. If *Sweet Sweetback* is [Richard Wright's] *Native Son*, *Ganja & Hess* is [Ralph Ellison's] *Invisible Man*. Some day it will take its rightful place in cinematheques and history books."[13]

The independent black film movement of the seventies started with *Sweet Sweetback's Baadasssss Song* and ended in three short years around the time of *Ganja & Hess*. What came in between were mostly thoughtless cookie-cutter action pictures. Those that dared to be different were usually lost in a logjam of exploitable flicks that—despite sex, violence, and soul—were rarely as much fun as their posters or soundtracks. Still, these were liberating years that moved the empowering themes of earlier race pictures one step further. For the first time, from fade-in to fade-out, black heroes and antiheroes got to triumph over the Man and subvert the System. Blaxploitation was a necessary cinematic catharsis.

Whitezploitation

The Man and the System had their own reaction to changing American mores and movies. One year after *Easy Rider* and *Woodstock*, indie studio The Cannon Group produced *Joe* (1970), a low-budget tale of hippie-killing and bigotry. And just as the radical *Sweet Sweetback's Baadasssss Song* challenged authority, its antithesis was found in the right-wing reactionism of the studio blockbuster *Dirty Harry* (1971). The wave of less political features inspired by *Sweetback* was mirrored by a smaller but more popular trend in the South. While there were urban action pictures with black antiheroes, a similar genre of rural action movies with white antiheroes also emerged.

Call it "whitezploitation." Such films are not necessarily conservative; in fact, most—like their blaxploitation counterparts—are essentially apolitical. What they share is a rural setting, a vigilante or otherwise criminal male antihero, corrupt authorities, and a distinctly Southern perspective. They were the illegitimate kinfolk of roughies and drive-in hillbilly flicks. These "southerns" did huge business on the drive-in circuit. Like blaxploitation, the studios made redneck pictures, including *Deliverance* (1972), *White Lightning* (1973), *Gator* (1976), and *Smokey and the Bandit* (1977).[14] And, like blaxploitation, much of the whitezploitation of the early seventies was independent.

Billy Jack (1972) isn't technically whitezploitation. It's set in the Southwest and supports the counterculture. Yet it probably did more than any other film to establish redneck movie conventions through its rural setting, stoic vengeful male, and surprisingly gargantuan profits. Smaller-market communities embraced this movie as no other; *Billy Jack* grossed more than $30 million in domestic theaters—a blockbuster figure at the time.

After his two forgotten indies in the early sixties, Tom Laughlin (1938–) wrote, directed, and produced (under various pseudonyms) *Born Losers* (1967), an amateurish biker flick in which a character named Billy Jack (Laughlin) is featured. Released by AIP, the movie was a surprise hit. Shortly thereafter, Laughlin and his wife, Delores Taylor, set out to place his character in a more political story. Together they wrote and produced *Billy Jack*; Laughlin directed (pseudonyms are used in all cases). Through a long struggle for creative control, the $650,000 production jumped from AIP to Avco-Embassy to Twentieth-Century Fox. Finally, nearly three years after production began, the Laughlins sold their film to Warner Bros. in 1971 for nearly $2 million.

Billy Jack is one of popular cinema's most manipulative propaganda pieces. The title character (Laughlin) is a half-Indian, ex-Green Beret martial arts expert who protects the counterculture Freedom School for children near a reservation in Arizona. He has a nonphysical relationship with the school's leader, Jean (Taylor). The good guys are really good: shy wounded children and nonviolent peace activists. The bad guys are oh so bad—slaughtering horses, racially tormenting kids, raping, murdering.

Into this mix the title character steps in as the messiah. Jean says, "We don't know how to contact Billy Jack. We communicate with him Indian-style; when we need him somehow he's there." And he always is. In a school play when the new Christ is born, kids give him a power salute. In the concluding shot, Billy Jack is led from a church to jail and hundreds of people give him, their martyred savior, that same salute. Thus, those taught pacifism on a commune—the Freedom School, no less—come to worship a man of violence.

Billy Jack is filled with overly earnest moments (the worst is a girl singing off-key about her dead brother), and it accepts every tenant of the counterculture without question. And yet—as with much propaganda—it's still fun. The real hoot is seeing the messiah take off his boots and kick the grins off rednecks. On the surface, Laughlin's exercise in narcissism was a kung fu western, and, despite zombified acting, it was superior to almost all of the chop-sockey coming out of Hong Kong at the time. The editing and karate choreography of a fight in and out of an ice cream parlor are electrifying. Young people thrilled to a superhero created as their champion. They saw this picture over and over again.

Laughlin sued Warner Bros. for some of *Billy Jack*'s profit windfall. After an out-of-court settlement, Warners released the movie again in 1973, splitting the profits equally with the Laughlins. This time, in even wider release, *Billy Jack* raked in millions again. Laughlin made and starred in two peace-through-violence sequels: *The Trial of Billy Jack* (1974), a hit despite being a three-hour mess, and *Billy Jack Goes to Washington* (1977), another lengthy ego trip. On *Billy Jack*'s profits, Laughlin tried to create a media empire in the mid-seventies. It collapsed with the dismal box office of *The Master Gunfighter* (1975), another tale of a violent pacifist (which, unfortunately, didn't have the name "Billy Jack" in its title). Tom Laughlin vanished from the film scene. In 1992 he ran for US President.

Walking Tall (1973) is a redneck classic. Helmed by B movie veteran Phil Karlson, it tells the true (but highly fictionalized) tale of crusading Tennessee sheriff Buford Pusser (Joe Don Baker), an ex-wrestler who carries a big stick to clean up corruption in his backwoods county. When his mission stirs up too much trouble, his wife (Elizabeth Hartman) is killed. Bandaged like the Invisible Man, Buford Pusser keeps on swinging. This is a throwback to old-style westerns and a modern plea for vigilantism. The real-life Sheriff Pusser was voted out of office during production because his tactics scared innocent people. Shot on a low budget in Tennessee, *Walking Tall* is crude and manipulative, with cheesy cinematography and music; the title song by Johnny Mathis is a howler. It was distributed by the same company (Cinerama) in the same year as the blaxploitation semi-indie *The Mack* (but not to the same audience) and was a great success, spawning two sequels and a TV series.

After years of playing Jethro on TV's "The Beverly Hillbillies," Max Baer, Jr., produced *Macon County Line* (1974), teaming up with director Richard Compton to write himself the role of a lifetime. Hunting season, Georgia, 1954: Baer turns a slyly malevolent deputy into a protector of the Old South. He torments Yankee strangers with a smile and shelters his polite racism behind closed doors. Baer's perfectly downplayed deputy is the Jethro we never got to know.

Variety originally dismissed *Macon County Line* as "a suitable dual bill exploitation item for lesser yahoo situations."[15] It's much better than that. Based on a true story, it sputters during the stretches when Baer isn't on-screen, but it's quietly effective throughout, eventually turning as dark as *Deliverance*. Made for a mere $250,000, *Macon County Line* grossed more than $19 million. The sequel, *Return to Macon County* (1975), is notable only for starring unknowns Nick Nolte and Don Johnson. Max Baer, Jr., went on to direct such films as *Ode to Billy Joe* (1976).

There were numerous whitezploitation pictures that failed to stir up much box office and rarely played in a non-Confederate state. *Preacherman* (1971), directed by Albert T. Viola, is the most amusing. It throws in all the usual hillbilly stereotypes—farmer's randy daughter, phony preacher, corrupt sheriff—and blends them Russ Meyer–style into a potent mix of rotgut. *The Legend of Hillbilly John* (1973), directed by John Newland, is notable for its bold attempt to create a G-rated fantasy film about Carolina folklore. With his coon hound and magical guitar, John (Hedge Capers) calls out the Devil to face him down. Satan is manifested in guises both prehistoric (a pterodactyl) and modern (exploiting industries). In the last scene, John is headed toward the White House. *The Legend of Hillbilly John* is a unique American fantasy.

Sharing screenwriting and directing chores, husband and wife Ferd and Beverly Sebastian have made a career out of whitezploitation. Ferd said in 1975, "We make our movies for the Sears-Roebuck kind of people. . . . We try to reach the working man who has a houseful of kids and is afraid of losing his $80-a-week job."[16] After producing industrials and softcore pornography, they made *The Hitchhikers* (1971), an awful flick about female drifters who rob men. Next came *Gator Bait* (1973), the story of a beautiful swamp woman (Claudia Jennings) and the violent fate of her admirers. Blessed with an exploitable title and exploitable star (Jennings was a *Playboy* Playmate of the Year), *Gator Bait* grossed $4 million. Ferd and Beverly had their recipe. A succession of redneck movies followed, including *Flash and*

Firecat (1975) and *Delta Fox* (1977). The Sebastians distributed their movies themselves, mostly to Southern drive-ins. Later they generated whitezploitation for the straight-to-video market.

Arkansas advertising man Charles Pierce had a vision. Though his only previous behind-the-camera experience was shooting local commercials, he wanted to make a G-rated docudrama about the fabled monster of a nearby swamp. He raised $100,000, gathered a crew of high-school students and a cast of local actors, and proceeded to produce, direct, shoot, and sing the theme song for *The Legend of Boggy Creek* (1972). When it was completed, Pierce rented and hand-cleaned an out-of-business theater. When the flick was a success there, he bought more prints and motored around the Deep South in his pickup truck, leasing theaters. Eventually *The Legend of Boggy Creek* was picked up by a small distributor. A runaway success below the Mason/Dixon line, the picture grossed more than $20 million.

Pierce followed *Boggy Creek* with two sequels (1977 and 1985). He also turned out several other low-budget films with a Southern or Western setting. The miraculous success of *The Legend of Boggy Creek* launched a whitezploitation subgenre: the drive-in documentary, typically about the "reality" of some fabled beast or previously unexplained phenomenon. Such exploitable nonstudio, pseudodocs as *Chariots of the Gods?* (1974), *Mysterious Monsters* (1976), and *The Legend of Bigfoot* (1976) did big business in the mid-seventies.

The Underclass

Just as blaxploitation overshadowed African-American dramas, whitezploitation obscured the artistic films that addressed the lives of the white lower class. There were several underappreciated pictures during these years that focused on marginal characters.

The Honeymoon Killers (1970) successfully bridges the gap between trash and art. It's based on the true story of Martha Beck and Raymond Fernandez, the "Lonely Hearts Murderers" who met their victims through singles clubs in the late forties. The couple were executed together in 1951. Opera composer and music professor Leonard Kastle researched the crimes and penned the melodramatic screenplay. Martin Scorsese was the original director, but he was fired by producer Warren Steibel after ten days of shooting (accounts vary as to why). Most of Scorsese's footage was reshot after Kastle, who had no filmmaking experience, took the directing reins. Both lead actors

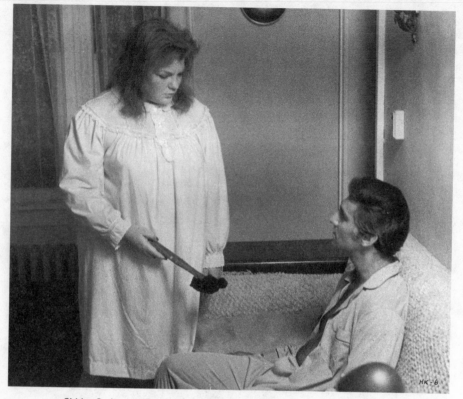

Shirley Stoler tells Tony LoBianco to get rid of his new wife in *The Honeymoon Killers*.

suggest that cinematographer Oliver Wood was the movie's true visual auteur. It's intriguing to ponder what the $140,000 film would look like if Scorsese had stayed onboard.

The Honeymoon Killers teams up ill-tempered 200-pound nurse Martha Beck (Shirley Stoler, in her debut) and her charming dim-witted Spanish lover Ray Fernandez (Tony LoBianco, in his debut). While pursuing their own volatile love affair, they travel across the country stealing from the forlorn ladies Ray seduces. Then they kill them. She's always jealous. Their love can't last.

The crimes and criminals are never glamorized. Instead, the picture maintains a sleazy, black-and-white claustrophobia; the camera always seems a little too close. The lighting and sound quality are sometimes sloppy, but such flaws feel at home in this tawdry love tale. Selections from Gustav Mahler dominate the soundtrack. Though the dialogue is frequently shrill, the acting by Stoler and LoBianco is excellent.

Cinerama sold *The Honeymoon Killers* as exploitation, but many critics championed its artistic qualities. On the strength of its reviews, *The Honeymoon Killers* was a small hit among hip moviegoers. Predictably, Europeans loved it. Michelangelo Antonioni praised its rare purity, and François Truffaut called it his favorite American film. Still, it wasn't the kind of success that made careers. Leonard Kastle returned to composing and teaching and has never made another film. Martin Scorsese, of course, went on to bigger things.

Barbara Loden had been a Tony Award–winning theatrical actress before marrying legendary director Elia Kazan. In 1970 she wrote, directed, and starred in a bleak $115,000 movie called *Wanda*. Shot in 16mm, it follows unskilled, uneducated Wanda (Loden) as she gives up her two children during a divorce and takes up with a small-time thief (Michael Higgins) in a degrading relationship. In the end, after an unsuccessful bank robbery, Wanda escapes to a bar. The camera freezes on her trapped in an industrial landscape of near poverty. Unable to find happiness or meaning, Wanda quietly gets by however she can.

Wanda was the only American feature at the 1970 Venice Film Festival, where it won the International Critics Prize. Though its depressing, neorealist tone limited its appeal, *Wanda*'s oblique message made it an intellectual favorite. Critic Stanley Kauffman wrote, "Wanda came out of a society that had ravaged her afferent powers and her adaptive intelligence long before she was on her own. Loden's triumph is that she has realized this truth without stopping at case history; her script, direction, and acting make *Wanda* a small, good work of art, and make Loden a very welcome addition to the film scene."[17]

Loden never really joined the scene. She died of breast cancer in 1980 at the age of forty-eight without making a second movie. Elia Kazan directed his own ultra-low-budget indie in 1972. *The Visitors* is a preachy Vietnam vet revenge tale, scripted by his oldest son, shot in and around his and Loden's Connecticut home, and featuring the debut performance of James Woods.

Tomorrow, based on a short story by William Faulkner (screenplay by Horton Foote), is one of the most precise and reverential motion pictures adapted from a literary master. Helmed by theater veteran Joseph Anthony, this $400,000 movie was shot in black-and-white on location in rural Mississippi.

The Depression-era story follows quiet, simple-minded handyman Jackson Fentry (Robert Duvall), who lives alone in a shack. He allows a pregnant woman (Olga Bellin) running from her husband to stay with him. He falls in love with her. She dies during childbirth. He raises the baby boy until the bleak conclusion. The subdued acting and writing are superb.

When it wasn't being ignored, *Tomorrow* was mostly dismissed as intolerably poetic. The early seventies were not the best time for such a literate Southern tale about the endurance of love. *Tomorrow* was rediscovered in 1983 when both actor Robert Duvall and screenwriter Horton Foote won Academy Awards for the similarly themed *Tender Mercies*. It has since been hailed as a small classic. Duvall, who has acted in some of the best movies of his generation, named Jackson Fentry his all-time favorite character.

Looking back more than a decade later, critic Judith Crist wrote, "The special beloveds are the unexpected films, the 'sleepers' that arrive without fanfare, are viewed without expectations, and make an indelible mark on memory and heart. *Tomorrow* is such a film."[18]

Payday (1973) was also overlooked by the general public, though critics sang its praises. Director Daryl Duke and writer/coproducer Don Carpenter fashioned a sad ballad about the final thirty-six hours in the life of fictional country singer Maury Dann (Rip Torn) as he tours the Deep South. Abusing booze, drugs, and people with equal abandon, Dann kills a man after seducing his date. He then spirals ever downward. Smirking like a gargoyle, Rip Torn is electric, and Duke correctly captures the ambiance of second-rate motels and diners.

Another ballad flopped at the box office despite the sensation it stirred at the 1973 New York Film Festival, and after being snatched up by Warner Bros. for nearly $1.1 million (about what it cost) and enthusiastically reviewed. Through the years, *Badlands* (1974) has been hailed as a masterpiece. Several publications, including *Time*, named it one of the ten best films of the decade.

Much of *Badlands*'s lingering attraction is focused on its mysterious producer/director/writer. With two previous credits for screenwriting and no directing experience, he made what critic David Thomson has called "the most assured first film by an American since *Citizen Kane*."[19] Terrence Malick (1943–), was the son of an oil executive raised in the Southwest. Before turning to filmmaking in his late twenties, Malick's intellectual pedigree was secure. He was a Phi Beta Kappa graduate of Harvard, a Rhodes scholar, and a philosophy instructor at MIT.

Badlands was executive-produced by Pressman/Williams at nearly the same time they financed De Palma's *Sisters*. Brian Probyn, Tak Fujimoto, and Steve Larner provided the shimmering color cinematography. Like *The Honeymoon Killers*, the story is based on a real murder spree in a more "innocent" America. This time it's the 1958 case of nineteen-year-old Charles Starkweather and his thirteen-year-old girlfriend. Starkweather gunned down ten people in Wyoming and Nebraska. He was executed; she went to prison.

Badlands features Martin Sheen as Kit, and Sissy Spacek (her second role) as Holly, who thinks Kit looks like James Dean. The movie's deadpan newspaper advertisement ended with the lines: "For a while they lived together in a tree house. In 1959, she watched while he killed a lot of people." They live in the tree house after he kills her overbearing father (Warren Oates) and he burns down the house, and before killing more innocent people, including bounty hunters who come looking for them. They drive into the barren Badlands of South Dakota. There's no escape.

Before he's captured Kit leaves a marking to be remembered by, a way to show he was special in an age of conformity. Holly's dispassionate yet often poetic narration punctuates the beautifully bleak landscapes. *Badlands* is about a society so culturally and emotionally bankrupt it can spawn casual killers and turn them into folk heroes. The performances are splendid. The photography is among the best in the history of cinema.

Terrence Malick went on to script and helm the visually stunning *Days of Heaven* (1978) for Paramount, another movie that found its principal audience among gushing movie critics. Then, discouraged by the ability to connect with a popular audience, Malick disappeared from view, neither interviewed nor photographed. He lived in Paris like his fellow underappreciated renegades, Sam Fuller and Orson Welles. For two decades, Terrence Malick was the J. D. Salinger of cinema. The World War II drama *The Thin Red Line* (1998) was Malick's third film in twenty-five years.

Gay

As the burgeoning gay rights movement struggled to find its voice, the first proudly homosexual features struggled to find a home. Hollywood served up *The Boys in the Band* (1970). Outside the studio gates, Mervyn Nelson's *Some of My Best Friends Are . . .* (1971) is a mawkish gay bar tract about oppression. The *Variety* review show-cases the uphill battle: "Laden with every type of fag character, today's audiences with this leaning should find it fascinating fare. For more normal patrons the going may be tough."[20] In *A Very Natural Thing* (1973), ex-monk Christopher Larkin crafted America's first unabashedly homosexual romance. Set in liberated areas of New York City, *A Very Natural Thing* came at least a decade too soon.

Underground Comedy

Comedy changed with the counterculture. It grew a hard satiric edge, it trampled previous boundaries of good taste, and it frequently tilted towards the left. As usual, independent film was at the vanguard.

Funnyman (1968) follows a young improvisional comedian (Peter Bonerz) from San Francisco's legendary group The Committee. He searches for meaning in a life that is one joke after another. John Korty directed, shot, cowrote with Bonerz, provided animation, and essentially self-distributed *Funnyman*. This was his second independent production; the first, *The Crazy Quilt* (1966), is an amateurish dramatic experiment. Korty made additional indies, including the generation-gap drama *Riverrun* (1969) and the documentary *Who Are the Debolts? . . . And Where Did They Get 19 Kids?* (1977), for which he won an Academy Award. He has also been a prolific, Emmy-winning director of TV movies.

Robert Downey, Sr. (1936–) was the Lenny Bruce of cinema, an underground filmmaker who made satirical, offensive, frequently incoherent movies. His earliest experiments—*Babo 73* (1964), *Chafed Elbows* (1966), and *No More Excuses* (1968), all produced for less than $25,000—never climbed out of the drug haze of the underground. Thanks to an industrialist investor, his fourth had a $200,000 budget, and its outrageous premise attracted national attention.

Downey's *Putney Swope* (1969) follows an African-American (gravel-voiced Arnold Johnson) who is accidently elected head of an ad agency. When he staffs it with black militants (and one token, underpaid white), the marketing campaigns change dramatically. Shot in black-and-white with color commercials, *Putney Swope* is a harsh satire of black radicalism and white expectations. It has not aged well. Unfunny segments involve the US President as a pot-smoking dwarf. Except for the wild commercials, there are many more groans than laughs.

Downey was never afraid of offending, and he proved it again with *Greaser's Palace* (1972), a rambling farce that places a Christ figure in a western setting and proceeds to impugn everything possible. Before it became a midnight hit with college students, *Greaser's Palace* made *Time* magazine's annual list of the ten best films. Robert Downey has attempted to revive his comedic anarchy, but none of his subsequent movies have attracted much attention. Actor Robert Downey, Jr., first appeared in his father's films as a child.

The satiric compilation movie began in the early seventies, growing out of underground comedy revues and the frenetic pace of TV's popular "Laugh-In." Directed, written, and produced by Ernest Pintoff, *Dynamite Chicken* (1971) was a collage of the era: Richard Pryor, Lenny Bruce, comedy skits from the Ace Trucking Company, Andy Warhol, John Lennon, music juxtaposed with images of politicians, Vietnam, Malcolm X as a soundtrack for Aunt Jemima, and on and on. Billed as "an electronic magazine of American pop culture," it now stands as an amusing time capsule. *Dynamite Chicken* was rereleased in 1982 as "a new Richard Pryor film," but Pryor successfully sued to keep the distributor from overemphasizing his role (he appears only for a few minutes).

Husband and wife Alan and Jeanne Abel made a sexual mockumentary, *Is There Sex After Death?* (1971). Buck Henry and Robert Downey, Sr., are among those featured in this collection of comic vignettes that explore sexual issues. It has not aged well. Slightly better is *The Groove Tube* (1974), directed, coscripted with Lane Sarasohn, and produced by Ken Shapiro. This medley of sketches satirizing television programs and commercials features Chevy Chase and Richard Belzer (both debuting). Shapiro distributed *The Groove Tube* himself after every studio turned it down. Surprisingly, it grossed millions. "Youth expert" Shapiro was then hired into an executive position at Paramount Studios.

Animator Ralph Bakshi (1938–) went to work for Terrytoons right out of high school, inking such cartoon characters as Mighty Mouse and Heckyll and Jeckyll. He was hired to head Paramount's animation department just before the division closed. In the late sixties, Bakshi struck out with producer Steve Krantz to create animation for adults. Bakshi's first such feature, the infamous *Fritz the Cat* (1972), is certainly adult. For its sexual and violent content, *Fritz the Cat* was the first animated movie to receive an X rating. With a budget of nearly

$1 million, fifty cartoonists in New York and Los Angeles inked the detailed anthropomorphic animals. Based on a character by underground cartoonist Robert Crumb, the acrid tale follows a feline through the sixties, from street singer to subversive. *Fritz the Cat* remains vulgar, but it was never very funny, and it's now hopelessly dated. Though it repeatedly jabs the youth culture, young people flocked to it anyway. The very novelty of an adults-only cartoon turned *Fritz the Cat* into a worldwide hit.

The R-rated sequel, *The Nine Lives of Fritz the Cat* (1974), helmed by Robert Taylor, also has not aged well. The second time out, the potsmoking feline imagines himself in eight other lives, most memorably as an aide to Henry Kissinger.

Bakshi's X-rated *Heavy Traffic* (1973) is the equal to *Fritz the Cat* in coarseness but superior in plot. In this semiautobiographical saga, a boy grows up in Brooklyn spending most of his time drawing cartoons. When he leaves his apartment, he finds a city festering with gangsters, hookers, and other derelicts. Live action is mixed with consistently impressive animation. *The New York Times* named *Heavy Traffic* one of the ten best films of 1973.

Bakshi made a misstep with *Coonskin* (1975), an animated and live-action feature about the status of blacks in America. The most offensive thing about it was its ironic title, but that was more than enough. Its preview was picketed by civil rights groups, and Bakshi was assaulted. Amid the controversy, Paramount dropped plans for distribution. In the years since, Ralph Bakshi has specialized in studio-produced animated features for mature audiences. Titles include *The Lord of the Rings* (1978), *American Pop* (1981), and *Cool World* (1992).

Oasis

The owner of an advertising agency in Dallas, Joe Camp made commercials and industrials before he got the urge to create a family feature. He raised half a million dollars and wrote, produced, and directed his debut, a simple tale told almost entirely from a dog's perspective. The one name actor was Edgar Buchanan (of TV's "Petticoat Junction"). When the film was completed, all the major distributors turned it down, believing that a G rating without Disney's name was box-office poison. So Joe Camp released it himself. Eventually it grossed more than $50 million.

The movie was *Benji* (1974), the story of a dog (also from "Petticoat

Junction") that saves two children held captive in a deserted house. Unlike previous canine heroes, Benji is an unassuming mutt, and that makes him all the more lovable. The dog became a marketing bonanza, launching scores of children's products and showing up on television and in three sequels, all helmed by Camp. Only the first and most successful retread, *For the Love of Benji* (1977), was produced autonomous of the studios.

Documentary

During these volatile years, the most significant documentaries were *cinema verité* portraits, filmed concerts, and political arguments.

After *Titicut Follies*, Frederick Wiseman continued his unnarrated institutional studies with *High School* (1969), an evocative view of life inside a middle-class Philadelphia academy. It premiered soon after his detached, Emmy-winning view of a police department, *Law and Order* (1969), aired on television. Subsequently, as part of a PBS television deal or through his own distribution company, Wiseman has produced, directed, and edited more than twenty *cinema verité* features—all without narration or music. All deal directly or indirectly with institutions. Titles include *Hospital* (1970) which won another Emmy, *Juvenile Court* (1973), and *High School II* (1993).

The Maysles brothers, Albert (1926–) and David (1932–1987), earned degrees in psychology from Boston University and served in the Army during World War II. They worked on *Primary* and other documentaries before capturing one of the all-time great *cinema verité* features, *Salesman* (1968). Editor Charlotte Zwerin is given equal credit as director with Albert (also cinematographer) and David (also sound technician and editor). In order to be less obtrusive, the Maysles brothers built their own quiet, lightweight camera. They then followed four Bible salesman peddling overpriced ($49.95 in 1967), durable ("washable and outlasts leather four-to-one"), gilt-edged Bibles door to door. The camera naturally gravitates towards the Willy Lomanlike Paul Brennan, a talkative, aging Irishman who is beginning to doubt his career choice.

Salesman is about loneliness, about people's need to confirm their faith, about the power of guilt in religion and consumerism, and, above all, about American values. *Newsweek* wrote upon its release: "It's an important film for the questions it raises: not merely esthetic and ethical questions about the documentary genre, but the central question of whether life in these United States is really as bleak as the peddlers and their customers suggest."[21]

Unable to secure a distributor, the Maysles brothers released *Salesman* themselves. With its account of the dying American institution of door-to-door sales, the unforgettable characters it introduces, and the unanswered questions that still linger, this spellbinding black-and-white movie has stood the test of time. The dialogue is richer than any screenplay.

The following year Albert Maysles and Richard Leacock were among the cameraman of the first major rock concert movie, *Monterey Pop* (1969), helmed by D. A. Pennebaker. They take us into the audience and onto the stage of the Monterey Pop Festival of 1967. Filled with classic rock, soul, fashion, and hairstyles, this is a vivid snapshot of the Summer of Love. Jimi Hendrix, Janis Joplin, Otis Redding, The Jefferson Airplane, and The Who are among those featured. Next came Woodstock, the monumental event, and *Woodstock*, the Warner Bros. feature. In December 1969, the Maysles brothers captured a free rock concert at Altamont Speedway, outside San Francisco. The Rolling Stones are in peak form in *Gimme Shelter* (1970), but attention is drawn to the drunken Hell's Angels working "security." A man with a gun is beaten to death by the Angels a few feet from the stage. Later, a dumbfounded Mick Jagger watches this chilling moment repeated.

Dusty and Sweets McGee (1971) is like an updated version of *On the Bowery*, an in-your-face docudrama about junkies and pushers. Debating writer/director Floyd Mutrux and cinematographer William Fraker recreated incidents and conversations with real drug users, including overdoses, hustling, arrests, and graphic shots of injections. Shooting took place on the streets of Los Angeles. Warner Bros. bought *Dusty and Sweets McGee* to compete with Fox's gritty heroin drama *Panic in Needle Park* (1971). William Fraker was a top Hollywood cinematographer before and after, nominated for six Oscars. He shot teen-oriented studio features which Mutrux directed.

Like the New Journalism movement that was taking hold, political documentaries often abandoned the posture of objectivity in favor of a clearly subjective—and arguably more truthful—approach. Self-described Marxist Emile de Antonio continued to raise hell. His Academy Award–nominated *In the Year of the Pig* (1969) is a leftist critique of the Vietnam War assembled from news footage and interviews. *Millhouse: A White Comedy* (1971) ridicules the President by detailing his various scandals—until then. And *Underground* (1976), captured with Haskell Wexler and Mary Lampson, is a penetrating exploration of the radical group the Weathermen that includes interviews with disguised fugitives. De Antonio made other nonfiction features, mostly political. His final film before his death was *Mr. Hoover and I* (1989), a reconstruction of his own life through the ten thousand pages on him in his FBI file.

Made by the Winterfilm collective and Veterans Against the Vietnam War, *Winter Soldier* (1971) was, and still is, a horrifying, eye-opening document. In black-and-white, it captures the testimonies of Vietnam vets as they detail the atrocities committed by some American soldiers. Accounts of the rape, mutilation, and murder of Vietnamese civilians are juxtaposed with war photos and footage.

No film better captures the fire of the early seventies than *The Murder of Fred Hampton* (1971), produced by the nonprofit Film Group and directed by Howard Alk and Mike Grey. The filmmakers set out to construct a portrait of charismatic Fred Hampton, twenty-year-old chairman of the Illinois chapter of the Black Panther Party. After documenting the work and words of the Panthers and the police harassment of the Chicago African-American community, the film was to end with a speech by Hampton. But in December 1969 Fred Hampton and another Panther were killed in a hail of hundreds of police bullets. Alk and Grey rushed to the scene, and their black-and-white feature became an examination of Hampton's death. Their footage of the crime scene contradicts official statements by police and the state prosecutor every step of the way. *The Murder of Fred Hampton* fueled the outrage felt by most blacks and many whites over what they believed was a premeditated execution.

Horror

These were the years when small-time horror struck it rich, pulling in huge crowds with gore and inventive shocks. Many such independent movies turned low budgets to their advantage, using shaky camerawork, amateur actors, and unpicturesque locations to prevent viewers from getting comfortable with their popcorn. The old Hollywood monster movie rules were flagrantly disobeyed. Anything was possible.

It crept up on the viewing public like a slow-moving zombie. Columbia turned it down because it was shot in grainy black and white. AIP rejected it because it lacked a romance and had a down-beat conclusion. Walter Reade's Continental Distributing eventually released it to the bottom bills of drive-ins and outdated theaters. Critics dismissed it. But fans of the horror genre discovered and championed it. They spread the word. When Continental realized what they had, they advertised it with the old William Castle gim-mick of an insurance policy (this time worth $50,000) for anyone who died from fright during a screening. It quickly became a worldwide success. It was even hailed as an art picture and was screened for film societies and at the Museum of Modern Art. It finally found its true home as a cult phenomenon, playing regularly on the midnight movie circuit for more than a decade. Made for a mere $114,000 by amateurs in Pittsburgh, *Night of the Living Dead* eventually grossed more than $50 million.

Its director, cinematographer, and editor was George Romero (1939–), who, growing up in the Bronx, began making 8mm shorts as a teenager. He went to Pittsburgh to study art and drama and formed, with two friends, an industrial and commercial film company. Though they were able to eke out a living, Romero dreamed of mak-ing a feature film. John Russo wrote the script for *Night of the Living Dead*; Romero is credited with the story. The cast and crew were all unknowns and still are. They shot off and on for nine months at and around a rented farmhouse near tiny Evans City, Pennsylvania.

Night of the Living Dead begins like a parody of a traditional gothic horror flick, complete with generic creepy music, lightning, odd cam-era angles, and a lumbering zombie. Things turn violent fast. Barbara (Judith O'Dea) escapes to a farmhouse and is joined shortly by Ben (Duane Jones, before *Ganja & Hess*). They barricade themselves against the relentless zombie attacks and are joined by four others who come up from the basement. Everyone is doomed.

Night of the Living Dead has been read as a parable about the American family consuming itself. Though its violent deaths, scenes of ghouls eating human innards, and full frontal nude zombie pro-pelled it to cult status, *Night of the Living Dead* is almost tame by today's standards. Much of the gore is suggested or takes place off-screen with flesh-eating noises. Included in the mix are some genuine jump-out-of-your-seat moments as well as campy humor, inventive camerawork and editing, and (except for Duane Jones) a lot of bad acting. The most terrifying element is that no satisfying explanation is

Ghouls attack the farmhouse in *Night of the Living Dead*.
© 1968 Image 10, Inc.

ever given for the zombies. *Night of the Living Dead* has echoes of fellow undead greats such as *Carnival of Souls* as well as the work of Herschell Gordon Lewis and Alfred Hitchcock. The final scene, in which the black hero Ben survives through the night only to be casually shot and thrown on a bonfire (shown in a series of news-style photos) by a band of white vigilantes, has real impact, especially given the racial climate in America in 1968.

George Romero's *The Crazies* (1973, aka *Code Name: Trixie*) is a gory tale of a plague, accidentally unleashed by the military, that strikes a small Pennsylvania town. When the Army is called in to contain it, the townspeople strike back. *The Crazies* and Romero's two nonhorror independents (*There's Always Vanilla*, 1971, and *Hungry Wives*, 1972) barely made a dent at the box office, but their director would rise again to unleash other thought-provoking scares.

The gory trend that Friedman and Lewis unleashed and Romero legitimized paid big dividends for cinematic outlaws in the early seventies. The barrage of independent horror is reminiscent of the nudie-cutie wave a decade earlier. Andy Milligan (*Bloodthirsty*

Butchers, 1970), Al Adamson (*Blood of the Ghastly Horror*, 1972), and Ted Mikels (*The Corpse Grinders*, 1971) were the most prolific hacks turning out Lewis-style (i.e. awful), no-budget gorefests. All three worked in other drive-in genres as well. David Durston's rabies rampage *I Drink Your Blood* (1970), Bud Townsend's cannibalistic comedy *The Folks at Red Wolf Inn* (1972, aka *Terror House*, etc.), and Larry Yust's murderous social satire *Homebodies* (1974), were among the better indie horrors. *Children Shouldn't Play With Dead Things* (1972), *I Dismember Mama* (1972), and *Three on a Meathook* (1973) were the most imaginatively titled.

One of the most memorable horror movies is *The Last House on the Left* (1972). Castration during oral sex and a chainsaw murder are hard to forget. When two teenage girls are tortured, raped, and killed by four sadists, their parents get bloody revenge. A perversion of Ingmar Bergman's *The Virgin Spring* (1959) with echoes of the Manson family murders, *The Last House on the Left* stirred up much controversy. Critics still use words like repulsive, repugnant, and reprehensible to describe the authentic-looking brutality that punctuates the last hour. Though there are no scares, just ugliness, and much of the acting, technical aspects, and hokey music is pitiful, *The Last House on the Left* used word of mouth and ominous advertising to become a teenage hit. It marked the debut of two horror giants: writer/director/editor Wes Craven (*A Nightmare on Elm Street*) and producer Sean S. Cunningham (*Friday the 13th*).

Other filmmakers of note debuted in the horror genre. Between stints assisting director Robert Altman, Alan Rudolph made the counterculture terror flick, *Premonition* (1971), and (under a pseudonym) an awful shocker with a sterling title, *Barn of the Naked Dead* (1973). Seven years before directing *Animal House*, twenty-year-old John Landis scripted, directed, and performed in a capable, no-budget spoof of B horror and sci-fi flicks called *Schlock* (1971). And long before *Platoon* or *JFK*, a cab driver and unsuccessful screenwriter named Oliver Stone cowrote and directed *Seizure* (1974), the disjointed tale of a horror novelist whose nightmares come to life. Stone had virtually no previous production experience; the movie had no money. In an effort to get paid, the crew mutinied, dwarf actor Herve Villechaize threatened Stone with a knife, and the cinematographer held the film negative for ransom. *Seizure* played in only one theater.

A publicity shot for *The Texas Chainsaw Massacre*.
Courtesy of Vortex, Inc./Kim Henkel/Tobe Hooper.

In the nineties, Austin, Texas—the progressive capital of a conservative state—became a surprising outpost for alternative cinema. In the seventies, the Texas Film Commission was launched, and its board members executive-produced, invested in, assisted on, and starred in the most notorious horror movie ever made. The director, cowriter, producer, and composer of that $140,000 feature was the only true professional filmmaker in Austin in 1973. Tobe Hooper (1943–) created PBS documentaries, industrial films, commercials, and *Eggshells* (1969), an unreleased art flick about the peace movement. He was ready to make something that would make money, so he and his friend Kim Henkel wrote a script called "Leatherface." They raised a meager budget through the Film Commission and assembled a cast of local amateurs and a crew of University of Texas students. The movie would eventually be titled *The Texas Chainsaw Massacre* (1974).

Five young adults are stranded near a farmhouse occupied by a cannibalistic family that includes Leatherface, a chainsaw-wielding brute who wears a face of human skin (his first appearance is truly shocking). Like *Psycho*, some script elements were inspired by Ed Grein, an infamous mass murderer who consumed and embalmed his victims. The plot resembles *Two Thousand Maniacs!* In both films a group of lost innocents are terrorized and slaughtered by Southern psychopaths merely because they're in the wrong place. But *Chainsaw* is far superior to *Maniacs*: more ferocious, better directed, and much more affecting.

The pain looks real, and some of it actually was. Production took place in 110-degree heat and near 100-percent humidity in insect-heavy woods, with little food or water. The actors were put through truly torturous scenes, and virtually all sustained injuries. Members of the crew—stripped to their sweaty shorts—worked until they dropped. Reading production stories, it seems like everyone hated everyone else.

The completed film feels frightfully authentic for another reason. After a series of well-publicized senseless murders in the late sixties and early seventies, it tapped into a collective fear of unmotivated slaughter by a deranged stranger. Michael Goodwin wrote in *The Village Voice*, "*Chainsaw* captures the syntax and structure of a nightmare with astonishing fidelity. The quality of the images, the texture of the sound, the illogic by which one incident follows another—all conform to the way we dream. No one's done that before, at least not in a commercial, mass market movie. . . . What makes *Chainsaw* interesting is that since we are watching it with our eyes open, it's a nightmare from which we can't wake up."[22]

The Texas Chainsaw Massacre certainly has its faults: too much unfunny black humor near the end, bad acting, and blanched cinematography throughout. Still, in the independent tradition, it subverted horror genre conventions. We have no faith that anyone will survive. A good (if obnoxious) character in a wheelchair would have always made it through a Hollywood movie, but in Hooper's nightmare he's disemboweled. Attacks come unprovoked, sometimes one after another. The blonde heroine (Marilyn Burns) is tortured relentlessly. We're never allowed to catch our breath.

When every major distributor passed, *The Texas Chainsaw Massacre* was picked up by a small company founded on the millions made from *Deep Throat*. Things got off to a good start. When *Chainsaw* played at a San Francisco preview in 1974, some viewers became ill. Others stormed the lobby in protest, provoking a fight, and a lawsuit was later filed by city officials on behalf of the offended audience. One couldn't buy better publicity for a movie that was advertised with a shot of a female victim dangling from a meat hook. Soon after the screening, *Chainsaw* became one of the most popular films in America. Many critics adopted it. It played at the Cannes Film Festival (out of competition), where it was hailed as a political document about cannibalistic America (everything was a political document in the year Nixon resigned). A print was even added to the permanent collection of the Museum of Modern Art. Through the years, *The Texas Chainsaw Massacre* grossed more than $50 million, making it one of the most successful independent features of all time, though the creators never enjoyed the windfall. Cheated by their distributor, the producers collected only thousands while *Chainsaw* made millions. Tobe Hooper went on to specialize in horror, helming frightening pictures big and small, including *Poltergeist* (1982). In 1986, Hooper made the first of three awful Leatherface sequels.

The effects of *The Texas Chainsaw Massacre* were profound. Like *Night of the Living Dead*, it is not nearly as gory as its reputation—most bloodletting is offscreen, and only the paraplegic character is killed with a chainsaw (virtually unseen)—but the violence is unremitting nonetheless. Screams of pain permeate the soundtrack. In perfecting the *Last House on the Left* formula, Hooper's movie further popularized the modern slasher film: innocent young people tormented by crazed killers. Variations on this scheme would propel more nonstudio horror flicks to tremendous box-office grosses in the next few years.

The black-and-white *Living Dead* feels like a perverse parable, while the color *Chainsaw* often plays like a slaughterhouse documentary. Still, they're similar in key regards: both were made with ultralow budgets (less than $150,000) and shot in 16mm, both were rejected by the Hollywood studios, and both went on to become phenomenal ticket sellers (more than $50 million). The most important elements they share, however, are a willingness to break rules and a relentless capacity to scare. Warner Bros.'s *The Exorcist* (1973) also came out during these years. It was gory, shocking, and among the most popular movies of all time. But it was a little independent flick from Pittsburgh and another from Austin that truly revolutionized the horror genre. The old limits were gone. No one could feel safe now.

Pornography

As sexual mores changed in America, the barriers of skin cinema, erected in the sixties, were about to be torn down. In the meantime, however, Russ Meyer continued making his special brand of big-breasted soft-core. *Finders Keepers . . . Losers Weepers* (1968) was a disappointment: a humorless, unerotic tale about a brothel and a strip club. That same year, *Vixen* (1968) catapulted its director to another level. As usual, Meyer directed, produced, and operated the camera; Robert Rudelson authored the script. Though it was shot in Northern California, the setting is Canadian "bush country." Erica Gavin plays Vixen, the racist, sexually insatiable, ball-busting wife of a bush pilot. She seduces every man and woman who comes her way, including her own brother. Eventually a bearded Marxist wanders into the nonexistent plot; the last eleven minutes consist of his hijacking a plane to fly to Cuba. Though void of full frontal nudity and far from sexually explicit, *Vixen* plays like a parody of earnest skin flicks. Still, after the Canadian travelogue opening, there are more uncomfortable moments (incest, racial epithets) than laughs.

Vixen was the first sexploitation picture to break through to wide public consciousness. Erica Gavin promoted it on the talk show circuit. National news stories were penned about it. Censorship efforts stirred up controversy. The film played in legitimate theaters, sometimes for more than a year. *Vixen* earned more than $15 million and cut a path for more explicit fare.

Meyer next made *Cherry, Harry and Raquel* (1970). Charles Napier plays sheriff Harry, trying to track down a snitch in between sexual encounters with Cherry (Linda Ashton) and Raquel (Larissa Ely). There's humor, action, and (as always) prodigious breasts.

While still collecting his windfall from *Vixen*, Meyer signed a deal with Twentieth-Century Fox. For the faltering studio, he directed *Beneath the Valley of the Dolls* (1970), an X-rated (though fairly tame) Hollywood spoof scripted by critic Roger Ebert. Also for Fox, he called the shots on *The Seven Minutes* (1971), a PG-rated drama. The latter and *Blacksnake* (1973), a blaxploitation/sexploitation flick for a different company, were box office duds.

The usual suspects kept churning out soft-core porn. Radley Metzger crafted classy features with European locales, beautiful actors, and simulated sex. He made *Therese and Isabelle* (1968), based on the memoirs of French author Violet Leduc; the futuristic fantasia *Camille 2000* (1969); and *The Lickerish Quartet* (1970). Metzger then crept into hard-core with the swinging spoof *Score* (1972). Sexploitation Queen Doris Wishman expanded on the Meyer formula. Her *Deadly Weapons* (1971) features (in the title roles) the 73-inch chest of stripper Chesty Morgan. In the endless pursuit of crime-fighting, Chesty uses her breasts as lethal clubs. Wishman followed with *Double Agent 73* (1974), in which Morgan's spying character has a camera surgically implanted in one of her deadly weapons. Such outrageousness attracted little attention. The scene had changed. While some continued to make fairly innocent titillation, the industry slithered into heretofore forbidden territory. By the time Russ Meyer was independent again, the skin flick market he nurtured would be a very a different place indeed.

In 1969, a Swedish movie called *I Am Curious—Yellow* made headlines in America for incorporating relatively explicit sex in a political drama. Originally banned from entry into the United States, it was routinely censored. Eventually it won most of its court battles. Fueled by the controversy, *I Am Curious—Yellow* was an art-house sensation, grossing more than $10 million. As an unfortunate result, "Swedish" became another euphemism for "smut." That same year, Matt Cimber's sexual how-to, *Man and Wife*—complete with anatomy charts, an austere narrator, and a copulating couple in a paneled room—ushered in the short but profitable run of "white coaters," pseudodocumentaries about hard-core matters. The stage was set for the swingin' seventies.

Founded in 1965 by Louis Sher, Sherpix distributed many of the most notorious cult movies and skin flicks of the era. Along with Andy Warhol's features, Sherpix released the work of San Francisco's hard-core pioneer, Alex de Renzy. In 1969, one year after Denmark abolished all censorship, de Renzy took a camera to the Pornography Fair of Copenhagen. The movie he assembled, *Pornography in Denmark* (1970), is a collection of interviews about the porn industry mixed with grainy footage of European hard-core. *Variety* noted that "the few remaining barriers to the depiction of the sex act on public screens have been shattered in a manner that makes *I Am Curious—Yellow* seem weaseling."[23] Opening to blockbuster lines, *Pornography in Denmark* became a huge American success. De Renzy rushed out *History of the Blue Movie* (1970), a collection of old stag clips, and *Sexual Encounter Group* (1970), a sex discussion that becomes an orgy, shot in one day for $10,000.

Meanwhile, the first hard-core fictional feature, *Mona: The Virgin Nymph* (1970), stirred up controversy and profits, while the less explicit but 3-D and X-rated *The Stewardesses* (1970) raked in millions. (Both were distributed by Sherpix.) Others hurried into the masturbation biz. Just before he directed *Joe* and a few years before helming *Rocky*, John Avildsen answered a "Wanted—Movie Director" ad that led to his debut: the skin flick *Turn on to Love* (1969). Rocky himself, Sylvester Stallone, performed in a nearly-hard-core movie that was later renamed *The Italian Stallion* (1971).

For the first years of the seventies, most XXX content existed on single 16mm reels (less than fifteen minutes long). These were grouped together and screened in continuous rotation in peep shows. As in nickelodeon days, small storefront theaters (often with flat floors and folding chairs) sprung up like weeds. There were

Sexual Revolution

Sexual mores and sexual movies traveled a nearly parallel course for three decades. The copulation revolution of the sixties and seventies had its roots in the fifties with the Kinsey reports, the birth of the Pill, and the founding of *Playboy*. Those years also marked the beginning of the innocent grindhouse craze for nudism.

A decade later, the Baby Boom generation came of age, leaving old precepts behind. "Free love" and "If it feels good, do it" became rallying cries for sex without obligations. Meanwhile, cinematic sexploitation went from nudism to sadism to almost orgasm.

At the dawn of the seventies, hardcore pornography arrived aboveground, following

continued

close to forty in New York City and more than one hundred in the Los Angeles area. They frequently charged a hefty $5 per admission. The raincoat crowd was expanding, but porno flicks had yet to reach mainstream consciousness.

In 1972, just before *Last Tango in Paris*'s X-rated (but nonpornographic) exploration of sex and loneliness hit middle America, a trio of independent features announced the official arrival of hard-core. Jim and Art Mitchell, owners of an adult theater chain based in San Francisco, had a stroke of luck when it was discovered that Marilyn Chambers, the star of their *Behind the Green Door*, was an "Ivory Soap girl" whose picture adorned the packaging for the "99 and $^{44}/_{1000}$ percent pure" soap. The film also benefited from a clothed, cameo appearance by Oakland Raider football star Ben Davidson, for which he received $500 (the NFL was not amused). The ensuing publicity brought large crowds, including many curious females, to this hard-core feature about a woman (Chambers) who, while forced to perform carnal acts in an exclusive club, becomes sexually "liberated." *Behind the Green Door* is shot like a dream and is more erotic than raunchy.

Ex-hairdresser Gerald Damiano helmed the other two porno blockbusters of 1972. *The Devil in Miss Jones* stars Georgina Spelvin as a spinster who kills herself and is sent to Hell. In Hades she performs various sexual acts but can never reach fulfillment. By the standards of porno, *The Devil in*

Sexual Revolution

continued

the counterculture of sex, drugs, and rock-and-roll. Though many feminists opposed pornography, the women's and gay liberation movements hastened the decline of conservative morality among young adults. For some, *Deep Throat* and company marked a welcome subversion of their parents' uptight, monogamous philosophy.

The proliferation of X-rated screens and the promiscuous lifestyles of a sizeable minority continued through the disco seventies, but easy sex on- and off-screen declined rapidly in the eighties when AIDS officially brought the sex rev to an end and when the expanding audience for "adult entertainment" switched from theaters to VCRs.

Such disparate, non-pornographic, indies as *Faces, Trash, Is There Sex After Death?* and *Remember My Name* address the sexual revolution.

■ ■ ■ ■ ■ ■ ■ ■

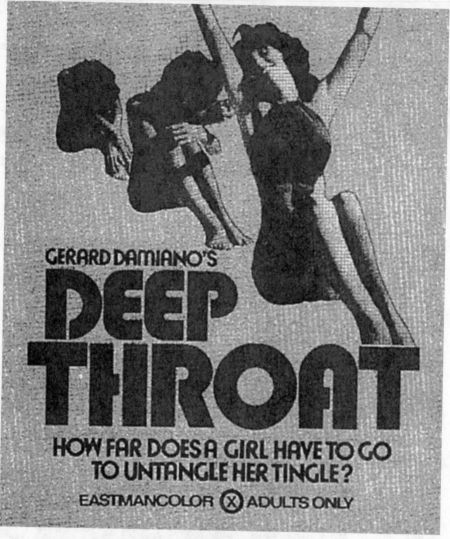

GERARD DAMIANO'S

DEEP
THROAT

HOW FAR DOES A GIRL HAVE TO GO
TO UNTANGLE HER TINGLE?

EASTMANCOLOR Ⓧ ADULTS ONLY

Advertising for *Deep Throat*.

Miss Jones is well produced, with a woman-centered fantasy and surprisingly competent production values and acting.

Damiano's first X-rated feature, on the other hand, is drab, stupid, and laughably acted. Yet *Deep Throat* is the most notorious American motion picture ever made—and one of the most successful. Despite a novel premise—a woman (Linda Lovelace) born with her clitoris in her throat can only experience ecstasy by giving fellatio—it is a typically ugly, boring skin flick, featuring barely attractive people (the norm from stag loop days) and unfunny humor.

Deep Throat's phenomenal success was mostly blind luck. When pornography first slithered aboveground it was suddenly chic, a radical affront to mom and dad and apple pie. Rococo theaters such as those in the Pussycat chain opened, along with storefront peep joints. Liberated couples attended hand in hand. Major critics analyzed hard-core in respected newspapers (*Variety* in 1972 was chock-full of straight and gay porno reviews). Of course, few people would admit to being a fan. After his second viewing of *Deep Throat*, Vincent Canby wrote in *The New York Times*, "The film itself remains junk, at best only a souvenir of a time and place. I'm sure if *Deep Throat* hadn't caught the public's fancy at this point in history, some other porno film, no better and maybe no worse, would have."[24]

Deep Throat continued right on capturing the public fancy, grossing tens of millions of dollars (totals vary greatly). It was *the* one XXX film to attend to see what all the fuss was about. Along the way it was also banned in twenty-three states. The federal government used *Deep Throat* as a test case in an attempt to stamp out pornography. Five corporations and twelve people, including costar Harry Reems, were named in a federal indictment in July 1974 for conspiring to transport "an obscene, lewd, lascivious, and filthy motion picture" across state lines. Reems, whose only involvement was performing on-screen, received a mere $100 for his acting duties and never shared in *Deep Throat's* immense profits. The defendants were convicted by a Tennessee jury in April 1976. Reems was granted a new trial, but the government declined to prosecute again. By that time, *Deep Throat* had already won most of its local appeals, the Supreme Court was about to allow adult theaters in restricted zones, and pornography was big business.

But hard-core porn was no longer chic. Shortly after 1972, the novelty wore off. X-rated movies, with their provocative titles and wretched quality, slipped on and off screens, unreviewed by the mainstream press. The acting, writing, directing, cinematography, editing, and music were almost always pathetic—but there was explicit sex, and that's all that mattered. Gerard Damiano said in 1973, "I created a monster . . . the financial success of *Throat* has caused these people to start cranking out sex pictures, making a lot of money with crap, with just garbage, making a lot of money without ever having paused to learn the craft, to learn what making a film is all about."[25]

After Louis Sher's conviction on an obscenity charge in 1973 (overturned in 1975), Sherpix ceased operations. Alex de Renzy and Gerard Damiano continued to create sexually explicit features. The Mitchell brothers made a few additional XXX movies, but they concentrated mostly on their adult theater empire and the various legal troubles it wrought. In February 1991, Jim Mitchell fatally shot his brother Artie; he was convicted of voluntary manslaughter. Linda Lovelace, the woman who went on a search for sexual pleasure in perhaps the most famous independent movie of all time, later claimed she was drugged, beaten, and forced to perform against her will. In a perverse but fitting tribute to those boundary-breaking years, *Deep Throat* was further immortalized—as the pseudonym for an unknown informant in the Watergate conspiracy.

Underground

The Anthology Film Archives was founded in 1970 to preserve and present avant-garde motion pictures. In the eighties, Anthology moved into a museumlike setting, with daily screenings, a collection of over 6,000 movies, and a reference library with more than one million art film documents. It was all initiated by Jonas Mekas, who continues tirelessly to fight the good fight for truly experimental cinema.

Despite Mekas's best efforts, in the Nixon era the noncommercial cinema of Brakhage, Markopoulos, and company (joined, most visibly, by John Lennon and Yoko Ono) was usurped by outrageous narrative features. As the underground came ever so slightly aboveground, it began to attract a wider college-aged audience. Bizarre stories and extreme antics could actually turn a profit, and soon they would make millions. What was originally cinema's intellectual domain was about to be usurped by the outer limits of exploitation.

But not yet. Jim McBride (1941–) wasn't in the underground to shock. He was there because he couldn't break into studio productions and he had no money. A graduate of NYU film school, he made the remarkable *David Holzman's Diary* (1968) for a mere $2,500. This black-and-white, mock *verité* feature was improvised from ten pages of notes. Though fiction, it plays like an autobiographical documentary by a young New York filmmaker named David Holzman (screenwriter L. M. Kit Carson). For nine increasingly bad days—job loss, love loss, loss of belongings—he records his own pathetic life, both by shooting his few friends and meager surroundings and by setting the camera down and talking to it. The result is a creative triumph, both amusing and perceptive.

David Holzman (and by extension McBride) blurs the line between fact and film. Viewers often think McBride's movie is real. After wowing them at film festivals, *David Holzman's Diary* became a cult favorite. When it premiered at the Museum of Modern Art, L. M. Kit Carson declared the death of the underground film. Actually, it was the reincarnation.

McBride struggled for years in near poverty. He made *My Girlfriend's Wedding* (1969), another tiny personal feature. Working with an independent company and $200,000, he crafted the thought-provoking *Glen and Randa* (1971), a futuristic adventure tale. *Hot Times* (1974) was a disappointing comedy. His films were barely released, but the cult for *David Holzman's Diary* remained strong. After years of teaching and driving cabs, McBride surfaced in Hollywood as the director and cowriter with L. M. Kit Carson of a disappointing remake of *Breathless* (1983). His best studio credit is for directing *The Big Easy* (1987).

Norman Mailer, though one of the great writers of the twentieth century (*The Naked and the Dead, The Armies of the Night, The Executioner's Song*), was one of the worst filmmakers. He directed, produced, and acted in *Wild 90* (1968), *Beyond the Law* (1968), and *Maidstone* (1971). Clearly influenced by Warhol and Cassavetes, Mailer's movies are improvisational experiments. All feature the author's friends making fools of themselves in nonsensical plots. Critic Pauline Kael wrote, "In movies, Mailer tried to will a work of art into existence without going through the steps of making it. . . . His movies trusted to inspiration and were stranded when it didn't come."[26]

Financed by Mailer, *Maidstone* has the biggest budget, cast, and production values, with D. A. Pennebaker (who worked on all three films) and Richard Leacock as cinematographers. *Maidstone* is also the most embarrassing of the three, a nonstop ego trip by Mailer, who plays a flamboyant presidential candidate. The only excitement arrives when actor Rip Torn, following instructions to ad-lib, surprises the writer/director/star by beating him with a real hammer. Both suffered injuries in the ensuing fight; Torn nearly lost his ear when Mailer chomped into it. Thankfully, Norman Mailer stuck mostly to novels and journalism after that.

While Mailer was struggling to distribute his Warhol-inspired flicks, the pop artist himself was recovering from his gunshot wounds. Paul Morrissey assumed the Factory's filmmaking reins. As the Factory's resident square, Morrissey was an enigma. He was prudish on sex, a critic of drugs and rock-and-roll, anti-avant-garde, anti-intellectualism, and politically conservative, yet he made avant-garde films fueled by sex-drugs-rock-and-roll that were championed almost exclusively by intellectuals and the counterculture. Morrissey simply loved movies. In lieu of a salary, he split any profits with Warhol.

Uncredited, Morrissey did most of the directing on *Lonesome Cowboys* (1968), a "pornographic western," which marks the debut of actor Joe Dallesandro and features a moving camera and crisp editing (both Warhol firsts). Its production stirred up press attention by transplanting the Factory freaks to rural Arizona. They were chased out of town by police and vigilantes for their drug use and for capturing a convincing rape scene.

In the summer of 1968, the United Artists film *Midnight Cowboy* was shot in New York City. Upon release the following year, it became an X-rated (nonpornographic) box-office hit that won Oscars for picture, director, and screenwriter. It deals with an otherwise underground topic—male hustling—and features a party scene filmed in the Factory with Warhol regulars (including Morrissey). While *Midnight Cowboy* was shooting and while Warhol was in the hospital, Morrissey rushed his own hustler story into production. *Flesh* (1968) was shot for $4,000 in two weekends. There isn't much of a plot, just a vagabond (Joe Dallesandro) making money any way he can in seedy New York. Still, *Flesh* is more accessible than previous Warhol productions. It played at one Manhattan theater for seven months. Dallesandro became a minor celebrity.

When he recovered, Warhol shot *Blue Movie* (1969, originally titled *Fuck*) in one day with his typical fixed camera. It's a one-hour-and-forty-five-minute study of two lovers (Louis Waldon and Viva) on and around a bed as they talk, watch TV, and have sex. Perpetually obscure, Warhol said it was about the Vietnam War. *Blue Movie* opened strong in New York but was quickly seized by police. It was held to be obscene in a case that went all the way to the US Supreme Court. The Court overturned it in 1973 (though the standards of seizure were upheld). Starting in 1969, Andy Warhol helmed one additional feature film, *Women in Revolt* (1972), which features three drag queens in a burlesque of women's liberation. This, Warhol's response to his would-be assassin, was barely distributed.

Trash (1970), scripted, directed, and shot by Morrissey, was made in two weeks for $25,000. It opened aboveground and earned a respectable $1.5 million. This squalid pseudocomedy follows a junkie ex-hustler (Joe Dallesandro) in search of an erection; his live-in girl-friend (female impersonator Holly Woodlawn) seeks sexual satisfaction and a welfare check. Offensive images and general ugliness mix with absurd dialogue and genuine poignancy. Some in the youth culture adopted *Trash* as a cult favorite, but mainstream critics were unim-pressed. Stanley Kauffamnn wrote, "I don't believe that Warhol and Morrissey believe in or care about the point of naturalism. I think they get a kick out of the suckers who drool in best Pavlovian style when the naturalistic bell is rung: the ones who believe that we are automatical-ly being told something about our society and its spiritual turmoil by candor and grubbiness. . . . *Trash* is disgusting, not for what is on the screen but for what is in the minds of the people who made it."[27]

Heat (1972), released with an R rating, was the most mainstream Warhol production yet. Again directed, written, and shot by Morrissey, it's a not very funny spoof of the already subversive clas-sic *Sunset Boulevard* (1950) in which a hustler/actor (Dallesandro) takes up with a faded star (Sylvia Miles). *Heat* was shown at the Venice and New York Film Festivals. Upon release, it was rejected by both general audiences and Warhol/Morrissey cultists.

Producer Warhol and writer/director Morrissey moved further into commercial cinema with the Italian/French-financed European fea-tures *Andy Warhol's Dracula* and *Andy Warhol's Frankenstein* (both 1974). Shot in Italy, they're bloody, campy renditions of the classic tales with Dallesandro in an otherwise European cast. *Dracula* is better, but *Frankenstein*, boosted by its 3-D gimmick and plentiful gore, was a worldwide blockbuster, grossing millions (figures are disputed)—not a dollar of which ever made it back to its American filmmakers.

The fiasco of trying to collect profits from European producers and a shady domestic distributor strained the relationship between Andy Warhol and Paul Morrissey, and they parted company. Since then, Morrissey has crafted a few movies on the fringe. He made the well-received *Mixed Blood* (1985), a multiracial gangland crime comedy, and *Spike of Bensonhurst* (1988), a Mafia/boxing comedy. Andy Warhol produced only one more motion picture, but it would be by far his most ambitious.

Warhol's original superstar, Edie Sedgwick, choked to death on her own vomit after a routine night of drinking and drugs in November 1971. Shortly thereafter, an independent film about her life, *Ciao! Manhattan* (1972), became an underground sensation. Black-and-white filming by John Palmer and David Weisman began in 1967 just after Sedgwick starred in the Warhol movies. Shooting broke down, but it picked up again in color in 1971 (the early footage is used as flashbacks). By then, the former fashion model was bloated, barely coherent, and near death. Whatever the filmmakers' intentions, *Ciao! Manhattan* plays like a depressing commentary on the destructive power of drugs and an alternate take on the lifestyle embraced in Warhol's movies.

It was up to a film school dropout from Baltimore to pick up the Warhol torch of campy outrageousness and proudly carry it to new lows. John Waters (1946–) is a fan of bad news and bad taste: destruction, mass murderers, the ugly underbelly of suburban life. While still a long-haired teenager, he turned his macabre obsessions into 8mm exploitation shorts. His first feature, *Mondo Trasho* (1969), is a collection of sometimes shocking, rarely humorous, and mostly boring scenes, shot without sound. It is mainly notable for marking the debut of Divine, a saucy 300-pound transvestite with kabuki-style eyebrows, huge wigs, and a fondness for cheap, skintight dresses. She (he) was a natural-born movie star.

Made for $5,000, *Multiple Maniacs* (1971) is an all-out assault on middle-class values. Divine runs a "Carnival of Perversions" that lures suburbanites into a tent where they can be robbed and sometimes murdered. The movie ends with a living room massacre and Divine being raped by a giant lobster! By this time, Waters had established his own Baltimore version of Warhol's Factory players, a stock company of local actors and creeps, including Divine, David Lochary, Mink Stole, the exceedingly ugly Edith Massey, Mary Vivian Pearce, and Cookie Mueller, all of whom appear in *Multiple Maniacs*.

The gang showed up again in the most infamous underground movie of all time: *Pink Flamingos* (1973). Waters, as usual, wrote, directed, produced, shot, edited, and financed (with his parent's $12,000). Waters's own home served as the Marble house. The plot follows a contest between trailer trash Babs Johnson (Divine) and baby farmers Raymond and Connie Marble (David Lochary, Mink Stole) to determine who is the filthiest person alive. After—among other assaults—sex with a chicken, cannibalism, incest, castration,

Divine in *Pink Flamingos.*/© 1997 New Line Productions, Inc. All rights reserved.
Photo appears courtesy of New Line Productions, Inc.

and the murder of the Marbles, Divine eats fresh dog excrement (for real) and smiles to the camera. John Waters, with his pencil-thin moustache, ghoulish tastes, and devious smile, fondly remembers the shock value: "Do you know how hard it is to horrify three generations? I know that when you left that movie, you may have hated it but you had to tell someone. You couldn't just be, like, What did you see last night?, and say, 'Oh, nothing.' "[28]

Reviews of *Pink Flamingos* ran the gamut. The *Los Angeles Times* wrote, "It makes as total an assault on conventional sensibilities as is imaginable without becoming downright morbid. That's because it is as funny as it is outrageous. And as we're being liberated by our laughter we're made aware how much more easily we can be offended by actually quite harmless scatological excesses. . . ."[29] On the other hand, *Variety*'s headline summarized, in bold type, "Dregs of Human Perversity. Draws weirdo element. Monstrous," before going on to call *Pink Flamingos* "one of the most vile, stupid and repulsive films ever made. Since such distinction is its relentless goal, it's a real perverse achievement."[30] Either review would suffice. Sick and hateful throughout, with awful acting and dialogue and trash/kitsch design, *Pink Flamingos* elevated bad taste to a hip aesthetic. It was a new way of offending the establishment. *Pink Flamingos* was the perfect underground flick for a generation coming of age during Watergate, devoid of the ideals of the late-sixties counterculture but equally disdainful of their parents' institutions.

New Line Cinema, founded in 1967 by Robert Shaye, first achieved attention when it rescued *Reefer Madness* from public domain and rented it to college communities as a campy classic. New Line also distributed Waters's *Multiple Maniacs*. Along the way, the midnight movie was born, a youthful diversion for Saturday nights. Among the 12:00 AM trailblazers with *Reefer Madness* and *Multiple Maniacs* were *Night of the Living Dead*, *Greaser's Palace*, *El Topo* (1971, Mexico), and Paramount's *Harold and Maude*. *Pink Flamingos* was the midnight movie queen. Screening in college towns after the church-going citizens turned out their lights, it steadily raked in millions throughout the seventies.

Female Trouble (1974) brought the Baltimore gang back together in the best of Water's independent features. Dawn Davenport (Divine) runs away from home, is raped by a pervert (Divine as a man), becomes pregnant, and raises her bratty daughter (Mink Stole) into a life of crime. After murdering for art's sake, Dawn is sent to the electric chair—the ultimate prize for someone with her severely twisted philosophy. *Female Trouble* has outrageous material—incest, vomiting, violence—but this time it doesn't overshadow the sustained attack on middle-class values, the delightfully tasteless production design, and Divine's appropriately over-the-top comedic performance. *Female Trouble* joined *Pink Flamingos* on the cult movie circuit.

John Waters would produce only one additional independent feature. As his budgets grew progressively larger, his subject matter became less outrageous. Eventually he would become almost (curse the thought) respectable. New Line Cinema, built on the profits of midnight movies, would focus more and more energy on foreign fare and American artistic independents, and it would continue to grow along with the art-house scene.

By the end of 1974, after *Pink Flamingos, Deep Throat,* and *The Texas Chainsaw Massacre* had shattered the last boundaries, there was nothing truly shocking to shoot anymore. As the slasher and, especially, the porno formulas were repeated thousands of times over the next ten years, such movies would lose their ability to scandalize. Instead, independent cinema would focus on the territory staked out by the American New Wave. In the last half of the seventies, while Hollywood developed its blockbuster mentality, outsiders would begin to build an infrastructure of festivals, organizations, and distributors that could nurture and promote smaller features. The course was about to be set.

Notes

---

[1] Ventura, Micheal, director, *"I'm Almost Not Crazy . . ." John Cassavetes: The Man and his Work,* film (Cannon Television, 1984).

[2] Rip Torn had a previous commitment to act in Norman Mailer's *Maidstone.* Additionally, there was an infamous confrontation in preproduction between Hopper and Torn. Hopper claimed on *The Tonight Show* in 1994 that he fired Torn because Torn pulled a knife on him, but sources maintained Hopper pulled the knife. In 1997, Torn won $475,000 in a defamation suit against Hopper.

[3] *New Yorker*, 27 Sept. 1969.

[4] *Filmmaker* 5, 1(Fall 1996), 40. Fifty films are listed in this myopic "expert" poll. Only two are pre-1960; none are pre-1940. The remaining top five in descending order are *Stranger Than Paradise; She's Gotta Have It; sex, lies, and videotape;* and *Return of the Secaucus 7* (all from the eighties).

[5] *New York Times*, 16 Dec. 1968.

[6] Kelly, Mary Pat, *Martin Scorsese: A Journey* (New York: Thunder's Mouth Press, 1991), 49.

[7] Kelly, 68.

[8] *Variety*, 3 Oct. 1973.

[9] *Time*, 16 Aug. 1971.

[10] *Variety*, 8 March 1972.

[11] *Variety*, 18 April 1973.

[12] Film doctor Fima Noveck did the re-editing. Not all of the changes are bad; some of them make the film more coherent and tense. Still, too much of Gunn's jagged poetry fell to the cutting room floor.

[13] Monaco, James, *American Film Now* (New York: Oxford University Press, 1979), 205.

[14] All four of these films star Mr. Whitezploitation, Burt Reynolds, who directed Gator and starred in such additional "southerns" as *W. W. and the Dixie Dancekings* (1975), *Smokey and the Bandit* II (1980), and *Stroker Ace* (1983).

[15] *Variety*, 24 April 1973.

[16] Kaminsky, Ralph, "Sebastians Rely on Common Folks as Key to Filmmaking, Distribution," *Boxoffice*, 28 April 1975.

[17] *New Republic*, 27 March 1971.

[18] Yellin, David G. and Marie Connors, eds. *Tomorrow & Tomorrow & Tomorrow* (Jackson: Univ. of Miss., 1985), ix.

[19] Thomson, David, *A Biographical Dictionary of Film*, 3rd ed. (New York: Knopf, 1995), 470.

[20] *Variety*, 8 Sept, 1971.

[21] *Newsweek*, 21 April 1969.

[22] Goodwin, Michael, "A Real Nightmare Makes a Great Horror Film," *Village Voice*, 9 Feb. 1976.

[23] *Variety*, 22 April 1970.

[24] *New York Times*, 21 Jan. 1973.

25 Turan, Kenneth and Stephen F. Zito, 154.
26 *New Yorker*, 28 Oct. 1972.
27 *New Republic*, 31 Oct. 1970.
28 Marc S. Malkin, "Idol Chatter: John Waters," Premiere, April 1997, 39.
29 *Los Angeles Times*, 13 Dec. 1974.
30 *Variety*, 11 Dec. 1974.

BUILDING

I'm a politician first, a filmmaker second.

—BARBARA KOPPLE

It's much easier to write something difficult off than it is to champion it.

—JAMES TOBACK[1]

For the country, the mid-seventies to early eighties was a time of economic insecurity. For Hollywood, the same period was marked by all-time box office champs *Jaws* (1975) on one end and *E.T.* (1982) on the other. *Star Wars* (1977) came in between. A giant, hungry shark officially marked the end of the American New Wave. Darth Vader obliterated it. Blockbuster mania was on.

On studio lots, those seven years were an escalating whirlwind of special effects and salaries that has continued nearly unabated to the present day. In 1975, no picture had ever been budgeted at more than $15 million, but a short five years later, eleven had been made for more than $30 million, including five for more than $40 million. *Superman* (1980) cost $55 million. Armed with computer marketing surveys, producers and executives reasserted their power, snatching it back from the auteur directors of the early seventies. After *Jaws* and *Star Wars*, the major studios swung for the fences, trying (usually in vain) to push a glossy "vehicle" towards a nine-digit worldwide total from ticket sales and merchandising. As the Hollywood factories weakly promoted or jettisoned lower-budgeted dramas and comedies altogether, the nascent independent scene sensed an opening. In 1975, the nonstudio sector was still just a few film festivals, a few specialized distributors, and a few hundred art houses. But things were about to change.

Grossing $2 million is a successful domestic box office take for most modern indies, but the majority fall short of even that meager mark. The audience for documentaries, ironic character studies, and bizarre cult flicks is minute when compared to the viewership for *Star Wars*. Such "small" films need nurturing to reach selective fans. While the studios churned out big-budget sequels and would-be blockbusters, the off-Hollywood sector developed a support system to cultivate talent and properly introduce small movies.

Key film festivals were born. Telluride, a tiny ski town in Colorado, started a cinema showcase in 1973 that steadily grew in influence. Toronto and Seattle both inaugurated fests in 1975. Montreal began an international event two years later. Between 1971 and 1986, Los Angeles's Filmex was a key showcase of the era, just as New Directors/New Films at the Museum of Modern Art (New York) rose in prominence as a screening series. Meanwhile, the festivals in New York City and San Francisco continued to attract attention. Cannes and Venice had not slipped in prominence, but by the late seventies it was possible to stir up interest without leaving North America.

To little fanfare, in 1978 a showcase was born—in of all places—Salt Lake City, Utah, 700 miles from Hollywood, more than 2,000 miles from Manhattan. In 1981 it moved to nearby Park City. Though it had an ambitious name, The US Film Festival, for years this indie showcase was known more for its ski slopes than for launching movies and moviemakers. In 1984, it was purchased by Robert Redford. A few years later the US Film Festival changed its name and became, with Cannes, one of the two most important film showcases in the world.

Festivals are where producers introduce their movies to potential distributors, and in the late seventies more and more distributors leaped into the fray. Samuel Goldwyn, Castle Hill, Triumph, Island/Alive, First Run Features, and Cinecom were among the new companies that specialized in art-house entertainment. Cinema 5 and New Yorker persisted until the early eighties but eventually found it impossible to thrive in an increasingly crowded marketplace. Likewise, the Walter Reade Organization sold off Continental Distributing in 1970 and filed for bankruptcy in 1977.

New Line continued to acquire various nonstudio features. And, in addition to pumping out the usual youth exploitation, Roger Corman's New World would sometimes pick up something for cinéastes. In 1983, four years after AIP merged itself out of existence, Corman sold New World and set up New Horizon Pictures, which has continued to produce mostly straight-to-video exploitable movies.

In 1980, United Artists became the first corporate victim of the blockbuster syndrome when its $44 million *Heaven's Gate* was an all-out bust. The factory that Chaplin, Griffith, Fairbanks, and Pickford built would never be the same. It merged with another decimated giant, MGM. Struggling to regroup, the severely wounded UA thought small once again and formed United Artists Classics to acquire and distribute (mostly foreign) art-house pictures. Fox and Universal followed with their own classics divisions. Within three years all were out of business. The studios would sometimes acquire features, but they generally had neither the patience nor the expertise to shepherd small movies to cinematheques.

Bulky, movie-loving brothers Harvey and Bob Weinstein started a New York company in 1979 named Miramax (combining the names of their parents, Mira and Max). They didn't truly join the bidding pack until the mid-eighties, but by the time the nineties rolled around Miramax would be the most important independent distributor in the world.

As festivals and release companies gained clout, a support structure for filmmakers developed at the end of the Carter years. In 1979, PBS started funding nonstudio features and shorts as part of its "American Playhouse" series. Projects deemed worthy were given crucial financing; in return, PBS received the initial television rights. Producers jumped at the chance to attain money *and* an unedited prime time TV broadcast. For the next fifteen years (until political pressure slashed funding), "American Playhouse" backed more independent motion pictures than any other single source.

The Independent Feature Project (IFP) began in 1979 as a nonprofit, member-driven organization whose goal was to nourish and promote nonstudio cinema. Based in New York City, it branched out to Los Angeles and other regions. The year of its birth, the IFP launched in Manhattan the Independent Feature Film Market (IFFM), an opportunity to show completed and uncompleted features and shorts to distributors, the press, festival programmers, investors, and a core audience. Many key American indies have scored their first break at the IFFM.

In 1981, actor/director Robert Redford formed the Sundance Institute to support autonomous cinema. He took the title from his skiing, art, and nature community in Utah, which was named after his character in *Butch Cassidy and the Sundance Kid*. The Institute staged various collaborative film workshops in rural Utah, but Sundance did not become the preeminent name in nonstudio cinema until it took over the US Film Festival. By that time the indie community was truly a scene.

John Cassavetes

John Cassavetes kept right on financing, directing, writing, and distributing his own feature films. *The Killing of a Chinese Bookie* (1976), as its evocative title suggests, was a departure for Cassavetes: a gritty crime story about strip joint owner Cosmo Vitelli (Ben Gazzara), who racks up $23,000 in gambling debts and reluctantly agrees to kill a bookmaker in order to clear the debt. After the murder, he learns that the thugs (including Seymour Cassel), who sent him on the mission, are now trying to eliminate him. Gazzara is terrific as the resigned loser, and the gaudy Los Angeles settings are appropriately evocative. After *A Woman Under the Influence*, this is Cassavetes's best feature, and for nonfans his most accessible.

Opening Night (1977) was pure Cassavetes, a tale of dependancy and self-destruction. The auteur again gave wife Gena Rowlands a scenery-chewing role, this time as Myrtle Gordon, an alcoholic theatrical actress on a rapid downward spiral. She's the star of a play that is auditioning out-of-town actors. Cassavetes is Maurice, the leading man; Ben Gazzara is the director; Joan Blondell is the playwright. After one of her fans is killed by a car while running after Myrtle's limousine, the drunken actress is haunted by the young woman's image. On opening night, Myrtle staggers on stage and falls and she and Maurice ad-lib the play's second act as a drunken farce. The curtain comes down to thunderous applause. A stage manager beams to Myrtle, "I've never seen anyone as drunk as you who could stand up. You're great." The ending suggests she will never stop drinking as long as those closest to her are willing to (literally) hold her up while others applaud. *Opening Night* is long and self-indulgent, but it's worth seeing for Rowlands's performance.

Between his regular Hollywood acting roles, John Cassavetes crafted two studio pictures, *Gloria* (1980) and *Love Streams* (1984). Filled with raw scenes, the latter is a favorite of Cassavetes fans. Like many final films, *Big Trouble* (1985) is not representative of its director's body of work. Instead, it's a ditsy kill-the-husband-for-the-cash comedy. *Big Trouble* had a troubled production history and was barely released.

Contemplating his films, Cassavetes explained: "What everybody needs is a way to say, 'Where and how can I be in love so that I can live with some degree of peace?' . . . And so that's why I have a need for the characters to really analyze love, discuss it, kill it, destroy it, hurt each other, do all that stuff in that war—in that word polemic and picture polemic of what life is. And the rest of the stuff doesn't really interest me. . . . That's all I'm interested in—is love."[2]

John Cassavetes died in 1989; he was fifty-nine. A true maverick, he presented his own pessimistic view of the quest for love. He sometimes trusted in his actors—close friends and family—too much and cared too little about pacing and story line. Other times, he let the camera run long enough to uncover the psychological truths— the sexual tension and middle-class anxieties. His is the ultimate oeuvre of personal filmmaking, and people who view his movies have a distinctly personal reaction. Some love them; some hate them; most have never seen them. Cassavetes kept the rights to the films he self-financed, and video versions are scarce. Nonetheless, Cassavetes's influence on independent cinema is great. You see it in handheld camerawork, in extemporaneous dialogue (or the illusion of such), in self-financing and self-distributing, in the emphasis on characters over the machinations of plots. If you look closely, you see John Cassavetes everywhere.

Period Pieces

The cinematheques received a wake-up call in 1975, when a little black-and-white period piece about immigrants that had failed to secure distribution earned more than $5 million and an Academy Award nomination. The film was *Hester Street*, and its writer and director was Joan Micklin Silver (1935–). Its producer was her husband, real-estate speculator Raphael Silver. The daughter of Jewish Russian immigrants, Joan Silver had been making educational and children's films. During her research for a short on immigration, she read a story called "Yekl" by Abraham Cahan, and it became the source for *Hester Street*.

Silver and her husband solicited funds and pitched in their own savings to come up with the $400,000 budget, a remarkably low sum for a motion picture set in the Jewish ghettos of turn-of-the-century New York City with all the necessary clothes, sets, and props. When they shot exteriors on lower Manhattan's Morton Street, residents literally propped up replicas of old storefronts and signs. The recreation of a unique culture and a different time is convincing, aided by an appropriate musical score by William Bolcom.

Hester Street follows Jewish Russian immigrant Jake (Steven Keats), who works in a sweatshop and is anxious to become Americanized. His wife Gitl (Carol Kane) and son arrive from Russia, bringing with them reminders of the Old World Jake is trying to leave behind. He rejects his wife and mocks her values when he cheats on her. Bernstein (Mel Howard) is the scholarly tenement boarder who falls in love with the pious and confused Gitl. The marriage of Gitl and Jake disintegrates.

Silver said of her characters, "I tend to see people as a mix, you know, the Jewish view is that people have the potential for good and evil and I really agree."[3] Every distributor rejected the sometimes rough (the boom mike haunts a lengthy shot) and distinctly ethnic *Hester Street*. So the Silvers released it themselves. It spread slowly to major markets. Aided by positive reviews and word of mouth, the film played for months in some urban centers. Carol Kane's Best Actress Oscar nomination also helped *Hester Street* at the box office.

The Silvers put their initial earnings from *Hester Street* into an independent follow-up, *Between the Lines* (1977). Helmed by Joan, produced by Raphael, and scripted by Fred Barron, it's an enjoyable tale about a failing alternative newspaper in Boston purchased by a print tycoon. Workers at the radical weekly are torn between their counterculture idealism and the realities of commerce. (Joan Silver wrote for *The Village Voice* in the late sixties.) The ensemble cast was made up of then unknowns (some debuting) who went on to great fame, including John Heard, Marilu Henner, Jeff Goldblum, and Bruno Kirby. The Silvers self-distributed *Between the Lines*, but it failed to find an audience.

The Silvers reversed roles—Raphael directing; Joan producing—on the forgettable prison melodrama *On the Yard* (1979), starring John Heard. Around the same time, Joan brought to the screen Ann Beattie's novel *Chilly Scenes of Winter*, a semi-indie from United Artists. Under the title *Head Over Heels*, this romance bombed upon general release. Without its happy ending and with its original name, United Artists Classics rereleased it more successfully to art houses in 1982. Joan Silver has since called the shots on studio productions, most notably *Crossing Delancey* (1988). The Silvers' daughter, Marisa, directed and wrote (and daughter Dina produced) the independent *Old Boyfriends* (1984), a slow-moving coming-of-age story.

The years 1979 to 1981 served up three highly praised, artistic independents set in earlier times. Period films are difficult to pull off with even a big budget, but by concentrating on the rural working class so often neglected by Hollywood, these low-priced renegades succeeded while *Heaven's Gate*—with a budget dozens of times larger—was failing for the opposite reason, emphasizing grandeur over substance.

Victor Nunez (1945–) writes, directs, produces, shoots, and edits unique features set in his native Florida. He remains steadfastly autonomous regardless of how long it takes to raise money for the films he wants to make. After working on educational and industrial shorts, his debut feature, *Gal Young 'Un* (1979), was produced for less than $100,000. Most of the actors were amateurs, including lead Dana Preu, a university professor who had never performed before.

Set in the Florida backwoods in the 1920s, the film follows a lonely middle-aged widow (Preu) who falls for a hustler (David Peck). They marry, and he uses her farmhouse to make moonshine. He is abusive when not neglectful. When he brings home a young woman (J. Smith) to live with them, the widow bides her time, forming a bond with the equally exploited young woman and plotting revenge.

Effectively acted, *Gal Young 'Un*, like *Tomorrow*, is a poignant tale that convincingly captures its period. Nunez was a founding member of the Independent Feature Project, and his debut screened at the inaugural IFFM. It was also one of the initial releases of First Run Features, a distribution collective created by Nunez and others. *Gal Young 'Un* was a modest art-house success.

Another movie at 1979's IFFM and another initial release from First Run Features was *Northern Lights* (1979), the result of a three-year collaboration between John Hanson and Rob Nilsson, who shared the major duties. They captured their gritty, incisive story in black-and-white for $350,000, filming entirely in the farmlands of North Dakota. Set in the winter of 1915, it tells the story of a man (Robert Behling) who works to politically organize Norwegian farmers. *Northern Lights* won the Camera D'Or (award for first film) at the Cannes Film Festival and eventually became a cinematheque success.

Since then, Rob Nilsson, who began his career as a leftist documentarian, has had trouble raising funds. Out of economic necessity he invented what he calls "direct action," which combines *cinema verité* with improvisation using videotape that is later transferred to film. His direct action features *Signal 7* (1983) and *Heat and Sunlight* (1988) won some acclaim but were not distributed theatrically.

Documentarians Annick Smith and Beth Ferris wanted to produce a series of motion pictures that would explore the roles of women in the settlement of the Old West. Beginning in 1977, Ferris and William Kittredge painstakingly researched and wrote a script on the life of pioneer Elinore Stewart. Executive producer Smith and producer Ferris (later joined by Michael Hausman) secured $600,000 from PBS for the first installment of a "Wilderness Women" series. Documentary cameraman Richard Pearce was hired as director. Smith mortgaged her ranch to secure another $200,000, and *Heartland* (1981) went into production in rural Montana.

Elinore (Conchata Ferrell) moves with her seven-year-old daughter (Megan Folsom) to Wyoming in 1910 and accepts work as a housekeeper for dour rancher Clyde Stewart (Rip Torn), who sports an Amish beard, a pipe, and a Norwegian accent. They eventually marry and bind together to survive a brutal winter. *Heartland* quietly presents special moments of a severely understated marriage and the realities of life on a farm. The birth of a calf is a highlight. The fall and winter color photography by Fred Murphy is evocative, and the casting of sturdy, average-looking people feels authentic. The simple story has few surprises and little conflict but remains compelling nonetheless. Depicting similar times and places, *Heartland* and *Northern Lights* both cut through western mythology to present the kind of hard-working, ordinary folks who actually homesteaded the West.

Heartland screened at the 1979 New York Film Festival to rave reviews. It also won the prestigious Golden Bear (Grand Prize) at the

Conchata Ferrell feeds wedding cake to Rip Torn in *Heartland*.

Berlin Film Festival and tied for first place at the US Film Festival. It played more than fifteen such events throughout the world. After two years, *Heartland* finally secured distribution from tiny Levitt-Pickman. Ads listed awards and review quotes and announced, "Few motion pictures have ever been so honored." Through a vigorous promotional campaign and consistently positive notices, this subdued movie quietly grossed millions. Richard Pearce went on to helm the similarly themed *Country* (1984) and other Hollywood movies.

Potpourri

A wide variety of fictional independent films were made during these years, covering topics from the apocalypse to gangster pianists to a dinner conversation. The nonstudio community strived to make the kind of thought-provoking movies that the factories were increasingly neglecting.

Several features that seemed to exist somewhere between the art house and the mall emerged. *A Boy and His Dog* (1975) was perhaps the most intriguing example. A faithful adaptation of science fiction author Harlan Ellison's award-winning novella, prolific character actor L. Q. Jones debuted as director and screenwriter (they were his only such credits in a career that spanned more than four decades). Don Johnson plays Vic and Tiger (the dog from TV's "The Brady Bunch") plays Blood. Together they made the kind of brave and peculiar movie that the studios assiduously avoid.

Vic and Blood the dog wander about a ravaged post–World War III earth in 2024. Vic finds food for both of them, and Blood—who communicates with Vic telepathically (with the voice of composer Tim McIntire)—sniffs out females for Vic to rape. When a woman, Quilla June (Susanne Benton), seduces Vic, Blood worries about his own future. Vic is taken to an underground commune where he is to mechanically impregnate thirty virgins before being killed. He escapes. Quilla follows him aboveground only to discover too late that there is nothing stronger than the bond between a boy and his dog.

A Boy and His Dog was blasted for depicting women as mere sex objects, but the story is clearly a satire of such thinking. Many viewers miss the movie's dark humor, probably because of the odd man/dog dialogue (the canine is clearly smarter than Vic).

Most critics were not impressed. *Variety* wrote, "*A Boy and His Dog* is a turkey . . . an amateurish blend of redneck humor, chaotic fight scenes, and dimwitted philosophizing. Director L. Q. Jones . . . should stick to playing cretins in Sam Peckinpah westerns. Commercial prospects are dim."[4] The last comment proved true. *A Boy and His Dog* was too cerebral, pedestrian, and mature (rated R) to attract the typically adolescent sci-fi fans, while its fantasy elements and childish title scared off adults. However, *A Boy and His Dog* managed to stir up a cult following that remained loyal throughout the Luke Skywalker years.

Pipe Dreams (1976) stars singer Gladys Knight as Maria Wilson, who journeys to Alaska to win back her husband (Barry Hankerson) on equal terms. She helps other women, including prostitutes, stand up for themselves in the male-dominated territory of the oil fields. Gladys Knight and the Pips perform on the soundtrack. Scripted, directed, and produced by Stephen Verona (*The Lords of Flatbush*), this plodding movie is notable mostly for its feminist theme.

Fraternity Row (1977) tells of the emotional and physical violence inside a college fraternity in 1954. Helmed by rookie Thomas Tobin, written and produced by USC student Charles Allison, the film features Gregory Harrison as a student who is sadistically hazed. This involving drama includes narration by Cliff Robertson and the music of Don McLean. Made with a cast and crew of mostly USC undergrads, *Fraternity Row* was picked up and released by Paramount Studios. It flopped.

Robert Young, coproducer and cowriter of *Nothing But a Man*, returned to independent cinema with two distinctly original features. *Short Eyes* (1977, aka *The Slammer*) was directed by Young and adapted by Miguel Piñero from his own brutally realistic play. Photographed entirely in the Tombs, Manhattan's infamous men's detention center, *Short Eyes* serves up the violence, racial tension, and desperation of life behind bars. Clark Davis (Bruce Davison) is a middle-class man awaiting trial for child molesting. No one is more abused by guards and fellow inmates than a "short eyes" (slang for child molester). Dimly lit, claustrophobic, and filled with uncompromising dialogue, cruelty, and the constant fear of rape and murder, this may be the most harrowing movie about incarceration ever made. Singer Curtis Mayfield and screenwriter Piñero are among those in the hellhole with Davison.

Robert Young also wrote, directed, and shot *Alambrista!* (1977). The simple story remains fresh today: a naive young Mexican man (Domingo Ambriz) crosses into America and is exploited as he seeks work to support his family. The fine cast includes Edward James Olmos, Julius Harris, and Ned Beatty. *Alambrista!* was well received at Cannes, but it failed to find a commercial audience. Small dramas with predominantly non-Caucasian casts were usually rushed in and out of art houses.

An excellent film by and about African-Americans couldn't get even such a perfunctory release. Charles Burnett (1944–) was born in Mississippi and grew up in South Central Los Angeles. While a film student at UCLA, he wrote, directed, produced, photographed, and edited a thesis film called *Killer of Sheep* (1977). In this deceptively modest black-and-white story, an African-American family in Watts struggles to stay together amidst poverty after the father loses his job at a slaughterhouse. Though the TV miniseries "Roots" was an unparalleled ratings phenomenon early in 1977, there were still precious few black-themed dramas on the big screen. *Killer of Sheep* failed to win theatrical circulation. Still, its legend grew. It won prizes at the

Berlin and the US Film Festivals in the early eighties and eventually reached the American public on PBS. In 1990, *Killer of Sheep* was named among the second group of twenty-five motion pictures added to the National Film Registry of the Library of Congress.[5]

Charles Burnett was the recipient of a MacArthur genius grant (for $225,000) in 1980, but he continued to fight a losing battle to get black dramas into theaters. He made *My Brother's Wedding* (1983), about a young man caught between the comfortable ghetto and the upwardly mobile life of his brother. It also failed to attain distribution. Such was the sorry state of African-American independent cinema during the twelve years between blaxploitation and Spike Lee.

Likewise, Joan Silver was virtually alone as a female fiction-film director in the late seventies (and one of very few since Ida Lupino). Three years after her debut, she was joined by another independent, Claudia Weill, who studied painting and photography and crafted experimental and documentary motion pictures. Weill made a $10,000 short and slowly raised additional money. Over the course of a year the short grew into a feature with the same name, *Girlfriends* (1978). It was a surprise hit at the Cannes Film Festival and Warner Bros. snatched it up and distributed it to good reviews and lackluster box-office receipts.

Girlfriends is the story of Susan (Melanie Mayron), an idealistic young woman in New York City struggling to make a career for herself as a photographer. Her roommate (Anita Skinner) wants to be a writer. They talk about guys and art and guys until Anne gets married, leaving Susan alone in an unforgiving city. *Girlfriends* is a likeable dramatic comedy, well acted by all (including Eli Wallach and Christopher Guest). Weill went on to helm the similarly angst-driven TV series "thirtysomething," starring Mayron.

James Toback was a Harvard-educated writer with one produced script to his credit (*The Gambler*, 1974) when he wrote and directed *Fingers* (1978). Made for $1 million, with strong use of New York locales, *Fingers* follows Jimmy Angelelli (Harvey Keitel), an aspiring concert pianist who is also a collector for his loan shark dad (Michael Gazzo).

As an independently produced, literate crime movie starring Harvey Keitel, *Fingers* fits into a continuum between Scorsese's *Mean Streets* and Quentin Tarantino's *Reservoir Dogs*, but it fails by comparison. Despite some surprising brutality, it's simply not that exciting as a gangster movie. *Fingers* did have its supporters. David Thomson wrote, "*Fingers* is ingrowing and wounding. It does not belong to any familiar genre: it is more like a psychological allegory or ordeal. The outward signs of a New York crime movie are only its vehicle—like the body that houses the shivers of a dream. *Fingers* is that genuine oddity: an American feature movie that treats plot as merely the imprint for compulsive passions of terrible but dynamic force."[6]

Difficult to categorize, *Fingers* was poorly distributed in North America and bombed at the box office. After being championed in Europe, it was reappraised by some domestic critics and hailed as a work of genius. Despite an Oscar nomination for scripting *Bugsy* (1991), James Toback has had a sporadic Hollywood career. He regained independence for *The Big Bang* (1990), a documentary in which folks contemplate the meaning of life.

Every now and then a celebrity's ego will expand to such prodigious dimensions that he or she feels divinely ordained to revolutionize moviemaking. A few years after Norman Mailer recovered, such dementia befell singer Bob Dylan when he wrote, directed, and (supposedly) edited four tedious hours of self-indulgence called *Renaldo and Clara* (1978). The completed film contains concert footage, but more than two-thirds of it is an incomprehensible chimera involving Dylan as the mysterious Renaldo, his wife Sara as Clara, 300-pound Ronnie Hawkins as Dylan, and Joan Baez as the Woman in White. Harry Dean Stanton, Arlo Guthrie, Alan Ginsburg, and Sam Shepard are also featured. It's a pretentious, confused mess about truth and beauty and slavelike audiences worshiping idols. *Renaldo and Clara* was later cut to two hours of mostly concert footage—it's still a wreck.

Playwright/actor Wallace Shawn and stage director/actor André Gregory have been friends since 1971. In the late seventies, they developed a most unique project. After they spoke at random about every subject that came to mind, Shawn took tapes of the conversations and shaped them into a two-character screenplay set at a meal. They acquired initial financing from PBS's "American Playhouse." Knowing that a nearly two-hour, two-person talkathon could very easily fall flat, they sought an expert filmmaker to bring it to life. Louis Malle—veteran of the French New Wave, director of such films as *The Lovers* (1958) and *Atlantic City* (1982)—accepted the challenge. A budget of $500,000 was raised. The script was rehearsed repeatedly, including a ten-performance run as a play in London.

Except for the rides to the meeting at the beginning and away at the end, all of *My Dinner With Andre* (1981) takes place at one table in an elegant New York restaurant. Courses are served as Gregory prattles on about his mystical excursions. Meanwhile the skeptical Shawn occasionally throws in a barb. The actors play fictional characters based on themselves. Eventually, Shawn opens up and presents his more earthbound philosophy.

My Dinner With Andre split critics and audiences. Many found it to be a mature and scintillating conversation; others thought it was a ponderous bore. Some of it is funny, the two men are engaging, and Malle's restrained direction is perfect. Still, *My Dinner With Andre* is a nearly two-hour staged yapfest. After successful screenings at the Telluride and New York film festivals, it received many rave reviews. Distributed by New Yorker Films, *My Dinner With Andre* was an arthouse smash, grossing more than $5 million.

Malle as director and Shawn and Gregory as actors teamed up again in the semi-indie *Vanya on 42nd Street* (1994), an adaptation by playwright David Mamet of Chekhov's *Uncle Vanya*. It was the late Louis Malle's final film.

Documentary

It's early on a cold misty morning in the Appalachian Mountains and thugs are rolling through a picket line in pickup trucks. A shot rings out. A flash in the darkness. A grimaced face. It feels like a nightmare, but it is all so very real. Among the combatants by the side of the road is a documentary filmmaker in her late twenties. She remembers: "The day the miners were lined up with their guns and the strikebreakers were coming through with their guns, my heart was beating so hard I couldn't hear anything else. They were pointing their guns straight at us and yelling. I kept the camera rolling. I didn't know I was screaming back until I saw the footage that I filmed that day."[7]

Barbara Kopple (1946–) grew up the daughter of a New York City textile magnate. She worked with the Maysles brothers and became politically aware in the tumultuous sixties. In 1972, Kopple as director, producer, and sound technician and Hart Perry as principal cameraman began filming the Miners for Democracy movement in Kentucky. They moved into Harlan County in 1973 when coal miners there launched a thirteen-month strike against the Brookside Mine.

Kopple befriended the strikers and joined them on dangerous picket lines and in contentious meetings. She even handed the warrant to the sheriff for the arrest of the thug leader. All the while, the camera was rolling. The Duke Power Company eventually conceded and signed a contract, ending the strike (the miners later learned that the agreement didn't include all the benefits they had expected). When Barbara Koppel finished her $350,000 movie four years after production began, she was seriously in debt.

Harlan County, U.S.A. premiered at the New York Film Festival in America's bicentennial year. It was the surprise hit, receiving a standing ovation. When released by Cinema 5 in 1977, reviews were mostly raves. Even that bastion of big business *The Wall Street Journal* found positive things to say about Kopple's unabashedly pro-union movie. In a category that has traditionally been dominated by sterile, apolitical footage compilations, it won the 1976 Academy Award for Best Documentary Feature.

And deservedly so. *Harlan County, U.S.A.* presents the kind of real, working-class citizens so often absent from movie screens. It takes the viewer into the black mines where men toil under brutally harsh and dangerous circumstances. It presents men dying from lung disease and shows rallies where previously quiet folks find their voices. Most dramatically, it hurtles the viewer into the center of a violent strike, where one man loses his life and where a slowly moving pickup is as ominous as an enemy tank. When strikers are limited as to how much picketing they can do and prevented from carrying guns, it is their wives who bravely march on (reminiscent of *Salt of the Earth*). Spellbinding, illuminating, and much more exciting than the typical Hollywood action picture, *Harlan County, U.S.A.* is a rare portrait of American people standing up for their dignity and their lives.

In addition to assisting on other left-leaning documentaries, Barbara Kopple helmed the union organization drama *Keeping On* (1981) for PBS's "American Playhouse" before beginning a five-year journey to capture another strike on film.

Kopple's mentors, Albert and David Maysles, continued to make documentaries, along with industrial and promotional shorts. They stirred up controversy with *Grey Gardens* (1976), a *cinema verité* portrait of Edith Bouvier Beale (age 79) and her daughter Edie (age 57), the peculiar aunt and cousin of Jackie Kennedy Onassis. Once society beauties, "Big Edie" and "Little Edie" prattle on amid the squalor of their decaying Long Island mansion as they face eviction from the health department. *Grey Gardens* was criticized for exploiting the "Edies," though it can also be seen as a liberating view of eccentricity. Alfred Maysles says, "Very few, if any, documentary filmmakers have the faith in people that my brother and I had. Even among documentary filmmakers, you'll hear, 'How wonderful—it's bigger than life.' As soon as you start to think it's better, worse, or different, then you're in trouble; you start losing the authenticity and tremendous power of what life really is."[8]

The Mariposa Film Group was a gay film collective in San Francisco. Six men and women from this group, including future notable Robert Epstein, crafted *Word Is Out* (1977). Twenty-six gay men and women talk about living in America. Filled with pain, joy, and perseverance, *Word Is Out* is a valuable historical document of people who had long been silenced.

Directed by George Butler and Robert Fiore, *Pumping Iron* (1977) is a fascinating view of bodybuilding. Centered on the 1975 Mr. Olympia contest held that year in South Africa, the filmmakers had the good fortune to capture the charismatic Arnold Schwarzenegger before he became a household name. He retires after winning the contest for the sixth time in a row, defeating a callow Lou Ferrigno. (Schwarzenegger returned to win the Mr. Olympia again in 1980.) It's great to see Schwarzenegger in his element: training, psyching out competitors, posing, and relaxing (he smokes a joint after winning), always supremely confident. Butler directed *Pumping Iron II: The Women* (1985), about the young sport of women's competitive bodybuilding; it, too, is fascinating.

"God is love—backward it's dog." Such are the lessons learned in *Gates of Heaven* (1978), a droll portrait of the owners and patrons of two California pet cemeteries. It marked the auspicious debut of Errol Morris (1948–), a documentarian with a master's degree in philosophy and little respect for the cult of *cinema verité* as ultimate truth. After bouncing from music to history to philosophy for his first twenty-eight years, Morris settled on cinema. Made with $120,000 raised from Morris's family and a college classmate, *Gates of Heaven* listens to Floyd McCure romanticize his failed pet cemetery before moving on to the Bubbling Well Pet Memorial Park of the Harbert family. Along the way, we learn about loneliness, positive thinking, and the American dream. Morris doesn't have the same respect for his subjects that Kopple does, but then he doesn't have the same subjects. Pet owners and pet cemetery owners are framed like potted plants and allowed to ramble on about animals and love and life. What they tell us is banal yet amusing, eccentric yet universal.

Errol Morris used the same deadpan technique to fashion *Vernon, Florida* (1981), a laid-back account of the residents of a tiny swamp town in the Florida panhandle. Worm farmers, wild turkey hunters, and other quixotic characters gaze towards the lens and talk openly about their lives. Morris has said of his work: "The idea is to allow each character to create a world for themselves, a dream. I've always thought of my portraits as my own version of the Museum of Natural History, these very odd dioramas where you're trying to create some foreign exotic environment and place it on display."[9]

Both *Gates of Heaven* and *Vernon, Florida* were deservedly well reviewed, though little seen. As Robert Flaherty learned, without grant money or government financing it's very difficult to sustain a career as a nonfiction filmmaker. Morris took a job as an investigator of Wall Street security fraud, but he would return to moviemaking again, putting his sleuthing skills to use while crafting an entirely new kind of documentary, one that would rescue a man's freedom.

German director Werner Herzog stated that if Morris ever finished *Gates of Heaven* he would eat his shoe. Herzog later boiled and consumed his boot, and director Les Blank captured the public event in a twenty-minute short called, appropriately, *Herzog*

Art Marketing

The success of art films is driven by reviews and word-of-mouth. Those who regularly attend nonstudio fare are typically more discerning than others and place greater emphasis on critical opinion.

Advertising is often literate and subdued, reflecting both an aura of quality and a lack of celebrities or explosions to hype. The black-and-white poster for *Stranger Than Paradise* is mostly blank, with an enigmatic photo on top, a purposely generic tagline: "A New American Film," a quote from Roger Ebert, and a small reference to its Cannes award. The poster for *Heartland* must hold the record for both film festival boasts and favorable notices. It lists eighteen festival appearances or awards and quotes from eleven reviews.

continued

Eats His Shoe (1980). Les Blank is a documentarian who specializes in catching the everyday life of his native South. His short movies pulsate with sizzling food and vibrant music. Werner Herzog, on the other hand, builds visually stunning, philosophical epics like *Aguire, the Wrath of God* (1972). After three years of preparation, Herzog led five hundred cast and crew members deep into the Peruvian jungles for nine months of treacherous production. Les Blank and sound person/editor Maureen Gosling went along with a camera.

The German-language movie Herzog made was *Fitzcarraldo* (1982), the visually astonishing true tale of a nineteenth-century Irishman who, trying to bring opera to the Amazon, leads Indians to drag a steamship over a hill. The movie Blank made about the making of *Fitzcarraldo* is *Burden of Dreams* (1982), and it is equally remarkable. Just as Herzog's epic recreates one of the most incredible quests in history, so, too, does Blank's. During *Fitzcarraldo*'s seemingly endless shoot, the original stars (Jason Robards, Mick Jagger) left the film when it was only halfway finished (shooting had to begin anew), a plane crash took lives, a tribal war broke out, and, most incredibly, Herzog tried to move his own ship over a hill only to have it get stuck in the mud. In the end, Herzog rants against nature and announces, "I shouldn't make movies anymore. I should go to a lunatic asylum." Life imitates art imitates life. *Burden of Dreams* captures an artist trapped in his own painting.

Art Marketing *continued*

Many artistic independents are released via a strategy called platforming. They open in New York and/or Los Angeles, hoping to generate a buzz. If they do, they'll move on to other cities. Directors and actors may travel to openings, giving interviews and appearing at promotional events. Platforming saves money on prints and marketing, and it allows small movies to grow. It also means that bad reviews in New York or L.A. can prevent a film from going any further.

Because art-houses frequently tackle difficult subjects, they replaced grind houses as the homes of celluloid sensationalism in the eighties and nineties. As with exploitation, controversy was sometimes part of an art marketing campaign. Films that have benefitted from such publicity include *Bad Lieutenant, Kids,* and *In the Company of Men.*

Best Boy (1979) deservedly won an Academy Award. Director/producer Ira Wohl convinced his aging aunt and uncle to let their fifty-two-year-old mildly retarded son, Philly, have more freedom. Wohl follows Philly as he attains some self-sufficiency, for the first time, running errands and attending a special school. Philly's parents are conflicted as their son needs them less. *Best Boy* isn't about pity; it's about real people experiencing real emotions. Wohl includes himself in the action, leading the way for more subjective, first-person documentaries in the eighties. A sequel, *Best Man: Best Boy and All of Us Twenty Years Later* (1999), presents Philly two decades later, more confident than ever.

Compiled by Howard Smith, *Gizmo!* (1977) is a whimsical, frequently funny collection of footage showing inventors and their various contraptions. *Atomic Cafe* (1982) is a darker comedy. Jayne Loader and Kevin and Pierce Rafferty assembled a collage of newsreel and government shorts from the early atomic age warning of the Soviet menace and describing how to survive a nuclear blast. Among the highlights are a cartoon turtle telling kids in a song to "duck and cover" when they see a white flash and a devoted father instructing his family not to leave their fallout shelter for *at least a minute* after they hear an explosion. Such clips are contrasted with footage of actual bombs and their effects.

Two excellent documentaries captured the essence of very different music. Penelope Spheeris made *The Decline of Western Civilization* (1981), which uncovers the then thriving Los Angeles punk scene. Included are such seminal nihilistic groups as Black Flag, X, and the Circle Jerks. There have been two sequels, and Spheeris has since called the shots on youth-oriented Hollywood features, including *Wayne's World* (1992). Meanwhile, far away from the mosh pits and heroin overdoses, movies made specifically for the Christian market have been a marginal independent genre, screened in church basements and parochial schools. The well-reviewed *Say Amen, Somebody* (1982) became a cinematheque hit. Director George Nierenberg documents the African-American gospel scene. He spends much time focusing on two legends, "Professor" Thomas A. Dorsey (age 83) and "Mother" Willie Mae Ford Smith (age 78). *Say Amen, Somebody* is an edifying combination of soaring songs and candid interviews.

A pair of documentaries about women also serve as appropriate companion pieces. The first, *The Life and Times of Rosie the Riveter*

(1980), assembled by Connie Field, follows the American women who labored in factories while men were fighting in World War II. Archival footage and current interviews present the "Rosies" doing their part on the home front. The second, set forty years later in a more liberated age, is *Soldier Girls* (1981). Directors Nick Broomfield and Joan Churchill were granted then unprecedented freedom to follow female Army recruits at Fort Gordon in Georgia. The military thought such a movie could help recruitment; they were wrong. *Soldier Girls* is both humorous and sobering as women are put through dehumanizing training while struggling to retain their identities.

Mainstream

During the mid-seventies to early eighties, several mainstream features were produced outside the studios. Some of these familiar titles may surprise art film purists, but they were created just as independently as a drama from John Cassavetes or a documentary from Frederick Wiseman.

Following the G-rated path of *Benji* and *The Legend of Boggy Creek*, a small herd of wilderness pictures emerged to exploit the children's market traditionally ceded to Disney. They also tapped into the back-to-nature/John Denver/granola fad, the popularity of TV's "Little House on the Prairie," and the bicentennial interest in American history. A combination of western and whitezploitation, wilderness adventures tracked rugged refugees fleeing modern society.

Originally shot in 1972, the tedious *Challenge To Be Free* (1975) was released after the success of Hollywood's superior mountain man romp, *Jeremiah Johnson* (1972). It was the final picture of veteran director Tay Garnett (*The Postman Always Rings Twice*). *The Adventures of the Wilderness Family* (1976), written and directed by Stewart Raffill, is a modern tale of a wholesome clan that leaves smoggy Los Angeles for a rustic life in the mountains. It was an innocent success that spawned two saccharine sequels. After playing a lone mountain man who befriends critters in *The Adventures of Frontier Fremont* (1975), bearlike Dan Haggerty was cast in a nearly identical role in *The Life and Times of Grizzly Adams* (1976). Richard Friedenberg directed both. Set in the mid-1800s, *Grizzly Adams* was photographed in Utah mountains near the future home of the Sundance Film Festival. It spawned a TV series.

Frontier Fremont, Grizzly Adams, and drive-in documentaries about

UFOs, Biblical prophecy, and the like were released by Sun International, an early exploiter of computerized market testing and a four-wall specialist. Four-walling is an independent distribution method wherein venues are rented outright. Typically the distributer keeps all the money from ticket sales, while the theater gets a hefty rental fee plus the food concession profits. Four-walled or not, there were other indie wilderness hikes, but the longing for unfettered rustic bliss dimmed when light sabers began to hum.

The inclusion of *One Flew Over the Cuckoo's Nest* in this book, among the zombies and nudists and art-house experiments, may seem surprising for such a "Hollywood" production. After all, it was the number-two box-office attraction of 1975 (after *Jaws*), eventually grossing more than $60 million in North America and twice that worldwide. It became only the second film in history to sweep all five major Academy Awards: picture, director, screenplay, actor, and actress.[10] It was nominated for four more: supporting actor, cinematography, editing, and original score. It had a substantial budget of $4 million and it starred Jack Nicholson, the hot actor who'd been nominated for an Oscar four out of the previous six years. Nicholson's salary for *Cuckoo's Nest* was also of Hollywood proportions: $1 million. Quite simply, *One Flew Over the Cuckoo's Nest* was an independent production because it was produced almost entirely outside the studios.

Ken Kesey's popular novel *One Flew Over the Cuckoo's Nest* was published in 1962. It became a Broadway play in 1963, starring Kirk Douglas as Randel P. McMurphy. Douglas optioned the film rights and for ten years tried unsuccessfully to get a movie made. When he became too old for the part, he turned it over to his then unknown son, Michael Douglas. Michael hooked up with Saul Zaentz, now a producing legend but then the head of a record company looking to diversify. Zaentz supplied the financial backing, and he and Michael produced *Cuckoo's Nest* together. They hired Czech immigrant Milos Forman as director. Bo Goldman and Lawrence Hauben adapted the book and play into a script. Nicholson was cast as McMurphy, and virtual rookie Louise Fletcher was given the crucial role of Nurse Ratched. A nonactor whom the casting director spotted at an Indian trade show, Will Sampson, plays Chief Bromden. Also in the cast are Brad Dourif, Scatman Crothers, Danny De Vito, and Christopher Lloyd.

The producers approached forty asylums before the Oregon State Hospital gave in and let them shoot inside. Even then, one of the conditions was that the head of the hospital, Dr. Dean Brooks, be given a part. Though he had no previous acting experience, he is excellent in the role of Dr. Spivey, head of the hospital. Hospital staff and patients appear as extras. Douglas remembers, "After eight weeks filming at the hospital, you could not tell the actors from the inmates."[11] The production took place with no strategy for distribution. United Artists got involved very late, buying the rights and providing some postproduction financing.

In 1963, R. P. McMurphy is sent to a mental hospital after feigning illness to get out of prison work duty and proceeds to shake things up at the regimented institution. McMurphy befriends his fellow inmates, especially the silent Chief Bromden and stuttering Billy Bibbit. He also squares off in a battle of wills with the emasculating Nurse Ratched—a battle he is doomed to lose.

In the 1998 American Film Institute list of the top 100 American films of all time, *One Flew Over the Cuckoo's Nest* ranked about right: number twenty.[12] Like *Titicut Follies*, *Cuckoo's Nest* is about an institution intent not on helping its patients but on keeping them sedate and impotent. McMurphy the liberator sees the absurdity of the situation but fails to comprehend its magnitude. The movie often has a comic tone that makes it easy to root for Nicholson's belligerent prankster and makes the ending all the more powerful. Great moments include McMurphy teaching the Chief to play basketball, McMurphy trying to get ten inmates to vote to hear the World Series on the radio, and a quiet "thanks" from the Chief. The acting throughout is splendid. Milos Forman went on to direct such studio features as *Ragtime* (1981) and *Amadeus* (1984).

Other mainstream independents during these years pulled in strong box-office numbers despite their dubious quality. *Harper Valley P.T.A.* (1978) is in the feeble tradition of movies based on popular songs. Barbara Eden stars in this broad comedy about a small-town mother who gets even with gossipy neighbors. It spawned a TV series. *Good Guys Wear Black* (1979) was the first of a steady stream of independently produced Chuck Norris action pictures. And in 1981, *Private Lessons*, the story of a virginal teen and his love tutor, tapped into the lucrative high-school demographic with sex just as slasher pictures did with violence. Distributed by a small Utah company, *Private Lessons* made more than $40 million worldwide. Together with the Canadian *Porky's* (1981), it launched a barrage of cheap teenage sex comedies.

When the word "independent" was appropriated as a marketing tool in the nineties, a *New Yorker* cartoon pictured a producer asking a studio mogul, "How's this for an idea—the first hundred-million-dollar independent film?" There was, however, an actual indie that cost a hefty $6 million in 1978. Its producer/director/cowriter was Richard Rush, a veteran of mostly action and youth pictures. Rush also held the option on *One Flew Over the Cuckoo's Nest* for a period in the early seventies, but, failing to find studio backing, he let the Douglas family assume control again.

In 1970 Columbia bought the rights to Paul Brodeur's novel *The Stunt Man*, hoping its existential, reality-versus-illusion theme would appeal to the counterculture. Rush eagerly accepted the job of writing and directing. He and Larry Marcus penned a script. But troubled Columbia dropped the film, so Rush purchased the option and shopped it to every studio in Hollywood; they all said no. After Rush had a hit directing the Warner Bros. feature *Freebie and the Bean* (1974), Warners agreed to make *The Stunt Man* if it was a straight action picture. Rush said no. (Rush held onto the name "The Stunt Man," forcing Warner Bros. to release its own fall guy comedy under the title *Hooper* [1978]).

Taking a fall in *The Stunt Man*.
© 1980 Simon Film Productions, Inc.

In 1977, Rush convinced supermarket kingpin Melvin Simon to finance *The Stunt Man*. When the movie was completed two years later, Rush knew he would need a wide release in order to recoup Smith's $6 million investment. Again, every studio turned him down. Nobody knew what to make of an existential action comedy. To prove *The Stunt Man* marketable, Rush began showing it at previews. Audiences raved. It won the top awards at the Dallas and Montreal film festivals. In 1980, the director opened *The Stunt Man* himself in Los Angeles. On the strength of word of mouth, it became the number-one movie in the city. Finally, ten years after Richard Rush began his journey, Twentieth-Century Fox purchased *The Stunt Man* for worldwide circulation. It was a box-office disappointment, but it earned three Academy Award nominations: director, screenplay, and actor (Peter O'Toole).

The Stunt Man sends a shell-shocked Vietnam vet and fugitive named Cameron (Steve Railsback) stumbling onto a real movie set where a World War I film is being shot. When he runs onto a bridge, he ruins a stunt, and the stuntman crashes and drowns. Eli Cross (Peter O'Toole), the movie's arch director, offers Cameron the fall guy's job and identity—thus protecting the production from investigators. Illusion and reality blend for Cameron as he performs stunts and has a dreamy romance with an actress (Barbara Hershey). He fears that Eli is plotting his death in the final stunt—the car crashing off the bridge again—leading to a showdown between the godlike director and the martyrlike fall guy.

The Stunt Man sharply divided critics. Some dismissed it as a simple "stunt," while others championed it as slyly wicked and dazzlingly vibrant. Critic Pauline Kael spoke for the latter: "*The Stunt Man* is a virtuoso piece of moviemaking: a sustained feat of giddiness that is at the same time intense. . . . Rush is a kinetic-action director to the bone; visually, he has the boldness of a comic-strip artist, and maybe because *The Stunt Man* is about subjects close to him—paranoia and moviemaking, which may be the subjects closest to almost all dedicated moviemakers—there's a furious aliveness in this picture."[13]

Railsback and Hershey are not ideally cast, slapstick music is misplaced, and the script—which connects sacrificial stuntmen to soldiers in Vietnam—lost cultural impact after sitting on a shelf for nearly a decade. Nonetheless, O'Toole is splendid (he won a National Society of Film Critics award), the cinematography by Mario Tosi is lively, and Rush's exuberance is contagious. Even those unimpressed by its philosophy and trickery concede that *The Stunt Man* contains unique pleasures. It stands as a terrific testament to personal film-making and perseverance of vision. Richard Rush did not helm another feature until 1994, when he directed the disappointing studio flick *Color of Night*.

Comedy

Comedy compilations remained a low-budget route to movie success. *Tunnelvision* (1976), directed by Neil Israel and Brad Swirnoff, is a crude parody of television programming in the future. Appearing in various clips are Chevy Chase, John Candy, and Betty Thomas. TV's "Saturday Night Live" was already doing a much better job of anarchic satire each week, and for free.

Kentucky Fried Movie (1977), which spoofs TV programs, commercials, and films is probably the funniest of the comedy revues, though even it is hit-and-miss. The best scenes are the kung fu spoof "A Fistful of Yen" and an elaborate black-and-white parody of courtroom dramas. *Kentucky Fried Movie* was directed by John Landis and scripted by Jim Abrahams and David and Jerry Jucker. The cast includes Donald Sutherland and Bill Bixby. The writers went on to make *Airplane!* and other rapid-fire comedies.

Arguably, the funniest motion picture of the Me Decade had no screenplay and only one performer. *Richard Pryor—Live in Concert* (1979) presents the comic genius at his uncensored best. Director Jeff Margolis captured the atmosphere of the live concert as Pryor masterfully used his voice and body to lay bare his pain, fear, and anger, with hilarious results. Bits include a recreation of his heart attack, his remembrance of fighting a boxer who was so mean he hit *himself* in the head, and whippings from his grandmother ("Boy, go get me something to beat your ass with."). The whole seventy-eight minutes is a highlight. Released without a rating (the language is "adult"), *Richard Pryor—Live in Concert* was a commercial hit. The filmmakers rushed out another concert film, *Richard Pryor Is Back Live in Concert* (1979), which is also good, but it covers much of the same ground. Studios produced the funny *Richard Pryor—Live on the Sunset Strip* (1982) and the less funny *Richard Pryor—Here and Now* (1983).

Horror

As usual, the Hollywood factories shied away from gratuitous gore and raw terror, so it was up to maverick moviemakers to give the teenagers what they wanted.

George Romero's efforts in the first years after *Night of the Living Dead* had failed to find an audience, and the *Living Dead* profits failed to find their way back to him. In a case that went to the Pennsylvania Supreme Court, his production company eventually won $3 million in *Living Dead* revenue from Walter Reade, but Romero failed to collect after Reade filed for bankruptcy. In an effort to jumpstart his career, he joined with producer Richard Rubenstein to form Laurel Productions. They planned a sequel to *Night of the Living Dead*, but it would take time to raise a substantial budget. So Romero wrote, directed, and edited a little vampire movie for $100,000 with a cast of Pittsburgh unknowns—at least it could be a vampire movie.

The most interesting thing about *Martin* (1978) is that the title character (John Amplas) is not a mythological monster. The shy, sexually repressed Martin puts his victims into a trance via hypodermic injections. He has no fangs, but he drinks their blood after cutting them with a razor blade. Furthermore, Romero mocks vampire conventions at every turn: the young Martin bites into garlic, moves about in daylight, grabs crosses, attends a church, and otherwise acts like a mere mortal. Still, his elderly cousin, Lincoln (Tata Cuda), a zealous Catholic, insists that Martin is an eighty-four-year-old vampire from the old country. Lincoln continuously condemns Martin until the fittingly violent conclusion.

Romero managed to turn this film into a provocative commentary on religion, repression, and the generation gap. Did the values of Martin's family turn him into a murderer or is his cousin correct all along? The bloody, harrowing *Martin* is stylishly photographed by Michael Gornick, including several gothic horror movie hallucinations in black and white. The film is also properly set in a decayed Pennsylvania steel town. The acting, by an inexperienced cast that includes friends and crew members, is effective; Romero himself stands out as the reformed Father Howard. *Martin* was well reviewed, and many consider it Romero's best film, but its box-office performance was hindered by a lack of promotion and a pedestrian title. It did become a midnight hit, however, playing at one New York theater for nearly a year.

George Romero's films are frequently satirical critiques of American capitalism and the traditional family structure. Nowhere is this more true than in *Dawn of the Dead* (1979), the bloody sequel to *Night of the Living Dead*. Romero wrote and directed *Dawn*; Rubenstein produced. The cast was again made up of Pittsburgh unknowns. The convincing gore effects were by Tom Savini. With a relatively hefty $2 million budget, *Dawn* was shot in shocking color.

Four human survivors hole up in a shopping mall, where they forge a utopian society to counter the mindless cannibalistic zombies (consumers) who plod through the mall. There are moments of perverse humor and genuine terror, and blood is everywhere.

Released without an MPAA rating (it would have received an X), *Dawn of the Dead* was notorious for its new standards in graphic violence: zombies are shot point-blank, a head explodes in a helicopter blade, etc. This was the main reason it became a huge cult hit, eventually earning even more worldwide than its predecessor's $50 million. Romero said of the gore, "The explicit violence is necessary because it's partially what the film is about. There's a violent underbed in America, and violence is certainly an integral part of any revolution. . . . I'm kind of playing around a little bit to see if the violence can be that dominant a factor in the film and still enable the audience to get past it and experience the storyline and the allegory.".[14] Some couldn't get past it; others, like Roger Ebert—who called *Dawn* one of the best horror films ever made—could. Some see the whole bloody experience as a catharsis. Author Stephen King wrote of shocking horror movies, "For myself, I like to see the most aggressive of them—*Dawn of the Dead*, for instance—as lifting a trapdoor in the civilized forebrain and throwing a basket of raw meat to the hungry alligators swimming around in that subterranean river beneath. Why bother? Because it keeps them from getting out, man. It keeps them down there and me up here."[15]

Dawn of the Dead reestablished Romero as an independent powerhouse. He followed with *Knightriders* (1981), an odd modern Arthurian tale about a traveling band of motorcycle jousters. After helming the nonindependent *Creepshow* (1982), he wrote and directed the third and easily the weakest installment in the zombie trilogy, *Day of the Dead* (1985). Rubenstein produced all. Since then George Romero has worked primarily on studio horror productions. He scripted and Tom Savini directed a needless color remake of *Night of the Living Dead* (1990).

John Carpenter (1948–) was a horror and science-fiction fan as a teenager in Kentucky. He made 8mm shorts with his friends and published a xeroxed monster movie fanzine with hand-drawn covers. While attending USC film school, Carpenter collaborated with Dan O'Bannon (now a noted screenwriter) on a short sci-fi satire called *Dark Star*. Shooting began in 1970. When they attracted an investor, Carpenter and company snuck their original footage out of school and expanded it into a $60,000 feature. Production ended four years after it began. Carpenter was director, producer, cowriter, and composer. O'Bannon was cowriter, editor, production designer, special effects supervisor, and, as Pinback, actor. A beach ball with claws plays an alien.

Dark Star is a bleak spoof of space exploration movies, especially *2001: A Space Odyssey*. Four scraggly-haired male astronauts and their dead, frozen captain cascade through the outer cosmos on an endless mission to blow up unstable planets with talking, conspiring, philosophizing smart bombs. Crew members annoy each other while trying to overcome boredom and avoid occasional catastrophes.

The interstellar special effects are surprisingly convincing in this shoestring effort. *Dark Star* was the first movie to present a spaceship interior that actually appears lived-in (the 1979 *Alien*, written by O'Bannon, perfected the design); sleeping quarters look like the world's grimiest dorm room. The scenes where Pinback chases the beach ball alien through ducts are the inspiration for the similar sequence in *Alien*.

As with *2001*, depicting the boredom of a long journey sometimes makes for a dull movie, and *Dark Star* is not as funny as it could be. Still, the explosive conclusion is as darkly joyful as *Dr. Strangelove*. Most importantly, *Dark Star* remains the best example of a creative, visually entertaining movie that looks like it cost dozens of times more than it did. It should be required viewing for current guerilla filmmakers who think they can afford to shoot only in their own homes and workplaces. The G-rated *Dark Star* was mishandled by its small distributor in 1975 and sold as an underground shocker. After *Star Wars*, it emerged as a cult picture, playing college campuses and revival houses.

John Carpenter subsequently wrote, directed, and composed the music for the independent feature *Assault on Precinct 13* (1976). Made with a cast of unknowns, this thriller follows the inhabitants of a nearly deserted police station under siege by a violent Los Angeles youth gang. The acting and production design are sometimes weak.

The boogeyman in *Halloween*.
© 1978 Compass International Pictures.

Nonetheless, this is an effectively violent homage to Howard Hawk's *Rio Bravo* with references to *Night of the Living Dead* and a dozen or so other Carpenter influences. A shocking scene where a girl is murdered while buying an ice cream cone is marvelously staged. Consistently tense, *Assault on Precinct 13* quickly disappeared at the box office, but it found many loyal supporters, especially in Europe.

Together with his then girlfriend, producer Debra Hill, Carpenter next made one of history's best and most successful horror films. The idea and the $320,000 budget (raised through a foreign investor) were supplied by Irwin Yablans, whose tiny Turtle Releasing had distributed *Assault on Precinct 13*. Hill and Carpenter penned the screenplay, originally entitled "The Babysitter Murders." Carpenter directed and composed the famous musical score. Cinematographer Dean Cundey guided the frequently moving camera. The one established performer in the cast, Donald Pleasence, was given top billing, though eighteen-year-old Jamie Lee Curtis, making her big-screen debut, is the clear star.

Halloween (1978) takes place before and during its namesake holiday in a small Illinois town fifteen years after six-year-old Michael Meyers stabbed his teenage sister to death. Michael (future filmmaker Nick Castle), who hasn't said a word since the initial crime, escapes from a mental hospital and returns to his hometown. He wears a mask (it's actually a cheap, latex mask of *Star Trek's* Captain Kirk) as he stalks three teenage girls: Annie (Nancy Loomis), Lynda (P. J. Soles), and the babysitting heroine Laurie (Curtis). Dr. Loomis (Pleasence) searches for Michael, convinced that he is pure evil.

Carpenter said, "*Halloween* is not about a crazy guy killing people. That's the story, but not what it's about. The movie is about evil, and it's about sex. In my opinion, evil never dies."[16] As for sex, *Halloween* has been criticized for killing off teenage girls immediately after they fool around. Carpenter counters—in an awkward defense—that Laurie (the one teen who doesn't fool around) is as sexually repressed as Michael, evident in the way she stabs her assailant with a (phallic) knife and then repeatedly drops it to be pursued again.[17] In fairness to Carpenter, the audience is never made to root for the death of teens (as in most of the *Halloween* imitators), and his young characters are treated sympathetically. The movie is also virtually blood-free; almost all of its violence is suggested. Like *The Texas Chainsaw Massacre*, it's so intense that viewers project blood onto the screen.

What makes *Halloween* such a frightening film is the expert work of its young director. Carpenter repeatedly uses a subjective camera point of view (which is at times unfairly manipulative), and he places Michael in the foreground and background of shots so that we see him before his potential victims know he's there—sometimes for an unbearably long time. We're denied peripheral views when we're struggling to see if the characters are safe in their surroundings. Throughout, Carpenter and cinematographer Cundey brilliantly utilize darkness. It haunts the frame. Even outside in the daytime, trees are used to create ominous shadows. Inside houses on Halloween night, the lights are invariably off; moonlight bounces off white walls and sometimes—just when you least expect it—illuminates Michael's creepy white mask. All of this is accompanied by Carpenter's relentless, piercing music.

Halloween was released by Irwin Yablan's tiny new company, Compass International Pictures. Initially, it was dismissed as just another maniac-on-the-loose slasher picture, but word quickly spread. *Halloween* was something different. It was a horror movie that genuinely delivered the scares. Young people went to see it over and over again. *Halloween* eventually earned more than $75 million in theaters worldwide. Both financially and artistically, it is one of the most successful independent movies of all time.

Halloween announced the arrival of Dean Cundey (who previously had no significant credits); he became a top Hollywood cinematographer, shooting big-budget bonanzas like *Jurassic Park* (1993). Debra Hill collaborated with Carpenter several more times and has produced such studio features as *The Fisher King* (1991). After *Halloween* (for which he received no up-front salary and little of the profits), John Carpenter gave up autonomy for bigger budgets. He has called the shots on more than a dozen features, mostly fantasy or horror films, including *Escape From New York* (1981), *The Thing* (1982), and *Starman* (1984). There have been five *Halloween* sequels, all made by studios, none directed by Carpenter; Hill and Carpenter wrote and produced the first (1981) and produced the second (1983).

Unfortunately, *Halloween*'s repeats followed the trend of its unimaginative imitators and stressed bloodshed over suspense, a trend that began with the countless independent imitators of *The Texas Chainsaw Massacre*. New ways to murder young people are explored in *Bloodsucking Freaks* (1976, aka *The Incredible Torture Show*), one of the most reprehensible of these films. In this sick comedy, nude women are tortured and killed in a Grand Guignol stage show that the on-screen audience believes is fake. *Bloodsucking Freaks* earned an X rating and was protested by women's groups. A girl having her brains sucked out with a straw represents the low point in the Herschell Gordon Lewis school of filmmaking.

The crudely made *I Spit on Your Grave* (1977) follows the same loathsome path of sadists brutalizing an innocent young woman for fun. She gets her revenge, castrating, hanging, axing, and ripping apart her attackers. The end. *Snuff* (1976) generated its own controversy by containing supposedly real footage of a female crew member being murdered and dismembered. It was staged. *The Toolbox Murders* (1978) and *Maniac* (1980) were two popular independent films that followed the hack-up-innocent-females formula. There were many more.

The Driller Killer (1979) supplied a minor twist. This time a frustrated male kills men. He may use a (phallic) drill because he fears he's a homosexual. *The Driller Killer* is mostly notable for marking the directorial debut of Abel Ferrara (1952-), who also edited the film, composed the score, and stars as the murderous artist under the pseudonym "Jimmy Laine." Ferrara next helmed *Ms. 45* (1981, aka *Angel of Vengeance*), a low-budget feminist thriller about a young mute woman (Zoe Tamerlis) who coldly kills her rapist and any men who exploit and degrade females. The movie won strong reviews and a cult following.

The Slumber Party Massacre (1982) was the mutilate-women version of *The Driller Killer*: a mass murderer escapes from prison and uses a power drill to gore girls (and some boys) at a sleepover. The interesting thing about this routine exploiter is that it was produced and directed by a woman, Amy Jones, and scripted by noted feminist Rita Mae Brown. Brown claimed she was trying to spoof and subvert the sexism of slasher films. She failed. Though Brown defended her screenplay and spoke out against censorship, she refused to see the movie and hated the woman-being-gouged ad campaign. Director Jones admitted there was very little about *The Slumber Party Massacre* that was feminist. There were two violent sequels, both written and directed by women.

Don Coscarelli made his first feature as a virtual one-man show at the age of nineteen, *Jim, the World's Greatest* (1976). It was picked up and released by Universal. After helming a film for Fox, the twenty-two-year-old prodigy then wrote, directed, and produced the independent *Phantasm* (1979), a moderately enjoyable horror movie despite its colorless characters and incoherent plot. Two brothers (Michael Baldwin and Bill Thornbury) investigate a creepy funeral home operated by the ghoulish "Tall Man." Inside are hooded zombie dwarves, an interplanetary transporter, and a rapid flying sphere that latches onto skulls, drills in, and pumps out a stream of its victim's blood. Coscarelli was out to have fun, and he supplies the kind of youthful giddiness that dreams up a quivering, severed finger that oozes yellow "blood" and transforms into a man-eating insect. Released through Avco-Embassy, *Phantasm* developed a loyal worldwide cult following. Coscarelli made two *Phantasm* sequels (1988 and 1994).

Another horror movie with loyal supporters is *Basket Case* (1982), the bizarre story of two separated Siamese twin brothers who communicate telepathically. Duane (Frank Van Hentenryck) appears normal, but his twin, Belial, is a hideous little mutant who lives in a basket and wreaks bloody havoc. Written, directed, and edited by debuting Frank Henenlotter, *Basket Case* is a juvenile mix of outrageous black comedy and gore. The New York City skid-row settings are suitably filthy; much of the film was shot in an actual fleabag hotel. In the year of *E.T.*, midnight movie audiences adopted Belial as the evil twin of Spielberg's extraterrestrial. Like that of *Phantasm*, the worldwide cult following for *Basket Case* has remained strong through cable TV and video. Since his debut, Henenlotter has specialized in freaky horror comedies, including two *Basket Case* sequels (1990 and 1992).

Wes Craven made a few horror flicks after directing *Last House on the Left*. Most notable was the independently produced atomic mutant cannibal tale, *The Hills Have Eyes* (1977) and the comic-book-style *Swamp Thing* (1982). Craven would soon reach the blockbuster level, but only after Sean Cunningham, the producer of *Last House on the Left*, had a monstrous success of his own.

"Paramount will have to do a yeoman's selling job to squeeze major cash from the sprockets of this sporadically gory but utterly suspenseless pickup. Lowbudget in the worst sense—with no apparent talent or intelligence to offset its technical inadequacies—*Friday the 13th* has nothing to exploit but its title and whatever oomph [Paramount] puts into the campaign. Quick, in-and-out playoff is in order."[18] So stated a *Variety* review just before the start of the most successful horror movie franchises in history.

And who could fault the critic? *Friday the 13th* (1980) is a bad movie. A group of teen counselors set out to shape up Camp Crystal Lake and are summarily murdered (often after sex) by hockey-mask-wearing Jason, who was neglected and drowned in the lake twenty-two years earlier. With a budget of $500,000, *Friday the 13th* was independently directed and produced by Sean Cunningham. The bloody makeup effects were by *Dawn of the Dead*'s Tom Savini. Kevin Bacon plays one of the counselors.

Cunningham screened his completed film for distributors in early 1980; Paramount scooped up the domestic rights (Warner Bros. bought the foreign rights). Paramount released the film one month before an actual Friday the 13th and while Fox's *The Empire Strikes Back* was dominating the youth market. It became a huge hit anyway. With the combination of teenage sex and teenage violent deaths, high-school kids paid to see *Friday the 13th* over and over again, often rooting for Jason as he stalked and murdered, accompanied by his own distinctive music. It grossed *Halloween*like numbers worldwide. And Jason just kept on slashing. Cunningham sold the sequel rights to Paramount, and Paramount pumped out repeats, one a year for five years, nine total so far, and a TV series. Sean Cunningham summed up the appeal of the *Friday the 13th* phenomenon: "It's primarily a social event, not a movie per se. . . . It's become sort of a roller coaster experience where audiences climb into a car. The guys who've done it before put their hands up in the air. Girls get scared and put their heads on their boyfriends' shoulders. There is social bonding going on. . . . The bottom line is it's just a place for kids to go." [19]

It took awhile for the studios to tap into the splatter horror genre. They held their noses and turned away from *Night of the Living Dead* and *The Texas Chainsaw Massacre*. But when America's youth went again and again to *Halloween* and *Friday the 13th*, Hollywood adopted the masked, indestructible killers Michael and Jason. The maniac-murders-teens formula was prepackaged. High-school audiences didn't want too much deviation. They wanted their roller-coaster ride to hit the same highs and lows and take the same turns every time.

When the film factories started pumping out slasher pictures, the independent sector was sent reeling. In the seventies, the horror genre had been one of the surest ways for an outsider to get rich and get noticed. These days were over. Now a lethal menace was about to strike. Just as sound and television had done in previous decades, this menace would deliver a deadly blow for some, while opening up greater opportunities for others. But to those with 35mm cameras and a bucket of fake blood, it was relentless, invading virtually every living room in the country. Within a few years, the proliferation of VCRs would virtually wipe out big-screen, low-budget horrors.

Pornography

Videotape would also kill off theatrical pornography, but not before blue movies made one last gasp for wider acceptance. Russ Meyer coaxed soft-core as far as possible without going all the way. *Supervixens* (1975) is a parody of his own style. Star Ann Marie is even more of a female caricature than usual: 67-25-36! The editing is faster; the comedy is broader. And it worked. Made for $200,000, *Supervixens* proved to be Meyer's biggest success, grossing more than $17 million worldwide.

Up! (1976), a color roughie, was the most graphic and tasteless Russ Meyer movie. Revolving around a young couple who run a rural diner, the film includes an S&M sequence with a Hitler clone, two rapes, and an outrageous final scene where nude women run through the woods trying to kill each other as they tie up the story's loose ends. Roger Ebert helped with the script (under the pseudonym "Reinholde Timme").

Unwilling to go hard-core, the fifty-seven-year-old Russ Meyer directed his final film, *Beneath the Valley of the Ultravixens* (1979), twenty years after his first. Again he served most major crew positions (he also acted); again he had pseudonymous script assistance from Ebert. Made for $240,000, *Beneath the Valley of the Ultravixens* is a typical big-breasted soft-core comedy, but it no longer had anywhere to play. It wasn't explicit enough for porno palaces, but it was too risqué for malls. It bombed.

Russ Meyer retired from moviemaking. He retained the rights to all but his two Twentieth-Century Fox films, and he has continued to self-distribute his unique oeuvre on videotape. In the long history of cinema, Meyer remains a singular auteur: a low-budget virtuoso, a masterful technician, a virtual crew of one, the greatest skin-flick artist of all time, visionary, gambler, maverick.

Meyer's female counterpart, Doris Wishman, also shunned hard-core. Struggling to get noticed, her last flick, *Let Me Die a Woman* (1978), was her most exploitable. In the tradition of the Forty Thieves, it features cringe-inducing surgical footage of a real sex-change operation!

Soft-core auteur Radley Metzger didn't buck the X trend. Using the pseudonym "Henry Paris," Metzger made movies like *The Opening of Misty Beethoven* (1976) and *Barbara Broadcast* (1977). He still shot in a consciously artful manner, emphasizing eroticism over raunch, and his pictures are among the best hard-core flicks ever made, but nobody really cared that much. Skin theaters were once again the nearly exclusive domain of lonely men and their fantasies.

Debbie Does Dallas (1978) was a run-of-the-mill X-rated picture with mechanical sex and horrendous acting. But by publicizing the fact that its star (Bambi Woods) was an ex-cheerleader, it capitalized on the Dallas Cowboy cheerleader phenomenon and raked in millions. Along the way, its title became as synonymous with hard-core as *Deep Throat*.

Insatiable (1980) brought the "99 and $^{44}/_{100}$ percent pure" Marilyn Chambers back to porn in a bigger-budgeted effort than most. Its huge box-office totals were due partly to Chambers's promotion of *Insatiable* across the country through nude interviews. The legendary John Holmes (who later died of AIDS) is featured.

In the early eighties, a few pornos tried to go legit, to slither out of sticky-seat dumps and onto mainstream screens. *Caligula* (1980), financed by *Penthouse* magazine and an Italian company and shot in Rome, was not an American independent. However, its $15 million budget makes it the most ambitious attempt ever at a mainstream movie with graphic sex. Though it had a major cast (Malcolm McDowell, Peter O'Toole, John Gielgud) and a script by noted author Gore Vidal (who had his name removed), the plot drowned in the depravity and violence. *Caligula* was a monumental flop.

With *Roommates* (1980), noted soft-core director Chuck Vincent tried to craft a porno that general audiences could accept. This tale of three female roommates was photographed in 35mm, played in some legitimate theaters, and was favorably reviewed by mainstream critics (who had mostly given up on hard-core after the early seventies). Still, it failed to reach a sizable nonraincoat audience. *Blonde Ambition* (1981) was another superior hard-core feature that played in some legit theaters at midnight.

The adult film that had the greatest success outside of porno palaces is *Cafe Flesh* (1982), a distinctly original, futuristic flick that never wanted to be hard-core. Cult movie expert Danny Peary calls it "the thinking man's porno film."[20] Director Stephen Sayadian (pseudonym: "Rinse Dream") and his cowriter, journalist Jerry Stahl (pseudonym: "Herbert W. Day"), felt that if they made the nonsex scenes impressive enough, the moneymen would drop the hard-core content and *Cafe Flesh* could be released with an R rating. It didn't happen that way, though some of the most explicit footage was excised from the theatrical version (but not the video), and the X-rated *Cafe Flesh* became a cult hit on the midnight movie circuit. It replaced *Pink Flamingos* in the 12:00 AM slot at Los Angeles's seminal art house, the Nuart.

Cafe Flesh is set in a postapocalyptic future where the majority of survivors are impotent "sex negatives." These miserable humans gather each night in clubs like Cafe Flesh to watch the few "sex positives" perform in highly stylized copulating cabarets. A man and a woman viewing a show become aroused and attempt physical contact, but, as for all sex negatives, touch makes them ill. Actually, the woman is a sex positive pretending to be sick to keep from being forced onto the intercourse circuit. Her secret is soon discovered.

Cafe Flesh dares to deride its audience. When the emcee of a sex club taunts the patrons, he's taunting us: "Hey, not too pathetic that the biggest night of your life is watching some strange palooka getting his hog washed by some bimbo you don't even know." The movie's writing predated popular knowledge of AIDS, but its equating sex with illness and its "negative" and "positive" terms make it all the more compelling. *Cafe Flesh* brings up questions about voyeurism, love, and sex. The acting is weak and the story is disjointed and interrupted by typical porno action, but *Cafe Flesh* is notable for its original theme, cabaret visuals, and avant-garde design.

Sayadian and Stahl again failed to be recognized as brave cinematic visionaries with the highly stylized horror flick *Dr. Caligari* (1989). By that time, Stahl was a top television writer ("Moonlighting," "Twin Peaks," "thirtysomething") and a heroin addict. The semi-indie *Permanent Midnight* (1998) is based on his memoir of the same name.

Cafe Flesh showed up ten years too late. Mainstream audiences and critics were primed for quality features with graphic content in the early seventies, but all they got was *Deep Throat* and its imitators. Most discerning viewers had long since turned away by the time *Roommates* and *Cafe Flesh* came along. Porno screens were for bumping and grinding and anatomical close-ups, not drama, and certainly not philosophy.

With VCRs being plugged into every other TV, XXX theaters were about to suffer the same death blow as low-budget theatrical horror. The once illicit industry that started in the days of Edison and continued through "Debbie Does Everything"—the business of Kroger Babb and Russ Meyer and Gerald Damiano—was killed, only to be reborn many times larger in the home video market. By 1983, adults who had shunned skin houses in the seventies were happily renting X-rated videotapes (typically shot in one day without a script) to gawk at in the privacy of their own homes. The pornographic industry experienced a boom of activity—all on TV screens. Americans rented more than six hundred million X-rated videos in 1998, but few adult movies, soft- or hard-core, were projected in theaters after the mid-eighties. The sexploitation film industry was over, leaving behind a twisted legacy of a few fun successes (mostly by Meyer), notable failures, and miles and miles of thoughtless dreck that never aimed higher than a man's crotch.

Underground

Mekas's message to the "old croaks" to stop fighting the inevitable was finally heeded. Underground movies were no longer shown principally by avant-garde cooperatives and film societies. A flop for Twentieth-Century Fox in 1975, *The Rocky Horror Picture Show*, was rereleased at midnight on April Fool's Day, 1976. With a transvestite from Transsexual, Transylvania, the campy, subversive musical and horror spoof became the most popular cult picture of all time. It was the ultimate audience participation show. Viewers recited dialogue and acted out roles in costume. At appropriate times they threw toilet paper and rice and fired water pistols. *The Rocky Horror Picture Show* was a simultaneous disco-era party every Saturday night in cities and college towns. It played weekend after weekend, year after year. The underground was big business.

Encouraged by the success of his *Frankenstein* but angered by his inability to share in the profits, Andy Warhol decided to create his own bigger-budgeted "underground" feature. Most of the $1.2 million dollars it took to make *Andy Warhol's Bad* (1977) came from the pop artist's bank account. Because Warhol and Morrissey had parted ways, Jed Johnson (Morrissey's assistant) debuted as director. The script was by Pat Hackett and George Abagnalo. A far cry from *Chelsea Girls*, *Bad* was produced with a union crew and featured legitimate actors.

Borrowing from John Waters, *Bad* is an outrageous black comedy about a housewife (Carroll Baker) and her ultradysfunctional family. She runs both a hair removal business and an all-female assassination ring that specializes in children and animals ("I want you to kill a dog and I want you to kill it viciously"). Everyone is mean to everyone. *Bad*'s most infamous moment is when a mother throws her baby out a window; a crowd gathers around the bloody remains (a watermelon).

Bad is a brazen attempt to offend. It can be seen as another Warhol satire of women's liberation and another shot at Valerie Solanas, but the outrageousness overwhelms any message. Vincent Canby wrote in *The New York Times*, "[*Bad*] presents the audience with a dilemma. If we become outraged and walk out, as one might in the baby murder scene, it laughs at us: This is, after all, only a film, so why don't we become outraged at the various real horrors in the world around us? If we don't become outraged, says the film, we may not be too different from the robots in the movie."[21]

Andy Warhol's Bad was picked up by New World. In order to avoid an X rating, Warhol wanted to cut the baby-goes-splat scene, but New World refused. (Usually it's the studio demanding such cuts, to the filmmaker's chagrin; Roger Corman's company did things differently.) *Bad* was initially released with an X rating. Advertised with hard-core porn, it never found its audience, nor did an R-rated version released later.

Andy Warhol was a frugal man, none too happy about losing so much money on one project. *Bad* was his last movie. From then on he occupied his time with society parties and overseeing the creation of Factory art. He died in 1987 after routine gallbladder surgery. His film oeuvre traces the history of cinema. Starting with static shots of everyday life, subsequent motion pictures added movement, music, talking, scripted content, plot, color, 3-D, and a million-dollar budget. Though only *Frankenstein* ever reached a wide audience, Andy Warhol was a crucial figure in independent cinema. He brought the underground sensibility aboveground and sold it to an ever-widening fan base. For Andy, nothing was too outrageous, anyone could be a movie star, and bad was beautiful.

John Waters, the Gomez Addams of cinema, carried Warhol's torch further into the mainstream. While *Pink Flamingos* was still a midnight favorite, he created his most ambitious feature to date, *Desperate Living* (1977). Divine is missing, but most of the other Baltimore freaks are there. Fresh out of a mental hospital, the deranged Betty Gravel (Mink Stole) and her maid (the obese Jean Hill) kill Betty's husband. Fleeing, they end up in Mortville, a town of lesbians and moronic men ruled by an evil queen (Edith Massey). Betty goes to work for the monarch, while others plot a revolution. As usual, there is violence, ugly whining characters, ridiculous dialogue and situations, and much offensive material. This time, however, the results are less repulsive and more competently realized. The controversial original advertising featured a dead rat (which Waters really cooked) on an elegant dinner plate with garnishes on the side.

John Waters has not made a truly independent film since, though he remains the antithesis of a Hollywood director. Starting with *Polyester* (1981), his movies have been produced by New Line Cinema. A middle-class satire, *Polyester* still features most of Waters's Baltimore players, including Divine, and it was released with the William-Castle-style gimmick of "Odorama," in which scratch-and-sniff cards coincided with appropriate moments on-screen (number two was amusing). In the ensuing years, Waters's pleasantly twisted films—*Cry-Baby* (1990), *Serial Mom* (1994), *Pecker* (1998)—have avoided gross-out material. His biggest hit, *Hairspray* (1989), was rated PG. It was the last film for Divine, who died in 1989 at the age of forty-one. As an independent, John Waters pushed the limits of campy outrageousness and dark humor. He proved that anyone anywhere with almost any slim budget could make a famous (or infamous) motion picture.

David Lynch (1946–) was born in Montana, the son of a tree scientist. His father's job moved the family around the Northwest and to Virginia. Lynch attended a fine arts college in Philadelphia and painted. For five years, he and his wife lived in an industrial neighborhood in near poverty in the City of Brotherly Love; Lynch hated it. Then Lynch earned a $5,000 grant from The American Film Institute using a bizarre four-minute art film and crafted an inventive thirty-five-minute picture without dialogue called *The Grandmother*. The story of a young boy, ignored by his parents, who grows a loving old lady from a seed, *The Grandmother* won several festival awards. It also helped Lynch earn admittance to the new graduate school of The American Film Institute.

Lynch, with his wife and his daughter, soundman Alan Splet, and art director/filmmaker Jack Fisk, moved to Los Angeles in 1970. He attended AFI while supporting his family with a series of odd jobs, and he developed an experimental script called "Eraserhead," which the school agreed to finance as a short. The artist proceeded, knowing his twenty-two-page screenplay would eventually be stretched to feature length. David Lynch was both innocent (sporting short hair, eschewing drugs, and favoring words like "neat" and "nifty") and peculiar (he wore a hillbilly hat and *three* ties). Mel Brooks later called him "Jimmy Stewart from Mars."

With an initial school stipend of $10,000, production began in 1972. Sets were built on the AFI campus. Props were raided from thrift shops and swap meets; many, such as the elaborate pencil machine, were meticulously built by Lynch. Unknown actor Jack Nance was cast in the lead role of Henry. His Don King hair was Lynch's idea after he saw it tousled up in the midst of styling. Industrial cinematographer Herb Cardwell was brought in from Philadelphia; when he left the project after nine months to earn a living, he was replaced by Cassavetes veteran Frederick Elmes. Production consumed nearly three years (Lynch initially told Nance it would take six weeks), and filming virtually shut down for all of 1973. AFI financing was erratic, and Lynch and Nance earned money by delivering newspapers in the wee hours. Near the end, when Lynch's marriage broke up, he literally lived on the set. The picture editing (by Lynch) and very precise sound editing (by Alan Splet) took another year.

The small, tight cast and crew of *Eraserhead* (1977) toiled through it all to make one of the most gloriously strange and ingeniously disturbing motion pictures in the history of cinema. It follows an emotionless man named Henry (Nance), who lives in a desolate, industrial city and fathers a monstrous baby with moody Mary X (Charlotte Stewart). All the while he dreams of escaping to be with the deformed but happy lady who serenades him from behind his radiator. No person's reaction is predictable. The scene in which Henry meets Mary's parents is like every dating guy's worst nightmare. Henry is asked to carve up a chicken the size of a baseball; it comes to life and spews a dark liquid; Mary's mom has an orgasm watching; and Mary's dad, with a blank grin, asks for the second time, "So, Henry, what do you do?" Henry's previous response: "Oh, I'm on vacation." The whole movie plays like this: perverse, disturbing, almost laughable, and perpetually hypnotic.

Eraserhead captured the illogic and the rhythm of a bad dream. Though Lynch refuses to discuss its meaning and many of its pieces clearly don't fit into a profound whole, the overriding theme is sexual repression. We see a nearly infertile world where spermlike worms fall in dreams, where Henry and the sultry woman across the hall

Jack Nance in the perpetual dream world of *Eraserhead*.

melt into a bed that turns to white fluid, and where the union of Henry and Mary creates a hideous, demanding mutant. Henry is so repressed in one apparent dream sequence that his head pops off, revealing the baby's deformed head beneath it. Henry's head is taken by a boy to a factory and turned into pencil erasers (hence the title).

The black-and-white cinematography and the audio with its evocative industrial sounds are stellar; the production design and special effects are spellbinding. Lynch believes that what he lacked in money he made up in time: some intricate props and effects were labored over for months during the extended production. At one point, Lynch even dissected a cat (he shot the carcass, but it didn't make it into the final film). Lynch stated: "I examined all parts of it, like membranes and hair and skin, and there are so many textures that on one side are pretty gross, but isolated in an abstract way, they are totally beautiful. . . . To me, a lot of these things are beautiful. And somehow, I think other people find the beauty in something that could be ugly in *Eraserhead*."[22]

Many people failed to see the beauty. *Eraserhead* was rejected for both the Cannes and the New York film festivals, though it was admitted to Filmex in 1976, where it was a sensation. Love it or hate it, *Eraserhead* was the one movie people couldn't stop talking about. Picked up by Libra Films, it opened slowly on the midnight circuit in 1977. Initially it was overwhelmed in a market pulsating to the happy camp of *The Rocky Horror Picture Show*. Critics skewered it as sickening and pointless. Lynch returned to repairing roofs and other odds jobs. But the cult of *Eraserhead* grew and, as with *Pink Flamingos*, everyone who saw it told their friends, and those friends—perhaps on a dare—had to see it too. *Eraserhead* became a midnight movie hit.

Sound editor Alan Splet won an Academy Award for his audio work on *The Black Stallion* (1979). Cinematographer Fred Elmes has had an accomplished career shooting idiosyncratic films, including several more by Lynch. Jack Nance, immortalized as the monosyllabic Henry, appeared in small roles in other Lynch productions but never broke through in Hollywood. He was murdered in 1996. On the assured visual strength of *Eraserhead*, David Lynch was given the writing and directing assignment for Paramount's *The Elephant Man* (1980). It was a huge success, nominated for eight Academy Awards, including Best Picture; Lynch was nominated twice (director and screenplay). After fifteen years of near poverty, of newspaper routes and roofing jobs, of meticulously pursuing his own disturbing dreams, David Lynch had finally arrived. *Eraserhead* represents one of the oddest springboards to the studios. But Lynch could never be truly comfortable in a Hollywood story conference, and whatever the budget or the medium, he has remained a renegade.

Underground U.S.A. (1980), as its title suggests, was a conscious attempt to make a cult film. Directed, scripted, coproduced, and starring Eric Mitchell, it, like *Heat*, is a pale retelling of *Sunset Boulevard*. Mitchell is the bisexual "Hustler" who latches onto a faded movie queen (Patti Austen). Future independent directors Tom DiCillo (cinematography) and Jim Jarmusch (sound) were in the crew. John Lurie contributed to the soundtrack.

Despite its exploitable title and story line, *Eating Raoul* (1982) wasn't exploitation. It was a film festival favorite and art-house triumph. Paul Bartel, veteran actor and director from the Roger Corman school, was unable to convince the Drive-In Deity or any studio to finance the droll script he wrote with Richard Blackburn. So he did it himself, directing and starring in *Eating Raoul*. Bartel plays Paul Bland; Warhol veteran Mary Woronow plays his wife. Wanting to both finance their own restaurant and reduce the "pervert" population, the prudish Blands lure swingers to their apartment, kill them, rob them, and sell them for dog food. Also in the cast are Robert Beltran, as Raoul, Buck Henry, and Ed Begley, Jr.

Eating Raoul is as bland as its lead characters, and despite its plot description, it's not shocking. The production design and camera-work are uninspired; the script is void of surprises. But *Eating Raoul* won over audiences that were titillated by the hip subject matter but shied away from Warhol/Waters visual nastiness. Bartel has contin-ued to act and occasionally direct.

Husband and wife experimental filmmakers Scott and Beth B. had their biggest underground success with *Vortex* (1982), a bizarre enig-ma about the unmotivated torture of a prisoner. Again Jim Jarmusch was in the crew and John Lurie contributed to the soundtrack.

In the early eighties, the so-called New York underground was thriving. It was a vibrant, disorganized collective of artists, filmmak-ers, and musicians who explored the juncture of avant-garde and pop. Punk, graffiti, New Wave, postmodern, rap—it struck a pose. The downtown scene included Warhol-influenced painters Keith Haring and Basquiat, musical groups The Talking Heads and The B-52s, and filmmakers Eric Mitchell, Beth and Scott B., and Charles Ahearn. Its future cinematic savior, Jim Jarmusch, had already made his NYU thesis film, *Permanent Vacation* (1981), and would soon begin work on a cool, detached, low-budget feature with Tom DiCillo as cinematog-rapher and John Lurie as star that would help define nonstudio cine-ma for the next generation. NYU graduate Susan Seidelman was the first of the downtown crowd to break through—but by then the term "underground" had been co-opted and commercialized by the old croaks and rendered virtually meaningless. The hot new cinematic term was "independent."

Microbudget

In a modern sense, microbudget movies are those budgeted at less than $150,000. In the early eighties there were three such films that set the stage for future trends. The first was by accomplished author and Roger Corman alumnus John Sayles (1950–). He grew up in upstate New York, the son of schoolteachers, and earned a degree in psychol-ogy. Sayles worked a variety of menial jobs while winning acclaim (including an O. Henry award and National Book Award nomination) but little money for his short stories and novels. In the mid-seventies, he began penning schlocky screenplays for Corman, including *Piranha* (1978) and *Battle Beyond the Stars* (1980). The left-wing populist dreamed of making small, personal movies.

Because Sayles had never directed so much as a short film, he envisioned his debut as an audition piece. He came up with the story in the fall of 1977; production began one year later. The $60,000 budget was raised from Sayles's screenwriting jobs. Shooting took place at and near a ski lodge in New Hampshire (which was cheap to rent out of season); the lodge also served as housing for the cast and crew of unknowns. Sayles's live-in girlfriend, Maggie Renzi, was a lead actress as well as production manager, and she later produced and acted in many Sayles movies. Sayles taught himself editing and cut the film in his and Renzi's house.

Return of the Secaucus 7 (1980) follows the reunion of seven Vietnam War protestors who were detained by police on the New Jersey

John Sayles.

turnpike while en route to the March on the Pentagon. Now approaching their thirtieth birthdays (as was Sayles, who acts in the movie), they've gathered to relive those times, gossip, flirt, play, and confront the choices they've made.

Return of the Secaucus 7 was well received at several festivals and picked up by a small distributor. Promotion compared Sayles's compelling $60,000 drama to the $44 million studio fiasco *Heaven's Gate*. Reviews were strong. Jack Kroll wrote in *Newsweek*: "Already Sayles' directing style reflects his writing style in its deceptive ease: you feel as if you're eaves-dropping on real people in real places with real relationships talking real talk. There are no sneaky pretentious attitudes about the fate of former radicals: Sayles understands and likes his characters; he captures the melancholy of inexorable normalcy as it overtakes these nice, ordinary people who once burned with world-changing zeal."[23] Some footage is poorly lit, and the sparse soundtrack screams out for music, but the characters are three-dimensional and the dialogue shines. *Return of the Secaucus 7* was a small success at theaters and showed up on numerous "ten best" lists for 1980.

Variety wrote: "Sayles has accomplished what many aspiring directors talk about doing but somehow never get around to undertaking—going off in the woods with some friends, a camera, some film and no money and producing something worthwhile."[24] More and more people would try similar routes in the future. John Sayles went on to become a major force in independent cinema. Hollywood had a mainstream success with *The Big Chill* (1983), an unauthorized, glossy copy of Sayles's audition piece.

(John) Wayne Wang (1949–) was born and raised in Hong Kong. He studied art and film in Oakland and returned to his homeland to make films and TV programming. Wang returned to San Francisco to create a 16 mm black-and-white feature with a budget of only $22,000. The wry, Zenlike script for *Chan Is Missing* (1982) was penned by Wang, Issac Cronin, and Terrel Seltzer. Wang produced, directed, and edited. The cast and crew were almost entirely of Chinese ancestry.

Chan Is Missing is a mystery about two cabbies, middle-aged Jo (Wood Moy) and young, hip Steve (Marc Hayashi), who become amateur investigators searching for a business partner named Chan who absconded with their money. With an affectionate sense of deadpan

(l-r) Marc Hayashi and Wood Moy in *Chan Is Missing*.
© 1989 New Yorker Video.

humor, the movie takes us into the kitchens, offices, and bars of
Chinatown (well-known community figures address the camera) on
an odyssey in search of Chan but indirectly investigating what it
means to be a Chinese-American. Perhaps Chan returned to China, or
maybe he was simply assimilated into his adopted country, thus losing his identity.

The often rough black-and-white cinematography adds to the documentary feel, and the chemistry of the two lead actors carries *Chan
Is Missing*; the rhythm of their overlapping, amusing banter feels too
natural to have been scripted (though it was). The Chan of the title
references American cinema's best known Chinese detective, and the
stereotypes of Charlie Chan pictures are indeed missing from Wang's
film. Like the race pictures of decades earlier, *Chan Is Missing* presents
a realistic, nuanced view of an ethnic group heretofore overlooked or
denigrated by Hollywood. And it accomplishes this with the barest of
budgets. If Wang and friends could make a well-reviewed movie for
only $22,000, then almost anyone could self-finance a motion picture.

After studying film at NYU and winning awards for her shorts,
Susan Seidelman, not yet thirty, raised $60,000 to make a feature. She
cowrote (with Ron Nyswaner), directed, produced, and edited

Smithereens (1982). Young and broke, Wren (Susan Berman) struggles to enter the music business and find a place to crash each night. She takes advantage of anyone who doesn't take advantage of her, mostly nice guy Paul (Brad Rinn) from Montana, who lives in a van. Eventually even Paul catches on and leaves. The rootless Wren begins to confront her sorry fate.

Some of the acting and dialogue of *Smithereens* is amateurish, and the mousy Berman is miscast as a selfish hustler. Nonetheless, Seidelman's movie provides a clear portrait of the downtown art and music scene where aimless souls live in poverty, waiting in vain for their big break. The casting of actual punk rock performers was inspired. Characters feel off-center without being cartoonish. Paul asks, "Isn't that guy a little bit weird?" Wren's response: "Everyone's a little weird these days. It's normal."

Smithereens was the most successful movie to date from the Manhattan indie scene of Mitchell, Jarmusch, and company. It was a surprise hit at the Cannes Film Festival and was picked up and distributed by New Line. *Smithereens* portrays the angst and aimlessness of twentysomethings delaying their entry into the world of responsibility. As so many

---

■ ■ ■ ■ ■ ■ ■ ■

Something for Nothing

In order to make a micro-budget movie there are some basic guidelines.

SCREENPLAY. Limit the number of locations and characters. Avoid special effects, stunts, extreme weather conditions, and any period but the present. Most importantly, take advantage of what you have. *Chan Is Missing*, *She's Gotta Have It*, and *Clerks* were written to use available settings.

FINANCING. Most indies made for six digits attract investors, but micro-budget fare is usually financed with bank accounts and credit cards.

BUDGET. Hire a nonunion cast and crew (or union members willing to work nonunion); use friends when you can. Salaries and some other expenses can be deferred, with the promise they'll be paid only if the project turns a profit. Skip insurance and permits. A student ID (even a fake one) can win you deductions on film stock and equipment, and you can buy discounted stock that was previously bought but unused. Some gear, clothing, and props can be purchased, used, and returned for

continued

Something for Nothing

continued

a full refund within thirty days. The $500 video camera that shot *The Blair Witch Project* was "borrowed" this way.

PRODUCTION. Shoot in 16mm or Super 16, and consider using black-and-white. Schedule eighteen (long) days or less. Limit complex setups and the number of takes.

POST-PRODUCTION. Edit when you can most cheaply rent a machine, perhaps on the graveyard shift. Utilize stock music or unknown bands willing to contribute for free. Show your 16mm or Super 16 film to distributors or investors in order to attain the money to optically blow it up to 35mm with a final sound mix (such completion costs may be several times what you spent).

young filmmakers experience those same feelings, it's a theme that independent cinema would return to repeatedly in the eighties and nineties. Susan Seidelman helmed *Desperately Seeking Susan* (1985), sort of a happier version of *Smithereens*, for Orion, and has continued to make movies about strong female characters.

By the end of 1982, American independent cinema was finally becoming an artistic genre unto itself, with its own distributors, festivals, theaters, and fans. With quality pictures being made for $60,000 or less, raising a budget was less of an impediment. Financing was still important, of course, but more and more potential filmmakers were realizing that the two most crucial ingredients in a film, the story and the artist's vision, could be had for free.

Notes

1. Gallagher, John Andrew, *Film Directors on Directing* (Westport, CT: Greenwood, 1989), 244.
2. Ventura, Michael.
3. Gallagher, 237.
4. *Variety*, 26 March 1975.
5. With the goal of preserving motion pictures deemed "culturally, historically, or aesthetically significant," the National Film Registry is eclectic. Among the films introduced in 1990 were

Meshes of the Afternoon, A Woman Under the Influence, and *Harlan County, U.S.A.* After its initial selections in 1989, the N.F.C. has chosen approximately four independent movies (out of a maximum of twenty-five titles) each year.

6 Thomson, David, 748. From a review which originally appeared in *The Real Paper.*

7 *Los Angeles Times,* 24 March 1977.

8 *New Times Los Angeles,* 13–19 August 1998.

9 Change, Chris, "Planet of the Apes," *Film Comment* 33, 5 (Sept./Oct. 1997), 69.

10 *It Happened One Night* (1934) was the only previous film. *Silence of the Lambs* (1991) also swept the five major awards.

11 Bergan, Ronald, *The United Artists Story* (New York: Crown, 1986), 277.

12 The controversial list, polled from mostly film industry professionals (who had 400 preselected titles to choose from), was touted as a celebration of the first one hundred years of American cinema. It was lamentably weighted towards modern, studio movies. No documentaries and only three silent films were included. In additional to *One Flew Over the Cuckoo's Nest,* only *The Birth of a Nation* (#44) and *Easy Rider* (#88) were independents. *Citizen Kane* was number one.

13 *New Yorker,* 29 Sept. 1980.

14 *Starlog* 21 (April 1979), 47.

15 King, Stephen, *Danse Macabre* (New York: Berkley, 1981), 177.

16 *Cinefantastique,* 10, 1 (Summer 1980), 40.

17 *Cinefantastique,* 10, 1 (Summer 1980), 40.

18 *Variety,* 14 May 1980.

19 *Cinefantastique,* 20, 1/2 (Nov. 1989), 91.

20 Peary, Danny, *Cult Movies 3* (New York: Fireside, 1988), 54.

21 *New York Times,* 5 May 1977.

22 Godwin, George K., "Eraserhead," *Cinefantastique* 14 4/5 (Sept. 1984), 64.

23 *Newsweek,* 22 Sept. 1980.

24 *Variety,* 26 March 1980.

COMING OF AGE

First public showing of sex, lies. I got up before-
hand to introduce the film and explained that the
sound mix was temporary, and that I was going to
redo the titles, but that everything else was fair
game. The audience seemed to like it.

—JAN. 22, 1989, FROM THE DIARY OF
STEVEN SODERBERG

It was a crisp, cold January in Park City, Utah (population 3000), twenty miles from Salt Lake City. The sidewalks of historic Main Street overflowed with filmmakers, actors, would-be producers, low-level studio executives, journalists, cinéastes, and hangers-on. Park City is a winter vacation community, home of ski resorts and art galleries and tony bistros. Once a silver boom town, its mountains were mined for all they were worth a century ago. The Hearst family made much of its fortune there. Now prospectors walked the streets again. Scribes and distributors sifted through films. Unknown directors, their futures invested, nervously suffered through screenings of their creations. Waiting, hoping, dreaming. Mining Park City.

Nineteen eighty-nine was the next to last year before The US Film Festival changed its name to the Sundance Film Festival. The event included a retrospective tribute to John Cassavetes, who died days later; a centennial celebration of Charlie Chaplin, born in 1889; and

Main Street in Park City, Utah during the Sundance Film Festival.
© 1999 Fred Hayes. Courtesy The Sundance Institute.

two programs honoring the work of animator Jay Ward, creator of *Rocky and Bullwinkle* and *Dudley Do-Right*. "Sundance" opened with a screening of a restored print of a moving picture created more than sixty years earlier, F. W. Murnau's *Sunrise*.

Among the movies playing in Park City that January were New World's fiendishly dark teen farce *Heathers*, the Native-American road trip *Powwow Highway*, the camera's-eye view of Vietnam combat *84 Charlie Miopic*, and the inspiring space documentary and winner of top nonfiction awards *For All Mankind*. The romantic comedy *True Love* won the Grand Jury Prize for dramatic features. Jodie Foster, Monte Hellman, and Debra Hill were among those on the jury; Paul Mazursky was the Master of Ceremonies.

This was also the year "Sundance" initiated a Filmmakers Trophy (voted by directors whose movies are screened) and an Audience Award (voted by viewers). Festival programmer Tony Safford remembers the submission of the fiction Audience Award winner: "[The] movie came in late, and I thought, nice film. I had no idea it would change things."[1] Change things, it did; in fact, no movie in the sound era has had a greater impact on independent cinema than that "nice" film with an eminently commercial yet artfully lower-case title: *sex, lies, & videotape*.

After it was shown at the Holiday Village Cinemas, unfinished, and with a temporary soundtrack, festival audiences stood and applauded. Tickets were scalped at ten times their value for its fourth and final screening on January 28. Phones in Park City worked nonstop with news about the movie and its tyro writer/director from Louisiana, just days past his twenty-sixth birthday. Sundance had arrived.

Nine distributors bid on *sex, lies, & videotape* after it played in Northern Utah. Universal and Columbia flirted with picking it up. Some faltering companies strived desperately to win the film in a last-ditch effort to save themselves. In early March, Soderbergh's debut went to Harvey and Bob Weinstein and their still fledgling Miramax. Ten years after they began, the Weinsteins had yet to release a film that grossed more than $2 million in domestic theaters. *Sex, lies, & videotape* would soon make more than ten times that much. Miramax had arrived.

Sex, lies, & videotape was admitted to the Director's Fortnight (the traditional showcase for first films) of the Cannes Film Festival in May and then squeezed into the main competition when another movie dropped out. Most thought the talkative picture would get buried amidst international heavyweights and Yankee efforts like Jim Jarmusch's *Mystery Train* and Spike Lee's *Do The Right Thing*. Instead, *sex, lies, & videotape* became the first American independent film to win the grand prize, the Palm d'Or. When writer/director Steven Soderbergh stepped onstage to accept the most cherished film festival trophy in the world, he said, "Well, I guess it's all downhill from here."

Sex, lies, & videotape, made for $1.2 million, opened in August and went on to earn more than $25 million in domestic theaters and more than $100 million worldwide. The film was the right festival favorite at the right time with the right marketing push behind it. Independent cinema had arrived.

Indie film is a tough racket, and most movies made without a prior agreement with a studio are never screened in a commercial theater. Their directors are never known. Even those that are projected domestically rarely stir up significant ticket sales. It's equally rough for the distributors, many of whom folded up shop in the eighties, suffering through too many lackluster releases while waiting in vain on a *sex, lies, & videotape* to arrive.

By the mid-eighties, it was almost all on the shoulders of festival independents. Soft-core porn was on cable TV; hard-core was on videotape. There were a few final stabs to revive the midnight movie, as in Paul Bartel's campy western, *Lust in the Dust*, (1985), but, with even John Waters making PG pictures, the underground, having been absorbed by VCRs, was no longer a significant cultural phenomenon. When people could experience *Faces of Death* in their living rooms, it was hard to get them to a Waters- or Warhol-style flick at 12:00 AM in an art theater. (There was a significant market for cult videos in the eighties, when, from the safety of their favorite chairs, many people viewed underground and exploitation movies for the first time.)

Horror

Horror catapulted New Line to another level a few years before Miramax arrived. *Last House on the Left* veteran Wes Craven wrote and directed *A Nightmare on Elm Street* (1984). Produced by New Line for less than $2 million, it was a sensation that spawned five highly profitable sequels and a TV series. Bloody studio efforts oversaturated the market. As with porn and the underground, after 1985 nonstudio terror was no longer a viable means for breaking onto the big screen. However, two final outsiders managed to squeeze through before almost everything cheap and gruesome moved to videotape.

Michigan native Sam Raimi (1959–) was just twenty when he wrote a *Friday the 13th*-style script. With his brother Ivan, producer Robert Talbert, and actor Bruce Campbell, Raimi then shot a short Super-8 version. Using it as proof that they could make a fun movie, the rookies solicited lawyers and doctors in the Detroit area, trying to secure financing. They raised $375,000. Location work took place in a century-old cabin in the steamy woods of Tennessee. Most of the impressive effects were captured in Detroit.

The movie Raimi and his young friends created was *The Evil Dead* (1983). In this typical slasher story, five college students, including overly earnest Ash (Campbell), are stranded in a remote cabin. They discover an ancient book that releases demons. Members of the group are creatively murdered, then come back to life to terrorize the others.

The script for *The Evil Dead* is predictable and ridden with clichés, but the movie wisely keeps its tongue in its cheek. Decomposing bodies and gratuitous splatter effects (*The Evil Dead* was released unrated to avoid an X for gore) distract from the incoherent character motivations. Raimi and cinematographer Tom Philo keep the camera roaming in vigorous tracking shots that are often ostentatious but enjoyable nonetheless. It makes for a campy, exuberant, over-the-top exercise in moviemaking.

The Evil Dead played in the open market at Cannes, where it was championed by critics. Released by New Line, it was a solid success, especially in Europe. Sam Raimi went on to helm two *Evil Dead* sequels (1987 and 1993), both featuring Bruce Campbell, campy gore, and hyperactive camerawork. Raimi's Hollywood features include *The Quick and the Dead* (1995) and *A Simple Plan* (1998).

Based on the writing of horror legend H. P. Lovecraft, *Re-Animator* (1985) also developed a cult following. It was directed and coscripted by Stuart Gordon, a Chicago theater director making his big-screen debut. Producer Brian Yuzna raised the funds. Charles Band's exploitation company, Empire Pictures, released it. (Band claims the film was made in-house because he contributed to the financing; Yuzna insists it was an acquisition by Empire and Band's contribution was a repayment of old debts.)

A gory black comedy, *Re-Animator* happily pushes horror to new lows. An impassive medical student (Jeffrey Combs) can bring the dead back to life. He resuscitates the school's decapitated chief neurosurgeon (David Gale), who spends the rest of the movie with his head literally in his hands. In one of cinema's most outrageous scenes, the doctor's lecherous head sexually assaults a woman. *Re-Animator* was released unrated to avoid an X for gore and sexual content.

Respected critics championed *Re-Animator*'s over-the-top absurdity. It won festival awards and became an "underground" favorite in theaters and on video. Brian Yuzna cowrote and directed the sequel, *Bride of Re-Animator* (1990). Stuart Gordon has since specialized in low-budget horror and fantasy movies, often for Charles Band's Full Moon Entertainment.

Veterans

Out of necessity or in search of creative freedom, established directors continued to work outside the studios. John Sayles was among the most prolific. *Lianna* (1983), which he wrote, directed, edited, and acted in, is the story of a married mother in her early thirties (Linda

Griffiths) who has a lesbian relationship with her college professor. *Lianna* focuses on emotions and, like *Return of the Secaucus 7*, is especially attuned to the dilemmas of the "do your own thing" generation. *Baby, It's You*, which Sayles made for Paramount, was released the same year.

Sayles has never shied away from unusual projects, as evidenced by *The Brother From Another Planet* (1984), which he wrote, directed, and edited. Future director and Spike Lee collaborator Ernest Dickerson was the cinematographer who captured the vibrant colors. *The Brother From Another Planet* is a contemporary fantasy about a mute black space alien (Joe Morton)—a slave on another planet—who hides in Harlem while being tracked by two goofy whites (Sayles and David Stratham) called the "Men in Black." The alien can perform miracles with a healing touch, but none of the people he meets in Harlem seek true magic. They mostly need someone to talk to, and the sweet, receptive stranger fills the void. A subplot with the Brother tracking a drug kingpin bogs things down, and tones change abruptly. Still, *The Brother From Another Planet* is a marvelous idea that accomplishes more with a slyly comic script, a meager budget, and a silent protagonist than any preachy drama on race could do. Joe Morton gives a touching performance reminiscent of Buster Keaton.

Sayles's semi-indie *Matewan* (1987) is a historical account of labor strife among the coal miners of West Virginia. The producers needed eight years to secure the $4 million in financing. Sayles had his biggest commercial success with the studio feature *Eight Men Out* (1988). The Hollywood detour was temporary.

Wayne Wang helmed *Dim Sum: A Little Bit of Heart* (1984) from a Terrel Seltzer script. It's a portrait of a Chinese-American family in San Francisco. Mrs. Tam (Kim Chew) is an older widow with one child at home, daughter Geraldine (Laureen Chew), who wants to marry but feels an obligation to stay with her mother. Uncle Tam (Victor Wong) would marry the mother if the daughter would get out of the way. *Dim Sum* is an amusing, well-acted tale about loneliness, risk, and the blending of Asian and American cultures.

Slamdance (1987) was a misstep for Wang, a plodding thriller about an underground cartoonist (Tom Hulce) who is framed for the murder of a young woman. Wang got back on track with *Eat a Bowl of Tea* (1989), directing a script by Judith Rascoe. From 1924 until the end of World War II, few Chinese women were allowed to accompany their immigrating husbands to America. *Eat a Bowl of Tea* is a charming comedy about life in New York City when the ban is lifted. American-born Ben Loy (Russel Wong) steps into an arranged marriage with Chinese-born Mei Oi (Cora Miao). Victor Wong is excellent as a gambling club owner. Wayne Wang went on to helm the bizarre, self-distributed thriller *Life Is Cheap . . . but Toilet Paper Is Expensive* (1990), shot in Hong Kong, as well as studio efforts like *The Joy Luck Club* (1993).

Again wearing many hats (director, writer, editor, cinematographer), Victor Nunez made a second independent feature five years after his first. Based on a novel by John D. MacDonald, *A Flash of Green* (1984) was produced by costar Richard Jordan with backing from "American Playhouse." Jimmy the reporter (Ed Harris) follows a tip that a Florida nature preserve is being threatened by a developer (Jordan). Kat (Blair Brown) steps in to stop the development. All three become entangled in a story of lust, greed, and the compromises of everyday life. This character study gets weighed down by its own plot devices. It would be nine years before the release of another Victor Nunez film.

Abel Ferrara continued to craft brutal movies that were seldom seen. With a cast that includes Tom Berenger, Melanie Griffith, and Billy Dee Williams, *Fear City* (1984) is a violent exploitation picture about a psychopath murdering prostitutes in the Big Apple. *China Girl* (1987), a Romeo and Juliet tale set amidst gang warfare in New York, is atmospheric but slight. The political thriller *Cat Chaser* (1989) never made it into theaters. Abel Ferrara would have his greatest success in the nineties.

Robert Duvall was a veteran independent director, having crafted *We're Not the Jet Set* (1977), a documentary about a Nebraska family. He was also one of America's greatest actors, shining in such classics as *The Godfather* and *Apocalypse Now*. The same year he earned the Best Actor Oscar for *Tender Mercies*, his dramatic directorial debut *Angelo, My Love* (1983) was released.

In the mid-seventies, Duvall encountered a young Gypsy boy hustling on the streets of New York and decided to make him the focus of a movie. Between acting gigs, Duvall researched, wrote the screenplay, and unsuccessfully attempted to raise the money for *Angelo, My Love*. He eventually financed it himself. Gypsies play themselves, and young Angelo Evans stars with his family. Duvall had a headache when Gypsies from all over North America heard about the production and showed up on the set. *Angelo, My Love*'s meandering plot about an attempt to recover a stolen ring is routine, but the neorealistic portrait of the Gypsy lifestyle is captivating.

Robert Altman and Alan Rudolph

After *The Delinquents* and *The James Dean Story* in 1957, Robert Altman toiled in television for the next decade. He later said his twenty years of industrials and TV episodes taught him precisely what he didn't want to do. From the late sixties to the mid-seventies the hard-drinking, goateed visionary was a seminal figure in the American New Wave, forging such acclaimed films as *M*A*S*H* (1970), *McCabe and Mrs. Miller* (1971), *The Long Goodbye* (1973), and *Nashville* (1975). With overlapping dialogue and expansive casts, Altman's best movies reinterpret cinematic genres and question American values; his worst are muddled bores.

By the late seventies, Altman found it increasingly difficult to work in the modern Hollywood system of corporate meetings and marketing strategies. He was the wrong director for the post–*Star Wars* era,

Robert Altman directs.

and his attempts at a science fiction saga, *Quintet* (1979), and a live-action comic strip, *Popeye* (1980), were expensive bombs. Altman has directed more than a dozen motion pictures since then, though not a single one was financed or released solely by the major studios.

Altman first ventured into the theater, directing plays on stage and on film. *Come Back to the Five and Dime, Jimmy Dean, Jimmy Dean* (1982) depicts the reunion of a James Dean fan club in a small Texas town and features Sandy Dennis, Cher, Karen Black, and Kathy Bates. It began as a play written by Ed Graczyk and directed by Altman, and it remains rooted to the stage. The inventive mise-en-scène and stellar acting transcend the predictable script. Pauline Kael wrote, "I doubt if a major film director has ever voluntarily taken on as thoroughgoing a piece of drivel as this one. Yet when Altman gives a project everything he's got, his skills are such that he can make poetry out of fake poetry and magic out of fake magic."[2] *Come Back to the Five and Dime, Jimmy Dean, Jimmy Dean* was a flop by the standards of the studios but a hit in Altman's new art-house home.

Altman filmed *Streamers* (1983), a play written by David Rose, using an Army barracks as his single set. The film features Billy (Matthew Modine), Roger (David Alan Grier), Richie (Michael Lichtenstein), and Carlyle (Michael Wright) as soldiers awaiting their orders to go to Vietnam. The men confront differences of race and sexual orientation in a powerful story about why young men go to kill each other in faraway lands. The entire cast won the best actor award at the Venice Film Festival. *Streamers* was unjustly neglected by American critics and audiences.

Another filmed play, *Secret Honor* (1984) is a one-man show. Philip Baker Hall plays Richard Nixon in a fascinating ninety-minute monologue that mixes fact with much speculative fiction. Wandering around the Oval Office, a post-Watergate Nixon prattles into his tape recorder about all manner of scandalous deeds. Limited to one actor and one set, producer/director Altman took the *My Dinner With Andre* formula one step further.

Altman adapted two plays for studios, *Fool For Love* (1985) and *Beyond Therapy* (1987). *O. C. & Stiggs* (1987) went unreleased. In the nineties, Altman directed movies for semi-indie studios. The most notable is *The Player* (1992). Written by Michael Tolkin, starring Tim Robbins, and featuring dozens of name actors in cameos, this scathing view of the modern Hollywood system was a solid success, nominated for three Academy Awards, including director. Other Altman semi-indies of the nineties include *Vincent and Theo* (1990), *Short Cuts* (1993), and *Kansas City* (1997).

Alan Rudolph was Robert Altman's protégé. After his initial horror efforts, Rudolph assisted on such Altman flicks as *California Split* and *Nashville*; he cowrote Altman's *Buffalo Bill and the Indians* (1976). Rudolph then scripted and directed *Welcome to L.A.* (1977); Altman produced. Based on rock songs by Richard Baskin, which, unfortunately, dominate the soundtrack, *Welcome to L.A.* is sort of a darker, slimmer version of *Nashville*. Rudolph, who grew up in Los Angeles the son of an actor/director, serves up a lot of poetic cynicism about his native city. Members of the standout cast (Keith Carradine, Harvey Keitel, Sissy Spacek, Sally Kellerman) hop from bed to bed in a desperate, cheerless attempt to connect.

Altman produced and Rudolph wrote and directed *Remember My Name* (1978), a moody movie about a spurned woman (Geraldine Page) who returns from a prison stint to disrupt her ex-husband's life. The blues vocals of Roberta Hunter dominate the soundtrack, and the stellar cast includes Anthony Perkins, Jeff Goldblum, and Alfre Woodard. After a very limited theatrical release, *Remember My Name* became a modern lost classic, with no prints or videos available.

For United Artists, Rudolph helmed and cowrote a pair of flops, *Roadie* (1980) and *Endangered Species* (1982). *Return Engagement* (1983) is a filmed account of traveling debates between LSD guru Timothy Leary and Watergate conspirator G. Gordon Liddy.

Returning to *Welcome to L.A.* terrain, Rudolph crafted *Choose Me* (1984), a stylized romantic comedy about confused but bright thirtysomethings searching for love but failing to communicate. Ann (Geneviève Bujold) works as a radio love doctor, dispensing advice even though she's unable to find her own fulfilling relationship. She moves in with bar owner Eve (Lesley Ann Warren), who doesn't realize that Ann is Dr. Love. Likewise, Ann doesn't grasp that Eve is a frequent caller. Pearl (Rae Dawn Chong) is another listener; her abusive husband (Patrick Bauchau) is pursuing Eve. Into this volatile mix wanders Mickey (Keith Caradine), a mental hospital escapee who seduces the three women and proposes marriage to Eve and Ann. Mickey serves as a positive, liberating force, though he claims to be a pathological liar.

Alan Rudolph says, "I don't do realistic films. I don't even believe they exist. . . . By definition, movies are a lie on reality."[3] With believable emotions and a preposterous story line, *Choose Me* has its own dreamy rhythm. Purposelessly artificial exteriors are bathed in neon light. Teddy Pendergrass's moody love songs haunt the soundtrack. *Choose Me* had many laudatory reviews, and it thrived through word of mouth.

Rudolph has since molded his own brand of semi-indies, often utilizing his trademark soft-focus lighting to create stylized ensemble pieces. Titles include *Trouble in Mind* (1985), *The Moderns* (1988), the Altman-produced *Mrs. Parker and the Vicious Circle* (1994), and *Afterglow* (1997). A true rebel and a highly literate filmmaker, Alan Rudolph continues to forge unique adult dramas outside the major studios.

Henry Jaglom

Depending on whom you ask, Henry Jaglom (1939–) is either a feminist or a male chauvinist, a truth-seeker or a self-indulgent bore, a genius or a fraud, the next Cassavetes or the second coming of Hugo Haas. Jaglom makes marginal improvisational movies that blur the line between fiction and fact. He turns his camera on people—mostly his friends—and agitates them from offscreen to see what happens.

Jaglom's cinematic career began with a few minor acting roles in the late sixties. For Columbia, in 1971, he wrote and directed *A Safe Place*. The independent *Sitting Ducks* (1980), is an energetic comedy in which two mob accountants (Michael Emil and Jack Norman) steal a day's collections and flee. Jaglom and his wife (Patrice Townsend) are featured. *Can She Bake a Cherry Pie?* (1983) is a slow excursion with a neurotic, jilted woman (Karen Black) who takes up with a talkative man (Michael Emil).

Jaglom crystalized his highly personal style and first drew attention to his developing oeuvre with *Always* (1985). He wears many hats: director, screenwriter, producer, editor, and actor. Three couples spend a fourth of July weekend together. A divorcing twosome is played by Jaglom and his then ex-wife Patrice Townsend, whom he prods into revealing the reason she left him. The cast is made up of the director's family and friends, and shooting took place in his home. Highly improvised, it all makes for a cringe-inducing comedy.

Someone to Love (1987) is a self-indulgent fictional documentary in which Jaglom, as a filmmaker named Danny Sapir, gathers his friends (including Sally Kellerman and Monte Hellman) in an auditorium on

Valentine's Day and questions them about love. Orson Welles (in his last film appearance) sits in the balcony and laughs at the absurdity of it all; he laughs alone.

Like his inspiration, John Cassavetes, the independently wealthy Jaglom formed his own production and distribution company (International Rainbow Pictures) to circulate his films. The first IRP release was *New Year's Day* (1988). Jaglom plays a writer reclaiming the apartment he rented to three female tenants. The threadbare plot is just an excuse for tedious talk about relationships.

Eating (1989) gathers a group of women together to celebrate the birthdays of friends turning thirty, forty, and fifty. Talk centers on food and men and men and food. *Eating* is sort of My Dinner with a Dozen Females, and it raises a key question about Jaglom: is he a feminist for making movies about women and their concerns or a chauvinist for making his women mostly concerned with men? Jaglom would provide more opportunities to ponder this question in the nineties.

Jim Jarmusch

It moved at its own laid-back pace, like a lazy hustler or a cocksure jazzman. Black-and-white with a static camera and laconic dialogue, it was unlike any other motion picture. Its auteur called it "a neo-realistic black comedy in the style of an imaginary East European director obsessed with Ozu and *The Honeymooners.*"[4] It hit the independent scene hard, launching the popular ascent of the modern art film that was brought to another level with *sex, lies, & videotape.*

The movie was *Stranger Than Paradise* (1984), written and directed by Jim Jarmusch (1953–). Jarmusch, who sports a white pompadour and a bohemian aura, grew up in Akron, Ohio and studied English literature at Columbia. He spent a year in France, where he became enamored with worldwide cinema. Upon returning to the states, Jarmusch earned a graduate film degree at NYU. He apprenticed with noted directors Nicholas Ray and Wim Wenders and worked various indie jobs. In 1983, Wenders gave Jarmusch some leftover black-and-white stock and, with producer Sara Driver (herself an experimental filmmaker), he put it to use one weekend, shooting a thirty-minute short called *New World*, about a recent immigrant to New York City. Screening it at a festival in Germany, the filmmakers raised the money to capture two additional thirty-minute segments and tie them into a feature film.

Gazing at the frozen lake in *Stranger Than Paradise*.

Willie (John Lurie) lives in a bleak apartment. He eats TV dinners, watches TV, gambles, and hangs out with his equally dull friend Eddie (Richard Edson). Willie's teenage cousin Eva (Eszter Balint) from Hungary stays with them, grows bored, and moves on to Cleveland. One year later, the two New Yorkers visit Eva and Aunt Lottie (Cecilla Stark) in Cleveland; The situation is even more mundane as they sit and stare at the frozen, snow-covered lake. Willie, Eddie, and Eva drive to Florida. Staying in an out-of-the-way motel in the cool wintertime, "paradise" is as lifeless as New York and Cleveland—at least for this lethargic threesome.

The humor of *Stranger Than Paradise* bubbles to the surface because nothing happens. The characters are incapable of breaking free of their boredom. Ironic dialogue is delivered deadpan. Long pauses often provide the biggest laughs. Production design is sparse, as is the cinematography by Tom DiCillo. The movie's main distinguishing feature is that the camera doesn't budge; it stays in a rigid wide shot.

There is no conventional editing; at the end of static scenes the picture simply fades to black. Long takes saved money on film stock, but they also complement the aimless story and languid dialogue. J. Hoberman wrote in *The Village Voice*: "Structurally, the movie is a tour de force—a succession of brief vignettes punctuated with opaque film stock. . . . Characters enter the frame as though it were a stage, and the effect is kabuki sitcom, yet powerfully naturalistic—an amalgam of Damon Runyon and Piet Mondrian that's a triumph of low-budget stylization."[5]

Stranger Than Paradise entranced critics and viewers who were ready to embrace something different, something in direct opposition to the big-budget gloss of Hollywood. After winning the Camera d'Or (best first film) at Cannes, it was picked up for circulation by the Samuel Goldwyn Company and became a hit at both the Telluride and the New York Film Festivals. Though *Stranger Than Paradise* grossed less than $3 million in North America, the National Society of Film Critics voted it the best picture of the year. It was a bigger sensation overseas.

The influence of *Stranger Than Paradise* cannot be underestimated. Countless independent filmmakers have been inspired by Jarmusch's ability to create—with a mere $110,000—an utterly original motion picture that's been championed around the globe. The aforementioned *Filmmaker* magazine poll proclaimed it the second most important independent film of all time.

Jim Jarmusch had arrived—at

Foreign Market

Modern studio movies typically make as much in foreign theaters as they do at domestic (U.S. and Canadian) box offices. All over the developed world, people clamor for American stars and big-budget spectacle—qualities most independent films lack. Many low-budget talk-fests are not even released with subtitles or dubbing. The erudite *My Dinner With Andre*, an art-house smash stateside, made only $150,000 away from home.

On the other hand, European audiences have been very receptive to some U.S. independents, especially those that play at a European film festival and those that are controversial or perceived as "cool." Since the auteur theory of the late fifties, the French have championed masculine mavericks and

continued

Foreign Market *continued*

quirky flicks that would otherwise go under-appreciated. Movies by Sam Fuller, Monte Hellman, and Quentin Tarantino have found their most welcoming venues in Paris. European countries have always been the key foreign markets for American indies, joined recently by Japan and Australia.

Kids ($8 million) and *Lost Highway* ($5 million) pulled in slightly more in Europe than they did in North America. *Sex, lies, and videotape* ($80 million) tripled its domestic revenue in foreign theaters, and *Reservoir Dogs* ($20 million) made eight times as much. Throughout their careers, idiosyncratic directors Jim Jarmusch and Hal Hartley have found their principal audience and financing outside their native land.

The foreign market remains unpredictable for American independents. An art-house hit may never get a foreign release, while a stateside indie flop can rake in millions across the seas.

■　■　■　■　■　■　■　■

least in the limited community of indie cinema. His follow-up covered similar terrain. *Down By Law* (1986) is a tranquil comedy about bad luck, lost jobs, tin roof diners, and swamp shacks. Small-time pimp Jack (John Lurie) and unemployed disc jockey Zack (Tom Waits) are both framed and end up together in a New Orleans jail cell. The narrative is as intentionally listless as that of *Stranger Than Paradise*, but it picks up when a third prisoner, life-loving, Italian Roberto (Roberto Benigni), joins them. As reluctant allies, the trio escape into the swamps. Roberto bumps into a diner that reaffirms his faith in the American dream. The two cynical Americans keep on rambling.

Down By Law works because of the inspired casting. The downtown jazzman Lurie and gravel-voiced singer Waits make a beguiling couple, and Italian comedic actor Benigni steals the movie with his confused English and amiable nature. Ellen Barkin also stands out in a tiny role as Zack's soon-to-be-ex-girlfriend. With the exception of a few long tracking shots, the camera is again static. The black-and-white cinematography was by Robby Müller. John Lurie provided the jazzy score, with the inclusion of Tom Waits songs over the credits. Writer/director Jarmusch stated he had never visited bayou country before filming there. Instead of authenticity, *Down By Law* is an amalgamation of B movie clichés and grimy atmosphere.

Reviews for *Down By Law* were mostly favorable, but it was a hard movie to sell. Made for ten times as much as *Stranger Than Paradise*, it grossed less in domestic theaters. Most of America had never heard of Jim Jarmusch (and still haven't), but *Down By Law* was again popular in Europe and Japan, where the auteur was correctly hailed as a major new force in cinema.

Jarmusch's *Mystery Train* (1989) also follows aimless, offbeat characters in an evocative locale. Three different stories are interwoven around a fleabag Memphis hotel. The first features a young, hip Japanese couple (Masatoshi Nagase and Youki Kudoh) on the trail of Elvis and Carl Perkins. The second (and weakest) focuses on an Italian woman (Nicoletta Braschi) whose husband has just died and who is visited by the ghost of Elvis. The third (and best) is a bumpy ride with three losers (Steve Buscemi, Rick Avilés, and musician Joe Strummer) who shoot a man and hide out in the hotel.

As always, the casting is offbeat (musician Screamin' Jay Hawkins plays the hotel's night manager) and the shabby decor and uncomfortable pauses are crucial. This time, however, the Southern night is captured in vibrant color (cinematography by Robby Müller), the camera movement and cutting have increased, and the overlapping story structure is unique.

Jarmusch's first features form a triumvirate examining the American dream as viewed by outsiders. The writer/director explains, "America's a kind of throwaway culture that's a mixture of different cultures. To make a film about America, it seems to me logical to have at least one perspective that's transplanted because ours is a collection of transplanted influences."[6]

The Coen Brothers

Minnesota natives Joel (1954–) and Ethan Coen (1957–) went to college in the East, studying film (Joel at NYU) and philosophy (Ethan at Princeton). Returning to the upper Midwest, the Coen brothers developed a working relationship with Sam Raimi. The three wrote the energetic independent flop *Crimewave* (1985), directed by Raimi. Like their Michigan predecessor, when the Coens decided to create their own feature, they shot an audition piece. For $2,000 they made a three-minute preview and showed it and their clever script to potential investors.

The Coens had never before directed even a short film. Cinematographer Barry Sonnenfeld had never looked through a 35mm lens. Still, after a year of soliciting, they managed to raise $1.5 million.

The shadows of film noir. Frances McDormand in *Blood Simple*.

Shots were meticulously storyboarded—a practice the brothers have maintained throughout their careers. Shooting took place in the indie outpost of Austin, Texas. The Coens shared screenwriting credit; older brother Joel is listed as director, Ethan as producer. (They've maintained this practice, though they share those duties; they also edit under the pseudonym "Roderick Jaynes.")

The title *Blood Simple* (1984) was derived from pulp fiction slang referring to the fearful state of confusion that follows the commission of murder. Joel said the movie was "about mistrust, double-cross, greed, jealousy and lust. The essential starting point of the plot was the notion of the pivotal double-cross. Supposing a guy hires a murderer and the murderer double-crosses him."[7] The guy is Julian (Dan Hedaya), owner of a roadhouse. The intended victims are his wife (Frances McDormand) and her lover (John Getz). The hired murderer is Visser (M. Emmet Walsh), a good ol' boy private dick. Untrusting and bewildered, the characters charge through a serpentine story, capable of killing or being killed.

Blood Simple was a sensation at the 1984 New York Film Festival and it won the Grand Jury Prize at the US Film Festival, but critics were split. Respected deans Pauline Kael and Stanley Kauffman denounced it as empty and overly clever, with script twists and camera pans designed solely to draw attention. Others couldn't help but get caught up in the filmmaking exuberance. David Denby wrote, "*Blood Simple* is indeed bloody (even, in spots, extravagantly bloody), so I suppose one must call it a gothic, but it has the suave, taunting fatalism of classic *film noir*—the wit, the shocks, the fascination with style that have marked the greatest examples of the genre. . . . It is also one of the most brazenly self-assured directorial debuts in American film history."[8]

Blood Simple's script and acting are focused; the camerawork is vibrant; the lighting is evocative. At one point the camera tracks down the roadhouse bar and rises up and over a drunk slumped on the counter, ostentatiously drawing attention to the filmmaking, but fun nonetheless. The finale, in which bullets fired through a wall lead shafts of light to penetrate a dark room, has often been copied. *Blood Simple* was a cinematheque triumph, championed by movie lovers worldwide.

Hollywood took note. Under various arrangements, the Coens have worked with studios big and small ever since, but yet they have remained "independent" by insisting on total creative freedom. They've made *Raising Arizona* (1987), *Miller's Crossing* (1990), the dark Hollywood satire *Barton Fink* (1991), *The Hudsucker Proxy* (1994), Oscar-winner *Fargo* (1996), and *The Big Lebrowski* (1998). All feature the Coen brothers' trademark quirky characters, plot twists, and exuberant camerawork. Cinematographer Barry Sonnenfeld shot several other movies, including the Coens's, before helming such films as *Get Shorty* (1995) and *Men In Black* (1997).

Hispanic-American

In the eighties, Hispanic-Americans stepped forward to tell the stories Hollywood had been neglecting for decades. The National Council of La Raza and producer Moctesuma Esparza developed a plan for a motion picture series about the literature and history of Latinos. Robert Young had been working in and out of the studios for twenty years. Now his adept handling of racial dynamics in *Nothing But a Man* and *Alambrista!* earned him another job on the outside.

With financing from the National Endowment for the Humanities and PBS, Esparza and Michael Hausman produced *The Ballad of Gregory Cortez* (1983), a film based on factual events. Young cowrote with Victor Villasenor and directed. Amazingly, with a budget of barely $1 million, this period film was shot in Texas with a cast of more than 1,500 costumed extras.

Set in 1901, the film follows Gregory Cortez (Edward James Olmos), who speaks only Spanish, as he is questioned in English about a horse theft. The language barrier leads Cortez to shoot a sheriff. In a saga that was closely followed in newspapers, he flees over hundreds of miles towards the Mexican border, managing to allude a posse of 600 men for eleven days. Finally Cortez is captured and brought to trial. Too slow for a western chase film, *The Ballad of Gregory Cortez* suffers from the weight of authenticity. Distribution was also mishandled; it was rushed in and out of wide release.

Hispanic-American Gregory Nava (1949–) was born and raised in Southern California. After attending UCLA film school, he made his first feature, *The Confessions of Amans* (1976), a medieval love story, for a mere $20,000 in Spain with costumes left over from Hollywood's *El Cid* (1961). It was barely distributed.

The movie that established Nava was *El Norte* (1983). Nava directed; his wife, Anna Thomas, produced; they cowrote. After a two-year

Poster for *El Norte*.

struggle, financing came via "American Playhouse" and private sources. The $850,000 movie was shot at more than one hundred locations in Mexico and California, with more than sixty speaking parts. Hostilities in the Mayan highlands (where Indian extras spoke neither English nor Spanish) resulted in the crew having to pay protection money. Later, when the production manager and film footage were kidnaped, Thomas had to hand over 1.3 million pesos ($17,000) in ransom to submachine-gun-toting bandits. For safety, future Mexican scenes were moved to Los Angeles, at additional expense.

El Norte ("the North" or, figuratively, "the United States") is told in Spanish, Mayan, and English. The principal actors were Latin Americans unknown in El Norte. Guatemalan Enrique (David Villalpando) and his sister, Rosa (Zaide Silvia Gutierrez), both in their early twenties, flee government violence in their primitive but beautiful Mayan village. "For the rich, the peasants are just a pair of arms," says their father before he is killed. Enrique and Rosa journey by bus and foot through Mexico and sneak into California in pursuit of the American dream. In Los Angeles they join the Hispanic cheap labor force and experience a new kind of oppression. Enrique gets a better job offer, but it will mean leaving Rosa. The ending is bleak.

Two hours and twenty minutes long, *El Norte* is an epic tale with a great sense of place and people. From Mayan jungle mills to American sweatshops, it takes us where other movies have never been. The Guatemalan section is the strongest, filled with poetry and hints of magic realism. There is a horrifying claustrophobic scene where brother and sister, crawling into America through miles of corrugated sewer pipe, are attacked by a pack of rats. The two leads give winning performances—naive, slightly wistful, and eternally optimistic. The one weakness is the presentation of gringos, almost all of whom come off as caricatures. Like *Alambrista!*, *El Norte* deals sympathetically with its topic while sidestepping overt politics.

El Norte was a substantial independent success. Buoyed by positive reviews and carefully marketed to both art-house patrons and the Latino population, it grossed more than $5 million in domestic theaters. In a category that has seen scant activity since the days of Edgar Ulmer, *El Norte* is history's most successful, American-made foreign language film. The screenplay by Nava and Thomas was nominated for an Academy Award.

The husband and wife team made *A Time of Destiny* (1988) for Hollywood; they assumed their regular roles on the semi-indie *My Family* (1995), a historical saga of a Mexican-American family in Los Angeles. Nava has since directed, for the majors, *Selena* (1997) and *Why Do Fools Fall in Love?* (1998).

Committed leftist and legendary cinematographer Haskell Wexler wrote and vibrantly directed another nonstudio narrative feature. *Latino* (1985) follows a Hispanic-American Green Beret (Robert Beltran), who experiences a change of conscience while assisting the US-backed Nicaraguan Contras. Though the story falls flat, this film, like *Medium Cool*, is a fiercely political document very relevant to its time.

Crossover Dreams (1985) was the second independent movie from Leon Ichaso. As codirector with Orlando Jiminez-Leal, Ichaso debuted with *El Super* (1979, in Spanish), the endearing fable of a homesick Cuban. *Crossover Dreams*, which Ichaso directed and cowrote with producer Manuel Arce and actor Ruben Blades, follows a salsa performer (Blades) who sheds his friends and Latin audience in an attempt to go mainstream. This conventional tale benefits from Blades's music and charisma. Ichaso went on to direct modestly budgeted projects like *Sugar Hill* (1994).

In 1983, recent film school graduate Ramon Menendez saw a newspaper article about Jaime Escalante, a math teacher at Garfield High School in East Los Angeles. Escalante's students had just passed a second advanced placement test in calculus after being accused of cheating the first time. Menendez and his film school friend, Tom Musca, met with Escalante for months before convincing the teacher to let them buy the rights to his life story. (Though the initial option was for $1 against a $10,000 purchase price, Escalante eventually received a bonus of $185,000 plus profit participation.) For months, Menendez and Musca pitched their idea in Hollywood with hopes of turning it into a TV movie. Nothing happened. They wrote a screenplay.

In the fall of 1985, "American Playhouse" came through with a proposed grant of $500,000 if the filmmakers could raise another $500,000. After a year and a half of pleading with various corporations and foundations, the rookie filmmakers raised a budget of $1.4 million. By that time they had their Escalante. Edward James Olmos spent months meticulously studying the techniques, mannerisms, and speech patterns of the gifted teacher. He gained forty-one pounds to mimic Escalante's body. With Menendez directing and Musca producing, *Stand and Deliver* was shot in the spring of 1987.

The completed film premiered at a small festival, followed closely by the IFFM. It was suddenly *the* hot property. All the major indie companies wanted it. With its uplifting story and straightforward filmmaking, the major studios were interested as well. It screened on studio lots, and Warner Bros. won the rights to *Stand and Deliver* (1988) with an advance of $3 million.

With humor, mockery, and respect, Bolivian-born Escalante (Olmos) inspires his surly Latino students to overcome their low self-esteem and meager expectations. The toughest teen to win over is Angel (Lou Diamond Phillips). Against all odds, the students pass the advanced placement exam, but they're accused of cheating by an exam representative (Andy Garcia). Rather than accept the perception of failure, the students take the test again.

Reviews were mostly favorable, though some rightly pointed out how potentially dramatic elements—crime, poverty, uninspiring teachers, even Escalante's heart attack—were not pursued with vigor. *Stand and Deliver*'s true story generated publicity. Advertising announced: "A New Troublemaker Hit Garfield High . . . He was tough. He was wild. He was willing to fight. He was the new math teacher." Sold to general audiences, the film was a solid box-office success, earning more than $18 million worldwide. Edward James Olmos was nominated for an Academy Award. Going Hollywood, Menendez helmed *Money For Nothing* (1993).

African-American

African-American independent cinema had been in hibernation since blaxploitation. For a decade, indie distributors saw predominantly black casts as box-office toxin, thus preventing quality films like Charles Burnett's *Killer of Sheep* from even reaching screens. John Sayles's *The Brother from Another Planet* was a rare exception, though it was not rigorously targeted to black audiences. Hollywood, too, was the same old story. Richard Pryor was a superstar in the seventies, followed by Eddie Murphy in the eighties, but they were invariably teamed up with a white buddy. "The Cosby Show" dominated television ratings from 1984 to the end of the decade, but for too long there were no motion pictures that spoke directly to African-

Americans. Thanks to a skinny, bug-eyed, twenty-nine-year-old from Brooklyn, things were about to change.

"We have to tell our own story. I am sick of these white people defining who we are. But there is nobody to blame but ourselves. I'm not naming names, but I think one of the things that holds us back is that we think it's not a film unless it's a $5 million picture. I think we have it backwards, and there are alternative means to doing this Hollywood stuff."[9] So said Spike Lee in 1986.

Spike Lee (1957–) grew up in Brooklyn the son of a jazz musician and a schoolteacher. He attended NYU film school, where his student short, *Joe's Bed-Stuy Barbershop: We Cut Heads*, won the Student Award of the Motion Picture Academy. He started an independent feature called "Messenger" in 1984 to star Larry Fishburne and Giancarlo Esposito, but it collapsed during preproduction. Lee then wrote a script for a less ambitious feature. Its provocative title was the first thing people noticed.

She's Gotta Have It (1986) was shot rapidly at limited locations in Brooklyn. Much of the dialogue is captured with stationary characters addressing the camera. Filming was completed in a brief twelve days for $80,000 (deferred pay and postproduction costs later doubled this

(l-r) John Terrell, Spike Lee, and Redmond Hicks argue Scrabble in *She 's Gotta Have It*.
© 1986 Island Pictures.

figure). Lee served as director, writer, editor, actor, and (credited under his given name, Shelton J. Lee) producer. He named his new production entity 40 Acres and a Mule after the property promised freed slaves. Ernest Dickerson was the cinematographer. Lee's dad, Bill, provided the music.

She's Gotta Have It is the sexy comedic story of Nola Darling (Tracy Johns), who juggles her three very different male lovers: dependable but dull Jamie (Redmond Hicks), narcissistic model Greer (John Terrell), and jiving bicycle messenger Mars Blackmon (Lee). The men turn possessive and insist Nola make a choice.

Photographed in black and white, *She's Gotta Have It* has one color dance sequence (which brings the film to a screeching halt) and fine use of photo montages. The film is funny and fresh despite its awkward acting and rough edges. The *Los Angeles Times* wrote, "There's something genuinely different here, a perspective we don't see enough—the joy and liveliness of an often neglected present. The movie's breeziness is tonic, refreshing. Even when some of the scenes aren't working so well, it grabs you."[10] Spike Lee as Mars Blackmon does most of the grabbing, screeching into the movie on a bicycle and leaping off the screen with his "Please baby, please baby, baby please" routine and other comic raps. The emphasis on a woman's enjoyment of sex (Lee had to trim some of the sexual content to avoid an X rating) and the foibles and insecurities of men is also inspired.

She's Gotta Have It was the hit at the 1986 San Francisco Film Festival. Island Pictures bought it when it stirred up international publicity at Cannes. Soon news of the film and its charismatic creator spread. Ads pronounced it "A Seriously Sexy Comedy." An incessant salesman, Spike Lee played up the racial and sexual themes of his debut and quipped that if it didn't make money he'd be hawking tube socks (a routine he used in the movie's trailer).

She's Gotta Have It was a hit, earning an eye-opening $7 million in American theaters, playing primarily to black audiences. In the process, it smashed the conventional wisdom about box-office poison. The repercussions from *She's Gotta Have It* were felt throughout the motion picture world, helping to open film up to more diverse cultural representations on both sides of the camera.

Mars Blackmon (and, consequently, Spike Lee) achieved his greatest fame in Nike commercials with Michael Jordan. Lee has gone on to have a highly visible, sometimes polemical filmmaking career.

Working for Hollywood studios, he has created such motion pictures as *School Daze* (1986), *Do the Right Thing* (1989), and *Malcolm X* (1992). He returned to independent filmmaking in 1996 with *Get on the Bus*, a fictionalized account of black men taking a bus from Los Angeles to Washington, DC for the 1995 Million Man March. *Get on the Bus*'s $2 million budget came from African-American businessmen. Spike Lee made the excellent HBO-funded, Oscar-nominated documentary *4 Little Girls* (1997), about innocent victims of the civil rights struggle.

Though comedian Robert Townsend (1957–) was coming off his most prestigious acting jobs, in *A Soldier's Story* (1983) and *Streets of Fire* (1984), there persisted a dearth of quality roles for African-Americans. In 1984 (a year before Lee launched *She's Gotta Have It*) Townsend took the money he'd earned from performing, gathered up his friends, and began to shoot some short movies to further his acting career. He had no filmmaking experience. Over the course of two and a half years, the material matured into a full-length motion picture called *Hollywood Shuffle* (1987). Robert Townsend and Keenen Ivory Wayans penned the script and acted; Townsend produced and directed. Filming took place around their homes and (without permits) on the streets of Los Angeles. When his savings ran out, Townsend financed the remaining $40,000 of the $100,000 production on credit cards. Just before the debt collectors came calling, and while *She's Gotta Have It* was packing in urban audiences, Townsend sold his movie to the Samuel Goldwyn Company.

Hollywood Shuffle is the broadly comedic tale of young black actor Bobby Taylor (Townsend) trying to make it in Hollywood while working at the Winky Dinky Dog hot dog stand. Along the way, Bobby auditions for a variety of demeaning roles and fantasizes about a system in which blacks get the best parts. Bobby's grandmother (Helen Martin) is critical of Hollywood; his girlfriend (Anne-Marie Johnson) is supportive of her man. The cast includes comedians Paul Mooney and John Witherspoon.

Hollywood Shuffle is uneven. Witherspoon and Martin are funny, and Townsend is a skilled actor, but many comedic moments fall flat. The further things travel from reality, the less successful they are. The disorganized script takes very broad swipes at black acting stereotypes, some of which were decades late. ("The Cosby Show" was the number-one TV show that year; "A Different World" was number two.) Townsend's satire would be more lethal if it focused on the

scarcity of black roles in front of and behind the camera in the eighties. *Variety* captured the movie's mixed bag: "Brimming with imagination and energy, *Hollywood Shuffle* is the kind of shoestring effort
more appealing in theory than execution. . . . Scattershot humor miss-
es as much as it hits, but the film is entertaining enough to lure an
audience looking for something different."[11]

By indie standards, it lured a large audience. *Hollywood Shuffle*
grossed more than $5 million in North American theaters. Townsend
got great mileage out of his "made a movie with credit cards" hook.
Virtually every news story and review mentioned it; Johnny Carson
highlighted it during Townsend's plum appearance on "The Tonight
Show." Although the financing was not any more inspiring than
that of the hundreds of other desperate mavericks (including Spike
Lee) who went into debt to get a movie made, the commonality of
credit cards clicked with the general public. It seemed like anyone could do what Townsend had done. The legend encouraged a
new generation of budding directors to get a feature made by any
means necessary.

Robert Townsend has gone on to have an uneven career as a filmmaker—*The Five Heartbeats* (1991), *Meteor Man* (1992)—along with
stints as a comedian and television actor. Cowriter Keenen Ivory
Wayans (TV's "In Living Color") has followed a similar path.

Except for a few moments at the conclusion, *Sidewalk Stories* (1989)
is silent. Producer/director/writer Charles Lane shot it in fifteen days
on the streets of New York in single-digit weather. Lane stars as a
Chaplinesque street artist who takes in an orphaned child (Lane's
daughter Nicole Alysia). With slapstick and pathos, *Sidewalk Stories* is
a comedic melodrama that brings the plight of the homeless to life.
Photographed in black and white by Bill Dill with music by Marc
Marder, the completed film has the look and theme of a Charlie
Chaplin silent. Lane went on to direct *True Identity* (1991) for Disney.

The success of *She's Gotta Have It* and *Hollywood Shuffle* delivered a
potent one-two punch to complacent Hollywood. By the end of the
decade, the studios were starting to come around. In 1989, the majors
served up such features as *Do the Right Thing, Harlem Nights, Driving
Miss Daisy, Glory, The Mighty Quinn,* and *Tap.* Movies would more frequently incorporate black actors and themes in the next decade, but
Hollywood continued to leave room for renegades to tell truly diverse
stories of the black experience.

Gay

Throughout its long history, with few exceptions, Hollywood has avoided gay themes and overtly homosexual characters—unless, of course, it was mocking them. Even the open-minded indie world had its closets. Though homosexual content had been a mainstay of vanguard filmmakers like Kenneth Anger, Gregory Markopoulos, and Andy Warhol, gay characters had only recently made it onto art-house screens for an extended stay, and only in the French/Italian cross-dressing farce *La Cage Aux Folles* (1978), and, at midnight, in the high camp of John Waters and *The Rocky Horror Picture Show*.

Things were about to change. Gay film historian Vito Russo wrote in 1987: "Independent features are beginning to routinely reflect what it traditionally takes Hollywood a decade to see, the writing on society's wall. There's an adult market for well-made films that aren't 'safe.' "[12] This pronouncement was made after the Brazilian/American semi-indie *Kiss of the Spider Woman* (1985) took cinematheques by storm on its way to collecting four Oscar nominations, including Best Picture. Playing a flamboyant homosexual, William Hurt won Best Actor.

Receiving much less fanfare, *Abuse* (1983) presents a homosexual graduate student (Richard Ryder) making a documentary on child abuse. He films a gay teenage boy (Raphael Sharge) who is brutalized by his parents. The two become lovers. Directed by Arthur Bressan, this microbudget, black-and-white production raises troubling questions about whether an adult romantically involved with a teen constitutes a form of abuse.

Bressan previously directed the documentary *Gay U.S.A.* (1978). Shooting in nine days, he next made *Buddies* (1985), the first feature film about AIDS. Robert (Geoff Edholm) is dying; yuppie David (David Schachter) is the man who volunteers to help him. They clash at first but eventually develop an emotional relationship.

In 1978 in San Francisco, conservative city supervisor Dan White shot and killed Mayor George Moscone and fellow city supervisor, openly gay Harvey Milk. The subsequent trial drew international attention for White's "Twinkie defense" that junk food had made him temporarily insane. The excellent, traditionally framed (file footage and interviews) documentary *The Times of Harvey Milk* (1984) does not dwell on the sensational trial. Instead, this labor of love, directed by Robert Epstein and narrated by Harvey Fierstein, serves as a tribute to Milk's life and to the flowering of gay pride in San Francisco in the seventies. *The Times of Harvey Milk* won the Academy Award for documentary feature. Two other 1985 documentaries, *Before Stonewall* and *Silent Partners,* highlighted previously closeted gay history.

The landmark independent movie *Parting Glances* (1986) is a portrayal of the last day two gay lovers (Richard Ganoung and John Bolger) spend together before one leaves. Steve Buscemi—a fixture of indie films in the following decade—steals the show as a cynical ex-lover dying of AIDS. The pedestrian *Parting Glances* was notable for the very matter-of-fact way it treated characters who happened to be gay. It was the only feature film by screenwriter/director/editor Bill Sherwood, who died of AIDS in 1990 at age thirty-seven.

Lesbianism, too, was featured in movies in the early eighties. Warner Bros. *Personal Best* (1982) and Sayles's *Lianna* both deal with the same theme as the independent *Desert Hearts* (1986): a previously straight woman becomes involved in a same-sex relationship. *Desert Hearts* was produced and helmed by Donna Deitch and penned by Natalie Cooper. Set in the fifties, a female professor (Helen Shaver) is seeking a divorce; her lesbian lover (Patricia Charbonneau) is a tomboy on a Reno ranch. Because of its female sex scene, the Samuel Goldwyn Company sold this film as erotica, and *Desert Hearts* became a surprising success. Donna Deitch has since made TV movies.

By the close of the eighties, what would soon be called the "New Queer Cinema" became its own independent genre. The first commercially successful gay-themed indies were out of art houses and into video stores in middle America. Gus Van Sant, Todd Haynes, and Gregg Araki had made their debuts (budgeted at a few thousand dollars and little seen). There were major gay film festivals in New York, Los Angeles, and San Francisco. And there was a new distributor, Strand Releasing, specializing in the gay and the marginal. As usual, the indie community was a welcoming refuge for those turned away at studio gates.

Gentility and Edge

In the eighties, a crucial split developed within the broader art-house community. On the one side were quiet, literate, affirming pictures. On the other were more startling, oblique, and challenging flicks. Merchant and Ivory and Victor Nunez were on the one side, David Lynch and Jim Jarmusch on the other. Call the genres "gentility" and "edge." Two 1986 art films with a British setting illustrate the schism: Ismail Merchant and James Ivory's *A Room with a View*, an elegant adaptation of an English romantic novel, and Alex Cox's *Sid and Nancy*, a harrowing punk-rock death trip. The audience age between the two genres split at around thirty-five, though there was crossover. Cinematheque consumers kept an open mind.

Gentility had its biggest patron in "American Playhouse," which specifically financed traditional dramas—often those based on a literary work and often with a sociological message. These were targeted to the check-signing segment of the PBS audience. In addition to *A Flash of Green*, *Stand and Deliver* and others previously mentioned, "American Playhouse" veterans include homespun historical tales by Horton Foote such as *1918* (1985) and *On Valentine's Day* (1986), both directed by Ken Harrison, and a disappointing, toned-down version of Richard Wright's explosive novel *Native Son* (1986).

One of the best projects "American Playhouse" backed was *Testament* (1983), helmed by TV veteran Lynne Littman and scripted by John Young. After a nuclear explosion, residents of a small town find themselves estranged from the rest of the world. They struggle to carry on but become ill and die. Carol Wetherly (Jane Alexander) struggles to keep her family strong and dignified while facing the bleakest of all futures. The film was a quiet but powerful testament against the nuclear buildup of the Reagan years. Kevin Costner and Rebecca De Mornay are featured. Jane Alexander was nominated for a Best Actress Oscar.

Expanded from a Joyce Carol Oates story by Tom Cole and directed by debuting Joyce Chopra, *Smooth Talk* (1985) also benefitted from "Playhouse" financing. A teenage girl (Laura Dern) struggles with new sexual feelings. While her family is away, she's terrorized by a manipulative predator (Treat Williams) who hastens the end of her innocence. There wasn't enough in the Oates story for a feature film, but *Smooth Talk* manages to stay afloat on its authentic teen dialogue and tense undertone.

New York native Nancy Savoca (1960–) made her full-length debut cowriting (with Richard Guay) and directing *True Love* (1989), the Grand Jury winner at Sundance the year of *sex, lies, & videotape*. Set in the Bronx, the film follows Donna (Annabella Sciorra) and her Italian-American family and friends as they prepare for her wedding. There is humor, but there is also the nagging feeling that

Donna and the immature Michael (Ron Eldard) should not be getting hitched.

After Savoca directed the overlooked *Dogfight* (1991) for a studio, she directed and cowrote her most challenging picture, the semi-indie *Household Saints* (1993), a modern fable about an Italian-American couple whose daughter (Lili Taylor) may be a saint. An odd combination of gentility and edge, *Household Saints* is the kind of unique film that has trouble fitting in anywhere. Savoca also made *The 24-Hour Woman* (1999).

Government financing is harder to come by for films closer to the edge. A veteran of the New York avant-garde, Charles Ahearn approached PBS for funds for what he called "an art movie that would play to a ghetto audience."[13] PBS declined. Ahearn raised almost half of the $250,000 budget for *Wild Style* (1983) from British and German TV; the remainder came from private sources.

Wild Style was the first feature-length view of the hip-hop culture that was then blossoming in New York. With a cast of unknowns, Ahearn made a docudrama about an outlaw graffiti artist ("Lee" George Quinones) who comes aboveground to have his work shown in galleries. Rap music, break dancing, and graffiti tagging are spotlighted. Fab 5 Freddy costars and was the musical director. A commercial disappointment in most theaters, *Wild Style* was a smash hit with young audiences in New York City, where the film was aided by a street-savvy marketing campaign. The visuals and editing are rough; the story is trite; but for its authentic feel alone *Wild Style* remains better than the lackluster hip-hop pictures that followed.

Wild Style was scheduled to open at New York's Waverly Theater in October 1983, but the bizarre little movie that was already there just kept playing, drawing a young audience week after week. An extraterrestrial ball of energy in a flying saucer lands in Manhattan searching for the chemical produced by humans during sex. It enters the life of a bisexual fashion model (Anne Carlisle) and feeds on her lovers. *Liquid Sky* (1983)—slang for heroin—will never be confused with Merchant and Ivory. Like *Smithereens* and *Wild Style*, it reveals a New York musical subculture. The new wave club and fashion scene are presented as a sordid, neon-lit netherworld of drugs and indiscriminate sex, of empty lives invaded by opportunistic others.

The New Wave/sci-fi amalgamation *Liquid Sky* was directed, produced, and cowritten (with his wife Nina Kerova and actress Carlisle) by Russian immigrant Slava Tsukerman. He, like Charles Ahearn, has yet to make a second feature. Yuri Neyman's colorful cinematography and special effects (on a $500,000 budget) are impressive. Rookie Anne Carlisle is excellent in the dual roles of Margaret and Jimmy, trendy models of different genders. *Liquid Sky* attracted the same avant-garde art and music crowd it savagely lambasts. Like *Cafe Flesh*, its equating sex with death in the club culture can be read as a metaphor for AIDS.

A graduate of Wellesley College and self-taught moviemaker, Lizzie Borden (born Linda Elizabeth Borden) creates challenging motion pictures from a feminist perspective. With a $30,000 budget, news footage, and a large cast of nonactors, Borden spent four years crafting *Born in Flames* (1982), a radical, improvisational jumble of narratives. It gained notoriety for its audacious theme about a violent female revolution in New York City (taking place when there is already a democratic socialist government). Though the first half feels fresh and exciting, *Born in Flames* eventually becomes repetitive. The rerunning of a squealing song throughout is especially annoying. Within the small genres of feminist and radical, *Born in Flames* is a classic.

Borden raised $300,000 from grants and a lesbian-owned production company for the movie *Working Girls* (1986), which she directed, edited, and cowrote with Sandra Kay. Prostitution is presented as an economically viable alternative to other jobs during one businesslike day in a New York City brothel. Awkwardly amateur moments mix with real compassion and insight. Clinically photographed in pallid color, the sex was purposely deglamorized by Borden, but the distributor, Miramax, emphasized it anyway. The marketing tag was taken from a prostitute: "The two things I love most in life are sex and money, I just never knew until much later they were connected." Released without an MPAA rating (it would have received an X), *Working Girls* was well reviewed and an art-house hit. Lizzie Borden has since had difficulty raising financing for her brave themes. She helmed the inept indie thriller *Love Crimes* (1992).

Documentary

As independent film in the eighties became almost exclusively a genre for festivals and art houses and trendy, educated audiences, some documentaries self-consciously tried to fit in with the cool kids. The jerky cameras and awkward spontaneity of *cinema verité* were no longer in vogue. Instead, a miniwave of stylized nonfiction features brimming with irony and careful camera composition was emerging.

The "cool school" of stylized docs was kicked off in 1983 with *Koyaanisqatsi*. Former Catholic priest Godfrey Reggio produced and directed. Taking nine years to get it just right, Reggio crafted a spellbinding visual feast of natural and manmade American vistas shown through the fast- and slow-motion cinematography of Ron Fricke that pulsates to the hypnotic music of Philip Glass. There is no narration or dialogue. The nearly impronounceable title is a Hopi Indian word meaning "life out of balance." Reggio tried to show that when nature is altered the world is disrupted. Closer to museum video art and the old avant-garde than a traditional documentary, the meditative *Koyaanisqatsi* became a cult film in theaters and on video. Reggio and Glass teamed up again for *Powaqqatsi* (1988), which uses stunning visual collages of cultures to show how Third World societies have been exploited.

Concert films featured art-house-friendly shows, thus appealing to the cosmopolitan audience that enjoys both indie cinema and the latest in music or theater. *Stop Making Sense* (1984), overseen by Corman veteran Jonathan Demme (*The Silence of the Lambs*), features a concert by the innovative new wave group the Talking Heads. *Home of the Brave* (1986) records a show by performance artist Laurie Anderson, who also directed. *Swimming to Cambodia* (1987), again helmed by Demme, was the first and best filmed record of a Spalding Gray monologue. As captured by noted photographer Bruce Webber, *Let's Get Lost* (1989) is a stylized black-and-white portrait of ultracool jazzman Chet Baker.

In the tradition of *Atomic Cafe*, compilation films served up stale, outmoded footage dripping with irony, now adding deadpan interviews with celebrities. An example of hipper-than-thou trendiness is *Heaven* (1987), an incoherent rumination on the hereafter by actress Dianne Keaton. *Heavy Petting* (1988), assembled by Obie Benz, is a peek at sexual mores in the fifties, featuring clips from "how to date" films.

On a dark road in 1976, Dallas police officer Robert Wood stopped a car for a traffic offense and was shot dead. Drifter Randall Adams was convicted of the crime and sentenced to life in prison, chiefly on the testimony of lowlife David Harris, who was later sentenced to death for another murder.

Errol Morris didn't know it yet, but he was about to free an innocent man. After *Gates of Heaven* and *Vernon, Florida* and his stint as a securities investigator, Morris went to Texas intending to make a documentary about Dr. James Grigson, a Dallas psychiatrist known as "Dr. Death" because his expert testimony in capital cases virtually assured the defendant a trip to the electric chair. Along the way, Morris interviewed Randall Adams, a prisoner who claimed innocence. His story clicked with Morris, so the documentarian/investigator went digging. Convinced that Adams was wrongly convicted and that Harris was guilty, Morris spent nearly three years making a movie about inconsistencies in the case.

The Thin Blue Line (1987) is the emblematic term for the police who stand between criminals and the rest of society. Morris's movie is a whole new kind of nonfiction feature—a "documentary" that is more consciously artificial than the products of Hollywood's dream factories. Moodily lit recreations present what may have taken place. A chocolate milkshake sails slowly through the air. Clocks tick away. Items are shown in jarring close-ups. Poetry is made. The traditional tools of documentarians appear—newspaper headlines, photos, interviews—but everything is shot like a (very good) music video. The cinematography was by Stefan Czapsky. The repetitive music of Philip Glass adds to the unique rhythm. Viewers become detectives, sharply attuned to the minute.

Near the end of *The Thin Blue Line*, David Harris essentially confesses to the crime for which Randall Adams was spending his life behind bars. The movie came out in August 1988. Reviews were great; box office grosses were disappointing. Most importantly, *The Thin Blue Line* brought intensified attention to the conviction of Randall Adams. The case was reopened by an appeals court in Dallas in December. Although his film was deemed inadmissible, Morris testified on Adams's behalf. Harris nearly confessed again on the stand. The judge ruled that Adams was convicted on dubious evidence; there would be no retrial. After having spent more than twelve years behind bars, Randall Adams was released from prison in March 1989, thanks chiefly to Errol Morris, detective/documentarian.

Anticipating his critics, philosophy grad Errol Morris said, "The whole idea of *cinema vérité* did tremendous damage to filmmaking in general, and to documentary filmmaking in particular because it carried this bogus metaphysical claim—nonsensical, if you stop and think about it—that style guarantees truth, that somehow if you juggle a camera around in the corners of rooms and hide behind pillars, the Cartesian riddle will be solved as a result."[14] With *The Thin Blue Line*, Morris invented the antithesis of direct cinema: a visually dazzling nonfiction film, meticulously plotted, shot, and edited. Few documentarians have followed his path, but the impact of *The Thin Blue Line*'s pulp poetry has been felt in fictional thrillers and on TV tabloid shows.

Meanwhile, in the corners of rooms and behind pillars, Sandi Sissel and nonfiction veteran Nick Broomfield made *Chicken Ranch* (1983), a *verité* peek inside the title bordello, the setting for *The Best Little Whorehouse in Texas* (1982). *Chicken Ranch* paints a grim picture of the world's oldest profession and serves as an antidote to the previous year's Hollywood musical and a precursor to Lizzie Borden's *Working Girls*.

Streetwise (1984) is an even bleaker portrait of disenfranchised lives. The camera follows teenage runaways in Seattle's skid row as they panhandle, prostitute, deal dope, eat from dumpsters, and sleep in abandoned buildings. The kids champion their freedom from abusive or neglectful parents—whom we also meet—but we see how dirty, demoralizing, and dangerous their lives are. (One teen committed suicide after filming.) *Streetwise* originated from a magazine piece by Cheryl McCall, who produced the film; it was directed by Martin Bell; the gritty music is by Tom Waits. Bell went on to helm the independent fictional feature, *American Heart* (1993), an effective drama about a kid (Edward Furlong) reunited with his ex-con dad (Jeff Bridges).

Sherman's March (subtitled: *A Meditation on the Possibility Of Romantic Love in the South During An Era of Nuclear Weapons Proliferation*) is a different kind of documentary, a first-person narrative that lands somewhere between the unblinking camera of Frederick Wiseman and the irony of early Errol Morris. A native of North Carolina, Ross McElwee started making nonfiction shorts while studying at MIT in the mid-seventies.[15] In 1981, he began a documentary about General Sherman's route through the South. When he was dumped by his girlfriend, McElwee's movie metamorphosed into something personal: his quest for a new love. The narrative is interwoven with Civil War history and Cold War fears. *Sherman's March* was finally released in 1986. At two and a half hours, the journey is lengthy, but the dating adventures of the romantic McElwee (a film crew of one) remain appealing. In making the real *David*

Holzman's Diary, Ross McElwee created a new from of documentary feature: the personal confession.

Nonfiction cinema had come a long way from *Nanook of the North* and *Grass*, and it was about to go even further. Michael Moore was a rabble-rousing alternative journalist, born and raised in Flint, Michigan. He was angered by the devastation caused to his hometown after General Motors closed auto plants. With no previous filmmaking experience, Moore raised money through foundations, donations, and Bingo games and made a movie. Like Ross McElwee, Michael Moore placed himself—with portly physique, shaggy hair, and "I'm out for Trout" baseball cap—at the center of his comedic documentary *Roger & Me* (1989). "Roger" is GM chairman Roger Smith, whom Moore repeatedly tries to bring to Flint to see the consequences of corporate decisions.

In addition to the running gag of Moore pursuing Smith, *Roger & Me* has several story lines. A Flint deputy sheriff is followed on his rounds near Christmastime as he evicts people who fail to pay their rent. Business boosters make desperate and doomed attempts to revive the community (bringing in "pro-American" entertainers like Pat Boone and Anita Bryant), and they steer the unemployed towards other jobs: Amway, Taco Bell, color coordinating. Meanwhile, residents of Flint get by however they can. Most humorous are a woman who sells rabbits for "pets or meat" and an every-day blood donator who explains the schedule of the plasma bank: "They're only open on Mondays and Tuesdays and Wednesdays and Thursdays and Fridays. Saturday and Sunday they're closed." Archival and news footage are mixed in for great effect; editors Wendey Stanzler and Jennifer Beman were also novices. Director/writer/producer Moore ambles through it all, looking to score laughs and political points in equal measure.

Roger & Me stood out like a class clown in the traditionally stuffy genre of documentaries. It was a hit on the festival circuit at the same time *sex, lies, & videotape* was drawing attention away from Hollywood. So Warner Bros.—a major corporation, no less—snatched up Moore's debut for an amazing $3 million (nearly twenty times its budget); the studio put another $6 million into promotion. Upon release, *Roger & Me* was fueled by enthusiastic reviews (it made more than one hundred "ten best of 1989" lists) and endless interviews with the quick-witted, irreverent Moore.

There was also a backlash. Starting with an article in *Film Comment*, journalists began to question the movie's loose treatment of the facts, how it compressed the events of the Reagan years and then manipulated the time sequence. *The New Yorker* and *Time* panned it as a fraud. Furthermore, Michael Moore, the committed leftist, took heat for what was perceived as his patronizing and exploitive attitude towards the poor residents of his hometown. There is truth to these charges, but all's fair in politics and comedy. Moore countered corporate image-making and doublespeak in kind. In the process he succeeded in forging a political document that is true in spirit to what happened to Flint, Michigan. More importantly, he made audiences laugh while focusing on the broader issue of corporate responsibility. Moore explains, "I figured, who wants to sit in a dark theater and watch people collect free federal surplus cheese. How's that going to be entertaining? How's that going to change anything?"[16]

Roger & Me went on to gross more than $7 million in domestic theaters. Though these were groundbreaking numbers for a nonconcert documentary, they were a disappointment to Warner Bros. Moore followed with a twenty-five-minute sequel, *Pets or Meat* (1992), which updates Flint and the characters of *Roger & Me* three years later. Roger Smith, no longer CEO of GM, claims to have never seen the film that bears his name.

By the end of the eighties, features like *The Thin Blue Line*, *Sherman's March*, and *Roger & Me* had reinvented the documentary just as *cinema verité* had in the sixties. The fact that few people noticed was hardly surprising. Documentaries—even when sold as murder mysteries, personal odysseys, or confrontational comedies—have always meant low turnout. Even art-house audiences tend to shy away from what are perceived as history lessons or political tracts. All the docs from these years combined grossed less than the average major studio release. Still, some of the most original, challenging, and entertaining movies of the decade were nonfiction.

Semi-indie

In 1986, the edge semi-indie *Blue Velvet* marked David Lynch's return to smaller nightmares after the big-budget flop *Dune* (1984). This disturbing exploration of the "bugs" below the surface of a Northwestern town was such a must-see among art film enthusiasts that it drew a broader audience. Many wished they'd stuck with *Top*

Gun. With vulgarity, violence, and weird flourishes, *Blue Velvet* is a difficult movie to embrace. Nevertheless, reviewers fawned over it. It was the National Society of Film Critics pick for best picture of the year; Lynch was nominated for a second directing Academy Award. Also in 1986, cinematheques were buoyed by the surprise success of Britain's *A Room with a View*, which collected eight Academy Award nominations (including Best Picture) and won three. Released by tiny Cinecom, it broke through the art-house glass ceiling with $20 million in box-office receipts. For the first time, Hollywood players looked at the modern indie scene with dollar signs in their eyes. The term "independent" was about to become very confused.

In 1987, fledgling company Hemdale produced *Platoon, Hoosiers,* and *River's Edge*. Feeling they weren't ready for solo distribution, Hemdale released the first two through Orion. They were solid successes, nominated for ten Academy Awards and winning four. Hemdale certainly wasn't a major studio, but it's difficult to view its movies as "independent." And thus definitions get muddled, because Oliver Stone's *Platoon* didn't just win a Best Picture Oscar. It also won the second annual Independent Spirit Award (from the IFP) for best independent feature; Stone won both the Oscar and the Spirit for directing. The nominally independent *After Hours* (The Geffen Company) won the IFP's top award the year before; *River's*

Semi-Indie Ten

In chronological order, these are ten of the most significant films that fall somewhere between the major studios and true independence.

The Gold Rush. Charlie Chaplin produced, directed, wrote, and starred in this classic, comedy epic, released by the studio (United Artists) which he partially owned.

Becky Sharp. Short-lived Pioneer films was formed to make color movies which RKO released. This 1935 Pioneer period piece was history's first Technicolor feature, and it uses color more creatively than virtually any film since.

Stagecoach. The seminal John Ford/John Wayne western was financed by producer Walter Wanger and released through Republic.

Detour. Edgar Ulmer's hard-edged, microbudget melodrama was shot in six days on Poverty Row.

continued

Semi-Indie Ten *continued*

Marty. Small-scale, nominally independent production made with United Artists. First American movie to win Palme d'Or at Cannes. Swept four Oscars in 1955.

Kiss Me Deadly. Robert Aldrich's pulp masterpiece continues to inspire film auteurs.

The Graduate. This landmark blockbuster from Avco-Embassy captured the young adult audience.

Blue Velvet. A weird and disturbing art-house smash that helped define modern independent film.

House Party. Produced by New Line, this 1990 African-American comedy is still the domestic box office champ of Sundance competitors.

Pulp Fiction. Tarantino's ultra-cool crime blockbuster rocked the independent scene as well as the studios.

Ten Honorable Mentions: *Sherlock, Jr.; Home of the Brave; The Killing; The Wild Angels; Kiss of the Spider Woman; River's Edge; Drugstore Cowboy; The Player; Menace II Society; Big Night.*

Edge won it the following year. And on and on. These are not independently produced films.

The distinction grew even murkier as major companies began to produce films specifically for cinematheques. Hemdale released *River's Edge* through Island, an art-house distributor. In the smaller-stakes indie world, it was a success. Shortly before going out of business, Hemdale even went into art film circulation with its bloodsucker comedy *Vampire's Kiss* (1989).

By 1989, several distributors were making and releasing their own quirky semi-indies. New World produced *Heathers*, a sort of comedic version of *River's Edge*. Vestron financed the underrated dark satire *Parents*. And Cinecom came out with Paul Bartel's bed-swapping romp, *Scenes from a Class Struggle in Beverly Hills*. The highest-acclaimed semi-indie of 1989 was *Drugstore Cowboy*, produced and released by the short-lived Avenue. Its director and cowriter, Gus Van Sant, was once a true independent.

Between crafting artistic gay shorts, Van Sant made his feature debut with the autonomous *Mala Noche* (1986), based on a poem by a skid-row resident. In this grungy, $25,000, mostly black-and-white tale, a male liquor store clerk falls in love with a heterosexual Mexican boy.

Made for two hundred times more ($5 million), *Drugstore Cowboy* maintains a similar hazy feel as it follows four junky thieves in Portland, Oregon in 1971. Van Sant has also directed the semi-indies *My Own Private Idaho* (1991), *Even Cowgirls Get the Blues* (1994), and *Good Will Hunting* (1997) as well as, for major studios, *To Die For* (1995) and *Psycho* (1998). The semi-indie arena would continue to grow through the nineties, with occasional bold leaps and stumbles.

Steven Soderbergh

Steven Soderbergh (1963–) grew up in Baton Rouge. Although his father was a dean at Louisiana State University, he skipped college for a career as a film director. After a few short films and an unproductive stint in Hollywood, eighteen-year-old Soderbergh returned to bayou country, where he penned screenplays and worked for a video production company. His concert video of the rock group Yes was nominated for a Grammy. After making a short film on sexual deception, Soderbergh penned the first draft of a feature-length script on the same topic during an eight-day period that included his return drive from Louisiana to Los Angeles. The screenplay would eventually be called *sex, lies, & videotape*, a talky character study with limited locations. He planned to shoot it for $75,000.

Soderbergh got his script to a small production company that promised $500,000. The sum expanded when a cast of rising semi-stars was secured for the principal roles. But it all fell apart three weeks before shooting was to commence, mostly because the rookie director insisted on filming in black and white. Scrambling, Soderbergh agreed to shoot in color. With producers Robert Newmyer and John Hardy, new financing was arranged one month later; RCA/Columbia provided $1.1 million in exchange for the foreign, video, and TV rights. The delay pushed the Baton Rouge production into the simmering days of August 1988. Walt Lloyd was cinematographer.

Sex, lies, & videotape follows four people in their early thirties with confused sex lives. A lawyer (Peter Gallagher) is no longer intimate with his frigid wife (Andie MacDowell). Instead, he is having a passionate affair with her sultry sister (Laura San Giacomo). Into this mix comes the lawyer's old college roommate, Graham (James Spader), and his video camera. Impotent Graham satisfies himself by videotaping women's sexual fantasies and watching the videos. He

Steven Soderbergh.
Photo by Amy Etra.

uncovers the true emotions of all four characters, including himself, with explosive results.

Sex, lies, & videotape could have been a ponderous exercise or a dirty joke. Instead, under Soderbergh's steady care and the excellent acting of the four leads, the movie soars. After the Sundance Film Festival, the distributor bidding war, and the Cannes Film Festival, it was a critical sensation. Jay Carr gushed in *The Boston Globe*: "Astonishingly, with one feature film, Soderbergh redefines romantic comedy for the late eighties, and probably for a good part of the nineties, too, with a distinct, original, and thoroughly contemporary sensibility. . . . The acting—which, by the way, achieves with insolent ease that much-cited but seldom realized ensemble idea—is flawless. I'd give them all Oscars in a minute."[17] Only Soderbergh was nominated for an Academy Award—for screenwriting.

In the final analysis, *sex, lies, & videotape* was simply the right movie at the right time: a polished, upscale conversation piece that captured the angst of thirtysomethings. And, of course, sex almost always sells—even if it's mostly sex talk. *Sex, lies & videotape* proved to be the perfect movie to expand the limited art-house audience of cinéastes into a broader base of literate adults. In this regard, it was also brilliantly marketed by Miramax. Most independent distributors barely have the money to buy film prints and newspaper ads, but Miramax went for broke. It launched saucy TV advertising, and it eventually built up *sex, lies, & videotape*'s release to more than 600 theaters simultaneously.

Art-house screens couldn't contain it. Soderbergh's and Sundance's and Miramax's movie entered America's consciousness. And so did independent film.

Notes

---

[1] Brodie, John, "Ten Days That Shook the Biz," *Premiere*, Oct. 1997, 31.

[2] *New Yorker*, 15 Nov. 1982.

[3] *American Film*, March 1986, 53.

[4] *Village Voice*, 2 Oct. 1984. Ozu is a reference to Japanese film director Jasujiro Ozu, a stylistic minimalist.

[5] *Village Voice*, 2 Oct. 1984.

[6] "Jim Jarmusch," *Microsoft Cinemania 97*, CD-ROM, Microsoft, 1996.

[7] *Chicago Tribune*, 3 Feb. 1985.

[8] *New York*, 21 Jan. 1985.

[9] *In These Times*, 25 June/8 July 1986.

[10] *Los Angeles Times*, 21 Aug. 1986.

[11] *Variety*, 18 March 1987.

[12] Russo, Vito, *The Celluloid Closet*, rev. ed. (New York: Quality Paperback Book Club, 1987), 307.

[13] Rosen, David, with Peter Hamilton, *Off-Hollywood: The Making*

and Marketing of Independent Films (New York: Grove Weidenfeld, 1990), 245.

[14] *Millimeter*, Oct. 1997, 136.

[15] Note the prestigious educations of great documentarians: Leo Hurwitz (Harvard), Lionel Rogosin (Yale), Frederick Wiseman (Yale), Emile De Antonio (Harvard), D. A. Pennebaker (Yale and M.I.T.), Ross McElwee (M.I.T.). Also noteworthy: Albert and David Maysles and Barbara Kopple have degrees in psychology. Errol Morris (Princeton) has a master's degree in philosophy from U.C. Berkeley.

[16] *Nation*, 30 Oct. 1989.

[17] *Boston Globe*, 11 Aug. 1989.

THE NEW SYSTEM

You know you're an independent filmmaker when
your fuck-you list is longer than your thank-you list.
—NEIL LABUTE

The attitude I grew up with was that everything
you've heard is lies.
—QUENTIN TARANTINO[1]

By the nineties, independent film was big business. Tiny distribution companies could now dream of having a true box-office hit. Maybe the next pickup at Sundance would make $100 million worldwide. Many of the biggest independent companies of the Reagan years didn't survive long enough to find out. Distributors like Island, Vestron, and Cinecom, which just a few years earlier were ruling the scene, were forced to fold up shop. Others moved in, and some previously tiny companies expanded into the big league.

New Line Cinema was the first to reach the next level. By 1990, riding the mainstream success of Freddy Krueger and Ninja Turtles, New Line was a true ministudio, endeavoring to create the same kind of commercial hits that the majors were. It launched its own art division, Fine Line Features, for lower-budgeted fare. Fine Line, in turn, became a major indie force. In 1994, New Line and Fine Line were acquired by media mogul Ted Turner, whose company merged with the massive Time-Warner organization, thus bringing the "Lines" into the Warner Bros. family.

Miramax just kept growing. With voracious Harvey Weinstein outbidding the competition at Sundance, the company became the principal acquirer of nonstudio features. In 1993, it was the first of the art-house distributors to be purchased by a major, becoming part of one-time indie and modern media conglomerate Walt Disney Studios. Since then, Miramax has added many modestly budgeted productions, such as *Scream* (1996) and *Good Will Hunting*, to their slate of acquisitions.

In a successful repeat of the short-lived "classics" divisions of the previous decade, major studios launched independent arms to bid on the hits of Sundance and to develop lower-budgeted productions. Sony birthed Sony Pictures Classics in 1992. In 1995, Fox formed Fox Searchlight. Universal purchased the independent company October Films in 1997. That same year, the Samuel Goldwyn Company was bought by the ghost of MGM. Paramount, the last of the majors without an art-house wing, created Paramount Classics in 1998. Meanwhile, Gramercy, a major semi-indie producer but not much of an acquirer, was part of the media giant Polygram.

There were another dozen or so truly independent companies that occasionally made noise, but, backed with the deepest pockets, the art-house arms of major studios were the most active indie companies of the nineties. They bid for the hottest properties on the festival circuit each year.

Independent movies went all-out to get admitted into the Sundance Film Festival in January. Shooting and editing schedules were arranged around the 'dance entry deadline. The competition for acceptance was fierce. In 1987, there were sixty dramatic features submitted; ten years later there more than 800. Geoffrey Gilmore, Sundance's programming director in the nineties, was an indie kingmaker. Other film festivals cropped up to compete for the attention and revenue Redford's event generated for tiny Park City: Long Island, Austin, Los Angeles, Orlando, and dozens more. In 1995, three directors whose films were rejected by Sundance started a festival held nearby and at the same time: Slamdance. (Two years later, some jokers staged Slumdance for those who couldn't get into Sundance *or* Slamdance. Movies were screened on the *ceiling* of a dingy basement with the audience lounging on moldy couches!) Still, in terms of prestige, only the Toronto Film Festival was in the same league with Sundance in North America. Though Cannes remained the world's grandest cinema showcase, the foreign events were no longer necessary for American indies. Despite limited screening venues, Sundance dominated everything. If not invited, it became increasingly difficult to sell a motion picture to even the smallest distribution company.

Sundance was the engine. After that, the indie system depended on the major distributors to give little movies the proper marketing push. It was as important in the nineties to have a company like Miramax or Fine Line advertise one's self-financed feature as it was in the thirties to be under contract with a studio like Paramount or Warner Bros. Without the proper promotion, movies got lost in the increasingly crowded marketplace. Producers' representatives—who sold movies to distributors—were suddenly key players, on a par with festival directors and acquisition executives. Successful producer's rep John Pierson (*She's Gotta Have It, Roger & Me, Clerks*, etc.) was one of the most influential people on the scene. Pierson is also the creator and host of the indie cinema show "Split Screen" on the Independent Film Channel.

By the time Bill Clinton was elected, all major cities and many college towns had art houses. New York City and Los Angeles had art multiplexes. Though smaller communities often had no screens regularly showing non-studio pictures, the influence of independent cinema was felt

Ancillary

In addition to domestic and foreign theatrical runs, modern independent films utilize the following ancillary markets.

VIDEO Sales to rental stores are usually tied to box office numbers, thus limiting art films. Still, several indies, including *Bad Lieutenant* and *Reservoir Dogs*, made more via videocassette and DVD sales than they did in North American theaters, and virtually every independent movie of the past three decades was seen by more people on video than on big screens.

TELEVISION. Other than horror movies, independents were seldom screened on TV until cable arrival in the seventies. In the nineties, between pay-per-view, premium channels, and basic cable, the best-known indies could make more than $1 million in three years. Limited to The Independent

continued

everywhere. Major cable TV channels like Cinemax, Showtime, and Bravo showed quirky festival winners. In the mid-nineties, two competing cable channels, the Sundance Channel and the Independent Film Channel, were born. Both specialized in off-Hollywood cinema. New national publications such as the glossy *Filmmaker*, were dedicated to the indie scene, covering how-to and who's who. And the mainstream press flocked to every success story. Perhaps most importantly, a century after Edison's first public screening, the VCR had become as common in homes as the toaster. People everywhere could rent or buy the latest from Abel Ferrara or Jim Jarmusch. Most movies found their biggest audiences via cable TV and videotape.

The proliferation of computers and the Internet also had an enormous impact. Megabytes changed independent filmmaking not only at the screenwriting stage and in editing rooms, where computers replaced manual machines, but also in marketing. In 1995, the independent *Party Girl* became the first film to be screened in its entirety on the Net prior to its theatrical release. Only a few people saw it in its tiny, low-resolution form, and not many more saw it on the big screen, but the event pointed the way towards new distribution methods for the next century.

At the beginning of the decade, popular interest in indie cinema rose at the same time that alterna-

Ancillary *continued*

Film Channel, The Sundance Channel, and PBS, the least-known made less than $30,000 initially. However, as with video, movies can collect money from TV sales until their copyrights expire.

STORY AND MUSIC. Story and character rights cover sequels, novelizations, plays, etc., and the money can be huge. Among the twenty-four non-porno independents that have generated at least one repeat are *Billy Jack*, *Halloween*, and *El Mariachi*. Original music for films like *Super Fly* and compilation albums for movies like *Swingers* have also done well, though much of the profit goes to the artists.

MERCHANDISING. A few small movies have made thousands via posters, T-shirts, and tie-in books. Surprisingly, *Clerks* spawned much stuff, including Jay and Silent Bob comic books and action figures. Among the more than two dozen official items *The Blair Witch Project* begat are a video on the "investigation" and witchcraft altar candles.

tive music groups like Nirvana were coming into vogue. Though both "independent" and "alternative" became diluted catchall marketing words, the basic impulse they fed on was healthy: consumers were looking for something different. And they now had a perfected system (festivals, distributors, theaters, press, TV, and video) to serve such movies to them. As the art-house arms of studios increasingly made bigger-budgeted festival films, the term "independent" became fuzzier than ever. Still, these were thrilling years of microbudget successes and important new cinematic visionaries. A once tiny and denigrated industry was reaching for the stars.

John Sayles

Like Cassavetes before him, John Sayles occasionally accepted studio checks, but he remained outside the walls when he wanted to tell his stories his way.

Sayles wrote, directed, edited, and acted in the ambitious *City of Hope* (1991), a complex story with more than thirty characters. Nick (Vincent Spano) is a confused young man who quits his cushy construction job and finds himself among people trying to grab their slice of a housing development in a fictional New Jersey city. Sayles weaves citizens of various ethnicities together in a convoluted plot about politics and money. Cinematographer Robert Richardson supervised the excellent camerawork. Among those in the large cast are Tony LoBianco, Joe Morton, and Angela Bassett. *City of Hope* was championed by some critics but overlooked by audiences.

Even with a $5 million budget, Sayles's *Passion Fish* (1992) was a wholly independent production. Aloof soap opera actress Mary-Alice Culhane (Mary McDonnell), divorced and unhappy in her career, is paralyzed in an accident. She returns to her family estate in Louisiana, drinking and feeling sorry for herself. After unnerving other nurses, she hires Chantelle (Alfre Woodard) and *Passion Fish* becomes a more nuanced version of *Driving Miss Daisy*: a struggle of wills between the bitter, wealthy matriarch, who needs companionship, and the economically dependent nurse, who stands up to her. Angela Bassett has a small role. Roger Deakins supervised the splendid cinematography.

In *Passion Fish*, Sayles adeptly avoids clichés and movie-of-the-week pitfalls. By contrasting his story with the canned melodrama of Mary's soap opera, he shows how much more complex his

(l-r) Alfre Woodard and Mary McDonnell in *Passion Fish*.
© 1992 Atchafalaya Films, Inc.

characters and situations are than most treatments of disability and discrimination. David Denby wrote, "Sayles has broken out of the current inane politicized discourse about sex and race and found out things for himself. A lot of junk had to be cleared away for people to talk so plainly to one another, but one feels the effort was worth it. Despite its limited setting, *Passion Fish* has a discursive splendor; everything is easy, flowing, and seemingly spontaneous, yet firmly shaped and dramatically relevant."[2] Mary McDonnell (for actress) and Sayles (for screenplay) were nominated for Academy Awards; Woodard was overlooked.

A Gaelic fairy tale shot on location in Ireland, *The Secret of Roan Inish* (1994) is Sayles's most ambitious film. Once upon a time, a girl (Jeni Courtney) goes to live with her grandparents on the coast of Ireland. There she learns that one of her ancestors was a Selkie (half-woman, half-seal) and that her little brother was carried away in his cradle by the waves. Investigating nearby Roan Inish ("Island of the Seals"), she spots her wee sibling, and she endeavors to move her skeptical kin back onto the isle where they once lived. *The Secret of Roan Inish* treats all of this with respect, avoiding the mawkishness of most children's movies. The pace is slow, and the brogue is occasionally a hindrance, but Sayles fully blossomed as a visual stylist in this movie. Cinematographer Haskell Wexler captures the lush scenery and dreamy tone. *The Secret of Roan Inish* earned $6 million in North America.

Sayles doubled that gross with *Lone Star* (1996), a sort of small-town version of *City of Hope* that explores the racial dimensions on the Texas border. Sheriff Sam (Chris Cooper) investigates a nearly thirty-year-old murder that everyone thinks was committed by his father (Matthew McConaughey) against the violent, racist sheriff (Kris Kristofferson). Just as they did in 1957, three communities mingle and clash: the dwindling, defensive white residents, the large and increasingly powerful Latino population, and the small black citizenry. The Oscar-nominated screenplay ties the past into the present as old wounds are opened again. The plot is convoluted, and the political elements are weak. Still, like most of Sayles's movies, *Lone Star* has a relevant message and a wealth of vibrant characters.

At the peak of his career, Sayles made his most difficult feature, *Men With Guns* (1998, aka *Hombres Armados*), the ponderous story of a Latin-American doctor who becomes entangled in politics and bloodshed. If nothing else, *Men With Guns*, in Spanish with English subtitles, exemplifies the uncompromising nature of its auteur. Away from Hollywood, Sayles has found the freedom to experiment and grow, forging a wide variety of unique stories. Proudly independent and critical of corporations, John Sayles is a renegade for life.

Jim Jarmusch

In the eighties, Jim Jarmusch carved out his own ultracool cinematic nook with small stories set in the South. In the nineties, he expanded his environment. Jarmusch wrote, directed, and produced *Night On Earth* (1992), an episodic film set in five different taxicabs on the same night in different cities: Los Angeles, New York, Paris, Rome, and Helsinki. Shooting took place in the five locations with casts from the respective cites; seven languages are heard.

Night On Earth floats along to the rhythms of the night with its own offbeat sense of humor and pathos. The New York segment is the funniest: a rider (Giancarlo Esposito) feels his German driver won't make it in the big city; a second passenger (Rosie Perez) chirps in. As with previous Jarmusch films, *Night On Earth* explores the clash of cultures and the influence and perspective of outsiders in a foreign land.

Cinematographer Frederick Elmes properly captures the nighttime lights. Jarmusch veteran Tom Waits provides the music.

Dead Man (1996) is a western, though, as envisioned by Jarmusch, it's no traditional cowpoke yarn. William Blake (Johnny Depp)—not the poet—is a mild-mannered accountant who travels West to a job that doesn't exist. He finds himself hunted for a murder as he dies from a bullet wound. Blake is joined on his existential journey by Nobody (Gary Farmer), a portly philosophical Indian.

Unlike Jarmusch's early work, *Dead Man* uses traditional techniques such as close-ups and over-the-shoulder shots, and a shocking amount of violence, yet it fits neatly into the auteur's body of work with its leisurely pace, eccentric character types, and wry dialogue. *Dead Man* was shot in low-contrast black and white (cinematography by Robby Müller), with emphasis on nontraditional western settings, filth, grime, and blood. In its bleak tone and visuals and its use of modern music, it's reminiscent of Robert Altman's *McCabe and Mrs. Miller*. Among those with small parts are Robert Mitchum (in his final role) and an unrecognizable Billy Bob Thornton. Neil Young's electric guitar rifts are *Dead Man's* most distracting element. *Dead Man* is one of the most visionary pictures of the decade. Unfortunately, American audiences barely noticed it.

Jarmusch made a black-and-white documentary called *The Year of the Horse* (1997), featuring murky concert footage of Young mixed with witless backstage interviews. It was his first artistic failure. He also made a series of talkative short films called *Coffee and Cigarettes* (1987, 1989, 1993).

Jarmusch has brought his famous pompadour and laconic style to cameo roles in nonstudio features that include *Johnny Suede, In the Soup*, and *Sling Blade*. For many cinéastes, he is the embodiment of modern independent film. Using primarily foreign financing and retaining ownership of his films' negatives, Jarmusch remains resolutely autonomous. Even the current indie system has little effect on his creative decisions. Jim Jarmusch has been able to do something few directors can do: craft his own distinct style—a cinematic language of slow rhythms, minimalist camerawork, and deadpan dialogue.

Hal Hartley

Postmodernism developed as a reaction to the sleek, simple modes of modernism. It's an elastic term, but typically postmodernism stresses the reinterpretation of traditional (even scorned) forms. Irony is at a premium. The typical Hollywood action flick is modern. Jim Jarmusch's work is postmodern. The most prolific postmodernist in American cinema today is Hal Hartley (1960–). Hartley works in the discarded genre of melodrama, bending tales into complex and ironic parables.

Hartley grew up in suburban Long Island and attended art and film school, making short movies and studying Jean-Luc Godard and playwright Bertolt Brecht. Hartley scripted, directed, and edited *The Unbelievable Truth* (1990). The $75,000 production lasted only eleven days. A mysterious man (Robert Burke) returns home after a stint in prison. A young woman (Adrienne Shelly) falls for him, and he gets the whole town talking about what criminal deeds he may have done. With his first feature, Hartley established his episodic style of languid humor, carefully composed shots, emotionless acting, and ironic melodrama. The dramatic technique—influenced by Godard, Jarmusch, and Lynch—is alternately off-putting and hypnotic.

Trust (1991) is Hartley's best movie. A teenager (Adrienne Shelly) announces she's pregnant. Her dad drops dead; her mom kicks her out of the house; and her football hero boyfriend dumps her. In the midst of this bad day, she meets a bookish slacker (Martin Donovan) who lives with his obsessive father and carries around an old hand grenade. Peter Rainer noted, "Despite the film's *outre* trappings, it's surprisingly conventional in structure. It's like a dour, crackbrained version of those '50s movies about misunderstood youth in rebellion against their uncaring parents. What saves it from sentimentality is Harley's tart, absurdist tone: He doesn't give in to bathos."[3]

In *Simple Men* (1992), two brothers (Robert Burke, William Sage) go in search of their fugitive father, a former Brooklyn Dodger and bomb-throwing anarchist. They meet various eccentric characters on their Long Island journey while struggling to come to grips with their past. As usual, Hartley's arch sense of humor repeatedly seeps in.

In *Amateur* (1995), an ex-nun (Isabelle Huppert) who authors pornography is both a nymphomaniac and a virgin (her explanation: "I'm choosy")! She helps an amnesiac (Martin Donovan) who's being hunted by hit men and who has a porn star wife and an unsavory sexual past. *Amateur* is neither as racy nor as captivating as this plot synopsis, but it is another carefully crafted, quirky clash of characters, situations, and dialogue.

Flirt (1996) tells the same tale in three different ways in three different locations: someone demands a commitment from his/her flirtatious lover. The stories are set in New York City, Berlin, and Tokyo, with role reversals in each.

Yet another postmodern tale, *Henry Fool* (1998), presents a Long Island garbage man (James Ubaniak) who passively supports his mother and sister until a failing ex-convict writer named Henry Fool (Thomas Ryan) inspires him to create.

It's a shame that Hartley's films have yet to prove popular even in American cinematheques. Like fellow laconic stylist Jim Jarmusch, he finds most of his financial and commercial support in Europe, especially in France and Germany (homes of Godard and Brecht), where he is hailed as a cinematic genius.

Abel Ferrara

Abel Ferrara makes movies like pulp novels: a mixture of poolroom parlance, graphic content, and modernized B movie plots. He finally received significant attention with the semi-indie *King of New York* (1990), helmed from a Nicholas St. John script. It's a stale tale about a crime lord and the drug dealers beneath him. The fine cast—Christopher Walken, Wesley Snipes, Laurence Fishburne—is mostly wasted amidst over-the-top violence and melodrama.

Ferrara stirred up much controversy with *Bad Lieutenant* (1992). As Janet Maslin wrote, "When Abel Ferrara calls something bad, better believe it: he means business. [Ferrara] has come up with his own brand of supersleaze, in a film that would seem outrageously, unforgivably lurid if it were not also somehow perfectly sincere."[4] Harvey Keitel plays The Lieutenant (as the credits read), a cop who investigates the gang rape of a nun who refuses to press charges. The plot is secondary. *Bad Lieutenant* is about a bad cop doing bad things: abusing drugs, buying sex, stealing, gambling (going into debt $120,000), tormenting the innocent. It's about his self-loathing, his Catholic guilt, and his desperate hope for salvation.

Bad Lieutenant was scripted by Ferrara and *Ms. 45* star Zoe Tamerlis Lund. The movie received an NC-17 for its adult content (there is also an R-rated version), and Ferrara displays everything without blinking,

Abel Ferrara directs Lili Taylor in *The Addiction*.
© 1995 Fast Films, Inc.

whether it's sleaze or over-the-top religious symbolism (Jesus makes a cameo). But *Bad Lieutenant* is Keitel's movie. He bares his character's soul and his own body, appearing vulnerable and tormented and lost. His is the most daring performance since Marlon Brando danced a *Last Tango in Paris* twenty years earlier. In the most infamous scene, Keitel is naked, whimpering and wailing with his arms outstretched in a crucifixion pose. For some, Ferrara's direction and Keitel's acting are too much, so raw and unrestrained that they become a parody of self-conscious directing and acting. Others found in this movie a liberating honesty.

Ferrara followed with two disappointing studio efforts, *Body of Evidence* (1993) and *Body Snatchers* (1994).

An allegorical vampire tale reminiscent of Romero's *Martin, The Addiction* (1995), written by Nicholas St. John, marked a return to independence and to the horror genre that launched Ferrara's career. It was photographed in black and white in Greenwich Village. Lili Taylor is excellent as Kathleen, a graduate student who becomes a bloodsucker. She mixes philosophy and Holocaust history while growing increasingly addicted to human hemoglobin. Anabella Sciorra and Christopher Walken are also undead. When not bogged down in drug metaphors and grad school discussions of good and evil, *The Addiction* sticks to the usual vampire clichés. The only twist is the happy ending.

Again tackling an overworked formula, *The Funeral* (1997) was Ferrara's take on a 1930s organized crime saga. One member of a mob family (Vincent Gallo) has been murdered; his two surviving brothers (Christopher Walken and Christopher Penn) seek revenge. Through flashbacks, we see what has brought them to this point as well as the madness that will boil over in the present. *The Funeral* broaches but then skirts over crucial issues—politics, love affairs, the crime business. Still, on a visceral level, it's amusing to watch Walken and Penn compete for scenery-gnawing honors (Penn wins). Veteran Ferrara collaborator Nicholas St. John penned the ambitious screenplay. Abel Ferrara will doubtless continue to make uncompromising, unflinching movies caught somewhere between exploitation and art.

Henry Jaglom

Feminist or chauvinist? Artist or hack? While at the Venice Film Festival with *Eating*, Henry Jaglom began filming *Venice, Venice*

(1990), a navel-gazing exercise in which he "plays" an independent filmmaker with a movie at the Venice Film Festival. He courts a pretty journalist (Nelly Alard), and her bizarre attraction to him continues at his home in Venice, California.

Babyfever (1994) listens in on a group of women at a baby shower as they converse about motherhood and men. Jaglom's real wife (Victoria Foyt) frets that she's pregnant but is unsure of the father.

The most approachable of Jaglom's self-made efforts is *Last Summer at the Hamptons* (1995). An extended family of theater professionals prepares for a performance. The film relies on much of the same improvisation and *verité* antistyle as other Jaglom flicks, but *Last Summer* benefits from a fine ensemble cast, including Roddy McDowell, Martha Plimpton, and Andre Gregory.

Déjà Vu (1998) features Victoria Foyt, who cowrote it with Jaglom. As an American traveling abroad, Foyt's character falls for a Brit (Stephen Dillane), though he's married and she's engaged and their partners are along for the trip.

Henry Jaglom inherited enough money to regularly craft noncommercial films, capturing his own independent vision while maintaining little regard for box-office rewards. He explains, "If there's one thing I'm trying to prove with my movies it's that there's no such thing as too personal" and "There's nothing better than the truth on film."[5] With all due respect, his movies more often prove the opposite.

Microbudgets

Sundance and the mainstream press alike reveled in finding the next "filmmaking prodigy" or "generational voice" in out-of-the-way places like Austin, Texas or Red Bank, New Jersey. Everyone rooted for fledgling rookies who'd pieced together budgets that were less than the cost of a new car, enlisted their friends in the cast and crew, and—against all odds— forged entertaining motion pictures. People loved the story of an unknown rookie suddenly thrust into movie premieres and Hollywood meetings.

The modern micro budget movement has a number of spiritual godfathers, including Edgar Ulmer, Jim McBride, and John Waters. Jon Jost (1943–) is another. Though few people have heard of him, Jost has remained in cinema's poorhouse for more than three decades. He started crafting experimental shorts in 1963, but his career was interrupted by two years in prison for failing to fight in the Vietnam War.

His Vietnam-era confessional feature, *Speaking Directly: Some American Notes* (1974) was made for $2,500. *Last Chance for a Slow Dance* (1977) was shot in the hobbyist format of Super 8mm. Jost created numerous microbudget sociological pictures throughout the seventies and eighties, featuring improvisation and leftist political slants.

Jost writes, directs, produces, and photographs his own films with his own equipment. He also often edits, composes the music, and self-distributes. He came slightly aboveground in the nineties with such admirable pictures as *All the Vermeers in New York* (1990), about art and commerce, *Sure Fire* (1990), and *Jon Jost's Frameup* (1995). The latter was shot in ten days. Jost will undoubtedly continue to craft seldom seen movies with precious little financing. He has whittled out his own noncommercial niche, closer to the old underground than the new indie system.

The most overhyped American dream tale of the nineties was that of Matty Rich, an African-American teenager from Brooklyn's tough housing projects who learned filmmaking from library books. Rich was only seventeen when he began *Straight Out of Brooklyn* (1991) and nineteen when it was released. The first $12,000 for the teen's debut came from his family's credit cards. An additional sum (bringing the total to $90,000) was raised through screening early footage for investors; "American Playhouse" helped with postproduction funding. The stop-and-go shoot took more than a year.

Everything beyond the back-story of *Straight Out of Brooklyn* was hyperbole. It's a bad movie. With bungled audio and murky cinematography, writer/director/producer Rich presents a black family in a housing project torn by violence and despair. The teenage son looks for a way out. The acting by amateurs is ineffective; the dialogue and story line are hackneyed. *Variety* correctly stated: "A production as no-frills as this one needed a script with some subtext or cleverness to hold interest, but pic is relentlessly blunt and repetitive. Talking scenes go on long after the point has been grasped. Screentime would have been better spent developing the characters, who come off as types rather than individuals, especially the stubborn son."[6] Still, some critics and audiences found a raw, authentic power in the subject matter. They wanted to believe in "Matty Rich the Success Story."

Straight Out of Brooklyn was released in the same summer as *Boyz N the Hood*, a studio production from much-hyped twenty-three-year-old John Singleton. The young black filmmakers were unfairly lumped together, with Spike Lee held as their doyen. (Lee supported Singleton while denigrating Rich.) Not surprisingly, Singleton's polished movie was the bigger hit (and he was nominated for two Oscars), but Rich's rough debut capitalized on his personal marketing hook to become an independent success. Rich went on to helm *The Inkwell* (1994) for Disney. It underperformed. Older and wiser, Rich now admits that arrogance and immaturity got the best of him.

Webster's definition: "Slacker, *n.* an esp. educated young person who is scornful of materialism, purposeless, apathetic, and usu. works in a dead-end job. [popularized by *Slackers* (sic) (1991), film by R. Linklater]"[7]

The most overly marketed story of the early nineties was the discovery of Generation X, a supposedly shallow, cynical, and unmotivated demographic group born between 1961 and 1972 and coming of age after the hippies and yuppies of the Baby Boomer set. Thousands of supposedly unmotivated members of Gen X would craft their own autonomous films, and more members of this supposedly shallow group would view art-house cinema than any previous demographic. Still, there was some truth to the label, as evidenced by the masses of floundering twentysomethings caught between college and the "real world" of responsibility. (It was nothing new, of course. See *The Graduate*.)

The movie that first spoke for the modern aimless was *Slacker* (1991). It has no plot. Instead, it's a structural chain letter. The camera simply follows one laid-back character after another, as though being passed around the college section of Austin, Texas over a lazy twenty-four hours. Nothing much happens. People talk about their various conspiracy theories and quirky philosophies and then someone else comes along and the camera follows that person for awhile. It makes for a mildly amusing, sometimes boring portrait of unmotivated young adults.

Slacker was written, directed, and produced by Richard Linklater (1962–), a Texas native, college dropout, and self-taught cinéaste. The unique structure of his debut worked to his economic advantage. Because the scenes are short and self-contained and because most characters appear only once, Linklater was able to shoot over an extended period, whenever he could find cheap equipment and enlist friends in the cast and crew. (Cast and crew were one and the same;

Linklater himself is the star of the first scene, expounding philosophy in the back of a taxicab.) There is a complex crane shot as well as continuous tracking moves and more than a hundred speaking parts, yet Linklater produced *Slacker* for a mere $23,000 up front, raised via family bank accounts and credit cards.

When it failed to win admittance to the Sundance Film Festival in 1990, Linklater opened *Slacker* himself in a theater in Austin. He managed to stir up attention, obtain a release from a major company, and get into Sundance the following January. *Slacker* was not a hit, but its title became part of popular culture, and its audacious style continues to inspire young mavericks.

Linklater made the semi-indie *Dazed and Confused* (1993), another essentially plotless, mildly amusing comedy. He narrowed his focus to only two lovers for the semi-indie *Before Sunrise* (1995), shot in Vienna, Austria. *SubUrbia* (1997), another view of slackers, fizzled. Linklater's $27 million studio western, *The Newton Boys* (1998), bombed.

Performing various production jobs, Nick Gomez (1963–) worked his way into the New York indie community. He then wrote, directed, and coedited a vibrant debut feature made for $38,000. *Laws of Gravity* (1992) is a streetwise crime drama without a traditional plot. It depicts three days in the lives of poverty-level Brooklyn hoods who steal, argue, fight, and dig themselves into a deeper hole. The dialogue sets a record for use of the word "fuck." The rhythm and setting are reminiscent of *Mean Streets. Laws of Gravity* contains hyperrealistic performances by Peter Greene and Adam Trese, but the real stars are Gomez's visceral direction and cinematographer Jean de Segonzac's pulsating handheld camerawork. Though this bleak, sometimes irritating movie was overshadowed by the buzz surrounding a $7,000 Spanish-language action flick and an upcoming "guys with guns" picture by some unknown named Tarantino, fellow filmmakers took note of Gomez and de Segonzac's kinetic style.

Spike Lee is a *Laws of Gravity* fan, and he executive-produced Gomez's next feature, the semi-indie *New Jersey Drive* (1995). Riding with young carjackers, it treads over familiar dramatic territory. Writer/director Gomez returned to the fully independent arena to again tag along with small-time hoods in *Illtown* (1997). Dope dealer Dante (Michael Rapaport) struggles to stay together with his girlfriend (Lili Taylor) and prevent his past from snuffing out his future. The acting and hypnotic cinematography (by Jim

Denault) are excellent, but, as usual, Gomez's screenplay is the biggest weakness. *Illtown* was distributed (in a limited manner) by The Shooting Gallery, the Manhattan production company and studio space started by Gomez and producers Bob Gosse and Larry Meistrich. In the mid-nineties, the company became a major force in the modern indie scene, financing *Sling Blade, Henry Fool*, and other low-budget pictures.

It was the greatest cinematic Cinderella story of all time. A twenty-three-year-old self-taught Hispanic-American filmmaker from Austin, Texas *sold his body to science* to raise most of his ridiculously low $7,000 budget! (*Titanic* cost *thirty thousand* times more!) He then proceeded—as a crew of one—to shoot a violent Spanish-language action flick in Mexico. Seen only on video, the movie sold to Columbia Studios for a worldwide theatrical release.

Robert Rodriguez (1969–) was Cinderella. After crafting short films with his family and friends, he wanted to produce a flick for the Mexican video market, but Rodriguez had no money. So he spent a month in a research hospital as a human guinea pig in a drug experiment, earning $3,000. During the stint, Rodriguez wrote the script for *El Mariachi* (1993). Another $4,000 came from a friend. With one assistant, Rodriguez shot with a borrowed camera for fourteen days in a Mexican border town. He was pushed around in a wheelchair for the frenetic "dolly" shots. Lighting was accomplished with 250-watt bulbs and aluminum foil reflectors. No sound was recorded with the picture (it was taped and synced up later). The cast was made up of amateurs, including star, coproducer, and assistant Carlos Gallardo. After the film was transferred to video, editing was accomplished with just two VCRs. Rodriguez managed this via a tedious process of recording the desired shots from a video in one VCR onto a master tape in the other VCR and going back and forth until he got it right.

The fact that editing took place under such rudimentary circumstances is all the more amazing because it's the pacing that makes *El Mariachi* shine. Cuts come at the frenetic rate of eighties Hong Kong action pictures. The mobile camerawork is also impressive. The plot is strictly formulaic, though it does possess a tongue-in-cheek sense of fun: a young mariachi is mistaken for a hit man and propelled into a breathless series of shoot-outs. Blood and bullets fly.

Upon completion of the film, Rodriguez traveled to Los Angeles to hawk his actioner to the direct-to-video Spanish-language market.

But a funny thing happened on his way to making a few grand. While waiting for a sale to go through, Rodriguez gave his tape to an agent. The agent gave the tape to some studio people. Everyone was bowled over by the breakneck pace and microscopic budget. *El Mariachi* sold to Columbia Studios for $150,000 and a 25 percent royalty, plus a development deal for Rodriguez worth another $600,000. Columbia promptly put several hundred thousand dollars into completing a final film edit for *El Mariachi* (until then, only the video was edited), as well as for remastering the sound and blowing the 16mm print up to 35mm for theaters. (This brings up an essential truth about microbudgets: much more money is necessary to prepare prints for commercial screens.)

El Mariachi was well received at Sundance and by critics, but it was a disappointment at the box office. In retrospect, the publicity surrounding the $7,000 budget probably hurt the release. People were amused by the production story, but they balked at paying $7 to see a subtitled "home movie" in the year of *Jurassic Park*. (Columbia might have done better had it pushed the film to the Spanish-speaking action crowd it was made for.)

Still, the production story launched Robert Rodriguez's career. Joining Hooper and Linklater, he completed a trinity of Austin rebels embraced by the studios. For Columbia, he wrote and directed *Desperado* (1995), a comparatively big-budget ($6 million) sequel to *El Mariachi*. Rodriguez made the best installment in the weak semi-indie compilation film *Four Rooms* (1995). He then dusted off an old Quentin Tarantino vampire-action scenario for *From Dusk Till Dawn* (1996) and followed it with *The Faculty* (1998). After his amazing beginning, Rodriguez settled into a comfortable Hollywood position. His script choices are less than inspired, but his directing and editing bring a dazzling pace to any story.

El Mariachi lowered the budget and raised the impoverished-production tale to such levels that, even if they could be topped, they would never be quite so amazing again. One film that came close was *Clerks* (1994). It was made for $27,000 by a twenty-three-year-old film-school dropout from Red Bank, New Jersey. He shot it almost entirely during off-hours in the Quick Stop convenience store where he worked. With money scrounged from his family and credit cards, Kevin Smith (1970–) wrote, directed, and, with Scott Mosier, coproduced his debut. *Clerks* is the nearly plotless story of a day in the life

(l-r) Brian O'Halloran and Jeff Anderson loafing in *Clerks*.
© 1994 Miramax Films, Inc. Courtesy View Askew Productions, Inc.

of a college-age convenience store clerk (Brian O'Halloran) and his friend (Jeff Anderson), an employee of the understocked video store next door. Both are listless when not abrasive.

Clerks was photographed in murky black-and-white (grainy after the blowup to 35mm). It is far from a visual feast, but the infectious charm of the two leads and the often vulgar but genuinely funny dialogue carry the movie. (There was originally a shockingly violent ending, wisely excised.) Janet Maslin wrote in *The New York Times*, "The upshot, an exuberant display of film-student ingenuity, is a classic example of how to spin straw into gold. To appreciate Mr. Smith's cleverness, you need only realize how little promise his basic elements provide. The stores look realistically drab, and this film's fuzzy, grainy production values place it at the garage-band level in terms of pure technique."[8]

Clerks was the surprise hit of Sundance 1994. Miramax snatched it up. It won over crowds and critics at Cannes. Due to its graphic sexual language, *Clerks* was originally slapped with an NC-17 rating by the MPAA board, but on appeal it was changed to a more palatable R. Ads read, "Just because they serve you doesn't mean they like you."

With a smart marketing campaign, Smith's easygoing repetition of his production story, and trailers playing before Miramax's megahit *Pulp Fiction*, *Clerks* became an indie success.

Kevin Smith's follow-up transplanted the aimless *Clerks* formula from a store to a full-scale suburban shopping center. Unfortunately, the semi-indie *Mallrats* (1995) had none of the charm of Smith's debut. It flopped. Smith wisely scaled back and conjured up a focused plot with a slim budget ($500,000). In *Chasing Amy* (1997), a comic book artist (Ben Affleck) falls in love with an effervescent lesbian (Joey Adams), much to the amazement of his crudely humorous best friend and business partner (Brandon Lee). Despite a limited visual palette, *Chasing Amy*, like *Clerks*, is buoyed by quick-witted, frequently vulgar dialogue. It was a critical and commercial success. Scott Mosier again produced. Smith next wrote and directed the controversial religious comedy *Dogma* (1999).

Bearded Smith appears in each of his films as Silent Bob, accompanied by his talkative sidekick Jay (Jason Mewes); they function as a sort of stoned Greek chorus. Kevin Smith is still more confident with his dialogue than his camera placement. He's also still young.

Like thousands of others, Ed Burns (1968–) struggled for years to break into the movie business. He penned unsold screenplays, slogged away as a production assistant, and made a movie that was never distributed. Then he wrote a simple romantic comedy. As director and one of the principal actors, the nasal-voiced Burns shot *The Brothers McMullen* (1995) on weekends over eight months for $24,000. Much of the filming took place in his parents' Long Island home with his mom "catering" the meals.

As opposed to an edge picture like *Slacker*, *The Brothers McMullen* is twentysomething gentility. It's the sort of tepid movie Hollywood makes with name actors and a budget hundreds of times larger. Burns chronicles the love lives of three Irish-American brothers, married-but-cheating Jack (Jack Mulcahy), easygoing Barry (Burns), and guilt-ridden Patrick (Mike McGlone). Like Scorsese's *Who's That Knocking At My Door*, Burns's movie is concerned with young adults wrestling with Catholic values in a modern world.

After originally being dismissed by distributors, *The Brothers McMullen* was the surprise hit at Sundance 1995, winning the Grand Jury Prize. New distributor Fox Searchlight made the movie its first release and pushed it tirelessly. *The Brothers McMullen* went on to gross more than $10 million in domestic theaters. Ed Burns wrote, directed, and starred in the semi-indie romantic comedies *She's The One* (1996) and *No Looking Back* (1998); both tiptoe over *McMullen's* safe ground. Burns had a key part in *Saving Private Ryan* (1998).

By the mid-nineties, the "wow" factor of producing a motion picture for less than $30,000 had dissipated, though the independent community, Hollywood, and the general public were still rooting for underdogs. The tale of a regular Joe or Joanne generating a movie that competes with multimillion-dollar Hollywood glamour products appeals to almost everyone. The industry and the public remained vigilant, always searching for the Next Big Thing.

Next Big Thing?

As usual, the independent scene was the launching pad for exciting new voices. Now, more than ever, a filmmaker with a hit at Sundance could quickly move up to a Hollywood assignment or attain the ability to make more independent or semi-indie features. As the stakes increased, so did the competition to get noticed. One or two directors each year were heralded as the Next Big Thing. Many have yet to distinguish themselves. Others have already made significant contributions to American cinema.

Like several other rookies in the nineties, Whit Stillman creat-

Sundancing

Nervously, you screen your creation for members of the Sundance selection committee. In November, yours is one of sixteen films admitted to the Dramatic Competition.

DAY 1: Thursday, late January. You arrive in snowy Park City, Utah. The hotels are booked, but you and your producers have rented a condo. Robert Redford addresses all filmmakers, and, except for the few directors and producers who signed deals before arriving, everyone looks as nervous as you. Your film's four shows sold out before you arrived, but that's not unusual. There will be nearly 10,000 festival attendees, but there's only three true movie theaters (and a few makeshift or out-of-town venues).

DAY 2: 1st screening. You introduce your creation before it screens and answer questions afterwards. In the lobby, small distributors talk to your agent and lawyer, but none of the big fish are biting.

continued

ed a very low-budget ($200,000) feature debut about young people, though there were a couple of key differences. First, unlike his twentysomething contemporaries, Stillman was nearly forty. Second, his debut deals not with underemployed slackers but with Park Avenue preppies during the annual ritual of debutante balls. The movie is *Metropolitan* (1990), a genteel social comedy about teenagers coming of age in Manhattan's upper classes. Stillman—a child of privilege, veteran of prep school and Harvard—knew of what he wrote, and he tackled his subject with both irony and affection. The screenplay for *Metropolitan* was nominated for an Academy Award. Stillman trod over similar terrain in the semi-indies *Barcelona* (1994) and *The Last Days of Disco* (1998). Both are dialogue-heavy, set in the early eighties, and curious about the mating habits of successful young adults. With three movies, Stillman carved out his own cinematic niche: the angst of financially secure WASPs in the Reagan/Bush years.

Karen Carpenter is played by a Barbie doll. A Ken doll stars as brother Richard. Todd Haynes (1961–) burst onto the independent scene in 1987 with the forty-three-minute *Superstar: The Karen Carpenter Story*. Plastic dolls are interspersed with newsreel footage and interviews to dramatize the life and death of the anorexic pop singer. Like Kenneth Anger and other underground forerunners, Haynes utilized songs without attaining the rights. This allowed the Carpenter estate

Sundancing *continued*

DAY 3–9: Constant barrage of interviews, screenings, panel discussions, and parties. You meet a hundred people a day. You can't find time to see many movies, let alone go skiing. The buzz on your film rises and falls. Studio executives attend the screening on Day 7, but they move on to the festival's hottest flick. On Day 9 you ink a deal with a small distribution company. You're lucky. Even most features that play Sundance never achieve a theatrical release.

DAY 10: Saturday night, awards ceremony. The Grand Jury prize is the most prestigious, but more than a third of the fictional features typically win something. You snag the directing award and thank everyone you can remember. You praise the courage of your fellow independent filmmakers. One or two of you will be a famous millionaire within a year. Most of you will never be heard from again.

and A&M records to order him to cease and desist the circulation of *Superstar*. Predictably, the movie's notoriety soared. *Superstar* became an underground video classic.

The openly gay Haynes started making shorts as a teen and experimented with controversial film topics for years. He stirred up a national debate with his first feature, *Poison* (1991). Inspired by the literature of Jean Genet, Haynes scripted and helmed a trio of interrelated allegorical tales. "Hero" is a mockumentary about an abused boy who murders his dad and supposedly flies out his window. "Horror," a metaphor for the fear of AIDS, is a horror movie parody about a scientist who becomes a leprous sex maniac. "Homo" presents the carnal obsessions of a men's prison.

After winning the Grand Jury Prize at Sundance in 1991, *Poison* was released with an NC-17 rating. At that time, controversy was growing around NEA's funding of the late Robert Mapplethorpe's photography and other homoerotic art. Because one-tenth of *Poison*'s $250,000 budget came from the government and because of the disturbing content of the prison segment (men spit into another's open mouth), the film became a prime target for conservative groups, bringing a certain select fame to its auteur.

Julianne Moore is withdrawn from husband Xander Berkley in a carefully composed shot from *Safe*.
© 1995 Chemical Films. Courtesy Good Machine International, Inc.

Unlike *Poison*, Todd Haynes's next feature slipped in and out of theaters virtually unnoticed. That's unfortunate, because *Safe* (1995) is one of the best motion pictures of the decade. Carol White (Julianne Moore) is a banal housewife in the sterile upper-middle-class suburbs of Los Angeles. Her biggest concerns are keeping her tummy firm and color-coordinating her furniture. One day she gets sick but the cause is unknown. She comes to believe her problem is caused by something in her environment. As the condition worsens, she checks into a retreat called Wrenwood, which isolates people from pollution and helps them heal themselves. She remains sick.

On its surface, *Safe* plays like a disease-of-the-week TV movie, but it's really a devastating critique of the self-help movement and the dehumanizing effects of modern society. *Safe* is a horror flick without violence, a political film void of ideology, a relationship story where a wife can't kiss her husband for fear of contamination. Many viewers and critics didn't get it. Some saw *Safe* as presenting Wrenwood and its New Age philosophy as a cure. Haynes never overtly condemns the retreat (as a studio movie would), but his intent is clear. Carol is worse off at the end than ever.

Safe is full of irony. It's also full of a creeping, lingering fear that one could be ill and never know why. Haynes explains that his movie is "really about a person who doesn't know who she is, whose illness forces her to look at her life and her self and her world in different ways. . . . I don't ever want to portray a sense of natural being—comfortable, unconscious, secure being. That's what I want to exclude from the film so that the whole time you're trying to think 'How do we get to that?' "[9] Julianne Moore gives a measured, subdued performance. Xander Berkley as her isolated husband and James LeGross as her Wrenwood friend are also great as the men who cannot help her. The cinematography by Alex Nepomniaschy and the direction by Haynes frame characters in wide shots, thus presenting them within their (possibly toxic) environments. The camerawork and lighting—and by inference the suburban world—feel cold and artificial. The soundtrack often has a hum, as from motors sending contagions into the air. *Safe* is a challenging, important movie—the kind the studios almost never make. Haynes next wrote and directed the semi-indie *Velvet Goldmine* (1998).

John Dahl (1956–) grew up in Montana. In Los Angeles, he attended The American Film Institute and worked his way up from storyboard artist to music video director. He helmed and cowrote an amusing film noir, *Kill Me Again* (1989), starring Val Kilmer and set in Nevada wastelands. It quickly headed to video shelves.

Dahl's next "western noir" would have met the same fate were it not for a last-minute twist. *Red Rock West* (1993), written with brother Rick, is another plot-heavy thriller set in the West with a name cast: Nicholas Cage, Dennis Hopper, and J. T. Walsh. Cage plays a drifter in a small town who is mistakenly hired to kill an adulterous wife (Lara Flynn Boyle). The twists multiply when the real psychopathic hit man (Hopper) shows up. *Red Rock West* premiered on HBO and stirred up attention. In an unusual move, it was given a theatrical release at the same time it hit video shelves.

Close on the heels of *Red Rock West*, Dahl called the shots on his third independent, small-town noir. Remarkably, it again played on cable television before being screened in American theaters; this time it was "discovered" by London critics. *The Last Seduction* (1994), written by Steven Barancik, pushes the classic femme fatale archetype to new extremes. Linda Florentino shines as Bridget Gregory, a cold-hearted vamp who steals the $700,000 her husband (Bill Pullman) made in a drug deal and hides out in a small town in upstate New York. There, she lures a rube (Peter Berg) into her murderous schemes. The fun of *The Last Seduction* comes from the liberating licentiousness of Bridget. Dahl directed *Unforgettable* (1996) for a major studio and *Rounders* (1998) for Miramax.

Growing up in Kentucky, Allison Anders (1955–) knew abuse and poverty as a youth. She later settled in Los Angeles and attended UCLA film school. Following an undistributed collaborative effort, she adapted a novel by Richard Peck into *Gas Food Lodging* (1992). A truck stop waitress (Brooke Adams) lives in a New Mexico trailer park with her two daughters, one too eager to get with men (Ione Skye), one too idealistic (Fairuza Balk). The oldest goes off to have a baby; the youngest grows up. *Gas Food Lodging* is a study of women frustrated by their environment, and Anders does a great job of capturing the claustrophobia of a small town.

Anders wrote and directed *Mi Vida Loca* (1994), composed of three separate but interrelated stories about girls in Latin gangs. The Spanish title means "My Crazy Life." The filmmaker based the limp script on the residents near her Los Angeles home; real gang members appear on-screen. Anders also contributed a weak segment to *Four Rooms*, directed *Grace of My Heart* (1996), and codirected *Sugar Town* (1999).

A graduate of NYU's film school, Tom DiCillo came out of the downtown indie scene of the early eighties. He was Jarmusch's first cinematographer, but he yearned to write and direct. Over the course of three years, while painting apartments and waiting tables, DiCillo raised $500,000 to make *Johnny Suede* (1991), a self-consciously odd tale about a young man with an enormous pompadour who wants to be a rockabilly star. The film garnered little attention upon release but has since achieved renown for the then unknown in the title role: Brad Pitt.

Unable to launch a more ambitious project, DiCillo next created an ultralow-budget black-and-white independent film about a subject he knew well: the trails and tribulations of making an ultralow-budget independent film. The cynical yet endearing comedy, *Living In Oblivion* (1995), was popular within the nonstudio film industry but barely noticed elsewhere.[10]

DiCillo was then able to launch the more ambitious *Box of Moonlight* (1997), an enchanting fable about straight-and-narrow Al (John Turturro) who stumbles into the magical life of Kid (Sam Rockwell), a free spirit who lives in the woods on his own psychedelic compound. Kid gets Al to question his previous path. *Box of Moonlight* could easily have become saccharine and shallow, but DiCillo and the small cast keep it tumbling forward with small pleasures. DiCillo's studio debut was the little seen *The Real Blonde* (1998).

Though the euphemistic title certainly grabs your attention, *Spanking the Monkey* (1994) is shocking for another reason. Teetering uneasily between family drama and black comedy, it follows college-aged Raymond (Jeremy Davies) as he spends a summer taking care of his bedridden mother (Alberta Watson). It's mostly about the banalities of home life, but what got *Spanking the Monkey* and its debuting screenwriter/director David O. Russell noticed is the universal sin of Raymond and mom: incest. Russell originally set up his controversial feature with his wife's employer, Fine Line, but the company balked when unable to secure name casting. So Russell and producer Dean Silver raised $200,000 and made *Spanking the Monkey* autonomously. Fine Line later purchased it. Russell wrote and directed the successful semi-indie *Flirting With Disaster* (1996), a comedic portrait of another (less) dysfunctional family, and the big-budget *Three Kings* (1999).

At twenty-one, James Mangold had it made. He created a short film that impressed the CEO of Disney and, just out of college, inked a development deal with the media conglomerate. Mangold cowrote

Liv Tyler and Pruitt Taylor Vince in *Heavy*.
© 1996 Available Light, Inc.

Oliver & Company (1988). But he was fired as director from a TV movie, and the Disney fairy tale ended quietly. Nine years after starting his studio career, Mangold finally made his directing and solo screenwriting debut—as an independent.

Mangold's movie is *Heavy* (1996), a bittersweet character study. Victor (Pruitt Taylor Vince) is a shy, overweight young man who lives with his mom (Shelley Winters) and cooks in their roadside tavern. Delores (Deborah Harry) is the hardened waitress. Carrie (Liv Tyler) is the young beauty whom Victor becomes infatuated with. *Heavy* is precisely scripted, helmed, and acted, pulling us into an empathetic portrait that avoids the obvious pitfalls of condescension or mawkishness. The screenplay supplies subtle surprises and conveys emotion through an awkward pause or a hand touching a face. Few who saw *Heavy* failed to recognize the talent of its creative force. James Mangold had arrived again. He next scripted and directed *Cop Land* (1997).

New Jersey's Todd Solondz took a route similar to Mangold's. After making award-winning student shorts at NYU, he was afforded the opportunity to script, direct, and star in an independent feature, *Fear, Anxiety and Depression* (1989), a neurotic New York comedy. It bombed. Solondz disappeared from the film business for six years.

Another day of hell for Heather Matarazzo in *Welcome to the Dollhouse.*
© 1996 Sony Pictures Classics.

He taught English to Russian immigrants. Eventually the gawky Solondz dusted off a script he had penned in 1989 entitled "Faggots and Retards." He hooked up with producers Ted Skillman and Dan Partland and raised an $800,000 budget.

The movie they made was *Welcome to the Dollhouse* (1996), a Sundance winner and art-house hit. Dawn Wiener (Heather Matarazzo) is an awkward eleven-year-old outcast, degraded in junior high and dismissed at home. Things only get worse when her adored sister disappears and Dawn absorbs the blame. *Welcome to the Dollhouse* is a wickedly comedic antidote to Hollywood's nostalgia for adolescence. Solondz, a nerd survivor himself, serves up the "wonder years" in all their brutality. "Why do you hate me?" Dawn asks a tormentor. The implacable reply: "Because you're ugly." Solondz finds humor in the pain. The cast of unknowns is superb, especially the young Matarazzo and Brendan Sexton, III.

An assistant director of *Dollhouse*, Morgan J. Freeman made two portraits of floundering teens, the independent *Hurricane Streets* (1998) and the semi-indie *Desert Blue* (1999). Both star Brendan

Sexton, III. The new indie system at work: October Films financed Solondz's next edge film, *Happiness* (1998) but refused to distribute it when parent company Universal balked at the pedophile content. The brutally funny *Happiness* was released by its production company.

Swingers (1996), a basic twentysomething romantic angst comedy, features male characters who talk and act like the Rat Pack on the make, though the movie is set in the present. *Swingers* was made by would-be Hollywood players who play would-be Hollywood players. Doug Liman served as both director and cinematographer; he includes film-savvy in-jokes along with technical glitches. Jon Favreau penned the slight script and stars effectively as Mike, a comic actor trying to heal his broken heart. Vince Vaughn plays Trent, producer wannabe and lady-killer. *Swingers* makes good use of its retro-hip Las Vegas and Los Angeles locations (the Dresden, the Derby) and soundtrack (Dean Martin, Big Bad Voodoo Daddy). The film's most extraordinary element, however, is that it was produced for $250,000 and sold to Miramax for $5 million, thus instantly turning Liman, Favreau, and Vaughn into real Hollywood players. Liman followed with *Go* (1999).

"Everyone in a relationship has hurt someone or been hurt, usually both. Men are trying to pass off the movie as a fantasy, while women are pretty sure it's a documentary. The truth is it's somewhere in between."[11] So says theater-trained writer/director Neil LaBute of his controversial feature *In the Company of Men* (1997). A converted Mormon, provocateur playwright, and college drama teacher, the frumpy, bearded LaBute shot his debut near his home in Fort Wayne, Indiana in a scant eleven days. Its meager $25,000 funding came through when his executive producers settled an insurance claim from a car wreck.

In the Company of Men is a harrowing emotional journey with two businessmen, handsome Chad (Aaron Eckhart) and mousy Howard (Matt Maloy), who agree to flirt, date, and dump the same woman in a vengeful act of cruelty. Chad says, "She'll be reaching for the sleeping pills within a week, and you and me, we'll laugh about this until we're very old men." Their victim (Stacy Edwards) is deaf. *In the Company of Men* is the kind of risky subject that Hollywood and Broadway leave for brave outsiders to tackle. With stinging dialogue, confident acting, and many static long shots, LaBute pulls it off. The result is painfully devastating and utterly unforgettable. Remaining in the same dangerous terrain of psychological sadism, LaBute followed with the semi-indie black comedy *Your Friends and Neighbors*

(1998). With two contentious features, Neil LaBute staked out unclaimed cinematic territory: gender tension in the Clinton years.

Quentin Tarantino

He was the biggest Next Big Thing of the decade. Born in Tennessee and raised in suburban Los Angeles, he was an only child who never met his father. Bright but hyperactive, he skipped classes and absorbed pop culture and didn't graduate from high school. Like thousands of others, the motor-mouthed, sharply featured young man struggled as an actor, lost in the casting cattle calls. For five years in the eighties, he worked in a video store, taking movies home at the end of the day, watching, studying—Hong Kong action flicks, French New Wave classics, American exploitation, Sam Fuller, Martin Scorsese, Jean-Luc Godard, Brian De Palma, Sergio Leone. It was his film school.

And like thousands of others, he wrote screenplays. With fellow video clerk Roger Avary, he tried to raise the funds to direct one himself. Three years later, he gave up and sold the rights to what eventually became the studio effort *True Romance* (1993), an outrageous black comedy with an all-star cast. The screenwriter/video clerk tried to direct another script, this one even more darkly humorous and violent. Again his inexperience proved to be the roadblock, and he sold the rights. That screenplay, after much rewriting, became the bloody mess *Natural Born Killers* (1994).

By the time *True Romance* and *Natural Born Killers* hit screens, the man who first dreamed them, Quentin Tarantino, had directed his debut and was being hailed throughout the world as an exciting new cinematic force. After selling the rights to his more ambitious work, Tarantino penned a heist script set in a warehouse (a cheap space to rent and an easy place to shoot in). He planned to direct it in black and white using the after-tax remainder of his $50,000 *True Romance* payday. (He'd begun to shoot an earlier project but aborted it after seeing the footage.)

On the way to making his microbudget flick, Tarantino met Lawrence Bender, a sometimes grip/sometimes actor who had a couple of very minor producer credits. Bender had at least been on a real film set. He gave the script to his acting coach who gave it to Harvey Keitel. Keitel loved it, agreed to star in it, and insisted that Tarantino direct. With a name actor onboard, producer Bender was able to secure $1.5 million from the video company LIVE Entertainment. Keitel (credited as coproducer) helped Tarantino find a gifted cast in

Slacker and Reservoir Dog. (l-r) Richard Linklater and Quentin Tarantino
attend a film festival in Austin, Texas.
Photo by John Carrico.

New York and Los Angeles. Polish Andrzej Sekula made his American debut as cinematographer.

Reservoir Dogs is the story of a diamond robbery gone wrong. For everyone's protection, the hard-boiled characters know each other only by the nicknames given to them by a crime boss (Lawrence Tierney): Mr. White (Keitel), Mr. Orange (Tim Roth), Mr. Blonde (Michael Madsen), Mr. Pink (Steve Buscemi), and, in smaller roles, the doomed Mr. Brown (Tarantino) and Mr. Blue (novelist Eddie Bunker). Nice Guy Eddie (Christopher Penn) helps organize the heist. Cops are waiting at the site for the colorful "dogs," and a bloody shoot-out ensues. The survivors, rendezvousing at a warehouse, are left to discover which of them set the others up.

Four elements distinguish *Reservoir Dogs*. First, the soundtrack pulsates to seventies pop tunes, sometimes used for ironic effect (reminiscent of *Mean Streets*). Most memorable is Mr. Blonde lip-syncing "Stuck in the Middle With You" to his razor. Second, the screenplay unfolds in a nonlinear fashion so that we often see consequences before actions. At

(l-r) Steve Buscemi and Harvey Keitel in the warehouse in *Reservoir Dogs*.

one point there is even a flashback within a flashback. Third, and most important, is the acting, which is universally great. The final and most controversial element is the blood. Characters literally slip in puddles of it. In the cringe-inducing "Stuck in the Middle With You" scene, Mr. Blonde saws off the ear of a policeman (offscreen) and douses him with gasoline. For many viewers it was too much. Tarantino explains the extreme brutality: "To me, saying you don't like violence in movies is like saying you don't like tap-dancing sequences in movies; it's just one of the many things you can do in movies. And it's a very cinematic thing. You may not like it—it may not be your cup of tea—but the fact that you should or should not do it is not up for question. You can do anything."[12]

Reservoir Dogs failed to win a prize at the 1992 Sundance Film Festival, but it made a huge splash, becoming the most talked about movie in Park City. Miramax snatched it up. Critic Todd McCarthy called it "a show-off piece of filmmaking that will put writer-director

Quentin Tarantino on the map. . . . Colorfully written in vulgar gang-ster vernacular and well played by a terrific cast, this piece of strong pulp will attract attention but looks like a modest [box office] per-former . . . Undeniably impressive pic grabs the viewer by the lapels and shakes hard, but it also is about nothing other than a bunch of macho guys and how big their guns are."[13] McCarthy may have over-estimated the impact at the box office, because, despite a strong push by Miramax, *Reservoir Dogs* made little more than $2 million in North American theaters. Yet it certainly got Tarantino noticed. The buzz spread through Hollywood. Overseas, *Reservoir Dogs* was a substan-tial hit, raking in over $20 million in deutsche marks, lira, francs, and yen. Like so many pulp-art pictures before it, *Dogs* was worshiped by the French; it played at one Paris theater for a year and a half. Most Americans saw it on videotape. (Miramax bought only the rights for domestic distribution; LIVE Entertainment retained the much more lucrative foreign and video rights.)

Tarantino wrote a new script with Roger Avary, and Lawrence Bender again produced. The film was originally set up with TriStar. When that studio balked at the violent, sordid plot, Miramax happily stepped in and ponied up the $7 million budget. Hollywood stars pleaded to work in the movie, for a fraction of their usual salaries. John Travolta, Samuel L. Jackson, Uma Thurman, and Bruce Willis are among those who signed on for *Pulp Fiction* (1994), a cluster of over-lapping, pulsating narratives about philosophical hit men, a double-crossing boxer, a drug overdose, a dead body, a restaurant robbery, and the meaning of loyalty. It grossed more than $100 million in American theaters ($200+ million worldwide), won the Palm d'Or at Cannes, and was nominated for seven Academy Awards, including picture and director; Tarantino and Avary won Oscars for original screenplay. After *sex, lies, & videotape*, the British *The Crying Game* (1992), and the Australian *The Piano* (1993), it marked the apex in Miramax's box-office ascent. *Pulp Fiction* was a cultural phenomenon and a blockbuster by any standard. It was also incorrectly labeled an independent film, thus bringing a new wave of attention and legiti-macy to the genre.

Quentin Tarantino took uncredited screenwriting assignments and starred in *From Dusk Till Dawn* (made from his old script) and the awful *Destiny Turns on the Radio* (1995). He wrote, directed, and starred in an irritating segment of *Four Rooms*. For Miramax again, he made *Jackie Brown* (1997). Another prestigious cast—Robert DeNiro, Michael Keaton, Samuel L. Jackson—stepped into a convoluted tale about money laundering and double-crossing. Blaxploitation icon Pam Grier performs in the title role. *Jackie Brown* didn't come close to the popular impact of *Pulp Fiction*, but Tarantino's reputation was set. Promoted everywhere and championed by critics and fans, the video store auteur was the "flavor of the decade."

The immediate impact of *Reservoir Dogs* was to inspire "guys with guns" indie copycats. *Killing Zoe* (1994) is the most obvious, because it was scripted and directed by Roger Avary and produced by Lawrence Bender, with Tarantino as a coexecutive producer. It's another violent, patently phony tale of a heist gone wrong, this time set in a Paris bank (though shot mostly in Los Angeles). Full of blood, self-conscious camerawork, and plot twists, *Killing Zoe* failed in its only true aim: to launch Roger Avary towards Tarantinodom.

The majority of Tarantino knock-offs never even made it to screens. One, however, launched two filmmaking careers. With a script from his childhood friend Christopher McQuarrie and meager foreign funding, Brian Singer directed *Public Access* (1993), a modest feature about a stranger who riles up a town with his cable TV show. *Public Access* was cowinner of the Grand Jury Prize at Sundance 1993, but it failed to find a domestic distributor.

With a better script by McQuarrie, director and coproducer Singer managed to secure a $5.5 million budget from Gramercy for *The Usual Suspects*. Despite the filmmakers' efforts to make a distinctive film, comparisons between *The Usual Suspects* and *Reservoir Dogs* were inevitable: character actors play criminals in a heist gone wrong; there are convolutions and flashbacks; survivors struggle to determine who set them up. The movie was a hit. Kevin Spacey (for actor) and Christopher McQuarrie (for screenplay) won Academy Awards. *The Usual Suspects* was again labeled an independent film, bringing still more attention to the indie scene. In the afterglow, the truly autonomous *Public Access* was given a very limited release.

The broader impact of *Reservoir Dogs* and *Pulp Fiction* was to inspire scores of sheltered twentysomethings to write scripts and rent cameras. Some of their films were original and compelling. Most were merely movies about movies. Like testosterone-fueled Hollywood at its worst (only without celebrities or explosions), such motion pictures were stylized collections of shots and characters and catch-phrases. They weren't stories inspired by real people or situations or emotions. As Martin Scorsese said in 1997, "There is a disturbing trend in the independents in the past few years, which is that the majority are basically just making calling cards to get pictures made in the studio, to dive into the mainstream."[14]

In the mid-nineties, the indie scene teetered from Tarantino aftershocks and the lingering slacker angst formula, but art-house audiences proved to be smarter than the marketing push. Selective viewers managed to locate the stories that truly mattered.

African-American

Shown the bottom line by Spike Lee and Robert Townsend, the studios made many more films by or about African-Americans. Most were gangbanger shoot-'em-ups or broad comedies, but mature pictures like *Waiting to Exhale* (1995) and *Soul Food* (1997) also proved successful. New Line Cinema—with in-house productions like the *House Party* series (1990, 1991, 1994), *Menace II Society* (1993), *love jones* (1997), and *The Players Club* (1998)—specialized in the genre.

Just as it was for race pictures forty years earlier, when Hollywood started turning out black-themed features with substantial budgets and name actors, it was difficult for indies to attract attention. Matty Rich did it with his production story. Rusty Condieff, with *Fear of a Black Hat* (1994), and Paris Barclay, with *Don't Be a Menace to South Central While Drinking Your Juice in the Hood* (1996), did it by spoofing black youth culture. Held back by script weaknesses, white filmmakers Anthony Drazen and Stephen Starr were less successful with the interracial romances *Zebrahead* (1992) and *Joey Breaker* (1993). Uncompromising indie veteran Haile Gerima circumvented mainstream channels altogether. He rented theaters and promoted his allegorical slavery tale *Sankofa* (1993) almost exclusively through the black press.

As the nineties began, Charles Burnett was best known for a few PBS showings of *Killer of Sheep*. He finally got a movie into theaters thanks to Danny Glover who (somewhere between *Lethal Weapon II* and *Lethal Weapon III*) agreed to star and coexecutive-produce. *To Sleep With Anger* (1990), scripted and directed by Burnett, is a modern fable about trickster Harry Mention (Glover), who visits a middle-class black family in Los Angeles and stays too long. He supernaturally stirs emotions, bringing up tensions and playing on weaknesses.

Doused with African-American folklore, *To Sleep With Anger* is a slow, evocative look at class and generational issues in the black community. The film was marketed to art film enthusiasts, ignoring the broader African-American audience, and despite Glover's presence, *To Sleep With Anger* grossed less in theaters than its $1.5 million budget. Burnett went on to craft the semi-indie *The Glass Shield* (1995).

Julie Dash's *Daughters of the Dust* (1992) found its audience primarily through a campaign of fliers and sermons in the black community. The movie, which has no real plot, is a poetic portrait of a day in 1902 when the Gullah women—descendants of slaves who live on islands off the coast of South Carolina—gather to celebrate their history before moving to the mainland. The hypnotic cinematography is by Arthur Jafa. Dash began making short films in the seventies. It took her ten years to finance and produce *Daughters of the Dust*. The result, undeniably beautiful, is tiresome if one fails to follow its lyrical rhythm, so unlike the driving narrative of most movies. *Daughters of the Dust* found its principal audience among educated black women.

Julie Dash was the first African-American female to direct a commercially distributed feature film; the second was Leslie Harris. She wrote and helmed the modestly budgeted *Just Another Girl on the I.R.T.* (1993), a drama about a spunky high-school student (Ariyan Johnson) living in a Brooklyn housing project. The teen must defer her college dreams when she becomes pregnant. The routine story of *Just Another Girl on the I.R.T* catches up with its unfocused second half.

One of the most successful indies with a predominantly black cast, *Fresh* (1994) was scripted and directed by white Boaz Yakim. Lawrence Bender was a producer. *Fresh*'s title character (Sean Nelson) is a twelve-year-old boy who works for Brooklyn drug dealers. His sister (N'Bushe Wright) is hooked on heroin; his chess-playing dad (Samuel L. Jackson) is an alcoholic. A violent event leads Fresh to set up the drug dealers. The subdued *Fresh* contrasts with the typical noise-and-bluster street movies of the nineties, but Yakim's script is a little too slow and neatly plotted. Yakim next made the independent *A Price Above Rubies* (1998), an emotional tale about a young Hasidic woman (Renée Zellweger) who wants to break free.

Once Upon a Time . . . When We Were Colored (1996) was another movie that followed the *Daughters of the Dust* marketing formula. In a limited release over an extended period, it steadily attracted African-American adults. Adapted from a book by Paul Cooper and directed by actor Tim Reid (his feature debut), *Once Upon a Time* presents a black boy growing up in a small town in the segregated South of the fifties and sixties. The meandering narrative includes many touching moments.

Christopher Cherot financed his $65,000 debut, *Hav Plenty* (1998), a romantic comedy filled with both fresh and stale African-American characters. *Hav Plenty*'s distributor, Miramax, made much more with the easily exploitable hood indie, *I Got the Hook Up* (1998), directed by Michael Martin and produced by rap mogul Master P.

Ethnic

Still craving blockbusters, studio executives kept their heads in the sand when it came to other ethnicities. It was, as always, up to off-Hollywood productions to present the nuanced characters and unique tales of hyphenated Americans. There were the Italian-American women of Nancy Savoca's films, the Russian-Jewish-Americans of James Gray's crime drama *Little Odessa* (1994); and the Hispanic-Americans of Miguel Artera's Hollywood hustle, *Star Maps* (1997).

American Indians have long been cinema's cardboard cutouts, almost always depicted as scalping villains or pitiable martyrs. More than a century after Edison first sold moving pictures, Indians found their voice in *Smoke Signals* (1998), a film by Native Americans Chris Eyre (director) and Sherman Alexie (writer).[15] Two twenty-two-year-old Indians, stoic Victor (Adam Beach) and talkative Thomas Builds-the-Fire (Evan Adams), team up to journey from Idaho to Arizona to bring back the remains of Victor's estranged father (Gary Farmer), seen in flashbacks. They gain a greater understanding of their culture and themselves. Somewhat underwritten, *Smoke Signals* is a genial portrait told from a fresh perspective.

Following the path of Wayne Wang, Asian-American narratives continued to reach screens independently. Mark Salzman spent two years in China, teaching English and studying martial arts. He wrote a book about the culture clash. With director Shirley Sun, Salzman turned it into a script and starred in *Iron & Silk* (1991). The photography of mainland China is gorgeous.

If *Iron & Silk* is a twist on the immigrant-in-America chronicle, *Combination Platter* (1993) is the formula straight up: an illegal Chinese immigrant (Jeff Lau) must marry to remain in the United States. Twenty-three-year-old Hong-Kong-born Tony Chan shot this microbudget debut mostly in his family's New York restaurant.

Two indie features tackled little known Asian-American history. Nancy Kelly's *1000 Pieces of Gold* (1991) deals with Chinese indentured servitude in the Old West and features an interracial love story. Kayo Hatta's *Picture Bride* (1995) focuses on the Japanese women who came to Hawaii in the early years of the twentieth century to marry men they had never met.

Gay

The major studios presented a few films like *Philadelphia* (1993) about homosexual characters, but, as usual, the indie community remained several steps ahead. The New Queer Cinema (aka the Queer New Wave) came of age in the nineties, presenting challenging and proudly gay movies for a predominantly gay audience.

The decade was kicked off with the most mainstream and commercially successful gay indie of all time ($5 million box office), *Longtime Companion* (1990). Directed by Norman René and scripted by playwright Craig Lucas, it begins in the early eighties with a group of healthy homosexual men. A mysterious new disease is mentioned. By the conclusion at the end of the decade, most of this group has died of AIDS. *Longtime Companion* does a good job of presenting diverse characters who are not defined by their sexuality. We care as they become ill and disappear from the story. Bruce Davison, Dermot Mulroney, and Campbell Scott are among those in the fine cast. Davison was nominated for an Academy Award as Best Supporting Actor.

Jeffrey (1995) was another mainstream effort that crossed over to a broader audience. Adapted by Paul Rudnick from his own play and directed by Christopher Ashley, it's a tepid romantic comedy about gay Jeffrey (Steven Weber) as he tries to abstain from sex and romance in the age of AIDS. Complications ensue. Sigourney Weaver, Olympia Dukakis, and Patrick Stewart—as a bitchy interior decorator—are featured.

The financial return for "safe" homosexual films was so promising that Paramount Studios purchased and released the independent *Kiss Me, Guido* (1997), a gay/straight male-bonding farce written and helmed by Tony Vitale. It underachieved. Another "safe" effort, *Billy's Hollywood Screen Kiss* (1998) is a light comedy by Tommy O'Haver about a gay photographer attracted to a male model/actor of unknown sexual orientation.

Asian-American Gregg Araki (1960–) is anything but safe. The Los Angeles native is the most audacious figure of the New Queer Cinema. He started with two Warhol-style underground features made for $5,000 each, *Three Bewildered People in the Night* (1987) and *The Long Weekend (O' Despair)* (1989). Araki wrote, directed, photographed, and edited *The Living End* (1992) for $20,000 with equipment borrowed from Jon Jost. It's a darkly comedic road movie about two HIV+ gay men (Mike Dytri and Craig Gilmore) who set out on a journey of gratification. With a title card announcing "An Irresponsible Film by Gregg Araki," *The Living End* is nothing if not provocative.

With typical indie budgets (still very low), Araki crafted three features known as his "teen apocalypse trilogy." The first, *Totally F***ed Up* (1993), which Araki also shot, is a portrait of gay Los Angeles teenagers raging against society. The second and worst, *The Doom Generation* (1995), was subtitled "A Heterosexual Film." This violently outrageous road movie, à la *Natural Born Killers*, rides along with a vacant teenage couple on a murderous joy trip. The third, *Nowhere* (1997), presents one tumultuous day with a multiracial, pansexual group of Los Angeles teens. All the movies in the trilogy feature actor James Duval in a lead role and present a palette of vibrant colors, imaginative pop-art production design, surrealism, outrageous dark comedy, social satire, and an overriding note of nihilism.

Producer Christine Vachon is the Queen of New Queen Cinema. She started as an assistant editor on *Parting Glances* and has since produced a host of independent movies with gay themes, characters, and /or directors, including *Poison, Safe, Stonewall*, and the ambitious $80,000 feature *Swoon* (1992). Helmed by Tom Kalin, who cowrote it with Hilton Als, *Swoon* retells the infamous case of Leopold and Loeb, two rich male lovers who kidnap and kill a boy in Chicago in 1924 for the thrill of it. Though they didn't get away with it, they did escape the death penalty when legendary attorney Charles Darrow successfully argued that their homosexuality proved they were insane. The story was brought to the screen earlier in *Compulsion* (1959), and it inspired *Rope* (1948), but those films glossed over the issues. *Swoon* dives right in.

Kalin's black-and-white movie is remarkably stylized (cinematography by Ellen Kuras). Shots are often constructed like photographs or stage plays; anachronistic modern props appear; and much is accomplished with sound effects and music. Kalin realized it would be impossible with a microbudget to effectively recreate Jazz Age Chicago, so he toyed with the lack of scope to give the film a dreamy feel. He focuses on the power dynamics between the controlling Richard Loeb (Daniel Schlachet) and the weak Nathan Leopold (Craig Chester), not on the criminality of their violent act. Kalin explains, "At the heart of *Swoon*, I think—and it's one of the things that makes many audiences disturbed by the film—is a kind of unrepentant quality to it or a refusal to moralize . . . *Swoon* tries to tell the film from inside the relationship, the chaotic, contradictory, complex relationship of Leopold and Loeb, so that in a certain degree you are made to participate."[16]

In 1992, *Poison, The Living End*, and *Swoon* launched the New Queer Cinema of bold, uncompromising movies. Other important films of this genre include Richard Glatzer's backstage look at a TV soap opera, *Grief* (1994); Todd Verow's exploration of violence and sex, *Frisk* (1996); and Nigel Finch's recounting of the 1969 riot that kick-started the gay rights movement, *Stonewall* (1996). Such films were mostly distributed by Strand Releasing; none of them broke out of their limited niche of gay festivals and theaters.

The most successful lesbian-themed movies avoided the controversy of the New Queer Cinema. Most lesbian filmmakers still felt the need to dispel stereotypes and thus tended to examine the ordinary lives of gay women. The microbudget, black-and-white *Go Fish* (1994) was directed and coscripted by Rose Troche. Cowriter Guinevere Turner stars. It's a standard romantic comedy talkfest (about lesbians), but it proved a surprising success, grossing more than *Reservoir Dogs* in domestic theaters. *The Incredibly True Adventures of Two Girls in Love* (1995), helmed by Maria Maggenti, was nearly as successful with another basic formula: high-school kids from different worlds (race and class) fall in love; the twist is that they're both female. More challenging works slipped by without fanfare. In a brave performance, Ally Sheedy plays a drug-addicted lesbian in *High Art* (1998). As conceived by Lisa Cholodenko, this is a seedy, romanticized portrait of a tortured artist.

On the gay-themed documentary front, Jennie Livingston captured *Paris Is Burning* (1991), an inside look at the elaborate vogueing drag balls of poor black and Hispanic men in Harlem. Alternating humor with poignancy, *Paris Is Burning* was a cinematheque smash. Barry Shils's *Wigstock: The Movie* (1995) covers similar territory, a giant drag ball in New York City. A few hundred outrageous cross-dressers are featured, but the movie lacks the insight and sorrowful undercurrent of *Paris Is Burning*.

The Celluloid Closet (1996) brings the theme of homosexuality in the movies full circle. Based on the perceptive book by Vito Russo, it was assembled by Robert Epstein and Jeffrey Friedman, the driving forces behind *The Times of Harvey Milk* and the Oscar-winning documentary about AIDS victims, *Common Threads: Stories from the Quilt* (1989). Lily Tomlin narrates. *The Celluloid Closet* documents the acknowledged and unacknowledged gay subtexts and characters throughout Hollywood's long history.

Documentary

They came from such unexpected places as a meat-packing plant in Austin, Minnesota, a dairy farm in Munnsville, New York, and the rough playgrounds of Chicago, Illinois. Some were genuine motion picture classics, but even when they fell short of that status, documentaries in the nineties proved invariably more absorbing than typical Hollywood fiction.

In the years after *Harlan County, U.S.A.*, Barbara Kopple kept right on capturing the struggles of working Americans. In 1984, the Hormel meat-packing plant in Austin, Minnesota proposed a workers' wage reduction from $10.69 to $8.25 an hour with other benefits cut 30 percent. The company had netted $29 million the previous year. The workers went on strike. As months dragged on, union negotiators made strategic mistakes and workers broke away from the picket line. A compromise wage was agreed to, but the majority of strikers were replaced. The company then closed half the plant and rented it to a business that paid $6.50 an hour. *American Dream* (1990) plays like a companion piece to both *Harlan County, U.S.A.* and *Roger & Me*. Strikers in the Reagan era are fought not with guns and scabs, but with downsizing and permanent replacements. They may be doomed to lose. *American Dream* was the second feature-length documentary by Barbara Kopple; she won a second Academy Award.

Kopple's third feature, *Wild Man Blues* (1998), was something completely different, a portrait of Woody Allen and new wife Soon-Yi Previn as Allen's jazz band tours Europe. The film is not as revealing as it should be about either the artist or his controversial romance.

In 1975, two FBI agents were shot dead at an Indian reservation near

Ogala, South Dakota. Though there was little evidence, Native American activist Leonard Peltier was convicted of the murders. Robert Redford executive-produced and narrated *Incident at Ogala* (1992), about the events and trial. The movie advances a convincing case that, at the very least, Peltier was unjustly tried. Noted British filmmaker Michael Apted (*Coal Miner's Daughter*) directed *Incident at Ogala* as well as Hollywood's fictional *Thunderheart* (1992), a film with a similar theme.

Another fascinating examination of a murder trial is *Brother's Keeper* (1992), by Joe Berlinger and Bruce Sinofsky. The four Ward brothers, ages fifty-nine to seventy, illiterate and barely verbal, lived in a two-room shack. They tended to their farm and stayed to themselves, never marrying, rarely bathing or shaving. Nobody in the tiny town of Munnsville in upstate New York ever paid much attention to the "Ward boys" until 1990, when William, the second oldest, was found dead in his bed. The local prosecutor charged Delbert, the youngest, with the murder. Did the sick William die in his sleep or did Delbert suffocate him to put him out of his misery? The odd case and the peculiar living arrangements of the Ward boys attracted national attention. Berlinger and Sinofsky won the trust of the brothers, following them through the murder trial. Most telling were the neighbors who rallied to Delbert's defense. *Brother's Keeper* is a gripping examination of human nature and media manipulation. The filmmakers distributed the picture themselves.

Berlinger and Sinofsky again chronicled the controversy surrounding a rural crime in *Paradise Lost: The Child Murders at Robin Hood Hills* (1996). Through interviews and courtroom footage, they examine the case of three teenage boys in Arkansas who are tried for killing a child, allegedly as part of a Satanic rite. The filmmakers were granted unprecedented access to strategy meetings for both the prosecution and the defense. Like *Brother's Keeper*, the case of *Paradise Lost* is riveting, exposing people's fears and prejudices. After a premiere on HBO, this movie was again self-distributed.

Robert Crumb was the leading underground comic artist of the sixties and seventies, creator of Fritz the Cat, "Keep on Truckin'," psychedelic album covers, and a seemingly endless stream of lewd, intricately rendered cartoons. Terry Zwigoff was a musician friend of Crumb's who constructed the documentary *Louie Bluie* (1985), about blues musician Howard Armstrong. In 1986, Zwigoff began a nine-year quest to bring the story of Crumb and his controversial art to the screen. His focus widened when he learned that Robert Crumb's two brothers were even odder than the eccentric legend. The older Charles still lives with their mother. Mentally unstable, he spends his days sedated, rereading novels and drawing elaborate cartoons. Max, also an artist, serves penance on a bed of nails. (Robert's two sisters declined to participate in the film.) The Crumb brothers open up about their artwork, mental instabilities, and sexual obsessions. *Crumb* (1994) is an unflinching inquest of an artist and his influences. Included is some of Robert Crumb's most offensive material, blatantly sexist and racist cartoons that are difficult to defend. The quietly disturbing *Crumb* is a triumph of documentary making. (Zwigoff himself was dangerously depressed during its long production.) Buoyed by rave reviews, it was an art-house success.

It began with an idea for a thirty-minute short to be produced in six days. Five years later they completed production, having shot for 160 days and compiled 250 hours of video footage. Over the next year, they cut it into a three-hour feature film. The epic movie *Hoop Dreams* (1994) became the most critically and commercially successful documentary of a generation.

In 1987, Steve James and Frederick Marx were filmmaking neophytes and basketball enthusiasts fresh out of film school. They wanted to make a short film about Chicago kids dreaming of success in basketball, but they had no money and no experience. They hooked up with cinematographer Peter Gilbert, who had shot footage for Kopple's ongoing *American Dream* production. He had his own professional video camera. They became a team: James as director, Marx as editor, Gilbert as cinematographer, all three as producers. The goal was to shoot on video and sell to PBS.

But when the filmmakers got to know incoming high-school freshmen William Gates and Arthur Agee, two inner-city teens recruited by a suburban private school, they knew they had something more than a video short. The filmmakers shot eleven days during the teens' freshman year and twelve during their sophomore year, when Agee returns to a Chicago public school. By showcasing their remarkably dramatic footage of the home lives of the teenagers, the producers acquired grants to capture much more video footage of the Gates and Agee families, through the boys' freshman year in college. They shot a remarkable eighty days during the teens' senior year of high school. After editing, the *Hoop Dreams* video was transferred to film.

It became a national sensation. Roger Ebert gushed, "A film like *Hoop Dreams* is what the movies are for. It takes us, shakes us, and makes us think in new ways about the world around us. It gives us the impression of having touched life itself. . . . It is one of the great movie-going experiences of my lifetime."[17] He and Gene Siskel lauded it on their TV show before it even played at Sundance in January 1994. It was the talk of the festival. New Line won the rights. Universally praised, *Hoop Dreams* went on to become both an arthouse triumph and a success in mainstream urban theaters—which initially showed it free to nonadults. James, Marx, and William Haugse were nominated for an editing Oscar. Inexplicably, the infamous Academy Award documentary committee failed to even nominate *Hoop Dreams* for documentary feature; the uproar was loud. *Hoop Dreams* was repeatedly a ratings winner when screened on PBS.

The praise is justified. *Hoop Dreams* has more drama and emotion than three typical Hollywood productions. It captures the most affecting moments of the five most crucial years of two teenagers struggling to realize their dreams. Effective scenes include Arthur's dad buying drugs on the court as his son plays basketball, William missing a crucial free throw, Arthur's family in a dark apartment with no electricity, William's callous coach giving him an impassive farewell speech, and his single mom telling him what not to do at college. *Hoop Dreams* serves up the poor and violent living conditions of inner-city Chicago, but it also presents the strength, faith, and determination of families persevering. Most of all, it cares enough to follow two boys as they become men. William Gates said in 1995, "*Hoop Dreams* is probably going to give me some of that lasting fame that I think every athlete is hoping for. . . . I wish it was basketball. But you know, basketball is still the reason all this is happening."[18]

Another sports documentary with wider implications is *When We Were Kings* (1997). Directed by Leon Gast, it's a vivid account of the Rumble in the Jungle boxing match between Muhammad Ali and George Foreman in 1974. Gast intersperses sometimes intrusive current interviews with classic footage he shot of the match and the weeks leading up to it in Zaire. The segments where an effervescent Ali comically harangues bystanders, Foreman, and the camera are priceless. Gast does a great job of locating the fight as a proud moment in African-American history. *When We Were Kings* won the Academy Award for Best Documentary Feature.

Errol Morris continued to explore the possibilities of nonfiction film. He spent $3 million to bring physicist Stephen Hawking's theories to the screen in *A Brief History of Time* (1992). With noted Hollywood cinematographers John Bailey and Stefan Czapsky, Morris creatively depicts Hawking's astronomical insights. We also learn about the brilliant Hawkings, who suffers from the disease ALS, moves via a motorized wheelchair, and talks through a computer. The movie makes complex science almost accessible. It documents Hawking's childhood but neglects his more interesting adult life. Philip Glass composed the score. Morris helmed a disappointing fictional feature, *The Dark Wind* (1994), about a mystery on an Indian reservation.

With *fast, cheap & out of control* (1997), Morris again sculpted a unique document. A topiary gardener, a robot scientist, an expert on African mole rats, and a lion tamer: what do they have in common? Morris blends the four stories together with old movie footage and other images. He often cuts the visuals from one occupation with the interview from another. Robert Richardson oversaw the splendid cinematography. A visually rich nonfiction montage, *fast, cheap & out of control* keeps revealing small pleasures.

Ross McElwee also continued to conjure up nonfiction features. He went far afield to document the fall of the Berlin Wall in *Something to Do with the Wall.* (1991). He then went up-close and personal with a sequel to *Sherman's March* called *Time Indefinite* (1993). McElwee captures his own life's passages—wedding, wife's miscarriage, deaths of relatives, birth of son—while simultaneously pondering how they're affected by the continuous intrusion of his camera. Combining a mismatch of footage (including stock nature shots) and subjective commentary, *Time Indefinite* is the apotheosis of personal filmmaking. In *Six O'Clock News* (1996), McElwee thrusts his intrusive camera at other intrusive cameras and the people who cover tragic, media-saturated events.

After the wide acclaim he received for *Roger & Me*, Michael Moore made the disappointing fictional film *Canadian Bacon* (1995) for a studio, and he was the driving force behind the muckraking television comedy *TV Nation*. Moore took on corporate America again with the satiric documentary *The Big One* (1998). Again, the rotund, dressed-down populist wields his microphone like a dagger. He seeks answers as to why companies (especially Nike) so eagerly disregard blue-collar Americans by shipping jobs elsewhere. Though not as consistently entertaining as *Roger & Me*, most of *The Big One*'s jabs and jokes hit home.

There were several other notable documentaries during these years, including *Hearts of Darkness: A Filmmaker's Apocalypse* (1991), directed by Fax Bahr and George Hickenlooper. It captures the tumultuous production of Coppola's *Apocalypse Now* with the kind of inside footage (provided by Mrs. Coppola) that made *Burden of Dreams* so compelling. Three decades after *Primary*, D. A. Pennebaker and his wife Chris Hegedus made *The War Room* (1993), taking us into the inner workings of the 1992 Clinton/Gore campaign. *Sick: The Life and Death of Bob Flanagan, Supermasochist* (1997), created by artist Kirby Dick, is an unflinching look at the title figure, a performance artist racked by cystic fibrosis whose act consists of feats like nailing his penis to a board. *20 Dates* (1999) is Myles Berkowitz's unflinching *Sherman's March* in search of Ms. Right. Eclecticism reigned in the nonfiction arena.

Gentility and Edge

Gentility and edge continued as twin cinematheque genres: *Smoke Signals* and *Lone Star* on the one side, *Bad Lieutenant* and *Poison* on the other. A knitting-club example of gentility is *The Spitfire Grill* (1996). Directed by Lee David Zlotoff, it's a docile New England melodrama that stirred up attention when it sold to Castle Rock for $10 million. Others not previously mentioned include *The Waterdance* (1992), about the recovery of a novelist who becomes a paraplegic; writer and codirector Neil Jimenz is himself paralyzed. *What Happened Was . . .* (1994) is a *My Dinner With Andre*-style conversation with two characters on one set during a first date; Tom Noonan penned, directed, and stars.

Great Britain provided American distributors with many of the most successful acquisitions of the era. Miramax benefitted from *My Left Foot* (1989) and *The Crying Game* (1992). *Howard's End* (1992) was the first release of Sony Pictures Classics. And both October Films (*Secrets and Lies*, 1996) and Fox Searchlight (*The Full Monty*, 1997) found their most profitable movies in England.

Stephen Frears had been filmmaking in Britain for more than twenty years. He came to America to helm *Dangerous Liaisons* (1988) and stayed to direct a substantially budgeted independent effort that caused a bid ding war at Cannes (Miramax won). The movie was *The Grifters* (1990), based on a Jim Thompson pulp novel and written by Donald Westlake. Martin Scorsese produced this modern film noir about three Southern California con artists: small-time Roy (John Cusack); his new girlfriend (Annette Benning), who likes big swindles; and Roy's previously estranged mother (Angelica Houston), who has been scamming the mob. *The Grifters* strips bare the trust and betrayal of lovers and family. The movie resembles a typical Hollywood production and isn't as clever as it should be, but it has its fans. Frears, Westlake, Houston, and Benning were nominated for Academy Awards.

Victor Nunez continued to make superior gentility pictures. After *A Flash of Green*, he had been trying to get a movie launched in Hollywood for nearly a decade. He finally gave up. Utilizing a $400,000 inheritance, he again wrote, directed, and edited his own independent feature set in Florida. The movie is *Ruby in Paradise* (1993). Ashley Judd plays Ruby, who leaves her stale existence in Tennessee and drives to Panama City, Florida. There she begins to blossom as a young adult. It's a simple story, poetically told and well acted by newcomer Judd and a cast of unknowns.

Nunez had his greatest critical and commercial success in 1997 with *Ulee's Gold*. After years in acting purgatory, "Easy Rider" Peter Fonda gives his all-time greatest performance. He stars as Ulee, an aging beekeeper and host to various emotions, wounded by his wife's death and his son's imprisonment. He's raising two granddaughters, nursing a drug-addicted daughter-in-law, and struggling to do the right thing as a pair of thugs come back for stolen money. Connie Hope (Patricia Richardson) is the benign neighbor who may be able to chisel through Ulee's stern facade.

Nunez weaves *Ulee's Gold* into a subdued yet powerful drama that hits all the right notes. Virgil Mirano oversaw the splendid cinematography; the results are soft and glowing. The camera lingers on faces, honey making, and the rural Florida landscape. Much is gained from understated acting and all the words that go unspoken. Critic David Ansen wrote, "What's startling about this quiet, un-hyped-up film is how moving it is. Fonda's performance—the best he's ever given— is haunted both by Ulee's past and by Fonda's father, whose physical mannerisms are eerily present in his son. *Ulee's Gold* possesses an attribute that's increasingly rare in American filmmaking,

Peter Fonda as a beekeeper in *Ulee's Gold*. Pictured with Vanessa Zima as his granddaughter.

independent or Hollywood: call it soul."[19] *Ulee's Gold* was a box-office success. Fonda was nominated for an Academy Award.

Veteran screenwriter/director Paul Schrader often works outside Hollywood: *Mishima* (1985), *Light Sleeper* (1992), etc. Adapting a Russell banks novel, he wrote and helmed *Affliction* (1998). In this icy drama, a small-town New Hampshire cop (Nick Nolte) investigates a hunting death and painfully unravels his own troubled emotions. Nolte's acting earned an Academy Award nomination. James Coburn won an Oscar as Nolte's angry, drunken father.

On the other side of the spectrum, few movies skirted the edge like the semi-indie *Crash* (1997), directed by veteran David Cronenberg. This disturbing ride with people who became sexually stimulated by automobile accidents stirred up attention when Ted Turner initially refused to let Fine Line release it.

The first film of the decade to stir up controversy was John McNaughton's deadpan tale of a mass murderer. Shooting in his native Chicago in the winter of 1985, McNaughton assumed his shocker would go straight to the exploitation video market. Instead, it lurched towards theater screens, only to get entangled in an MPAA ratings fight. When it was slapped with an X for violence, McNaughton refused to make a single cut. Finally, in 1990, *Henry: Portrait of a Serial Killer* was released without a rating but with an "Adults Only" warning.

The movie stars Michael Rooker as Henry, a lethal drifter who videotapes his crimes. Based on the confessions of a real serial killer, *Henry* is a *Honeymoon Killers*-style slice of tabloid chic. *The New Yorker* called it a "hybrid of *Blood Feast* and *Stranger Than Paradise*."[20] The script combines droll, bored dialogue ("Where you going?" "Nowhere. You wanna come?") with shocking violence perpetrated in a detached manner. The mix of brutality and banality is anything but entertaining, and yet when *Henry: Portrait of a Serial Killer* finally hit theater screens, critics and hip viewers championed it. It made numerous "top ten of the year" lists, including those of *Time* and *USA Today*. There was a sequel in 1998. McNaughton directed a low-budget sci-fi effort called *The Borrower* (1991) and *Sex, Drugs, Rock & Roll* (1991), a concert film of performance artist Eric Begosian. He called the shots on the studio efforts *Mad Dog and Glory* (1993) and *Wild Things* (1998).

Edge maven David Lynch kept right on brewing his own brand of self-conscious weirdness. He created the cult television series "Twin Peaks," which further explored *Blue Velvet* territory, and he made the semi-indie *Wild at Heart* (1990), a twisted road movie and an exercise in excess. *Twin Peaks: Fire Walk With Me* (1992) was intended to wrap up his canceled TV series.

Unable to make motion pictures his way, Lynch concentrated on his other artistic projects, including photography, painting, furniture design, and music. His daughter Jennifer wrote and directed the independent *Boxing Helena* (1994), a mess about a surgeon who lops off the limbs of the woman he obsesses over. Its fame came only when Kim Basinger was successfully sued by the production after she opted out of the lead role.

David Lynch returned to the independent arena in 1997 with the foreign-financed *Lost Highway*. A jazz musician (Bill Pullman) apparently murders his wife (Patricia Arquette) and then transforms into someone else (Balthazar Getty). The movie floats along in a dark Los Angeles dream state where everything is discombobulated and nothing is quite as it appears. Is it schizophrenia? Ghosts? A manifestation of the unconscious? Lynch wasn't talking. An overly designed mixture of film noir, existentialism, and imponderables, *Lost Highway* was Lynch's most experimental work since *Eraserhead*. It only added to its auteur's unique legend as America's most visible avant-garde filmmaker. Most surprising of all, Lynch next made the G-rated *The Straight Story* (1999). David Lynch remains one of the few cinematic figures to have spawned an adjective, "Lynchian," meaning "obsessively peculiar, often at the expense of coherence."

A rare voyager in Lynchian territory is Darren Aronofsky. With a look and feel reminiscent of *Eraserhead*, Aronofsky's π (Pi) (1998) is a $60,000, black-and-white thriller about mathematics, madness, mysticism, and the meaning of life.

"Jesus Christ, what happened?" So says Casper, waking up in a stupor after a day of drinking, doping, bashing, and indiscriminate sex. It's the last line of the *Kids* (1995), one of the most controversial films of a generation. *Kids*, a portrait of aimless, amoral New York City teens and preteens, marked the directing debut of fifty-two-year-old photographer Larry Clark. Nineteen-year-old Harmony Korine wrote the hyperrealistic script. All of the actors were nonprofessional "real kids" found on the streets of New York.

Kids follows Telly (Leo Fitzpatrick) as he "de-virginizes" young girls, joined on his daylong romp of booze, drugs, and copulation by skateboarding pal Casper (Justin Pierce). The only real plot device is supplied by Jennie (Chloe Sevigny), who, after learning she is HIV+ attempts to find her one sexual partner, Telly, before he beds someone new. *Kids* simply follows its characters through a twenty-four hour period. Its matter-of-fact presentation makes it riveting and disturbing (it earned an NC-17 rating). As in *Laws of Gravity*, the naturalistic acting, dialogue, and handheld photography (cinematography by Eric Edwards) give *Kids* the feel of a *verité* documentary. It's a difficult movie to enjoy but equally hard to forget. The self-inflated *enfant terrible* Harmony Korine spawned the disturbing, experimental features, *Gummo* (1997) and *julien donkey-boy* (1999). Clarke directed the seedy independent *Another Day in Paradise* (1998) about a group of outlaw junkies.

Steven Soderbergh may have been right when he proclaimed after *sex, lies & videotape*, "Well, I guess it's all downhill from here." He was the boy wonder, the messiah who delivered art films to mainstream America. As such, he was afforded the capital to do almost anything, and Soderbergh couldn't seem to make up his mind whether to turn toward the edge or more typical Hollywood plots.

With a substantial budget from Miramax, Soderbergh helmed the psychological storytelling experiment *Kafka* (1992) in Czechoslovakia. In black and white and color with period production design and a paranoid plot mixing biography and fantasy, *Kafka* was nothing if not ambitious. It flopped.

Soderbergh moved to the new semi-indie studio Gramercy for his third film, *King of the Hill* (1993). This poignant historical tale was highly praised, but it failed to find an audience. Staying in Hollywood, Soderbergh helmed *The Underneath* (1994). It also bombed. Reminiscent of Orson Welles, Steven Soderbergh was no longer the toast of cinema; he was the fading one-hit wonder.

In 1997, Soderbergh returned to the independent arena. The two movies he directed had combined budgets of less than half of the $1.2 million he used for *sex, lies, & videotape*. *Gray's Anatomy* is the third filmed Spalding Gray monologue. (The second, *Monster in a Box* [1992], was directed by Nick Broomfield.) The wholly experimental *Schizopolis* is an incomprehensible farrago of Dadaist comic vignettes. For Soderbergh, the two pictures were conscious attempts to refuel his independent zest. He next called the shots on *Out of Sight* (1998) and *The Limey* (1999).

Commercial Ascent

The most successful independent movies were those that attracted fans of both gentility and edge. On rare occasions such movies could transcend art-house altogether. With their combinations of critical and commercial success and approachable yet distinctly original content, four independent films in the last half of the nineties took the movie industry by storm. They heralded the marketing of truly independent pictures and their ascendancy into multiplexes everywhere.

Leaving Las Vegas (1995) hit America like a three-day binge, sucking in audiences who would normally never have sidled up to the bar with such a bleak movie. Ben (Nicholas Cage) is an alcoholic who's drunk himself out of a marriage and a job. He goes to Las Vegas to drink himself to death. He hooks up with Sara (Elisabeth Shue), a pretty prostitute unable to shake her own demons. Life seeps downhill.

The beauty of *Leaving Las Vegas* is its simplicity and uncompromising purity. In this sad love sonnet, two wounded adults cling to each other out of desperation. *Leaving Las Vegas* is an independent film in the best sense, because the elements that Hollywood would have focused on are nowhere to be found. The subplot about Sara's brutal pimp would have been played to the hilt in a studio movie; here it's discarded offscreen. There is never a moment when Ben tries to stop drinking. A hot desert sex scene ends abruptly and embarrassingly. Most importantly, a happy ending is nowhere to be found here.

Elizabeth Shue and Nicolas Cage in *Leaving Las Vegas*.

Leaving Las Vegas was adapted from a partially autobiographical novel by John O'Brien that originally sold only 2,000 copies. O'Brien committed suicide two weeks after the movie rights sold (for a $2,000 option). The screenwriter and director was Mike Figgis, a British film-maker whose biggest previous effort, *Internal Affairs* (1990), was a Hollywood disappointment. With French financing, *Leaving Las Vegas* had a substantial indie budget of $4 million. Still, Figgis chose to shoot in Super 16mm so that he could more easily and unobtrusively capture scenes in busy Vegas. Declain Quinn was responsible for the simmering cinematography. Figgis also composed the evocative jazz score, with singing by Sting.

Leaving Las Vegas is an acting piece par excellence. The most hack-neyed roles in drama—the self-hating drunk and the hooker with a heart of gold—are brought to life by Nicholas Cage and Elisabeth Shue with dynamism and sincerity. Cage and the script teeter on the edge of absur-dity, but the actor manages to toe the thin line without faltering. Shue imbues her role with a steely sadness, vulnerability, and resignation.

The film was picked up by MGM before it was completely edited. It was a critical triumph. Film historian David Thompson effused praise: "*Leaving Las Vegas* is that rare thing—a great film and a very dark experience. It will not easily let you go; it could drive you to drink; it might make you hopeful again. For it lives in that lonely place—to invoke one of the greatest of noir titles—where we are our own best enemies."[21] *Leaving Las Vegas* was nominated for four Academy Awards: director, screenplay, actor, and actress; Nicholas Cage won Best Actor. The movie expanded into wide release and earned more than $30 million in American theaters. Many who saw it left shaking their heads, wondering how such an unrelenting and depressing motion picture could receive rave reviews and Oscar attention. For millions of Americans, so used to Hollywood happy formulas, it was the first "art film" they'd ever seen.

Many of those same viewers returned to their local multiplex the following year to view a directing debut from a self-described hillbilly. Billy Bob Thornton moved to Los Angeles from his native Arkansas in the late eighties. He cowrote and costarred in the excellent semi-indie crime sojourn *One False Move* (1992), cowrote *A Family Thing* (1996), and had a few small acting roles, usually as a Southern villain. Thornton remembers, "I was working on a crummy movie that I had a little nothing part in. I was broke at the time. I started talking to myself in the mirror about what a creep I was. I started making faces at myself. I made that Karl face and started talking in that voice. All of a sudden I had this weird character."[22] Thornton played that character in a short black-and-white film that he scripted, *Some Call It a Sling Blade*. Then he inserted the character into a feature-length screenplay that expanded on the mental-institution setting of the claustrophobic short. He would direct it himself. Thornton enlisted his Hollywood friends for major roles and his Arkansas pals for smaller ones (no one had to read for a part). *Sling Blade* (1996) was shot in Benton, Arkansas (population: 18,000) for $1.2 million.

Karl Childers (Thornton) is a mentally retarded man with a protruding jaw and sloped posture. He has been in a "nervous hospital" for twenty-five of his thirty-seven years for killing his mother with a machete. Now he's returning to his hometown. No one remembers him. He goes to work repairing lawnmowers, and he befriends a boy, Frank (Lucas Black), the boy's mother, Linda (Natalie Canerday), and Linda's gay coworker (John Ritter). Linda's violent boyfriend (singer Dwight Yoakam) isn't so friendly. When Karl fears that Frank may be in danger, he serves up his own form of preemptive justice.

Writer/director Billy Bob Thornton as Karl in *Sling Blade*.
© 1996 Shooting Gallery, Inc.

As in most Southern gothic fiction, the past weighs heavily on the present, and it gives *Sling Blade* an ominous feel. There is a measured sense of humanity to each of the people we meet. The relationship between Karl and Frank is especially touching. Karl is a marvelous Forrest Gumplike creation, simple-minded but possessing a strict moral code and a dose of common sense. When a man brings a "broken" lawnmower in, fix-it-wiz Karl immediately spots the problem: no gas. Karl's boss comments, "See, he always goes for the simplest things first." And then there's Karl's gravelly voice—a slow, deep rumble interspersed with "I reckon" and nervous affirmative grunts. Footage is often captured in long, static, wide shots reminiscent of Jim Jarmusch. The evocative cinematography was by Barry Markowitz. Thornton wanted to maintain the black-and-white feel of the short film, so there are no bright hues; wardrobe clothing was faded. Robert Duvall makes a brief appearance, and the late J. T. Walsh repeats his role from the short as a sex-obsessed inmate.

Screened for distributors, *Sling Blade* sold to Miramax for an eye-opening $10 million. The movie, the character, and the writer/director/star became the little Southern outsiders who made good. Most critics sang the praises. *Time*'s Richard Corliss wrote: "*Sling Blade* is about the difficulty good folks have living with rotten ones. . . . Karl is a memorable, affecting creature—so gentle he daren't sleep on an offered bed for fear of spoiling the room's perfect primness, so righteous he will consider killing to protect his adoptive family. *Sling Blade* meanders when Karl isn't driving it, but for the first half hour and the last it has the long, clean lines of an American classic."[23] *Sling Blade* followed a box-office course similar to that of *Leaving Las Vegas*, riding critical accolades and word of mouth into a wide release. Thornton was nominated for two Academy Awards, actor and adapted screenplay; he won the latter. He has had several plum acting roles since. After years of struggling, Billy Bob Thornton finally established himself as a Hollywood player—by traveling the independent path.

Like Thornton, a number of actors chose the Cassavetes route and made their directorial debuts with festival-friendly films, including Tim Robbins (*Bob Roberts*, 1992), John Turturro (*Mac*, 1993), Steve Buscemi (*Tree's Lounge*, 1996), Al Pacino (*Looking for Richard*, 1996), Stanley Tucci and Campbell Scott (*Big Night*, 1997), and Vincent Gallo (*Buffalo 66*, 1998).

Actor Robert Duvall was bitten again. Shortly after *Angelo, My Love*, he got another character in his head and had to make a movie. He was in a small Arkansas town in 1984, researching a role, when he wandered into a church and heard a firebrand sermon. Five years later he finished a script. As before, when every studio and indie company rejected his idea Duvall opened up his own bank account. He withdrew a hefty $5 million. The movie Duvall financed, wrote, directed, and starred in is *The Apostle* (1997). When it first screened at the Toronto Film Festival, an announcement was made to distributors: "Bidding will commence after the completion of the opening titles." There were many eager buyers (October won).

Duvall plays Sonny Dewey, a zealous Pentecostal preacher who kills his wife's lover with a baseball bat. He leaves Texas for Louisiana in search of redemption. He rebuilds a small church, pursues romance, and goes about saving souls with uncompromising passion. The transcendent conclusion is especially powerful.

Farrah Fawcett, Miranda Richardson, and various nonprofessionals round out the cast, but this is Duvall's movie from start to finish.

Robert Duvall leads a tent revival in *The Apostle*.
© 1997 Butcher Run Films, Inc. All rights reserved. Courtesy of October Films, Inc.

Bellowing scripture or quietly contemplating the right thing to do, his performance is electrifying. Like his friend Billy Bob Thornton (who returns the *Sling Blade* favor and plays a small part in *The Apostle*), Duvall cast himself in the plum sort of role that almost never comes around in Hollywood. As writer/director, Duvall remains respectful of religious zeal while presenting a highly charged, atmospheric parable.

Ads read, "Lust, Obsession, Revenge . . . Redemption." *The Apostle* appeared on more than fifty top ten of '97 lists, including *The New York Times* and the *Los Angeles Times*. It made more than $20 million in domestic theaters. Duvall won the National Society of Film Critics prize for best actor and was nominated for an Academy Award for acting.

Three college students disappeared in the woods of northern Maryland while shooting a documentary film on a legendary witch. One year later the footage they shot was found and assembled into a movie. This is the premise of *The Blair Witch Project* (1999), a microbudget breakthrough and the most harrowing horror film of the nineties. The making of *Blair Witch* was itself harrowing, blurring the line between fact and fiction.

Cowriters/codirectors Daniel Myrick and Eduardo Sanchez attended film school together in central Florida. After graduation and years of menial jobs, they were inspired by *The Legend of Boggy Creek* and other drive-in documentaries to create a pseudo-authentic horror film. Eduardo Sanchez, a 6'7" Cuban-American, explains, "*Blair* just happened to be the best low-budget idea we had at the time. It used all the weaknesses of independent film—used them in its favor—like shaky camera work, no lighting, no-name talent."[24]

Myrick and Sanchez took a year to audition nearly two thousand actors for the roles won by twentysomethings Heather Donahue, Joshua Leonard, and Michael Williams. (The actors share their names with their characters in the film.) It was the big-screen debut for all. For eight days, Donahue, Leonard, and Williams hiked and camped in the Maryland wilderness. The movie had no script; the actors improvised. Their only direction came from notes left along the way (example of a note to Leonard: "You don't trust Heather, take control"). The weary threesome shot themselves with a 16mm black-and-white camera and a Hi8 camcorder in the typically sloppy style of home movies. Events took them by surprise, and much of their frustration is real. Myrick and Sanchez spent eight months cutting the twenty hours of footage down to the eighty-one minute feature. Editing expenses made up most of the film's $35,000 budget.

Many of the people interviewed near the beginning of *The Blair Witch Project* were non-actors (some of whom were asked unawares about a witch). After these sequences, the film is made up of footage shot by Heather, Joshua, and Michael in the bleak wilderness as they become increasingly certain they will

Internet

The Internet began to impact independent filmmaking, along with the rest of society, in the last half of the nineties. Sites like indieWIRE dished out daily news. Kevin Smith was among the directors with an official site for merchandising and news updates. Others, including Quentin Tarantino, had unofficial fan sites. Movie reviews and rumors were posted on a seemingly endless sea of electronic pages. And otherwise undistributed indies were broadcast in their entirety in low resolution.

Web pages promoting movies, big and small, became obligatory in the late nineties, but most were little more than print advertisements. The first film to truly exploit this high technology was one of the

continued

Internet *continued*

lowest tech features ever made: *The Blair Witch Project*. Its state-of-the-art, official site contains a thorough background on the people and events of the film, never once letting on that it's all fake. Included are a timeline from 1785 to 1997 of the mythology of the witch; biographies and photo scrapbooks (including baby and prom photos) of the missing filmmakers; evidence and search photos; video interviews with Heather's mom and with investigators; TV news reports on the missing threesome; Heather's twenty-five page journal; and clips from the discovered 16mm and Hi8 video footage (which made up the feature film). The information works in conjunction with the film, adding to the horror. The site became a runaway phenomenon, receiving millions of hits before *Blair Witch*'s release, fueling rumors, positive word-of-mouth, and print and TV publicity. Fan sites quickly followed. It all helped turn the micro-budget movie into a must-see event.

never get out alive. There is no violence and only one brief moment of gore. Ominous sounds, oblique symbols, and darkness supply the chills.

The Blair Witch Project was an ingenious idea, but it could have been scarier. Additional background information may have helped us fear the witch more and care more about the characters. Asked to improvise, the actors reveal little, but mostly curse and shout. That said, *Blair Witch* benefits from its rawness, leaving mysteries to burrow under your skin. Some of the things it can make you fear (the sound of cracking wood, bundled sticks, piles of rocks) are so ordinary that you may never go into the woods again without remembering this movie.

As the first *cinema verité* horror film, *Blair Witch* represents a melding of the exploitation and artistic yin and yang of independent cinema—a union previously made by such directors as Abel Ferrara and Quentin Tarantino. It also builds upon the horror realism of *Night of the Living Dead, Halloween,* and others, reaffirming once again that the greatest scares are found closest to ordinary life. Daniel Myrick says, "I think we've undermined the system in a way. Some Hollywood types are taken aback that five broke dudes from Orlando could make a movie on a shoestring that scares the hell out of them."[25]

The Blair Witch Project played out-of-competition in the midnight

screening series (a dumping ground for cult films) at the Sundance
Film Festival. Snatched up by new distributor Artisan Entertainment,
it was masterfully promoted for months before its release, mostly via
a popular website. Like *The Birth of a Nation* eighty-four years prior
and a few horror films in the seventies, *The Blair Witch Project* became
a genuine blockbuster by even Hollywood standards. It appeared
simultaneously on the covers of *Time* and *Newsweek*, and it was the
first independent film to make more than $100 million in domestic
theaters. What's equally notable is that this little movie—consisting
mostly of shaky footage shot with a home video camera—was first
released exclusively to art houses. Thus, in the final months of the
twentieth century, a pseudo-documentary horror flick came out of
cinematheques and into the American mainstream. The commercial
ascent of independent cinema was complete.

In the wake of Soderbergh, Quentin Tarantino, and the Blair Witch,
more people than ever are creating their own independent movies.
The "just do it" route is now the preferred path for entering the motion
picture industry. And experienced professionals are opting for autonomy, as well. Of course, with over one thousand nonstudio features
being produced each year, the vast majority of them are never commercially projected, and most of those that are disappear fast.

But the dream continues—the dream of sudden success, the dream
of telling a unique story to a receptive audience, the dream of doing
it without interference and without pandering to the lowest common
denominator of the widest possible audience. As long as there has
been a motion picture industry there have been renegades working
outside the walls, telling the stories the studios can't or won't tell—
challenging, shocking, inspiring. More than a century after it all
began, the next great director—with a small budget and a big
dream—calls "Action!"

The lights go down. The curtain goes up.

Notes

[1] *Premiere*, Nov. 1994, 100.
[2] *New York*, 15 Feb. 1993.
[3] *Los Angeles Times*, 16 Aug. 1991.

[4] *New York Times*, 20 Nov. 1992.

[5] Rubin, H. Alex and Jeremy Workman, directors, *Who is Henry Jaglom?*, film (Calliope Films, Inc., 1995).

[6] *Variety*, 4 Feb. 1991.

[7] *Random House Webster's College Dictionary* 2nd Ed. (New York: Random House, 1997), 1212.

[8] *New York Times*, 25 March 1994.

[9] *Filmmaker* 3, 4 (Summer 1995), 42.

[10] *Living in Oblivion* was one of seven distributed nonstudio features in four years about the struggles at the bottom of the movie industry—a subject most screenwriters and directors know well, but one audiences assiduously avoid. The other films were: *In the Soup* (1992), *Mistress* (1992), *Inside Monkey Zetterland* (1993), *. . . And God Spoke* (1994), *My Life's in Turnaround* (1994), *Swimming With Sharks* (1995).

[11] *Details*, August 1997, 138.

[12] "The Edge of Hollywood," *American Cinema*, 10 episodes (PBS, A New York Center for Visual History Production in co-production with KCET and the BBC, 1994).

[13] *Variety*, 27 Jan. 1992.

[14] *Premiere*, Oct. 1997, 98.

[15] The first independent film with a modern Native-American theme was *Powwow Highway* (1989), written and directed by whites, based on a novel by an Indian. It was barely released by Warner Bros.

[16] "The Edge of Hollywood."

[17] *Chicago Sun-Times*, 21 Oct. 1994.

[18] Danphin, Barry, "Burden of Dreams," *Village Voice*, 23 May 1995.

[19] *Newsweek*, 16 June 1997.

[20] *New Yorker*, 23, April 1990.

[21] *Los Angeles Magazine*, Oct. 1995.

[22] *Boston Phoenix*, 7 Feb. 1997.

[23] *Time*, 9 Dec. 1996.

[24] Timberg, Scott, "Fresh Blood," *New Times Los Angeles*, 8–14 July 1999.

[25] Timberg, Scott.

Timeline

1896

first publicly screened motion pictures in America

1903

Edison's *The Great Train Robbery* (first popular film)

1908

Motion Picture Patents Company (the "Trust") formed to battle
    independents with patent suits

1912

Oliver Twist (first feature film)

1915

The Birth of a Nation (first blockbuster)

1916

Trust falters; rise of modern studios, Hollywood, feature films,
    and movie stars
Intolerance

1919

United Artists formed
The Homesteader (Oscar Micheaux's debut)

1922

Nanook of the North (Robert Flaherty's debut)

1924

radio reaches wide public

1926

first art-house theaters open in New York City and Washington, DC

1927

Warner Bros.'s *The Jazz Singer* premieres (first sound feature)

1928

Steamboat Willie (Walt Disney's breakthrough)

1930

Depression and expenses of sound technology hurt independent
companies; rise of studio system

1931

Venice Film Festival founded (Italy)

1932

Film Forum begins in New York
Independent Motion Picture Producer's Association formed
New York Film Society begins

1933

first drive-in theater opens in Camden, New Jersey
The Emperor Jones

1934

Production Code is strictly enforced
Our Daily Bread

1935

"March of Time" series of newsreels begins, influences
    documentaries
The Museum of Modern Art (New York) establishes film library
Pioneer/RKO's *Becky Sharp* (first Technicolor feature)

1939

MGM's *Gone With the Wind* and *The Wizard of Oz*

1941

Revenue Act of 1941; Hollywood stars want out of contracts
RKO's *Citizen Kane*

1942

Native Land

1943

Meshes of the Afternoon (Maya Deren's debut)

1945

after WW II 16mm projectors flood schools, museums, etc.
Art in Cinema screenings begin in San Francisco
Italian neorealism begins

1946

Walter Reade Organization formed (–1970)

1947

Cannes Film Festival launched (France)
Cinema 16 in New York City starts (–1963)
HUAC begins searching for Hollywood communists

1949

Supreme Court announces first consent decree in Paramount case;
    studio system breaking down
I Shot Jesse James (Sam Fuller's debut); *Not Wanted* (Ida Lupino's
    debut)

1950

Berlin Film Festival begins (Germany)
race picture industry fades

1951

television reaches wide public ("I Love Lucy" premieres)

1952

The Miracle case establishes First Amendment rights of motion
    pictures
This Is Cinerama (first Cinerama feature); *Bwana Devil*
    (first 3-D feature)

1954

AIP formed (–1980)

The Monster from the Ocean Floor (Roger Corman's debut); *Salt of the Earth*

1955

drive-in theaters reach wide public
Film Culture magazine begins (–1966)

1957

San Francisco International Film Festival launched

1958

Jonas Mekas's "Movie Journal" column first appears in *The Village Voice* (–1964)

1959

The French New Wave; rise of the auteur theory
The Immoral Mr. Teas (Russ Meyer's debut)

1960

TV's *Primary* and the rise of *cinema verité*

1961

The Connection (Shirley Clarke's debut); *Shadows* (John Cassavetes's debut)

1962

Film-Makers' Cooperative formed
The New York Film Festival begins

1963

Cinema 5 formed

Blood Feast (first graphic horror film); *Sleep* (Andy Warhol's debut)

1965

Sherpix formed (–1974)
Super 8mm film introduced to amateur market

1966

Chelsea Girls (underground breakthrough)

1967

The American Film Institute founded
New Line Cinema formed

1968

MPAA ratings system instituted; Production Code ends
Night of the Living Dead; Who's That Knocking at my Door (Martin
   Scorsese's debut)

1969

Sweden's *I Am Curious—Yellow* is an X-rated art-house hit
Easy Rider

1970

Anthology Film Archives formed
film study accelerates in America
Roger Corman's New World formed

1971

Los Angeles's Filmex festival begins (—1986)
Billy Jack; Sweet Sweetback's Baadasssss Song (blaxploitation genesis)

1972

X-rated films reach wide public: *Deep Throat,* and others

1973

Telluride Film Festival begins (Colorado)
Pink Flamingos (underground sensation)

1974

HBO begins, cable TV taking off
Benji; The Texas Chainsaw Massacre

1975

Toronto and Seattle film festivals launched
Universal's *Jaws*
One Flew Over the Cuckoo's Nest

1976

Fox's *The Rocky Horror Picture Show* becomes underground hit

1977

Fox's *Star Wars*

1978

Samuel Goldwyn Company formed
The US Film Festival launched (Utah)
Eraserhead (David Lynch's debut); *Gates of Heaven* (Errol Morris's
    debut); *Halloween*

1979

Independent Feature Project (IFP) and its Independent Feature Film
  Market (IFFM) begin
Miramax formed
PBS starts funding films as part of its "American Playhouse" series
Gal Young 'Un (Victor Nunez's debut)

1980

Friday the 13th; Return of the Secaucus 7 (John Sayles's debut)

1981

The Sundance Institute begins

1983

VCRs taking off; theatrical porn, horror, and underground fading

1984

Stranger Than Paradise (Jim Jarmusch's debut)

1985

The US Film Festival incorporated by Sundance Institute

1986

British *A Room with a View* and American *Blue Velvet* are art-house
  hits
She's Gotta Have It

1987

Weekly "Vanguard Cinema" showcase launched on Cinemax

1988

Stand and Deliver

1989

Strand Releasing formed
sex, lies, & videotape

1990

The Unbelievable Truth (Hal Hartley's debut)

1991

Filmmaker magazine launched
New Line Cinema forms Fine Line Features
The US Film Festival officially changes name to the Sundance Film
    Festival

1992

"New Queer Cinema" takes off
Sony Pictures Classics is born
Reservoir Dogs (Quentin Tarantino's debut)

1993

Miramax acquired by Walt Disney Studios

1994

The Independent Film Channel launched
Miramax's *Pulp Fiction* is a major hit
New Line Cinema absorbed by Warner Bros.
Hoop Dreams

1995

Fox Searchlight is born
Los Angeles Independent Film Festival launched
Slamdance Film Festival begins (Utah)
The Sundance Channel launched
Leaving Las Vegas

1996

the Internet reaches wide public
Sling Blade

1997

Lions Gate formed
October Films acquired by Universal
Paramount & Fox's *Titanic*

1998

Artisan Entertainment founded

1999

The Blair Witch Project

COST-TO-GROSS RATIOS

This chart presents the most profitable independent features as measured by cost to gross. Column A is the filmmakers' costs. Column B is the domestic (US and Canadian) box-office gross in millions. Column C reflects the ratio of column A to column B. Hard-core pornography is not included because its figures are very difficult to validate. (*Deep Throat* would be in the top five.) Many soft-core porn, horror, and pre-1960 films are excluded for the same reason.

Note that modern films make much more than their domestic box-office gross through foreign distribution, video sales, TV fees, etc. (Some figures in the text reflect this.) Also note that the wide cost-to-gross ratios that appear on this chart can only be seen in the independent arena. As a frame of reference, *Titanic* made three times its cost in domestic theaters. Before its rerelease, *Star Wars* made thirty times its cost—a phenomenally huge ratio for the studios.

		A	B	C
1999	*The Blair Witch Project*	$35,000	$140	4000
1928	*Road to Ruin*	$2,500	$2.5	1000
1915	*The Birth of a Nation*	$105,000	$60	571
1974	*Pink Flamingos*	$12,000	$6	500
1995	*The Brothers McMullen*	$24,000	$10	417
1968	*Night of the Living Dead*	$115,000	$40	348
1993	*El Mariachi*	$7,000	$2	286
1968	*Vixen*	$72,000	$15	208

1933	Damaged Lives	$10,000	$2	200
1972	The Legend of Boggy Creek	$100,000	$20	200
1978	Halloween	$320,000	$50	156
1972	Last House on the Left	$87,000	$13	149
1997	In the Company of Men	$25,000	$3	120
1994	Clerks	$27,000	$3	111
1974	Benji	$500,000	$50	100
1974	The Groove Tube	$200,000	$20	100
1971	Sweet Sweetback's . . .	$150,000	$15	100
1979	Friday the 13th	$500,000	$45	90
1975	Supervixens	$200,000	$17	85
1974	Macon County Line	$250,000	$19	76
1959	The Immoral Mr. Teas	$24,000	$1.5	63
1969	Easy Rider	$500,000	$30	60
1977	Kentucky Fried Movie	$250,000	$15	60
1970	Trash	$25,000	$1.5	60
1972	Billy Jack	$650,000	$33	51
1987	Hollywood Shuffle	$100,000	$5	50
1998	π (Pi)	$60,000	$3	50
1979	Richard Pryor—Live in Concert	$300,000	$14	47
1973	Walking Tall	$500,000	$23	46
1986	She's Gotta Have It	$160,000	$7	44
1989	Roger & Me	$160,000	$7	44

Appendix B

ACADEMY AWARD NOMINEES

The independent films below have been nominated for Academy Awards. Winners are in boldface. Only documentaries mentioned in the text are included. The Academy Awards began in 1927. The documentary award was initiated in 1941. Dates reflect the year of release, with the awards ceremony held the following spring.

1931	*Tabu*	—**cinematography**
1948	*Louisiana Story*	—screenplay
1949	*The Quiet One*	—screenplay
1952	*The Medium*	—musical score
	Navajo	—documentary, cinematography
1953	*The Little Fugitive*	—screenplay
1957	*On the Bowery*	—documentary
1962	*David and Lisa*	—director, screenplay
	Long Day's Journey Into Night	—actress
1963	*The Balcony*	—cinematography
1964	*One Potato, Two Potato*	—screenplay
1969	*Easy Rider*	—screenplay, sup. actor
1969	*In the Year of the Pig*	—documentary
1974	*Phantom of the Paradise*	—musical score
	A Woman Under the Influence	—director, actress
1975	*Hester Street*	—actress
	One Flew Over the Cuckoo's Nest	—**picture, director, screenplay,**

		actress, actor
		sup. actor, editing
		cinematography
		musical score
1976	*Harlan County, U.S.A.*	—**documentary**
1977	*Who Are the Debolts?*	—**documentary**
1980	*The Stunt Man*	—director, screenplay, actor
1983	*Testament*	—actress
1984	*El Norte*	—screenplay
	Streetwise	—documentary
	The Times of Harvey Milk	—**documentary**
1988	*Let's Get Lost*	—documentary
	Stand and Deliver	—actor
1989	*Common Threads*	—**documentary**
	For All Mankind	—documentary
	sex, lies, & videotape	—screenplay
1990	*American Dream*	—**documentary**
	The Grifters	—director, screenplay, actress, sup. actress
	Longtime Companion	—sup. actor
	Metropolitan	—screenplay
1992	*Passion Fish*	—screenplay, actress
1993	*The War Room*	—documentary
1994	*Hoop Dreams*	—editing
1995	*Georgia*	—sup. actress
	Leaving Las Vegas	—director, screenplay, actress, **actor**
1996	*Lone Star*	—screenplay
	Sling Blade	—**screenplay**, actor
1997	*The Apostle*	—actor
	Ulee's Gold	—actor
1998	*Affliction*	—actor, **sup. actor**

INDEPENDENT SPIRIT AWARD WINNERS

The Independent Feature Project began honoring indie filmmakers in 1986. Listed below are the award winners that meet this book's definition of an independent film. Semi-indie productions are excluded. (Eight of thirteen best feature winners have been semi-indies.) A "first feature" is the director's debut. Awards for debut performance (male or female in a first feature) and first screenplay began with 1994 films. Dates reflect the year of release, with the ceremony held the following March (the weekend before the Oscars).

1985	*Blood Simple*	—director, actor
1986	*She's Gotta Have It*	—first feature
1988	*Stand and Deliver*	—feature, director, screenplay, actor, sup. actress, sup. actor
1989	*sex, lies, & videotape*	—picture, director, actress, sup. actress
1990	*The Grifters*	—feature, actress
	Longtime Companion	—sup. actor
	Metropolitan	—first feature
	To Sleep With Anger	—director, screenplay, actor, sup. actress
1991	*City of Hope*	—sup. actress
	Straight Out of Brooklyn	—first feature
1992	*Bad Lieutenant*	—actor
	Gas Food Lodging	—actress
	Night on Earth	—cinematography

	Passion Fish	—sup. actress
	Reservoir Dogs	—sup. actor
	The Waterdance	—first feature, screenplay
1993	*American Heart*	—actor
	El Mariachi	—first feature
	Ruby in Paradise	—actress, cinematography
	Twenty Bucks	—sup. actor
1994	*Fresh*	—debut performance
	The Last Seduction	—actress
	Spanking the Monkey	—first feature, first screenplay
1995	*The Brothers McMullen*	—first feature
	Georgia	—sup. actress
	Kids	—debut performance
	Leaving Las Vegas	—feature, director, actress
1996	*Lone Star*	—sup. actress
	Sling Blade	—first feature
	Welcome to the Dollhouse	—debut performance
1997	*The Apostle*	—feature, director, actor
	Chasing Amy	—screenplay, sup. actor
	In the Company of Men	—first screenplay, debut performance
1998	*High Art*	—actress
	The Opposite of Sex	—first feature, screenplay
	Π *(Pi)*	—first screenplay
	Smoke Signals	—debut performance

Bibliography

Acker, Ally. *Reel Women: Pioneers of the Cinema 1896 to the Present*. New York: Continuum, 1991.

Balio, Tino, ed. *The American Film Industry*. Madison: University of Wisconsin Press, 1976.

Barsam, Richard Meran. *Nonfiction Film: A Critical History*. New York: E. P. Dutton, 1973.

———, ed. *Nonfiction Film Theory and Criticism*. New York: Dutton, 1976.

Bergan, Ronald. *The United Artists Story*. New York: Crown Publishers, 1986.

Bergman, Andrew. *We're in the Money: Depression America and Its Films*. New York: Harper & Row, 1971.

Bernard, Jami. *Quentin Tarantino: The Man and his Movies*. New York: HarperPerennial, 1995.

Biskind, Peter. *Easy Riders, Raging Bulls: How the Sex-Drugs-and-Rock 'n' Roll Generation Saved Hollywood*. New York: Simon & Schuster, 1998.

Bockris, Victor. *The Life and Death of Andy Warhol*. New York: Bantam Books, 1989.

Bodeen, DeWitt. *From Hollywood*. Cranbury, NJ: A. S. Barnes and Co., 1976.

Bogle, Donald. *Blacks in American Film and Television: An Encyclopedia*. New York: Garland Publishing, 1988.

———.*Toms, Coons, Mulattoes, Mammies, & Bucks: An Interpretive History of Blacks in American Film*. 3rd ed. New York: Continuum, 1995.

Bouzereau, Laurent. *The DePalma Cut: The Films of America's Most*

Controversial Director. New York: Dembner Books, 1988.

Bowser, Eileen. *The Transformation of Cinema 1907–1915*. New York: Charles Scribner's Sons, 1990.

Brownlow, Kevin. *Behind the Mask of Innocence*. New York: Alfred A. Knopf, 1990.

———. *Hollywood: The Pioneers*. New York: Alfred A. Knopf, 1979.

Cook, Raymond Allen. *Fire from the Flint: The Amazing Careers of Thomas Dixon*. Winston-Salen, NC: John F. Blair, 1968.

Corman, Roger, with Jerome, Jim. *How I Made a Hundred Movies in Hollywood and Never Lost a Dime*. New York: Random House, 1990.

Cowie, Peter. *Coppola*. New York: Charles Scribner's Sons, 1990.

Cripps, Thomas R. "The Evolution of Black Film." *Hollywood's America: United States History Through Its Films*, eds. Steven Mintz and Randy Roberts. St. James, NY: Brandywine, 1993.

de Grazia, Edward, and Newman, Roger K. *Banned Films: Movies, Censors and the First Amendment*. New York: R. R. Bowker, 1982.

Donati, William. *Ida Lupino: A Biography*. Lexington, KY: University Press of Kentucky, 1996.

Durgnat, Raymond, and Simmon, Scott. *King Vidor, American*. Berkley: University Of California Press, 1988.

"The Edge of Hollywood." *American Cinema*. 10 episodes. PBS. A New York Center for Visual History production in coproduction with KCET and BBC, 1994.

Flaherty, Robert J., with Flaherty, Frances. *My Eskimo Friends*. New York: Doubleday, 1924.

Frasier, David K. *Russ Meyer: The Life and Films*. Jefferson, NC: McFarland & Co., 1990.

Goldman, Eric A. *Visions, Images, and Dreams: Yiddish Film, Past and Present*. Teaneck, NJ: Ergo Media, 1979.

Gomery, Douglas. *Shared Pleasures: A History of Movie Presentation in the United States*. Madison: University of Wisconsin Press, 1992.

Grey, Rudolph. *Nightmare of Ecstacy: The Life and Art of Edward D. Wood, Jr*. Portland, OR: Feral House, 1992.

Henderson, Robert M. *D. W. Griffith: His Life and Work*. Oxford: Oxford University Press, 1972.

Jacobs, Diane. *Hollywood Renaissance*. New York: Delta, 1980.

James, David E., ed. *To Free Cinema: Jonas Mekas & The New York Underground*. Princeton, NJ: Princeton University Press, 1992.

Jones, G. William. *Black Cinema Treasures: Lost and Found*. Denton, TX:

University of North Texas Press, 1991.

Katz, Ephraim. *The Film Encyclopedia*. 2nd ed. New York: HarperPerennial, 1994.

Kelly, Mary Pat. *Martin Scorsese: A Journey*. New York: Thunder's Mouth Press, 1991.

King, Stephen. *Danse Macabre*. New York: Berkley, 1981.

Knight, Arthur. *The Liveliest Art: A Panoramic History of the Movies*. rev. ed. New York: Mentor, 1979.

Lee, Spike. *Spike Lee's Gotta Have It: Inside Guerrilla Filmmaking*. New York: Simon & Schuster, 1987.

MacGowan, Kenneth. *Behind the Screen: The History and Techniques of the Motion Pictures*. New York: Delacorte, 1965.

Manvell, Roger. *The Cinema, 1950*. Hardmondsworth, England: Penguin Books, 1950.

McCarthy, Todd, and Flynn, Charles, eds. *King of the Bs*. New York: E. P. Dutton & Co., 1975.

———, ed. *The Sleaze Merchants: Adventures in Exploitation Filmmaking*. New York: St. Martin's Press, 1995.

Meade, Marion. *Buster Keaton: Cut to the Chase*. New York: HarperCollins, 1995.

Medved, Harry and Michael. *The Golden Turkey Awards*. New York: Perigee, 1980.

Mekas, Jonas. *Movie Journal: The Rise of the New American Cinema 1959–1971*. New York: Collier Books, 1972.

Miller, Don. *B Movies*. New York: Ballantine, 1973.

Monaco, James. *American Film Now*. New York: Oxford University Press, 1979.

Muller, Eddie, and Faris, Daniel. *Grindhouse: The Forbidden World of "Adults Only" Cinema*. New York: St. Martin's Press, 1996.

Naha, Ed. *The Films of Roger Corman: Brilliance on a Budget*. New York: Arco Publishing, 1982.

Peary, Danny. *Alternative Oscars: One Critic's Defiant Choices for Best Picture, Actor, and Actress—From 1927 to the Present*. New York: Delta, 1993.

———. *Cult Movies: The Classics, the Sleepers, the Weird, and the Wonderful*. New York: Dell, 1981.

———. *Cult Movies 3: 50 More of the Classics, the Sleepers, the Weird, and the Wonderful*. New York: Fireside, 1988.

———. *Guide for the Film Fanatic*. New York: Fireside, 1986.

Pierson, John. *Spike, Mike, Slackers & Dykes: A Guided Tour Across a Decade of American Independent Cinema.* New York: Hyperion, 1995.

Pitts, Michael R. *Poverty Row Studios, 1929–1940.* Jefferson, NC: McFarland & Co., 1997.

Riordan, James. Stone: *The Controversies, Excesses, and Exploits of a Radical Filmmaker.* New York: Hyperion, 1995.

Robinson, David. *From Peep Show to Palace: The Birth of American Film.* New York: Columbia University Press, 1996.

Rodriguez, Robert. *Rebel Without a Crew: Or How a 23-Year-Old Filmmaker with $7000 Became a Hollywood Player.* New York: Dutton, 1995.

Rosin, David, with Hamilton, Peter. *Off-Hollywood: The Making and Marketing of Independent Film.* New York: Grove Weidenfeld, 1990.

Rotha, Paul. *Robert J. Flaherty: A Biography.* Philadelphia: University of Pennsylvania Press, 1983.

Russo, Vito. *The Celluloid Closet.* rev. ed. New York: Quality Paperback Book Club, 1987.

Sanderson, Lennox, Jr. "The Black in Silent Film." In *Magill's Survey of Cinema: Silent Films,* vol. 1, edited by Frank N. Magill. Englewood Cliffs, NJ: Salem Press,

Schatz, Thomas. *The Genius of the System: Hollywood Filmmaking in the Studio Era.* New York: Pantheon, 1988.

Schickel, Richard. *The Disney Version: The Life, Times, Art and Commerce of Walt Disney.* Revised and updated. New York: Touchstone, 1985.

———. *D. W. Griffith: An American Life.* New York: Simon & Schuster, 1984.

Server, Lee. *Sam Fuller: Film Is a Battleground.* Jefferson, NC: McFarland & Co., 1994.

Sherman, Eric, and Rubin, Martin. *The Director's Event: Interviews with Five American Film-Makers.* New York: Atheneum, 1969.

Silver, Alain, and Ursini, James. *What Ever Happened to Robert Aldrich?: His Life and His Films.* New York: Limelight Editions, 1995.

Sitney, P. Adams. *Visionary Film: The American Avant-Garde 1943–1978.* 2nd ed. Oxford: Oxford University Press, 1979.

Sklar, Robert. *Movie-Made American: A Cultural History of American Movies.* New York: Random House, 1975.

Slide, Anthony. *The American Film Industry: A Historical Dictionary.* New York: Greenwood Press, 1986.

———. *The Silent Feminists: America's First Women Directors.* Lanham,

MD: Scarecrow Press, 1996.

Snyder, Robert L. *Pare Lorentz and the Documentary Film.* Norman: Oklahoma University Press, 1968.

Soderbergh, Steven. *sex, lies, & videotape.* New York: Harper & Row, 1990.

St. Johns, Adela. *The Honeycomb.* Garden City, NY: Doubleday, 1969.

Thompson, Frank. *Lost Films: Important Movies That Disappeared.* New York: Citadel Press, 1996.

Thomson, David. *A Biographical Dictionary of Film.* 3rd ed. New York: Alfred A. Knopf, 1995.

Turan, Kenneth, and Zito, Stephen F. *Sinema: American Pornographic Films and the People Who Make Them.* New York: Praeger Publishers, 1974.

Vidor, King. *A Tree Is a Tree.* New York: Harcourt, Brace and Co., 1952.

Walker, Alexander. *Stanley Kubrick Directs.* New York: Harcourt Brace Jovanovich, 1971.

Waters, John. *Shock Value: A Tasteful Book About Bad Taste.* New York: Delta, 1981.

Wagenknecht, Edward. *The Movies in the Age of Innocence.* Norman: University of Oklahoma Press, 1962.

Yellin, David G., and Connors, Marie, eds. *Tomorrow & Tomorrow & Tomorrow.* Jackson: University of Mississippi Press, 1985.

Yule, Andrew. *Picture Shows: The Life and Films of Peter Bogdanovich.* New York: Limelight Editions, 1992.

INDEX

I

I Am Curious-Yellow 106, 245, 418
I Call First 212-213
I Conquer the Sea 66
I Dismember Mama 240
I Drink Your Blood 240
I Got the Hook Up 389
I Hate Your Guts! 166
I Shot Andy Warhol 188
I Shot Jesse James 115-116, 416
I Spit on Your Grave 291
Ichaso, Leon 331
Iguana 172
Illtown 368-369
Imitation of Life 89
Immoral Mr. Teas, The 147, 178, 417, 424
In the Company of Men 277, 381, 424, 428
In the Soup 360
In the Year of the Pig 236, 425
Inauguration of the Pleasure Dome 132
Ince, John 32
Ince, Thomas 18, 25, 35
Incident at Ogala 394
Incredible Torture Show, The 290
Incredibly Strange Creatures Who Stopped Living and Became Mixed-Up Zombies, The 178
Incredibly True Adventures of Two Girls in Love, The 392
Independent Votes for Women 14
Industrial Britain 76
Inkwell, The 367
Insatiable 295
Inside of the White Slave Traffic, The 14
Interim 184
Interiors 62
Internal Affairs 404
International Burlesque 99
Interviews with My Lai Veterans 201
Intolerance 15, 20-22, 42, 54, 108
Introduction to the Enemy 201
Intruder in the Dust 102
Intruder, The 166
Invasion of the Body Snatchers 114
Ireland, John 115, 121, 125
Iron & Silk 389
Is There Sex After Death? 233, 247
Israel, Neil 284
It Conquered the World 127-128
Italian Stallion, The 246
Ivory, James 338
Iwerks, Ub 56

J

Jack-Knife Man, The 35
Jackie Brown 386
Jackson, Mahalia 150
Jackson, Samuel L. 386, 388
Jackson, Shirley 133
Jafa, Arthur 388
Jagger, Mick 236, 277
Jaglom, Henry 320-321, 364-365
Jail Bait 141
James Dean Story, The 138, 317
James, Steve 395
Jamestown Baloos 132
Jarmusch, Jim 302-303, 307, 312, 321-325, 338, 356, 359-362, 377, 406, 420
Jarrico, Paul 129
Jaws 220, 260, 280, 419
Jazz on a Summer Day 150, 188
Jazz Singer, The 56, 414
Jeffrey 390
Jeffrey, Herbert 87
Jennings, Al 32
Jennings, Claudia 226
Jeremiah Johnson 279
JFK 240
Jim, the World's Greatest 291
Jiminez-Leal, Orlando 331
Joan of Arc 100
Joe 223, 246
Joe's Bed-Stuy Barbershop: We Cut Heads 333
Joey Breaker 387
Johann the Coffin Maker 53
John Barleycorn 11, 44
Johnny Suede 360, 378
Johns, Tracy 334
Johnson, Anne-Marie 335
Johnson, Ariyan 388
Johnson, Arnold 232
Johnson, Don 226, 269
Johnson, Fred 79
Johnson, George 28-29
Johnson, Jed 297
Johnson, Lyndon 209
Johnson, Noble B. 27-28
Johnson, Tor 141-143
Jon Jost's Frameup 366
Jones, Amy 291
Jones, Duane 221, 238
Jones, L. Q. 269
Jones, Quincy 220
Jones, Tommy Lee 124
Joplin, Janis 236
Jordan, Louis 102
Jordan, Michael 334
Jordan, Neil 106
Jordan, Richard 316

About the Author

Greg Merritt has an M.F.A. from The American Film Institute. He is a journalist, filmmaker, and screenwriter. His previous book was *Film Production: The Complete Uncensored Guide to Independent Filmmaking*. He lives in Los Angeles.